strategic management of eBusiness

JUDY MCKAY

Monash University

PETER MARSHALL

Mt Eliza Business School

John Wiley & Sons Australia, Ltd

First published 2004 by
John Wiley & Sons Australia, Ltd
33 Park Road, Milton, Qld 4064

Offices also in Sydney and Melbourne

Typeset in 10/12.5 pt Giovanni Light

© Judith McKay and Peter Marshall, 2004

National Library of Australia
Cataloguing-in-Publication data

McKay, Judy, 1955–   .
    Strategic management of e-business.

    Includes index.
    ISBN 0 470 80292 8.

    1. Electronic commerce — Management.
    I. Marshall, Peter, 1945–   . II. Title.

658.054678

Cover and internal design images:
Digital Vision/Copyright 2002/Nic Miller

All URLs were correct at time of publication.

Edited by Cathryn Game

Printed in Singapore by
Kyodo Printing Co (S'pore) Pte Ltd

10 9 8 7 6 5 4 3 2 1

contents

CHAPTER 1

Introduction to e-business 1

CHAPTER 2

Adopting appropriate e-business models 22

CHAPTER 12

IT governance: delivering
value from e-business   329

preface

We have been collaborating as researchers and authors now for more than a decade, during which time we have witnessed the spectacular rise of e-commerce, the demise of many dotcoms, and the subsequent concerns bordering on pessimism and cynicism in business about e-commerce, all at a time when we have witnessed the uptake of a form of technology — the Internet — and its infusion and diffusion into everyday business routines and activities at a rate unparalleled in history. As academics, we were party to the furious activity in establishing a range of e-commerce courses and units, only to find ourselves sometimes wondering in what fundamental ways these new units and courses were different from more traditional information systems courses. As we sought textbooks to help shape our lectures and discussions with our students, we felt sometimes frustrated because there did not seem to be a single text that covered the material we believed to be important or that approached the subject and content from the perspective and 'tone' that we felt was required. Then, of course, we became concerned that there was a need for a text that took a reflective and realistic perspective on the dotcom crash and its lessons. It was in this climate that the idea for this book was spawned.

First of all, we wanted to create a textbook that was almost obsessive in its focus on the delivery of business value from IT investments, including the Internet. Many texts, we felt, presented an overly optimistic and simplistic portrayal of e-commerce. We were uncomfortable with the image presented whereby, if organisations were just to buy the right hardware and software, and put up a corporate website, success would be theirs as millions of online purchasers would flock to their site. Long before the demise of the dotcoms, we believed passionately that the key to long-term success would rest with thoughtful strategising about the business cognisant of the capabilities required to identify, develop and effectively utilise information systems using traditional as well as Internet-based forms of technology. A pervasive theme in this book, then, is that the Internet and associated forms of technology offer exciting prospects for organisations, but that sober assessment and informed decision-making is necessary in order for targeted investments to be made in e-business initiatives and benefits realised for the organisation.

Second, we felt that some texts were lacking a clear focus in terms of the perspective on e-commerce adopted (i.e. organisational, marketing, technical and so on). Also lacking was a clear focus and emphasis on the management of the technology involved in such a way to create business value for the organisation. Our intention with this text was to adopt an organisational perspective and to approach e-business from both a business and an IT management perspective.

Third, we had been actively researching in the areas of e-business and IS/IT management for some time, and recognised that a textbook such as this would provide a coherent framework in which we could draw together the disparate threads of our research interests and activities over a number of years.

The aim of this text is to describe, analyse and understand the e-commerce phenomenon from an organisational perspective, recognising that articulating and implementing IS/IT strategies in alignment with business objectives and appropriate management of information and IS/IT resources in organisations underpins the successful exploitation of the Internet and modern technology in contemporary business organisations. The text offers a conceptual view of the e-business landscape, but it is populated with many practical yet simple and straightforward tools and techniques to support analysis and decision-making. In most chapters the frameworks, tools and techniques are based on an amalgam of our experiences as teachers and researchers. The illustrative examples and cases in each chapter are often fictitious, but elements in each case are most certainly drawn from real-life experiences.

We have used draft and early versions of chapters of this text ourselves with MBA and coursework masters students at Monash University and Mount Eliza Business School, and students and courses of this type were certainly part of our intended audience. However, we have tried to write the text without assuming years of business experience or knowledge, and hence we feel that the text will be equally helpful for undergraduate students in business and IT management courses.

With any project of this nature, there are always many people in the background who play an invaluable role in helping to create the final book, and we would like to acknowledge briefly their help, support and advice. In particular, we would like to express our thanks to our research colleagues, especially Adi Prananto for his contributions to chapter 1; Roger Sor for his friendship, advice and 'Devil's advocate' role, which helped us so much in the work reported in chapters 4 and 10; Craig Valli for his enthusiasm and energy, which are also reflected in chapter 4; Janice Burn for her contributions to chapter 10; and to Lisa Smith and her awesome capabilities, which contributed so greatly to chapter 12. Special mention must be made of the help we received from Helana Scheepers, for her insight and willingness to share her research initiatives from which parts of chapter 11 were crafted. Although there are too many to list individually, our thanks are also due to all the organisations that have allowed us to conduct research.

There are other friends and colleagues who have, over the years, been willing to enter into many spirited debates about aspects of IT management and e-business, and we would like to thank them for their advice, thoughts and support on so many occasions. We need to mention particularly Rudy Hirschheim, Thomas Siu, Donald McDermid, Dieter Fink, Phil McGuigam and Rens Scheepers. Thanks are due also to all our students who willingly offered many helpful insights into earlier drafts of this text.

A special thankyou is extended to the reviewers who spent many hours reviewing the developing manuscript, in particular, Dennis Hart, Australian National University; Iain Morrison, University of Melbourne; Pat Auger, University of Melbourne; Kay Bryant, Griffith University; and Roger Jenkins, University of Technology, Sydney.

A final word of thanks must go to the staff at John Wiley & Sons Australia, Ltd, in particular Darren Taylor, who believed in our ideas and who has so skilfully and amicably herded us towards the finish line!

Judy McKay
Peter Marshall

about the authors

▶ **Dr Judy McKay** has a PhD from the University of Queensland. She is currently in the School of Information Management and Systems in the Faculty of Information Technology at Monash University. Judy teaches e-commerce and IT management to MBA students and to students in the Master of Information Management and Systems.

▶ **Dr Peter Marshall** is a Senior Fellow in e-business at Mt Eliza Business School and an Associate Professor of e-business at the University of Queensland. Peter teaches courses in e-business and managing information and knowledge to MBA students. He also supervises students in Mt Eliza Business School's Executive MBA.

Both authors are active researchers in e-commerce and IT management, carrying out field research in contemporary business. They are both regular contributors to information systems conferences and research journals, particularly in Australia.

acknowledgements

Images

P. 8: copyright © 1995–2001 ComputerScope Ltd. All rights reserved. http://www.nua.com/surveys/analysis/graphs_charts/comparisons/ecommerce_us.html; p. 11: © J. McKay, A. Prananto, and P. Marshall. Australasian Conference on Information Systems, QUT, 6–8 December 2000; pp. 28, 58, 59 (below), 71 (top), 78, 83, 352: © J. Ward & J. Peppard, *Strategic Planning for Information Systems*. John Wiley and Sons, Chichester, 2002. Reproduced by permission; pp. 32, 279, 290, 291, 355: © McKay, J. & Marshall, Idea Group Publishing. www.idea-group.com; p. 59 (top): *Electronic Commerce 2002: A Managerial Perspective*, by Turban, King, Lee, Warkentin, Chung, © Reprinted by permission of Pearson Education, Inc., Upper Saddle River, NJ; p. 65: Copyright © 2001, by the Regents of the University of California. Reprinted from the *California Management Review*, vol. 44, no. 1. By permission of the Regents; p. 71 (below): adapted with permission from *Perspectives*, no. 66. *The Product Portfolio* by Bruce D. Henderson. Copyright The Boston Consulting Group 1970; p. 74: adapted with the permission of The Free Press, a Division of Simon & Schuster Adult Publishing Group, from *Competitive Strategy: Techniques for Analyzing Industries and Competitors* by Michael E. Porter. Copyright © 1980, 1988 by Free Press, Macmillan, New York, p. 4. ISBN 0–02–925360–8; p. 76: adapted with the permission of The Free Press, a Division of Simon & Schuster Adult Publishing Group, from *Competitive Advantage: Creating and Sustaining Superior Performance* by Michael E. Porter. All rights reserved; p. 79 (top and below): *The Essence of Information Systems*, 2e, by C. Edwards, J. Ward and A. Bytheway. Pearson Education Limited. © Prentice Hall International (UK) Ltd, 1991, 1995; p. 80: © Tim Lincoln, *Managing Information Systems for Profit*. John Wiley and Sons, Chichester, 2001. Reproduced by permission; p. 81: Copyright © 1999, by the Regents of the University of California. Reprinted from the *California Management Review*, vol. 41, no. 3. By permission of the Regents; pp. 103, 107, 112: originally published in INFOR 40 (1); p. 135: © E. Turban, E. McLean, J. Wetherbe. John Wiley & Sons Inc, New York, 2002; pp. 136, 350: © Dutta & Manzoni. *Process Re-engineering, Organizational Change and Performance Improvement*, McGraw-Hill, London; p. 160: From *Information Systems in Management*, 4th edn by SENN. © 1990. Reprinted with permission of Course Technology, a division of Thomson Learning: www.thomsonrights.com. Fax 800 730-2215; pp. 179, 182: reproduced from 'Developing Market Specific Supply Chain Strategies', by Christopher, M. and Towill, D. *International Journal of Logistics Management*, 2002, vol. 13, no. 1; p. 181: reprinted by permission of *Harvard Business Review*. From 'Syncra systems', by Andrew McAfee, Harvard Business School, 25 June, p. 14. Copyright © 2003 by the Harvard Business School Publishing Corporation; all rights reserved; pp. 188, 189: © F. Reichheld, W. Sasser/*Harvard Business Review*; p. 202: reprinted by permission of *Harvard Business Review*. From 'Interactive Technologies and Relationship Marketing Strategies'. 19.1.00. Copyright © 2003 by the Harvard Business School Publishing Corporation; all rights reserved; p. 206: reprinted by permission of *Harvard Business Update*. From 'A Crash Course in Customer Relationship Management'. Copyright © 2000 by the Harvard Business School Publishing Corporation; all rights reserved; p. 247: reproduced from

'Core IS capabilities for exploiting information technology', by Feeny, D. F. and Willcocks, L. *Sloan Management Review*, Spring, p. 11, 1999. Tribune Media Services; p. 255: © M. Lacity & L. Willcocks, *Global Information Technology Outsourcing*. John Wiley and Sons, Chichester, 2001. Reproduced by permission; p. 260 (top): reproduced from 'The value of selective IT sourcing', by Lacity, M. C., Willcocks, L. P. and Feeny, D. F. Sloan Management Review, Spring, 1996. Tribune Media Services; p. 260 (below): *Academy of Management Executive: The Thinking Manager's Source*, by R. C. Insinga and M. J. Werle. Copyright 2000 by Academy of Management. Reproduced with permission of Academy of Management via Copyright Clearance Center; pp. 283, 284, 287: reproduced from *E-Commerce and V-Business*, S. Barnes and B. Hunt, pp. 172–8, copyright 2001, with permission from Elsevier; p. 322: 'Issues and Challenges in Ubiquitous Computing', by Lyytinen and Yoo. *ACM*, vol. 45, no. 12. © 2002 ACM, Inc. Reprinted by permission; p. 335: from Board Briefing on IT Governance, published June 2001 by IT Governance Institute, www.itgi.org; p. 348: reproduced from *Strategic Information Management*, R. D. Galliers and B. S. H. Baker, p. 369, copyright 1994, with permission from Elsevier; p. 349: reproduced from *Strategic Information Management*, R. D. Galliers and B. S. H. Baker, p. 376, copyright 1994, with permission from Elsevier.

Text
Pp. 35–6, 103, 104–5, 105–6, 106, 108, 110, 110–11, 111, text throughout chapter 4: originally published in INFOR 40 (1); p. 158: reprinted by permission of *Harvard Business Review*. From 'What is the Right Supply Chain for Your Product?', by Marshall L. Fisher, Mar–Apr 1997. Copyright © 2003 by the Harvard Business School Publishing Corporation; all rights reserved; p. 252: © M. Lacity & L. Willcocks, *Global Information Technology Outsourcing*. John Wiley and Sons, Chichester, 2001. Reproduced by permission; p. 288: reproduced from *E-Commerce and V-Business*, S. Barnes and B. Hunt, pp. 172–8, Copyright 2001, with permission from Elsevier.

Every effort has been made to trace the ownership of copyright material. Information that will rectify any error or omission in subsequent editions will be welcome and the publisher will be happy to pay the usual permission fee. Please contact the Permissions Department of John Wiley & Sons Australia, Ltd.

chapter 1

Introduction to e-business

After reading this chapter, you should be able to:

- define e-commerce and e-business and understand the relationships of e-commerce and e-business to the existing IT resource in an organisation
- understand some fundamental concepts surrounding e-commerce and e-business
- appreciate the extent and diffusion of e-commerce
- discuss business uses of the Internet, and appreciate the costs and benefits for an organisation of adopting e-commerce and e-business
- understand the determinants of success for e-commerce and e-business.

chapter overview

For the purposes of this book, **e-commerce** is defined as the buying and selling of goods and services over computer networks, including the Internet. This chapter discusses the division of e-commerce into business-to-consumer (B2C) e-commerce and business-to-business (B2B) e-commerce, pointing out that these definitions can lead to confusion. **B2C e-commerce** refers to e-commerce transacted between business organisations and end consumers, whereas **B2B e-commerce** refers to e-commerce transacted between business organisations.

For the purposes of this text **e-business** is defined as the utilisation of information technology in organisations. Thus e-business includes the e-commerce systems that electronically connect the organisation to suppliers and customers, as well as the pre-Internet internal systems of the organisation, such as accounting and financial systems, inventory and manufacturing systems, order processing systems and the like.

The advent of the **Internet** led to changes in business that some academics and business writers saw as revolutionary. Such talk was encouraged by the convergence of three trends: the increasing use of the Internet and computer networks as vehicles for commercial transactions, the sustained boom in the US economy and those of other developed and developing countries in the mid to late 1990s, and the concomitant surge in productivity led by the United States and many other developed and developing economies.

The view adopted is that these trends can be viewed as primarily evolutionary, and the increasing use of computers for all aspects of business was seen well before the mid 1990s. Further, arguably the economy of the United States and other Western democracies in the mid to late 1990s was not 'new' in a fundamental sense, except that the rate of productivity growth increased at levels not seen since the 1950s and 1960s.[1]

The chapter covers some basic introductory concepts that are essential to developing an understanding of e-commerce and e-business. In particular, it discusses confusion surrounding many contemporary definitions of e-commerce and e-business, and identifies problems with terms commonly used, such as B2C and B2B. The chapter argues that organisations need to consider fundamental issues related to the advent of the Internet: namely, how to adopt the Internet and associated technologies to support the achievement of business goals and objectives. Doing this effectively will require organisations to be cognisant of the costs and benefits associated with any proposed uptake of e-commerce and e-business.

In an effort to assist and enable an understanding of the increasing maturity of organisational uses of computers, computer networks and the Internet, the Stages of Growth for e-business model is presented in this chapter. This model follows the style of earlier computing stages of maturity models, but extends the thinking to encompass the Internet and Internet-based commerce.

This chapter, and indeed this book, adopts an organisational perspective on e-commerce and e-business. Thus, e-commerce and e-business interactions, transactions and activities are typically described from the perspective of an organisation rather than from the perspective of its customers or its suppliers.

Introduction

> e-commerce, e-money, e-Bay, e-Trade...it's e-topia! (Kemp 2000, as cited by Willcocks & Plant 2000, p. 19)

> E can stand for electric or electronic, but at some point it will also have to stand for earnings (Chairman, New York Stock Exchange, May 2000, as cited by Willcocks & Plant 2000, p. 19)

The world has now entered the 'post-dotcom' era. In the space of a few short years preceding the dotcom crash, there was quite unprecedented hype surrounding e-commerce and what has been described as 'irrational exuberance' (Shiller 2000) about new paradigms of business, about the so-called 'new' economy, about the changes and transformations that organisations and individuals would need to make to adapt and survive in electronic, globalised, technology-driven environments that were predicted to emerge. The then-vice president of the United States, Al Gore, declared on the White House website:

> We are on the verge of a revolution that is just as profound as the change in the economy that came with the Industrial Revolution. Soon electronic net-works will allow people to transcend the barriers of time and distance and take advantage of global markets not even imaginable today, opening up a new world of economic possibility and progress. (Gibbons 1997)

Other pundits suggested that e-commerce could be likened to a 'tsunami' (Tapscott 1996, p. 4) that would sweep away all in its path who chose to ignore it. It was argued that traditional business fundamentals would no longer hold sway, and that businesses would rapidly have to adopt new business models involving substantial investments in information technology (IT).

Since the demise of the dotcoms in 2000, however, such technological optimism has been replaced by a more gloomy, pessimistic view of e-commerce. Greater cynicism surrounds the future prospects for the Internet and the changes that it was predicted to bring about in our society. Although the prevailing mood in the late 1990s was undoubtedly somewhat irrational in its advocacy of e-commerce, it is also a concern if this buoyancy is replaced by 'irrational pessimism' regarding the role and importance of e-commerce.

The purpose of this chapter is to discuss and analyse some of these issues. The chapter aims to provide a reality check of the importance and contribution of e-commerce currently and introduces the key impacts of e-commerce that will be explored throughout the book, namely the potential for e-commerce to offer efficiency, effectiveness and competitive gains in interacting with customers, suppliers and internal operations. Before considering these important issues, however, it is proposed to establish carefully what in fact is meant by the terms *e-commerce* and *e-business*. Experience suggests that a deal of confusion surrounds these terms and very little consensus exists on what is meant by them.

Defining e-commerce and e-business

Before reading this section, consider what the terms *e-commerce* and *e-business* mean to you. Jot down your ideas.

Now consider these scenarios. Decide whether or not you believe the activity described represents e-commerce or e-business. Discuss and justify your answers.

The Wong family need to buy a new washing machine. After extensive searching on the Internet during which they compare brands, features, prices and availability, they decide that a SPINMASTER 360i will be ideal for their purposes and budget, and find that such a machine is available at their local whitegoods store. They then drive to the store, where an assistant helps them to buy their desired washing machine.

Dominic Antonelli wants to buy flowers for his wife to celebrate her birthday. He telephones a florist close to his wife's place of work, describes his requirements and pays for the floral arrangement by credit card over the telephone. Dominic asks the florist to have the arrangement ready at 5.00 pm, as he wants to collect it and give it to his wife when he meets her at her office.

Kate Wilkinson hurries into her favourite department store to buy a dressing-gown for her sick father who has been admitted to hospital. She finds a suitable one and pays by credit card. She also takes advantage of the stores EFTPOS facilities to withdraw $100 cash as part of the transaction. Kate pays an additional fee to the store for them to deliver the dressing-gown to the hospital.

The term *commerce* denotes some transaction, an exchange of goods and/or services for money or other goods and services. Should we expect, then, that e-commerce thus implies commercial transactions taking place electronically? If this is the case, then using a telephone (which now relies on electronic networks) to order and pay for a pizza via credit card, or flowers in Dominic Antonelli's case above, would constitute e-commerce. So too would purchasing an item in person in a department store using EFTPOS facilities as Kate Wilkinson did. But is it helpful to consider buying goods in this manner in Wal-Mart or Tesco or Coles as e-commerce? The danger of doing so is that there is no apparent difference between e-commerce transactions and the way we have conducted transactions now for many years.

Another issue to consider is whether or not e-commerce necessarily involves the completion of a transaction. Hence consideration needs to be given to whether Internet-based advertising and marketing activities, Internet-enabled information provision and exchange that generate demands for goods and services, Internet-based after-sales support and customer service, and even Internet-enabled collaborative design and other activities that facilitate the production and distribution of goods and services (i.e. all activities that support the commercial transaction) should all be taken into account when the term *e-commerce* is used. If so, then the Wong family could be argued to have engaged in e-commerce in the process of obtaining their washing machine. Then we must also consider whether, in deriving our definition, what we mean is literally 'electronic' or whether indeed what we mean is 'Internet-based'.

Consider some of the following definitions of e-commerce.

> ...e-commerce can be formally defined as technology-mediated exchanges between parties (individuals, organisations, or both) as well as the electronically based intra- or interorganisational activities that facilitate such exchanges. (Rayport & Jaworski 2001, p. 3)

If the definition of Rayport and Jaworski (2001) is accepted, then e-commerce would include telephone, fax and even manual cash register-based transactions, as these could all be described as technology-mediated exchanges. This is unacceptable as it is far too inclusive for analysing e-commerce and e-business. By contrast, Kalakota and Robinson (1999, p. 4) describe e-commerce as 'buying and selling over digital media', emphasising that e-commerce must involve a transaction which must be effected via the Internet, an interorganisational computer-based system or some other digital device. This definition reflects that which is counted in national statistics on e-commerce, but seems restrictive in that it excludes all other Internet-based activities such as product design, interorganisational collaboration, advertising, marketing and so on, which are vital in supporting a transaction, irrespective of whether that transaction occurs over digital media.

Similar questions can be posed regarding e-business. Is *e-business* identical in meaning to *e-commerce*, and can the terms therefore be used interchangeably? Is it a more encompassing term, or is it narrower in scope than e-commerce?

For the purposes of this book, the term *e-commerce* will be used to denote commercial transactions mediated via the Internet, including all those computer-mediated activities involved in supporting that revenue generation. Thus direct sales of goods and services that take place over the Internet would be regarded as e-commerce, including the sales of goods and services from suppliers to an organisation as well as sales from the organisation to its end consumers. Also considered as e-commerce would be the advertising and marketing activities that take place over the Internet to support such sales, the provision of information and after-sales service over the Internet, and any other Internet-based activity that supported or enabled the transaction to take place.

E-business takes on a much broader meaning and includes the use of Internet-based technology and other information technology to support commerce and improve business performance. This can be achieved through increased connectivity and through deploying these technologies via **intranets**, **extranets**, the Internet and dedicated EDI-based interorganisational systems to improve efficiencies and effectiveness along the entire supply chain, to create internal efficiencies, and thus to create value directly and indirectly for the customer. Thus e-business not only embraces e-commerce but also includes the applications, systems and technology that were traditionally called information systems or information technology (IS/IT). This is captured in figure 1.1.

Given the above, an e-business therefore is a business that creatively and intelligently utilises and exploits the capabilities of IT and Internet technologies to create efficiencies, to achieve effectiveness gains such as flexibility and responsiveness, and to create strategic opportunities through competitive uses of IT to alter market and industry structures.

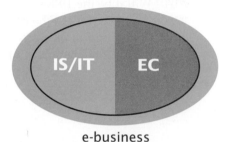

e-business

Figure 1.1 ▶ The relationship between e-business and e-commerce

Issues to consider regarding e-commerce and e-business

As soon as an attempt is made to differentiate e-commerce and e-business clearly, the difficulties in so doing become apparent. The matter is complicated further if one attempts to draw distinctions between e-commerce, e-business and what has traditionally been called IS/IT. Making such a distinction is probably therefore becoming less and less useful, and arguably all three terms will merge in time so that we will refer once again to the deployment of IS/IT (including the Internet and communications technologies) in business. Hence most businesses will be 'e-businesses' in that various IS/IT components will play a vital role in supporting and enabling a range of business activities. It is argued, then, that thinking about e-commerce or e-business primarily in terms of dotcoms, or 'pure play' start-ups, is not very helpful for the majority of organisations that need to grapple with issues of how best to embrace the new technologies to improve business performance and/or customer service. Arguably, the distinction between 'traditional' businesses and 'online' businesses is also rapidly fading. Thus the challenge facing all organisations is to make effective decisions about how and what information and communication technologies can be employed to support the achievement of organisational objectives.

With the increasing maturity of e-business, the questions for all existing organisations and new businesses will be:

• How can the Internet and other associated information technologies be effectively employed in our organisation to improve our performance in some way? Can these technologies be harnessed to increase efficiencies, improve the effectiveness of our operations, and/or to improve our flexibility and competitiveness?

- Can our business (established or new) effectively harness the potentialities of the Internet and associated technologies to help us achieve our business goals?

E-business: new phenomenon or natural progression?

Imagine it is now the year 2020. What will be remembered in the history studied in 2020? Will it be the 1960s, for the advent of the computer in business, or will it be the 1990s, for the advent of the Internet? Did the more fundamental change occur through the computerisation of business or through the widespread adoption of the Internet? The sequence of diagrams in figure 1.2 clarifies the position adopted in this text.

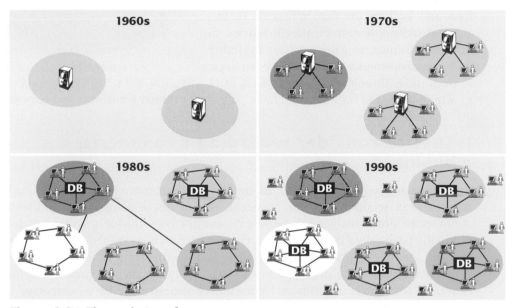

Figure 1.2 ▶ The evolution of e-commerce

The 1960s saw the introduction of mainframe computers in a relatively few, large organisations. At this stage, data-processing remained in the realm of IT specialists and, generally speaking, few end-users had direct access to computer technology. By the 1970s, there was greater diffusion and infusion of mainframe computers, and some end-users had direct access to computer processing via dumb terminals linked directly to the mainframe. This enabled some rudimentary processing power to be placed directly in the hands of end-users. The 1980s era was characterised by the emergence first of the personal computer (PC) and second of database technologies, both of which became more prevalent throughout that decade. The 1980s also saw the emergence of private leased lines being used to establish private networks, often between various branches of multinational corporations, and to facilitate trade between large business partners using EDI-based interorganisational systems. These systems tended to be expensive and technically moderately complex, which generally precluded all but the larger organisations from investing in them. The 1980s were also characterised by the emergence of networked PCs in some organisations. Throughout the 1990s, the proliferation of networked PCs increased rapidly as most knowledge workers were equipped with computer technology to support their work. The decade was also marked by rapid developments in computer networks and the wide-scale adoption of the Internet by business. Many households also had invested in PC and Internet capabilities.

Thus, the 1990s was marked by the emergence of an 'internetworked' world, with some important consequences. First, computer networks linking organisation to organisation via the Internet became cheap enough and readily available to mean that most organisations could access other organisations electronically. Second, with the rapid uptake of the Internet by private individuals at home, organisations could now communicate directly with individual end consumers electronically. Third, the emergence of internetworked organisations helped, to some extent at least, to remove barriers of time and place that had previously limited the availability of goods and services to customers and end consumers. The impacts and implications of these developments infuse each of the chapters of this book.

Arguably, therefore, we have been moving inexorably towards the current e-business environment since the early 1960s, and the current potentiality of e-business is much more of a natural progression or evolution than a recent revolution. This does not, however, mean that e-business is unimportant. The Internet and associated technologies potentially offer enormous benefits to business as it is now possible to access so many people, organisations and so much information quickly over the Internet. The key changes that are so significant in contemporary business environments are:

- first, the business environment is now highly interconnected via computer networks of various types (but primarily the Internet)
- second, for most businesses, electronic linkages to players all along the supply chain allows the achievement of substantial efficiencies and better service as a result
- third, direct access to customers and end consumers provides opportunities for goods and services to be better targeted towards specific customer needs, and for information regarding customer preferences to be fed back into internal decision-making about production, product and service design and development
- fourth, internal efficiencies can be achieved through the provision of more timely information and streamlined business processes.

Perspectives on e-commerce and e-business

In many developed countries, substantial proportions of the population are online (more than 50 per cent, for example). In the United States, Scandinavia and many Western European countries substantial proportions of the population are online and, in Asia, Singapore, Hong Kong and Taiwan lead the way. In Australia, studies suggest that the typical profile of home users of the Internet is employed, relatively affluent couples with children, who live in cities. The most popular purchases over the Internet are books, followed by computer hardware and software, clothing, music, event tickets and so on (NOIE 2001). Despite the rapid rate of growth in e-commerce in many of these countries, e-commerce remains a small proportion of the total retail trade. Estimates suggest that it comprises around 1 per cent in most developed countries.

How significant is e-commerce? On the one hand, the achievement of 1 per cent of retail sales is more moderate than some forecasters had suggested. The achievement of what was a very conservative target (and widely criticised at the time of publication) of e-commerce reaching 15 per cent of total retail trade (Markham 1998) now seems quite challenging. However, statistics record only Internet-based transactions and make no account of transactions carried out via other channels but informed by the Internet. It would seem that the figure would be very much higher if these could be included. As is shown throughout this book, however, the impact of e-commerce and Internet-based technologies is much more significant than can be evidenced currently in direct and Internet-based sales.

Two broad categories of e-commerce can be identified: these are known as business to consumer (B2C) e-commerce and business to business (B2B) e-commerce. Thus when a business sells goods and services via the Internet to individual end consumers, this constitutes B2C, whereas B2B implies that the commercial transaction is taking place between two organisations. B2B e-commerce has grown much more rapidly than B2C e-commerce, as reflected in figure 1.3, and is now estimated to be between 10 and 20 times larger than B2C e-commerce (Cunningham 2001).

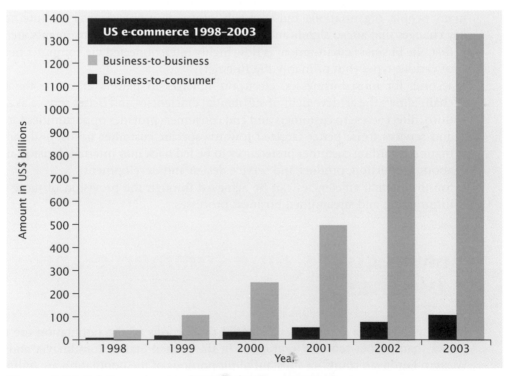

Figure 1.3 ▶ Relative volumes of B2B and B2C e-commerce
Source ▶ Nua.com 2002.

This distinction between B2C and B2B e-commerce, however, can be confusing (see figure 1.4). Imagine a scenario in which our organisation sells office paper both online and via our own stores. Our organisation sells bulk volumes of office paper to C, who on-sells to organisations F and G. F and G then consume the paper they have purchased from C. We also supply smaller volumes to organisation D, which consumes that paper internally, and in very small quantities to E, who uses the paper in her home office. Interactions and transactions between our organisation and end consumer E would be regarded as B2C e-commerce: all other online interactions (between A, B, C, D and our organisation) would be considered B2B e-commerce. This causes confusion in distinguishing between different types of customers and even between different types of end consumers.

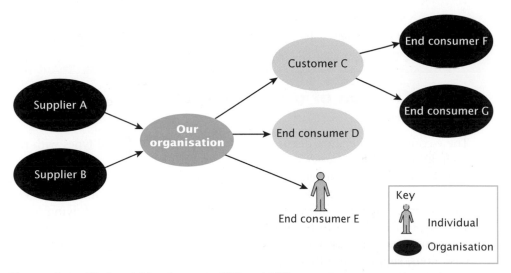

Figure 1.4 ▶ Distinguishing between B2B and B2C e-commerce

In this book, for many of the subsequent discussions, we prefer to adopt a much simpler distinction, as illustrated in figure 1.5 (p. 10). Both online and offline interactions and transactions are more simply conceived of as occurring between an organisation and its customers (of varying sorts and purposes), known as *customer* or *demand-driven transactions*, and between an organisation and its suppliers, known as *supply-driven transactions*. Customers of all types like — and possibly expect — to be treated as customers. Managing one's interactions with customers is a different thing from sourcing suppliers, negotiating arrangements with them and then trading with them.

B2B and B2C are helpful concepts when it is important to distinguish between the volume of transactions occurring (B2B e-commerce can involve a much higher volume of transactions than B2C), the power relations existing between trading partners (an organisation can typically exert more power than an individual), the nature of exchanges and so on. However, B2B and B2C are less helpful when it is important to distinguish between organisations that supply another organisation with goods and services (**supply-oriented interactions**) and those who claim to be customers of an organisation (**demand-oriented interactions**).

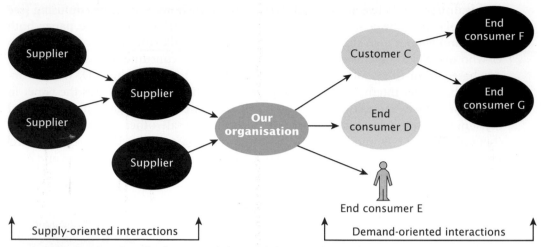

Figure 1.5 ▶ Supply-driven and demand-driven relationships

Classification of organisational types and e-commerce

The e-commerce literature discusses a number of organisational types with respect to their adoption of e-commerce technologies and behaviours.

A **'bricks and mortar'** enterprise presents itself to its customers through its factories, warehouses, office blocks, retail stores and sales force. If it is a retail company, its customers transact with it by visiting its physical stores and buying its products via face-to-face interactions. Bricks and mortar organisations have not adopted e-commerce to any substantial degree (there are no electronic interactions with their customers, suppliers or other major stakeholders).

A **'pure dotcom'** or **'Internet pure play'**, however, essentially presents itself to its customers via its web page. Its customers purchase and pay for products via mouse clicks and data entry on its web page and, although it is likely to have a physical office, warehousing and the like, its interactions with customers are accomplished over the Internet.

Enterprises that offer the customer both a physical presence in the form of retail stores where customers can buy goods in face-to-face interactions with sales staff, and a web page on which mouse clicks and data entry can constitute a sales transaction, are often referred to as **'bricks and clicks'** or **'clicks and mortar'** organisations.

Business uses of the Internet

There is wide variation in the ways in which business can adopt and use Internet technologies for both supply-oriented and customer-oriented e-commerce, from relatively simple, unsophisticated approaches to highly complex, mature appropriation and utilisation. This can perhaps best be illustrated by considering how the SOGe (Stages of Growth for e-business) model explains various stages of maturity or sophistication and suggests a progression to more mature stages as appropriate (see figure 1.6).

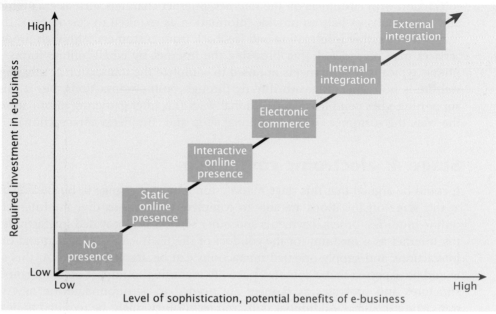

Figure 1.6 ▶ The Stages of Growth for e-business model (SOGe)
Source ▶ McKay, Prananto and Marshall 2000.

Stage 1: no presence

Organisations at this stage may be characterised as adopting a 'wait and see' approach. Despite reports of rapid growth in e-commerce, and the accompanying expectation of substantial returns on investment, the strategy adopted here is to wait for competitors or business associates to go online, assess their results, and then act when business benefits and/or profitability accrue from the e-commerce investment. The 'no presence' approach might stem from ignorance of the Internet. However, preliminary research results (Marshall, Sor & McKay 2000) suggest it is more typically associated with uncertainty about the costs and benefits of e-commerce (as opposed to the costs and benefits of *not* establishing a web presence), issues of risk and security associated with e-commerce, and uncertainty as to whether an organisation's goods or services are suited to advertising and sale over the Internet.

Stage 2: static online presence

At this stage, the organisation establishes an initial presence on the Internet. However, it is limited to a static, information provision role whereby information dissemination and communication is essentially uni-directional from the organisation out to interested parties. Information published online at this stage might take the form of corporate brochures or 'brochureware' (Berryman 1999), contact details, product/ service information and catalogues, information for shareholders, job opportunities with the organisation and the like.

Stage 3: interactive online presence

This is the first stage at which organisations enter into two-way communication and interaction with customers on the Internet. Internet channels such as email, browsers and web databases help to provide information as required to customers and might also serve to gather information and feedback from customers. Although products or services may be ordered after browsing the Internet by email, online forms, fax or phone, typically the Internet is not used to complete the transaction at this stage. The website is not generating cash directly through online transactions, but it might be supporting sales completed in traditional ways (i.e. after gathering information from the Web, the customer visits a traditional shop and completes a transaction).

Stage 4: electronic commerce

It could be argued that this stage marks a fundamental change in business activity as at this stage organisations are able to complete transactions over the Internet. Thus online inquiries, orders, payments and other services are provided interactively using the Internet as a medium for the conduct of the transaction. Both demand-oriented interactions and supply-oriented interactions can be accommodated. At this stage it would be expected that e-commerce activity is starting to impact on an organisation's structures and processes as changes are needed to accommodate the new way of transacting business. Additional skills and technology might be required to deal with round-the-clock trading and distribution issues.

Stage 5: internal integration

At stage 5, progress has been made in integrating the 'front office' Internet transaction capabilities and accompanying technologies with 'back office' IS/IT business support systems and technologies, thus representing the emergence of e-business. There is a consciousness throughout the organisation of the need to align IS/IT investment with business strategies and that processes and structures might have to be re-engineered to accrue the true benefits of modern technologies (Premkumar 1999). Discontinuities between e-commerce trading activities and traditional trading activities can occur when the two are not closely integrated both from an IS/IT perspective and/or from a business perspective. At this stage, however, discontinuities typically disappear as organisations achieve better levels of integration across all the IS/IT and e-commerce investments. In this regard, e-commerce can act as a catalyst to remove duplicated effort and truly integrate intra-organisational IS/IT initiatives and investments.

Stage 6: external integration

IT plays a key role in transforming entire business networks at this stage. Hence, blurring and extension of traditional organisational boundaries will occur, giving rise to such notions as the extended enterprise (Harrison & Pratt 1998; Tapscott 2001), and the virtual organisation (Marshall, McKay & Burn 2001). Evident at this stage is the integration of business processes and technologies of networks of buyers and sellers, resulting in close and mutually beneficial relationships between trading partners.

Extranet technologies can be usefully employed at this stage. Business strategies and IS/IT strategies must be closely aligned, both internally, to provide a seamless process of placing and receiving an order, making appropriate logistical arrangements, and making and receiving payments electronically, and externally, among all players in strategic business networks. The resultant 'internetworked enterprise' (Tapscott 2001) is responsive, flexible, dynamic and opportunistic in its business activities.

As organisations progress from less to more mature levels of e-commerce adoption, generally speaking, the potential benefits derived from e-commerce increase, but so do the costs and the risks associated with these initiatives. Careful analysis and strategising is thus required to ensure that costs and risks are carefully monitored and controlled and thus minimised, and benefits are carefully managed to ensure their realisation. These issues will be covered in more detail in chapters 2, 3, 4 and 12.

From a consideration of the types of activities that are enabled by the various increasing levels of maturity in the SOGe model, it can be deduced that businesses are using the Internet in general terms for the following purposes:

- direct dialogue with suppliers and customers, interactive marketing and customer relationship management
- commercial transactions
- communication and collaboration with customers, suppliers, business partners and possibly competitors
- formation of strategic business alliances and networks to influence the competitive environment
- management of procurement and the supply chain
- operational efficiencies.

Potential costs and benefits of e-commerce

Costs and benefits of e-commerce vary according to the stage of the SOGe model an organisation embraces. However, certain generic benefits can be identified. Many organisations look to the Internet as a means of increasing their revenue generation. This can be achieved via direct sales over the Internet (SOGe model — stages 4, 5 and 6) or through an increase in traditional sales resulting from Internet-based marketing and advertising efforts and through provision of information online. Increased revenue streams can also result if e-commerce enables an organisation to reach a new or additional market successfully, which is sometimes achieved through the global reach of the Internet. Additionally, increased revenues could result if the Internet is used to add value to a good or service from the customer perspective, if that added value serves to increase customer retention rates and build customer loyalty.

Appropriate use of Internet technologies could also improve a firm's performance if they serve to reduce costs for the organisation. Efficiencies can be achieved through improved internal processes, and costs can be reduced through efficient Internet-based transactions with suppliers and customers.

Opinions differ as to whether the Internet itself is a source of competitive advantage for an organisation. Before the dotcom collapse, there was a tendency to view the Internet in that light. However, more recent advice suggests that any source of competitive advantage in fact stems from the way the Internet technologies are deployed by an organisation rather than residing inherently within the technology itself (see Porter 2001).

Costs also vary according to the stage of uptake of the SOGe model. By stages 4, 5 and 6, substantial investments could be required, especially if existing internal IS/IT needs to be integrated with web-based trading activities and processes. In work reported by Oz (2000), for example, an average figure of the US$1.3 million was reported for the adoption of e-commerce, although the stage of adoption was not made clear. Research into the costs incurred by small and medium enterprises (SMEs) adopting e-commerce in Australia suggested figures ranging from as little as $2500 for stage 2 sites to in excess of $100 000 for stage 4 websites (Marshall & McKay 2002). For discussion of the costs involved for SMEs adopting the basic levels of e-commerce refer to the paper by Marshall and McKay (2002) in the Suggested Reading list at the end of this chapter.

The types of costs that need to be considered in properly estimating the costs of a move to e-commerce are as follows:
- computer hardware and software
- telecommunications hardware and software
- development or acquisition and implementation of systems
- systems integration
- use of consultants
- additional personnel (such as specialised IS/IT staff, web designers, network specialists and the like) and/or training (both of IS/IT staff and general business staff)
- security
- ongoing technical support
- operating costs and maintenance
- process re-engineering costs
- enhancement of business strategy and development of e-business vision and strategies
- change management.

thinking strategically

The florist's dilemma: adopt e-commerce or not?

You are a consultant to the owner-manager of City Flowers, a small florist shop. The owner-manager has been reading a lot about the promise of e-commerce and e-business recently, and is naturally concerned about whether he would benefit from adopting e-commerce and e-business in some form.

City Flowers is located close to the central business district. Although there are many office blocks and retail stores close by, there are also an increasing number of trendy,

up-market apartment blocks. About 40 per cent of City Flowers' business currently comes from meeting standing orders (usually on a weekly basis) from corporate clients who require floral arrangements for their reception areas and executive suites. Another 30 per cent of his business comes from individuals who buy on impulse or for special occasions, either when passing the shop or by telephone. The remaining 30 per cent are for orders to be delivered interstate or internationally.

The owner-manager attended a short computer course at a TAFE college and has a PC to run basic financial packages that support the accounting and GST (Goods and Services Tax) needs of his business. However, the owner-manager currently buys his flowers over the telephone and relies on visiting sales reps to replenish supplies of soft toys, balloons, gift wrapping, ribbon and the like.

Questions

1. What would you advise the owner-manager of City Flowers to do? Should he adopt e-commerce? Use the SOGe model to recommend a level of adoption. Justify your choice. What would be the main benefits of it? Where would the major costs be incurred?

2. How certain are you that such an initiative would prove profitable for the owner-manager of City Flowers?

Determinants of e-commerce and e-business success

Despite its rapid growth, e-commerce and e-business are still relatively immature disciplines, and the understanding and appreciation of these disciplines is still evolving. Writing definitive critical success factors (CSFs) is therefore difficult, if not impossible. However, based on ever-expanding research findings and experiences with e-business, a number of factors and issues are emerging that appear to be pivotal to the success of such initiatives. Each of these is considered briefly in turn, as they form the basic structure of this textbook.

Profitability

To be successful in the long term, all businesses, including e-businesses, must make a profit. (An e-business is defined here as a business that creatively and intelligently utilises and exploits the capabilities of IT and Internet technologies to create efficiencies, achieve effectiveness gains such as flexibility and responsiveness, and create strategic opportunities through competitive uses of IT to alter market and industry structures.) An analysis of the dotcom euphoria of the late 1990s suggests that in many cases, this business maxim, and the careful decision-making that it implies, might have been overlooked or forgotten. But experience now suggests that being profitable is not a certainty in the e-business world.

What, then, lies at the heart of e-business viability, success and profitability? First, a sound understanding of e-business models, or a blueprint for the e-business, is essential. From that understanding can come recognition of the sources of costs and revenues in e-business and, importantly, of the risks associated with the move into e-commerce and e-business. Understanding e-business models and their implications forms the basis of chapter 2 of this text. Second, another key component of ensuring viability and/or profitability is understanding the sources of value in e-business. Once value creation is clearly understood, appropriate performance measurement can become a core component of e-business success. These notions of e-business value and performance measurement are more fully explored in chapter 12.

Planning

At the height of the dotcom euphoria, it was fashionable to suggest that in highly dynamic, turbulent and uncertain business environments, it was impossible, or at the very least undesirable, to spend time in planning. Experience now suggests that this thinking was folly, as sound planning appears to be a vital ingredient in successful e-business ventures. However, it does appear that the nature of planning is changing. Planning for e-business needs to resemble day-by-day thinking and acting rather than being a heavy, bureaucratic undertaking. That day-by-day 'sense and respond' mode of planning (McNurlin & Sprague 2002) requires a clear vision for the organisation, the support of senior executives for the e-business initiatives, and a strategy by which this vision, along with the organisation's goals and objectives, is communicated throughout the organisation.

Another vital component of successful planning activities is the notion of alignment: ensuring that IS/IT investments and initiatives directly enable the achievement of business goals and objectives, or support this through building an appropriately flexible infrastructure that forms the basis of future business growth and development. These aspects of planning are addressed in more detail in chapters 3 and 4.

Re-engineering of processes

The Internet and associated technologies offer an organisation an opportunity to reorient itself in highly competitive markets to become a customer-centric organisation, geared to being responsive to the needs and preferences of its customers. This inevitably means that core business processes might change, and long-term viability and profitability imply a need to analyse opportunities to re-engineer such processes. Many organisations are using Internet-based and/or communication technologies to bring about fundamental changes in the way they interact with their suppliers (and indeed their suppliers' suppliers and so on). Others realise opportunities to re-engineer their interactions with customers, using the Internet and other technologies to develop closer relationships with customers, to add value to the experience of their customers and to compete in the marketplace in fundamentally new ways. Organisations are also finding that such technologies are providing outstanding opportunities to increase internal efficiencies and to build flexibility and responsiveness. Exploring these opportunities to re-engineer business processes forms the bases of chapters 5, 6 and 7.

Management of knowledge resources

Another vital factor for successful e-businesses appears to be their ability to manage their knowledge resources. The knowledge resources of an organisation include information and knowledge about its customers, suppliers, business processes, technologies and 'know-how', and it is argued that sharing and distributing such knowledge resources allows them to be better utilised and exploited as a source of competitive advantage. Knowledge of information technology and the Internet obviously plays a vital role in the successful exploitation and management of the knowledge resource of an organisation. This notion is exploited more fully in chapter 8.

Developing and sourcing capabilities

The challenge for successful e-businesses is to combine the strengths typically associated with large enterprises (efficiency, power and resources) with those we associate with small enterprises (speed, agility and responsiveness). This is clearly a very subtle balancing act, implying that carefully considered decisions need to be made as to whether required skills, knowledge and activities should be accessed via the marketplace or outsourced or whether they should be fostered in-house. Arguments for and against insourcing versus outsourcing can be raised, but the trend seems to be for organisations to move away from traditional vertically integrated structures to more flexible partnerships and alliances through which requisite knowledge, skills and resources are accessed. Hence organisations must successfully negotiate entry to and manage relationships with other organisations in order to access required resources and capabilities. Developing e-business capabilities and managing strategic business networks are the foci of chapters 9 and 10.

Proactive uptake of technologies

E-businesses remain successful while they exploit appropriate technologies and while they regard technological innovation and change as an opportunity rather than a problem. Of particular interest currently for many e-businesses is the extent to which mobile computing (or m-commerce) offers opportunities to enhance customer service, create new customers, seek efficiencies in operations and so on. Mobile computing is explored further in chapter 11.

IT and e-business governance processes

Organisations have traditionally struggled to manage and exploit their IT resource, and this issue becomes more difficult and more pressing with the added IT investments associated with the Internet and e-business. This has often been attributed to poor governance processes or the processes by which it is ensured that IT and Internet investments add value to the organisation, support and enable the achievement of corporate goals, and through which exposure to IT risk is minimised. Hence viability for e-businesses depends on ensuring alignment between IS/IT and corporate goals, on appropriately allocating IS/IT resources, on managing risks, and on ensuring excellence and consistency in decision-making with respect to IS/IT. The requirements for good IT governance are explored in chapter 12.

Overall, most businesses today need to find ways to adopt the Internet and other communications and IT to achieve and maintain a competitive position. The Internet itself is not a source of competitive advantage: this has been learned from the dotcom debacle. But it does appear that if appropriately utilised and managed, in tandem with other IT, the Internet can play a significant role in modern organisations, both as a source of efficiency and effectiveness and in fundamentally altering the nature of competition.

What must be borne in mind, however, is the fact that no direct link can be made between investing in IT and in improved outcomes for the organisation. The organisation acts as something of a 'black box' in which sometimes excellent outcomes are achieved whereas at other times results are disappointing. One of the objectives of this book, then, is to explore the 'inner workings' of the black box that is e-business and e-commerce in an attempt to identify those organisational activities that enhance the benefits derived from IT and Internet investments.

Summary

This chapter has introduced some of the basic concepts about e-commerce and e-business and, in particular, has attempted to explain the relationship between the 'e' phenomenon and what traditionally was known as IS/IT. The overall conclusion was that all businesses will evolve to become e-businesses and almost seamless integration will occur between the adoption and use of Internet-based technologies and other information technologies in the organisation. Arguably the move towards e-business has been evolutionary rather than revolutionary, but nonetheless a significant challenge facing organisations is how best to incorporate these newer technologies into their business activities to improve efficiency and effectiveness and to influence the strategic positioning of the organisation.

The concepts of B2C and B2B e-commerce were clarified and some potential areas of confusion highlighted. The preferred distinction between the adoption of IT to support relationships with suppliers and the adoption of IT to support relationships with customers was drawn. Various options for adopting e-commerce were discussed and illustrated with the SOGe model, and the various costs and benefits associated with e-commerce were outlined. The importance of deriving business value from e-commerce was also discussed, and a number of critical success factors that support the achievement of profitability and/or viability for organisational e-business initiatives were identified.

key terms

bricks and mortar	extranet
business-to-business (B2B) e-commerce	Internet
business-to-consumer (B2C) e-commerce	Internet pure play
clicks and mortar, or bricks and clicks	intranet
demand-oriented interactions	pure dotcom
e-business	supply-oriented interactions
e-commerce	

In answering the discussion questions for this chapter, you are expected to give very broadly based answers rather than venture into the detail of each topic.

1. Much of the excitement and interest related to the Internet came from the idea of selling an organisation's products to remote consumers who connected to the organisation's web page. In fact, a very similar activity had been going on in an unspectacular fashion for many years. Many organisations had catalogues that were distributed to remote or potential customers. The customers would choose items from the catalogue and close the sale by mail, telephone or fax. Discuss the similarities and differences between catalogue-based retailing and Internet retailing. (You might like to do some research to establish the relative sizes of catalogue-based retailing and Internet retailing.)

2. An organisation's suppliers need to communicate and collaborate with the organisation to ensure the timely flow of raw materials for production or, in the case of retailers, finished goods into the organisation. General supplies such as computers, office paper and the like, as well as materials for maintenance and repair operations, also need to be procured to ensure the smooth and efficient operation of the organisation. The management of these activities is called supply chain management, and it could involve coordination and cooperation not only with the organisation's suppliers but also their suppliers' suppliers and so on, thus creating a chain of linked organisations, all involved in the supply process.

   An organisation and its suppliers need to coordinate the flows of raw materials and supplies such that these are obtained when needed and in the minimum required quantities so that inventory carrying costs are minimised. This requires the synchronisation of the production schedules of both organisations. Joint product development, so that appropriately designed raw materials are developed, is also important. Synchronising the production schedules of an organisation and its suppliers as well as arranging distribution and product development activities appropriately takes much effective communication, coordination and collaboration. Discuss the potential contribution of IT and the Internet to these activities (i.e. to supply chain management). Discuss the role of IT before the Internet with regard to these activities.

3. 'Knowledge management' became a popular term in the Internet era of the late 1990s. The idea was that the knowledge that an organisation possessed regarding its business processes, its customers, its technology and the like was a very important source of competitive advantage. Some writers saw IT and the Internet as important tools in the storage and diffusion of knowledge throughout an organisation. Other writers saw this viewpoint as too strongly emphasising the role of technology and pointed out the important role of people as the source and repository of knowledge. These writers also pointed out the importance of tacit knowledge or 'know-how' that could not be made explicit in documents and could not be transferred to other persons without personal mentoring and coaching. Discuss the role (if any) of IT and the Internet in managing and increasing the knowledge in an organisation.

4. Outsourcing is the contracting out of tasks, activities, processes and even business functions such as accounting, IT, all human resource management to third parties. Writers on e-commerce have suggested that in the era of e-commerce and the Internet, outsourcing has increased and will continue to increase. This increase in outsourcing is partly attributed to the availability of the Internet. It is implied that the Internet will improve the ability of businesses to identify appropriate outsourcing partners, as well as enabling the monitoring and control of outsourcing arrangements to be carried out more efficiently and effectively. Discuss this proposition, examining carefully where the Internet will make an impact and where the Internet will only have a marginal effect because the mode of interaction it permits is inappropriate.

5. It is argued that the Internet makes possible more efficient — and possibly also more effective — communication between the members of an organisation. The Internet is also argued to make possible more efficient and effective communication between the organisation and its customers. Discuss the idea that IT in general and the Internet in particular might enable more efficient and effective communication and interaction between the organisation and its customers. Further, discuss the proposition that an organisation might, with the help of IT and the Internet, better manage the relationship between an organisation and its customers.

6. Select any five organisations with websites that you are familiar with. Use the SOGe model to analyse each website and attempt to establish their level of maturity with respect to e-commerce. Be prepared to justify your decision. Are there any weaknesses with this type of analysis? How certain are you that the level of maturity you have identified is accurate?

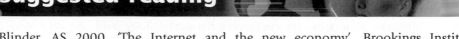

note

1. Although the advent of the computer is typically associated with productivity gains, statistics suggest that productivity between 1975 and 1995 (a time of rapid increases in investment in IT) grew by approximately 1.5 per cent per annum on average, whereas during the 1960s (a time of small investment in IT), it had been increasing at about 4.5 per cent per annum on average (*The Economist* 1999).

suggested reading

Blinder, AS 2000, 'The Internet and the new economy', Brookings Institution, Washington, USA. www.brookings.edu, accessed May 2002.

Coltman, T, Devinney, TM, Latukefu, A, & Midgley, DF 2001, 'E-business: revolution, evolution or hype?', *California Management Review*, vol. 44, no. 1, pp. 57–86.

Gordon, RJ 2000, 'Does the new economy measure up to the great inventions of the past?', *Journal of Economic Perspectives*, vol. 4, no. 14, pp. 49–74.

McKay, J & Marshall, P 2002, 'Current approaches to realising the benefits from e-commerce investments amongst SMEs', *Australian Journal of Information Systems*, vol. 9, no. 2, pp. 135–47.

references

Berryman, E 1999, 'Getting on with the business of e-business', PriceWaterhouseCoopers, www.pwcglobal.com, accessed 10 June 2001.

Cunningham, MJ 2001, *B2B: How to Build a Profitable e-Commerce Strategy*, Perseus Publishing, Cambridge, MA.

Economist, The 1999, *Economics: Making Sense of the Modern Economy. The Economist*, in association with Profile Books, London.

Gibbons, J 1997, 'NGI testimony — John H. Gibbons', Next Generation Internet Initiative, United States, www.ngi.gov/testimony/gibbons-10Sep97.html, accessed June 2003.

Harrison, DB & Pratt, MD 1998, 'A methodology for re-engineering businesses', in V Sethi & WR King (eds), *Organisational Transformation Through Business Process Re-engineering*, Prentice Hall, Upper Saddle River, NJ, pp. 67–74.

Kalakota, R & Robinson, M 1999, *E-business: roadmap for success*, Addison-Wesley, Reading, MA.

Markham, JE 1998, *The Future of Shopping: Traditional Patterns and Net Effects*, Macmillan, London.

Marshall, P, McKay, J & Burn, J 2001, 'The three S's of virtual organisations: structure, strategy and success factors', in B Hunt & S Downes (eds), *E-commerce and V-business*, Butterworth Heinemann, London, pp. 171–92.

Marshall, P, Sor, R & McKay, J 2000, 'Electronic commerce and car retailing: an industry case study', *International Journal of Electronic Commerce Research*, vol. 1, no. 1, pp. 1–12.

McKay, J & Marshall, P 2002, 'Current approaches to realising the benefits from e-commerce investments amongst SMEs', *Australian Journal of Information Systems*, vol. 9, no. 2, pp. 135–47.

McKay, J, Prananto, A & Marshall, P 2000, 'E-business maturity: the SOGe model', Australasian Conference on Information Systems, Queensland University of Technology, Brisbane, 6–8 December.

McNurlin, BC & Sprague, RH 2002, *Information Systems Management in Practice*, 5th edn, Prentice Hall, Upper Saddle River, NJ.

NOIE 2001, *The Current State of Play*, National Office for the Information Economy, Canberra.

Nua.com 2002, US Ecommerce 1998–2003, www.nua.ie, accessed March 2002.

Oz, E 2000, *Management Information Systems*, 2nd edn, Course Technology, Cambridge, MA.

Porter, ME 2001, 'Strategy and the Internet', *Harvard Business Review*, vol. 79, no. 3, pp. 62–78.

Premkumar, G 1999, 'Supply chain management and inter-organizational systems: an integrated perspective', in *Proceedings of the Fifth Americas Conference on Information Systems*, Milwaukee, WI: Association of Information Systems, 13–15 August, pp. 621–3.

Rayport, JF & Jaworski, BJ 2001, *E-commerce*, McGraw-Hill/Irwin MarketspaceU, NY.

Shiller, RJ 2000, *Irrational exuberance*, Scribe Publications, Carlton North, Vic.

Tapscott, D 1996, *The Digital Economy: Promise and Peril in the Age of Networked Intelligence*, McGraw-Hill, NY.

—2001, 'Rethinking strategy in a networked world (or why Michael Porter is wrong about the Internet)', *Strategy + Business*, issue 24, Third Quarter, pp. 1–6. Available online at http://www.strategy-business.com/press/prnt/?ptag-ps=$art=14904&pg=0&format=print, accessed 18 June 2003.

Willcocks, LP & Plant, R 2000, 'Business strategy: moving to the net', in L Willcocks & C Sauer, *Moving to E-business*, Random House Business Books, London, pp. 19–46.

chapter 2

Adopting appropriate e-business models

learning objectives

After reading this chapter, you should understand:

- what constitutes a business model
- why understanding and articulating a business model is vital to an organisation achieving profitability and sustainability
- the essential components of a business model, and some generic business models
- how managers can use business models and the implications of business models for managerial decision-making and action-taking
- the relationship between business models and organisational strategy.

chapter overview

The advent of the Internet has presented business organisations with new opportunities and challenges. It offers a new, interactive channel by which to reach out to trading partners and individual consumers, and hence decisions need to be made about whether and how to embrace the new technology and the opportunities it creates. On the other hand, in the short history of the wide-scale adoption of the Internet in business, it seems apparent that there are no guaranteed successes, and that great care and judgement needs to be exercised if Internet technologies are to be successfully adopted and integrated into business activities.

This chapter explores the proposition that underpinning the successful incorporation of Internet technologies is, among other things, a sound e-business model. The e-business model provides a blueprint for the operation of the business: it clearly articulates the value that customers (of all types) derive from the bundle of products, services and relationship that is established between the organisation and its customers. Furthermore, the e-business model must identify the sources of profitability and viability of the e-business initiative, which implies a need for careful management of the activities and processes and the resources and capabilities required to deliver value to customers. The chapter will consider the key elements of an e-business model and explain their implications for managers.

Introduction

> The terms 'business model' and 'strategy' are amongst the most sloppily used in business. People use them interchangeably to refer to everything — so they mean nothing. (Magretta 2002, p. 2)

In starting a chapter on business models, the words of Magretta (2002) contain both an undeniable truth and an important warning. The truth is that *business model*, as a term, has become one of the buzzwords associated with hype surrounding the Internet, e-commerce and e-business, and, as is so often the case when phenomena become hyped, important terminology loses its meaning as it is sprinkled through the literature to refer to a whole range of concepts. Hence the warning from Magretta (2002): there is a danger that terms like *business model* start to mean nothing much at all because of their routine misappropriation. One of the aims of this chapter, then, is to define what is meant by a business model and, from that, to discuss why this concept is so important in e-business.

Why the upsurge in interest in business models? Is there something inherent in e-commerce, e-business and the new economy that requires us to talk about business models? Before addressing this second question, let us consider why, since the mid 1990s, there have been widespread discussions about business models in the literature.

Simply expressed, a **business model** is an attempt to identify an organisation's customers and, from there, to discuss how the organisation will achieve profitability and sustainability by delivering goods and services (or 'value') to those customers. Before the widespread advent of the Internet, businesses were typically adopting models of business that had been developed and refined over more than a hundred years of the so-called industrial age. The models were familiar, and therefore the customer value and the means by which an organisation achieved profitability were generally obvious. Thus, in talking about a car dealership, or a clothing manufacturer, or a charitable organisation, for example, there was a sense in which the guiding framework or principles by which these organisations delivered 'value' to their customers or clientele and the means by which they achieved profitability or sustainability were familiar. Detailed explanation of the goods and services provided, the skills and processes required for success and so on were not required as it was generally accepted that such concepts were well understood and did not require further explication.

With the advent of the Internet and associated communications technologies, however, new and unfamiliar possibilities emerge. For example, the Internet offers a new medium and an additional channel by which organisations can 'reach' their customers, by which organisations procure goods and services, and by which organisations can distribute digital goods and services. The Internet facilitated the emergence of businesses that did not have a pre-Internet existence and could not exist as they do without the Internet (think of Amazon and eBay, for example). It also changed the way previously existing organisations could operate (such as Dell Computers, some supermarkets and other retailers, and government departments, for example). The **value**

proposition of these organisations (the value they deliver to customers), the capabilities they need to deliver the value proposition successfully, their sources of costs and revenues, and so on are generally much less obvious and therefore need further analysis and articulation.

The concept of a business model is not a new one. But as we move more and more into the so-called information age or the new economy, new possibilities emerge for the conduct of business that are not familiar or obvious and which therefore need to be discussed. For businesses to make sensible decisions about appropriate technologies to adopt and incorporate into their operations, they must understand the potentialities, issues and risks associated with new business models, so that Internet-based technologies can be exploited to enhance the value generated for customers while ensuring the viability of the enterprise. There is nothing inherent in the Internet *per se* that requires a discussion about business models. Rather it is the new business possibilities that arise as a result of the new technologies, prominent among which is the Internet, which imply a need to revisit familiar business models and explore new and unfamiliar business models. Finding a creative approach and an integrated mix of new and old is a challenge that faces most contemporary organisations.

Think about the Internet-based organisations mentioned in the introduction to this chapter (Amazon, eBay, Dell). For each organisation, what do you know about:
- their target customers or customer groups?
- their sources of revenue?
- what goods and services they offer?
- how they deliver value to their customers?
- what business processes they excel at?
- what skills, competencies, or resources are crucial to their business success?

On each of these points compare your thoughts and ideas about those e-commerce organisations above to your ideas about traditional businesses. Think of a bookshop (e.g. Blackwells, Borders, Dymocks), an auction house (e.g. Sothebys, Christies) and a computer company (e.g. IBM, HP). What are the differences and similarities between these largely traditional businesses and e-commerce-based businesses in each of these categories?

What is a business model?

Analysis of some definitions of business models is an excellent way to start to understand the core components of a business model. Consider the following definitions.

> A business model...explains who your customers are and how you plan to make money by providing them with value. (Magretta 2002, p. 2)

Magretta's definition (2002) is one of the simplest and emphasises two key aspects of business models: customers and profitability.

> ...companies need a robust business model to knit together the different activities required for creating and distributing unique value to customers. (Sandberg 2002, p. 3)

In a similar vein to Magretta, Sandberg (2000) emphasises customers but in addition argues that a business model needs to incorporate a discussion about the activities needed to be successful.

> An operating business model is the organisation's core logic for creating value...since organisations compete for customers and resources, a good business model highlights the distinctive activities and approaches that enable the firm to succeed — to attract customers, employees, and investors, and to deliver products and services profitably. (Linder & Cantrell 2000, p. 2)

Linder and Cantrell (2000) add to our understanding the notion of scarce resources, including customers, employees and investors for which an organisation must compete. They also stress the importance of goods and/or services as being pivotal to the value delivered to customers and ultimately to the profitability of the organisation.

> A business model is nothing else than the architecture of a firm and its network of partners for creating, marketing and delivering value and relationship capital to one or several segments of customers in order to generate profitable and sustainable revenue streams. (Dubosson-Torbay, Osterwalder & Pigneur 2002, p. 7)

In this textbook, the definition of a business model offered by Dubosson-Torbay, Osterwalder and Pigneur (2002) is the one adopted by reason of its comprehensiveness. It seems to incorporate the major themes contained in all the other definitions. Thus, a comprehensive business model is seen as consisting of six major elements:

- It contains a consideration of the customers and/or customer segments that an organisation intends to serve, the nature of relationships with customers that will form the basis of its trading in future and what constitutes 'value' from the perspective of its customers.
- It contains a consideration of the mix of product and services offered by an organisation and may also include reflections on product and service innovation in that organisation.
- It contains a high-level architecture of the activities and processes required to create or obtain goods and services and to market and deliver them to customers.
- It contains a consideration of the internal resources and capabilities by which goods and services are produced, marketed and distributed to customers. This will include decisions about whether these resources and capabilities should be available in-house or whether the marketplace should be seen as the source of these elements.
- Allied to the previous point, it contains a consideration of the organisation's suppliers and the types of relationships it needs to develop with those suppliers. This would include a clear picture of the types of **strategic business networks** in which the organisation participates and its role within such networks.
- It contains a consideration of the financial aspects of the proposed transactions, operations and interactions. Sources and magnitudes of revenues and the time frame for their receipt are key considerations of an organisation's business model. Also requiring consideration are sources and magnitudes of costs and the time frame in which they are incurred and the resultant profitability and sustainability.

Figure 2.1 ▶ Business model architecture

These elements are illustrated in figure 2.1. A more detailed discussion of each of these elements is contained in the following section.

Customer management

The term *customer management* is used here as an umbrella term to cover a number of different aspects to do with customers and the relationship an organisation maintains with its customers. Each of these aspects will be considered below.

▶ Customer identification

It is essential for organisations to understand who their customers are or, in other words, which customer segment or segments they intend to target and service as opposed to those they do not intend to target or service. Thus, customer identification will include an understanding of the geographical reach of the organisation and whether its customers are other organisations or end consumers. Questions for an organisation to consider at this stage include:

- Who are our customers? Are they other organisations and/or end consumers?
- Are we targeting a mass market or some sort of niche market (which needs to be clearly defined)?
- Are we servicing a global market, or are we focusing on a purely regional market (which needs to be clearly defined)?
- Do we understand the demographics of our target set of customers?

▶ Value proposition

The idea of a value proposition is one of the most important concepts included in a business model. This anticipates one of the fundamentals of the business. The value proposition defines and describes the value that organisations deliver to their customers. It stems from the perceptions of customers as to what an organisation does or provides that is important to them.

Think about shopping for groceries. What do you value about shopping:
- at a large supermarket that opens from 8.00 am to 8.00 pm Monday to Saturday?
- at an upmarket delicatessen?
- at an open-air market?
- at an online supermarket?
- at a small, one-owner store that opens from 6.00 am to midnight, seven days a week, 365 days a year.

Jot down your ideas, and then compare them with others.

From the perspective of the authors, a large supermarket offers one-stop shopping, it is easy to find items and it offers a large product range. The extended hours of the small one-owner store offer great convenience. The upmarket delicatessen offers quality products and specialisation in its product range. The open-air market is expected to be cheap and a fun experience. The online experience offers convenience in its constant availability and delivery options. These are all examples of value propositions.

Nowadays, organisations must also consider the role of technology, including the Internet, in changing, enhancing or offering new value for customers. For example, customisation, or the ability to offer customers the opportunity to personalise an organisation's goods and services, is enhanced through the application of technology. **Disintermediation**, by cutting out the intermediaries, or **reintermediation**, adding an agent to simplify complexity, are other examples of the technology potentially transforming the value proposition for customers. From the customer's perspective, disintermediation or reintermediation may represent greater access, greater convenience and value, and so on. From an organisation's perspective, disintermediation or reintermediation may mean different ways of interacting with customers, implying a need for different processes and activities, different skills and resources, and so on.

Organisations often strive to offer a distinctive or unique value proposition to their customers. They may offer additional service, for example, or may seek efficiencies to be able to offer lower prices or better quality at no additional cost.

Questions that can be posed at this stage include the following:
- Are we sure of our customers' needs and wants, and hence that our products and services are appropriate for fulfilling those needs and wants?
- Do we clearly understand the value proposition of our customers?
- What is distinctive or unique about the value proposition that we offer our customers?

▶ Understanding and servicing customer requirements

Most organisations today recognise the need to be customer-centric, to focus on meeting the needs of their customers. Information technology plays a crucial role in helping an organisation to gather, store, manipulate and distribute large amounts of information about its customers, their buying habits, their (changing) preferences and their profitability to the business. This information can be fed back into R&D initiatives, thus ensuring that products and service innovations are even more closely attuned to meeting the needs of customers in a timely fashion and to attracting additional customers.

This virtuous cycle of product and service innovation or refinement, providing value to existing customers and attracting new customers, is premised on excellence in lfilling customer orders and in providing customer support. Here again technology an play a vital role in helping to manage the 'touch points' at which an organisation directly interacts with a customer and in helping to build and manage a relationship with the customers over time.

▶ Developing brand awareness

Successfully delivering on the value proposition and in building and maintaining relationships with customers depends on targeted markets being aware of the products and services offered by an organisation. Hence building brand awareness is a critical consideration in a business model design. Brand awareness can be achieved through advertising and marketing activities, through public relations initiatives and through viral models (Taylor & Terhune 2001), for example.

The key questions to be posed at this stage are:
- How do we reach our customers?
- How do we build brand awareness among existing and potential customers?

Product and service portfolio

Pivotal to a business model is an understanding of the portfolio of products and/or services offered by an organisation. The key question then for the organisation to pose at this juncture is: what do we offer our customers?

Included in the understanding of the organisation's offerings are such questions as:
- Do we offer our customers products, services or experiences or a combination of them?
- Do we offer a broad or narrow range of goods and services?
- Do we offer stand-alone or tightly integrated goods and services?

Another key issue to the result at this stage has to do with the notion of a product or service lifecycle. It is argued that all products and services pass through lifecycles, from initiation through rapid growth, maturity, and finally decline and ultimately termination (see figure 2.2).

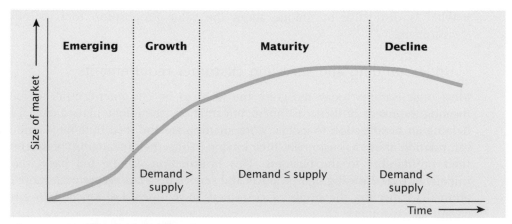

Figure 2.2 ▶ The product lifecycle
Source ▶ adapted from Ward and Peppard 2002, p. 88.

The concept of the product lifecycle has two key implications for business model design. First, it is essential to appreciate where in the lifecycle existing products and services are situated, and to consider this against estimates of how long or short the lifecycle is expected to be. Second, attention must be paid to the issue of product and service innovation, such that some notion of a process of innovation is included in the business model. For example many fad items, or items subject to the whims of fashion, enjoy very short lifecycles, which implies that a continuous process of innovation is required if an organisation that sells such items is to sustain itself in future.

Processes and activities

Having established notions about its customers, the type(s) of relationships that need to be managed with its customers, the value proposition its customers derive from bundled offerings of product and service, and about the product and service portfolio of an organisation, attention needs to be turned to the core business processes and activities by which that value proposition is delivered to customers. This is often described as the business configuration (Philipson 2001).

In defining and describing an organisation's business model, it is not expected that detailed mapping of precise steps and activities involved in a particular process is conducted. The thinking and analysis required takes place at a high, strategic level. An example might help to clarify this point. As academics, the authors value the services offered by Amazon.com. It offers us excellent search facilities and a range that comprises a large number of technical and academic books, and it is accessible twenty-four hours a day, seven days a week, from any computer that has Internet access. Also, for those occasions when books are required urgently, Amazon offers delivery across the world in three to five days. Hence, from our perspective, the value offered by Amazon can be summarised thus:

- excellent search facility
- large range of books
- accessibility
- fast delivery.

Let us assume that our perspective is shared by a whole segment of Amazon's customers. What does this imply for the management of Amazon when they are thinking at a high level about processes and activities in the business model?

If search facilities are one of the reasons customers come back to Amazon, then a business model should acknowledge the importance of a process of ongoing innovation and development of search techniques and technologies. If Amazon becomes complacent about its current search facilities and simply maintains its current system, then it puts itself at risk of being surpassed in this respect by a competitor. If the value proposition is built to some extent around the search facility, then a process of continual improvement and upgrade of this facility is essential.

If customers value access to a large range of books, then the business model needs to articulate the requirement for a process by which the range continually increases. Hence establishing close links with publishers and being able to add new and forthcoming publications constantly are vital components of continuing to deliver value and thus remain competitive.

Likewise, if accessibility is vital, then achieving 100 per cent uptime of their website is highly desirable for Amazon. From a business model perspective, it might imply a need to articulate a process by which the operations and maintenance of Amazon's website to ensure 24/7 operations is conducted so as to achieve constant availability for its customers. In addition, it might also imply articulating a need for excellent backup and recovery processes and procedures and for business continuity and disaster recovery planning.

If fast and efficient delivery is part of the business that Amazon is in, then once again managers need to think about the high-level process(es) by which this aspect of the value proposition is delivered. Hence effective and efficient processes that support the efficient internal handling of orders and the delivery of those orders to desired destinations are vital.

Note that some of these processes and activities are internal to the organisation (efficient handling of book orders) whereas others reach beyond the traditional boundaries of the organisation (links to publishers, delivery to customers). Those activities and processes that stretch across and beyond an organisation's boundaries are an important aspect of a business model, and will be discussed shortly (see the section Suppliers and Business Networks on p. 31). Another decision to be considered in articulating a business model is whether these processes and activities should be performed and managed using internal resources or whether they should be outsourced to an external, expert provider.

The example given of Amazon should not be regarded as an attempt to give a comprehensive analysis of the processes and activities of the business model: clearly it was not. It was intended only as illustrative of the arguments and ideas in this section. The key point to remember is that a business model should describe at a high level the main processes and activities by which the business operates and delivers value to its customers. How the business is configured largely affects how it can go about delivering value to its customers, and hence whether it is able to meet customer expectations.

The major questions for consideration in this stage, then, are:

- What are the key processes and activities by which we deliver on the value proposition for customers or, in other words, how should we configure our business?
- Should these processes and activities be performed internally using in-house resources and capabilities, or should they be outsourced and rely on external resources and capabilities?
- Do these processes and activities imply a need for us to develop external relationships and linkages to ensure delivery of the value proposition?

Resources, capabilities and assets

In order to deliver on the value proposition, an organisation needs more than efficient, appropriate processes and activities. Clearly appropriate and timely access to resources of all types, including capabilities and assets, is necessary if an organisation is to create value for its customers. The term *resources* is used here to cover a range of things that are obviously specific to particular industries and firms. The types of things to be considered would include physical assets (buildings, plant and equipment), financial assets (access to operating cash), intangible assets, such as brand name, reputation, intellectual property (copyrights, patents) and knowledge as human resources.

Let us briefly return to the Amazon example used above. Given the value proposition, and the processes we identified, what resources and assets would be essential? Jot down your ideas.

In thinking about the Amazon example, you probably identified the need for appropriate IT skills, capabilities and assets. (Would your local bookstore require the same IT skills, capabilities and assets?) You probably also identified the need for one or more automated warehouses, operations management skills and the resources to deliver goods. You might also have recognised that Amazon would need the capability to negotiate and manage relationships, for example with publishing companies, such that win–win outcomes can be achieved for all parties. Again, this is not intended to be a comprehensive list, but rather provides an example of identifying required resources as part of the overall development of a business model.

In considering required resources, organisations might need to consider how they are to recruit, train, motivate and retain the talented people who will underpin their success and drive innovation processes. They might consider how vital knowledge assets can effectively be managed. They might consider the resource implications of wanting to streamline their supply chains, automate warehouses and so on. The key here is to link this thinking directly to the previously identified sources of value for their customer segments.

Again, an important consideration at this stage is to consider whether these skills and resources need to be nurtured in-house or whether external parties can or should be relied on to supply requisite capabilities and resources. There are those who argue that in this modern information-based network economy, an organisation can better manage rapid change, uncertainty and turbulence by concentrating on core competencies and relying on the marketplace for access to other required resources and capabilities (Hamel & Prahalad 1994). This tends to result in the formation of highly interconnected, interdependent webs of organisations referred to as business webs or b-webs (Tapscott, Ticoll & Lowry 2000) or strategic business networks (McKay & Marshall 2001). These will be discussed in the next section.

In considering the needs for resources, assets and capabilities in articulating a business model, questions that can be posed are:

- What resources, assets and capabilities do we need in order to create value for our customers?
- Should these resources, assets and capabilities be built in-house or should external providers in the marketplace be relied on for their supply?
- Where and how are we going to recruit and retain the human resources we need to be successful?

Suppliers and business networks

In discussing processes, activities and resource requirements, we raised the issue of whether business success (profitably delivering value to customers) might not be dependent on successfully entering into a variety of relationships. Increasingly, organisations are relying on other organisations to contribute in various ways to the process of creating value. So, in modern business environments, the trend has been for organisations to move away from the traditional vertically integrated organisation to the virtual organisation.

The virtual organisation typically is one that identifies its core competencies and capabilities, and relies on the relationships it builds with other organisations for other skills and resources it needs in delivering its value proposition (Chesborough & Teece 1996; Marshall, McKay & Burn 2001). Thus, the value proposition for customers is no longer the preserve of just one firm. The organisation enters into a variety of relationships and arrangements with others to create goods and services of value jointly. These relationships can take the form of business partnerships, strategic alliances, joint ventures, long-term understandings and so on (Gulati, Nohria & Zaheer 2000), and the resultant interconnected set of organisations is known as a strategic business network. Figure 2.3 provides an illustration of a strategic business network.

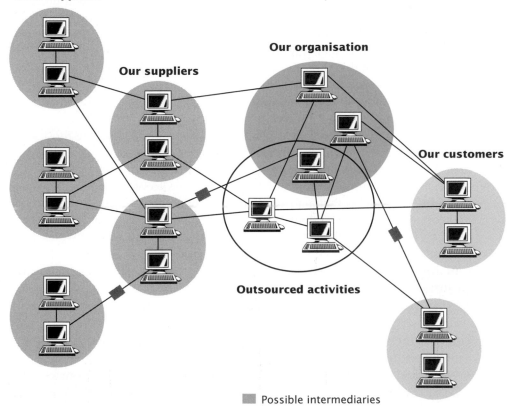

Figure 2.3 ▶ An example of a strategic business network
Source ▶ adapted from McKay and Marshall 2001, p. 29.

The key considerations for management in thinking about the role of strategic business networks in their business models are contained in such questions as:
• Do we need to rely on close relationships with other organisations in order to deliver value to our customers?

- How will we find suitable partners and manage the resultant strategic business network?
- Will a strategic business network arrangement enhance our ability to be responsive, flexible and agile in changing and competitive marketplaces?

Financial viability

The financial aspects of the business model are absolutely essential to the development of a sound, viable blueprint that will drive the organisation's operations in future. There are essentially four components that need to be considered: profitability and sustainability, sources of revenues, a consideration of the costs incurred, and an understanding of the risks associated with the business model.

▶ Profitability and sustainability

Profitability stems from the difference between all revenues and all costs. In order for an organisation to be profitable, its incoming revenues for a particular period must exceed its outgoing costs. An issue for businesses can stem from the fact that traditionally costs are often incurred (say, for producing or obtaining a particular good) before revenues are received from the sale of that item. Hence one challenge is to manage the cash flows of the organisation so that it is able to sustain this period between incurring costs and receiving revenues.

A change in business model and creative application of technology can change this situation quite substantially. For example, encouraging customers to order and pay online, and producing or obtaining that good only after the order is confirmed and paid for, mean that revenues are received before costs are incurred, and this represents a favourable shift for the organisation. If this type of approach also constitutes value from the customers' perspective (through lower prices or the ability to customise, for example), then it might represent a very robust business model.

▶ Sources of revenues

If profitability is to be achieved, revenues must exceed costs. Clearly, then, identifying all potential revenue streams, their time frames (i.e. when these revenues are going to start flowing into the organisation) and their magnitude is vital. Sandberg (2002) identifies four broad categories of revenue streams: selling products and services produced by the organisation (including subscription fees), stocking and selling products and services of other organisations, deriving revenues from ownership of required infrastructure (e.g. telcos), and providing access to services and information (e.g. on-selling a list of clients or customers to an interested third party), all of which were available before the emergence of e-commerce and e-business. However, the advent of the Internet has seen other possibilities emerge or, indeed, become much more popular. For example, an organisation can generate revenues by selling online advertising or sponsorship opportunities to interested third parties, by receiving commissions for all customers referred to another website, by charging commissions on arranged sales and services (such as eBay), or by capitalising on its knowledge assets, for example.

This list is not meant to be exhaustive but rather is illustrative of some of the possibilities in terms of revenue flows. The key point to remember here is that a sound business model must be clear about sources of revenues and when those revenues are likely to occur. It should be noted that when value creation occurs across a strategic business network, it might be necessary to apportion some of the incoming revenues to members of the network. Managing this element successfully is quite fundamental to business success.

◗ Costs

In developing a business model, it is also important to identify all costs that will be incurred in the total set of activities involved in ultimately delivering a product or service of value to a customer. Total costs could include all costs involved in the design, development, and/or procurement of goods and services, including raw materials, production, marketing, delivery and service; that is, all costs incurred in delivering the value proposition to the customer. Costs could also be incurred in forming and maintaining strategic business networks, in investing in technologies, in developing and implementing websites, and so on. A clear understanding of costs is essential in establishing pricing mechanisms and policies.

◗ Risk considerations

The elements that have been grouped thus far under financial aspects (profitability, revenues, costs) are necessarily uncertain, and therefore an assessment of the associated risk is essential. For example, many assumptions are generally embedded in estimates of revenue streams for an organisation, such as volume, magnitude and frequency of sales, and it is critical to examine these assumptions and the validity of the grounds on which they are based. Further, analyses need to be conducted to consider the implications if some of the bases of the financial model prove to be inadequate. An example of this would be to scrutinise the implications of sales volumes being half or twice the anticipated levels. It might sound unusual to argue that higher than expected sales volumes could be a risk, but issues such as the ability to meet demand, to deliver goods and to provide adequate service all then become potential sources of risk to the organisation.

At the basis of a sound business model is adequate attention to a number of financial considerations, including profitability, revenues, cost and risk associated with the proposed initiative. Questions that might be posed at this stage include:

- How is the price customers are expected to pay for products and services being established, and is the basis of price determination reasonable and appropriate?
- When is each of the products and services offered expected to turn a profit? Is this time frame realistic given the anticipated lifecycle of the product/service?
- Have all areas of cost been identified? Have all potential revenue streams been explored? Is there an opportunity for the organisation to leverage knowledge, technology or physical assets?
- Has consideration been given to the riskiness of various aspects of this initiative and the consequences of adverse events or occurrences?
- Has the profitability of this initiative been clearly demonstrated? How sustainable is this profitability?

thinking strategically

The importance of understanding your business model

The case that follows could only be described as a dotcom debacle! Read the case carefully, and then think about the business model that was used as the basis for this enterprise.

SportsBiz

SportsBiz was established in 1997 by two friends, Graham Ross and Peter Blackmore, who decided to form a partnership and establish an Internet retail business. The partners in this venture were both professional people with a love of sports, and they decided to start selling sports clothing and equipment via the Web. The partners intended to maintain their current careers, with the dotcom acting as a lucrative sideline, or so they hoped. One of the partners was IT literate and used his skill to develop a web presence to enable two-way communication (information exchange and orders placed online, transaction completed offline). His plan was to migrate to a full transactional capability on the Web as soon as practicable.

Both partners were members of a number of different sporting or recreational clubs, and as parents they were also involved in a number of junior sporting activities. For example, Graham and Peter were active members of cricket, hockey and football clubs, and their partners were keen squash and netball players. Children from the two families were involved in athletics, swimming, football and pony clubbing. Sport played a very important role in all their lives, and Graham and Peter believed that they could quite ethically benefit from selling a range of sports goods and clothing online to friends and acquaintances at the various clubs they belonged to. It was felt that these contacts and interests would be a vital source of business for their fledgling enterprise and that orders would come primarily from members of the various clubs in which they and their families had an active interest. They thought that orders would be placed online, or handed to them directly, and that they could then source the goods and deliver them to the customer next time they attended that club or possibly by driving around to their home to deliver the goods. They recognised a need to offer online payment facilities eventually, but did not make arrangements for credit card payment as they believed that most transactions would be COD; that is, that customers would pay them cash when they delivered the goods to them.

To avoid the difficulty of such a small player attempting to negotiate directly with the various sports goods and sports clothing manufacturers, the partners instead went to a large, successful sporting goods retail chain and negotiated with them to obtain stock. They did not intend to maintain any inventory (in order to avoid having capital tied up), planning instead to source the required items from the warehouse of the sports chain once orders had been received over the Web. The sporting goods retailer maintained one large warehouse in Perth, which supplied eight retail outlets at various prime locations across the city. During the negotiations, SportsBiz had reached agreement with the management of the retailer that it could source supplies from the warehouse, and a pricing mechanism was agreed to by both parties. The only condition was that the needs of the retail outlets would be given priority over SportsBiz.

Interest in and commercial activity on their website proved to be much less than anticipated. However, orders did start to trickle in. As an order was received, one of the partners had to take the time off from his job to obtain stock from the warehouse, and these goods then needed to be packaged and delivered to the customer. Over time, problems occurred. Staff at the warehouse of the sports chain were often unfamiliar with the negotiated arrangement and were frequently difficult about making supplies available. Individual outlets of the chain also had priority in terms of being supplied with goods, thus making it difficult to guarantee supply, particularly of fast-moving, popular items. For example, special events such as the football World Cup would stimulate demand for relevant memorabilia, sometimes resulting in demand far outstripping supply for a short period of time. As the needs of the retail outlets had priority over SportsBiz, Graham and Peter often experienced trouble in obtaining the stock they required, and they were spending increasing amounts of time arguing their case with successive warehouse managers. Hence an increasingly fractious relationship developed with the sports chain, and increasingly orders received by SportsBiz failed to reach their customers in a timely manner.

Furthermore, the belief that most orders would be received from customers locally via their sporting club contacts proved inaccurate. For some reason, friends and acquaintances at the various clubs seemed a bit coy about ordering goods from SportsBiz. This puzzled Graham and Peter for quite some time, until one of their team members confided that he preferred to browse through the large range of stock held by the larger retail outlets, to try on clothing and to get the feel of equipment before purchasing. Accordingly, orders received typically came from geographically distant customers, meaning that issues of delivery had to be addressed. The costs and effort associated with doing so had not been properly factored into the prices quoted to potential customers online, and severe problems arose as a result.

In designing the website, both partners felt that it was important to display prices. Once they knew what they would be charged by the warehouse, they could add on their margin and display the selling price on the Web. But incompatible IT systems reduced the flow of information between the sports chain warehouse and themselves to a manual exchange, often by telephone. This proved very time-consuming, and it usually had to be done during normal office hours when both partners were supposed to be doing their regular jobs. It was also sometimes difficult to negotiate a price on stock that had yet to be received at the warehouse. By far the biggest issue, however, was that they had not factored in delivery charges in the prices they advertised on the Web, as they had imagined they would personally be handing over the items to customers at the various clubs.

It was not long before the venture became untenable and was closed down.

Question

Use figure 2.3 and the discussion in this section to analyse the case and identify the business model. Consider particularly where major weaknesses in the business model seem to be. Be prepared to discuss your thoughts with others.

Examples of business models

The previous section identified and discussed the six major components of a business model (refer to figure 2.1). From that discussion it should be clear that there is an almost infinite number of ways the various elements can be combined to form workable business models, blueprints of what the organisation is, the value it delivers to customers and a high-level view of the key elements of the organisation's operations. A sound business model, of course, does not guarantee business success. A business model must be implemented via particular strategies and managed effectively. The major purpose of the business model is to provide a coherent framework for managers to think through key elements of their business and to avoid overlooking something that is vital to their success.

New technologies can offer new possibilities for organisations and thus have a fundamental influence on the design of the organisation. Arguably the Internet and associated communications technologies are examples of this. The Internet offers not only efficiency or effectiveness gains but also new possibilities for organisations. Because of the pervasiveness of the Internet, most businesses must analyse its influence and consider whether its potentiality can be creatively exploited. Few players can totally ignore the Internet; some will experience radical change in their industry and their way of doing business, whereas others will be assisted to make fundamental changes to the nature of their business. For the vast majority there will be important considerations of how to incorporate the Internet effectively into their operations. This implies a rethink of business models and therefore an understanding of the emerging business models that underlie Internet commerce.

In this section, some typical examples of Internet business models will be considered, particularly those that typify new business opportunities. Once again these will serve as exemplars rather than being an exhaustive list. (For interested readers, some of the references listed in the Suggested Reading section on p. 48 provide a comprehensive coverage of a range of Internet business models. See Weill and Vitale (2001), Eisenmann (2002), Applegate (2001) and Philipson (2001)). The challenge for organisations is to recognise those models that offer potential and then to incorporate suitable elements creatively into their existing business models. Understanding the strengths and weaknesses of some of the basic Internet business models will assist this process.

Three generic Internet commerce models will be considered in this chapter: the Direct-to-Customer model (Weill & Vitale 2001), the Marketplace model, and the Content Provider model (Weill & Vitale 2001). These will be discussed almost as 'pure' types, as though they were quite separate stand-alone models. In reality, models are often mixed and/or used in part only. The challenge for many existing organisations lies in how to combine their existing business model effectively with the appropriate elements of Internet commerce business models.

The Direct-to-Customer model

This model lies at the heart of commercial transactions over the Internet, describing the business of selling direct to the customer via the Internet. The model is also frequently referred to by different names; for example 'online retailer' (Eisenmann 2002), 'online sales' (Philipson 2001) or 'e-tailer' (Turban et al. 2002) are often used to refer to similar concepts.

The **Direct-to-Customer business model** describes a process of selling goods and/ or services direct to a customer via the organisation's website. Hence there is a direct linkage via the Internet to the customer. Note that the customer could be an individual (and the end) consumer, or it could be an organisation, which might or might not be the end consumer. Goods and/or services essentially flow from the seller to the buyer, whereas money (payment) flows from the buyer to the seller (see figure 2.4). The seller might be a retailer, but it could also be a wholesaler or a producer or manufacturer. In other words, this model represents a basic online transaction between seller and buyer. It incorporates both the supply-oriented transactions in which the organisation occupies the buyer role and demand-oriented transactions in which the organisation occupies the seller role (refer back to figure 1.5).

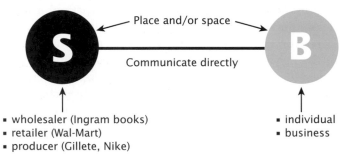

Figure 2.4 ▶ The Direct-to-Customer model

The Direct-to-Customer business model needs to be analysed by considering each of the six components of the business model framework (see figure 2.1) in turn.

▶ Customer management

In developing a robust Direct-to-Customer business model, consideration needs to be given to the anticipated customer base online. For example, organisations need to consider carefully whether the move to online selling expands their existing market and hence allows them to reach additional customers, or whether in effect it cannibalises their existing market, in that some existing customers move to purchase online but essentially the customer base does not expand. This latter situation poses difficulties for an organisation, as it might end up requiring substantial investment in IT, having to maintain two channels by which to reach the customer and having to manage significantly increased complexity in their business without a substantial increase in their customer base. Hence they might need to be able to demonstrate that the additional service delivered online increases satisfaction and loyalty in some way so that it is demonstrated to be a viable option for the organisation.

In these calculations, however, the risks and potential costs of not going online need to be factored in. Organisations might lose customers and market share through not offering online services. As an analogy, think of banks and ATMs (automatic teller machines). It is debatable whether banks attract new customers or increase their market share through having ATMs. Not having them, however, could be deleterious to their ability to hold on to customers and might put them at a competitive disadvantage.

In addition, it is important to establish clearly a customer's value proposition. For many organisations adopting the Direct-to-Customer business model, it appears that availability (24/7) and the associated convenience are major sources of value for customers. So too is the potential to have access to a large and global range of products and services with some ability to customise some of those products and services. In some cases, having goods delivered adds to the attraction from the customers' perspective. Whatever the source of value for a particular product and/or service, it is essential that the organisation understands this and ensures its delivery to customers.

Product and service portfolio

Irrespective of whether the organisation in question is a dotcom (i.e. it trades only on the Internet) or whether it is an existing bricks and mortar organisation wishing to start selling online, a case must be clearly established that there is a demand for its goods and/or services online. Even a short history suggests that some goods and services experience greater consumer acceptance of being sold online than do others. For example, software, which can not only be purchased online but also digitally distributed, seems to be much easier to sell online than a man's suit or a wedding dress, which are purchases that involve fit, feel, an experience and an emotional connection.

Processes and activities

The Direct-to-Customer business model implies a need for excellent order fulfilment and, often, for delivery. So all the activities and processes associated with accepting and processing a customer order, linkages to inventory and pricing information, and delivery need to be very good. Processes associated with website design, development, enhancements and maintenance are also likely to need to be exemplary.

Note that manufacturers and/or wholesalers might also elect to start selling online via the Direct-to-Customer business model and might also sell directly online to end consumers. For these organisations, a new set of activities and processes is implied. The attractiveness of this type of business model for manufacturers and wholesalers stems from a number of sources. First, the Direct-to-Customer business model might enable them to establish and manage a direct relationship with end consumers, which might help them to be more responsive to changing consumer preferences. They might also be attracted by the prospect of being able to sell more cheaply by cutting out various intermediaries. However, unilaterally deciding to bypass such trading partners as retailers could provoke a backlash from the retailer, which is known as *channel conflict*. The size and power of the various players and whether the existing relationship needs to be maintained will have an impact on whether this proves feasible.

Resources, capabilities and assets

The Direct-to-Customer business model clearly implies a need for access to excellent IT skills. For many dotcoms there might also be the question of whether to invest in automated warehousing, some logistics capability and so on. Existing businesses might already have these capabilities and, if so, decisions need be made as to whether they have sufficient capacity and are suited to the needs of online customers. For example, some traditional toy manufacturers were accustomed to making relatively few deliveries, but those they did make were of very large quantities to regional distribution warehouses for some large retail chains. This capability (and the underlying business process) proved to be totally inept when their online customers (end consumers) expected rapid delivery of single items to their doorstep: meeting their customers' demand required investment in and development of a new set of capabilities and the associated logistics.

Suppliers and business networks

The Direct-to-Customer business model does not absolutely require an organisation to form a strategic business network. However, particularly for dotcoms, a decision is often taken to rely on the expertise of people external to the organisation for performance of some key aspects of the delivery of value to the customer. One obvious area is in distribution and delivery. For example, Amazon.com relies largely on external expertise for the delivery of all its orders. Australia Post has expanded from its traditional role of delivering mail and does some of the home deliveries of groceries for the Coles Myer group, and it is actively promoting its warehousing, sorting and distribution skills to other organisations that need to develop a logistics capability.

Decision-making with respect to strategic business networks is clearly dependent on some of the decisions taken in relation to resources and capabilities. An organisation that judges that it has essentially adequate resources and capabilities internally to accommodate the Direct-to-Customer business model might not feel much of an imperative to form strategic business networks. By contrast, however, with all the complexities of modern business to deal with, many organisations are choosing to focus on core business and thus concentrate on developing core capabilities while relying on the marketplace to provide all other requisite resources and capabilities. This decision clearly implies a need to enter into and manage a variety of relationships, alliances and partnerships with other organisations on an ongoing basis. In such circumstances, understanding the requirements for successful strategic business networks is a key to developing a robust, sustainable business model.

Financial viability

With the Direct-to-Customer business model, one of the main sources of revenue is likely to come from the direct selling of goods and/or services to customers (both end consumers and businesses). Hence the organisation might place online some sort of catalogue of goods and services available for purchase online, together with product information, availability, delivery options and details of how to place an order and payment options.

Another source of revenue can stem from charging for advertising space on the organisation's website. Particularly in cases of 'popular' sites, those enjoying a larger number of visitors to the site, or 'niche' sites, those attracting a particular type of audience, substantial revenues can be generated by careful selling of advertising space to potential advertisers. Revenues can also be generated via referrals. For example, a gardening website could recommend a number of gardening books. Clicking on those books takes the potential customer direct to an online bookshop, such as Amazon.com, where the purchase can be transacted. If appropriate prior arrangements have been negotiated, the online bookshop could pay the gardening site a referral fee for all referrals who go ahead and purchase the book.

The Direct-to-Customer business model implies substantial costs to an organisation, as it involves the establishment of a website with full transaction capabilities as a minimum. It is highly likely that, to be successful, substantial integration of the existing back-office systems (such as inventory, order processing, fulfilment, payment and so on) with the web-based front-end system providing direct electronic access to customers is necessary. Substantial costs could be incurred for the required hardware, software, networks and telecommunications, and personnel. Not only are there setup costs but costs for enhancements and maintenance must also be factored in. Building brand in online environments has also proved very costly.

It is clear that decisions about pricing must take into account costs, cash flow projections and estimates regarding revenues in order to ensure profitability and viability. However, risks are obviously associated with estimates of costs and revenues, and their likely occurrence and concomitant consequences need to be taken into consideration.

The Intermediary model

The Intermediary business model differs in one fundamental respect from the Direct-to-Customer business model. Whereas in the Direct-to-Customer business model, there was a direct electronic linkage between the organisation and its customers, with the **Intermediary model** there is literally some sort of intermediary who mediates the interaction between organisations and their customers. Figure 2.5 below depicts this situation.

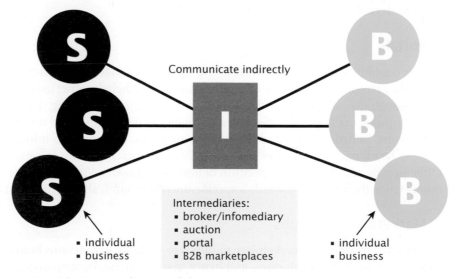

Figure 2.5 ▶ The Intermediary model

The nature of the intermediary and the role it plays in facilitating or orchestrating a transaction can vary depending on the circumstances. Thus, four broad types of intermediary are recognised here: the broker or infomediary, auctions, portals and B2B marketplaces or hubs.

Broker or infomediary

Brokers and infomediaries act as intermediaries in transactions. They are typically retained by clients and act in the client's interest in facilitating a transaction. Both rely on gathering information and then on using the information to facilitate an exchange. A classic example might be an online insurance broker. It is expected that insurance brokers gather and keep current information about a range of insurance products and options. The client then engages the broker to locate the most suitable insurance product for them, giving certain parameters (cost, type of coverage, etc). Thus, in essence, an online broker is trying to provide a service to clients by matching the requirements of the client to available goods and services.

Infomediaries in a sense operate in the reverse direction: they typically gather information about particular customers and groups of customers, which is then provided to interested organisations for the purpose of target marketing or subsequent product and service refinement and development.

Auctions

Classic examples of successful online auctions are eBay and sold.com.au. eBay and other online auctions essentially function by providing the infrastructure by which would-be sellers and would-be buyers can come together. Potential buyers can place bids for goods and services for a specified period. Typically, sellers pay a listing fee and a commission on the sale of the item. Storage and delivery of the item is negotiable but is usually the responsibility of the seller, meaning that for typical online auctioneers, they never own a good or service, never need to warehouse it and do not need to develop logistics capabilities.

Portals

Portals could be considered gateways to the vast content that resides on the World Wide Web. They typically offer a range of services, designed to help Internet users navigate their way through the complexity of the Web to find what they are seeking. Thus, portals can offer shopping malls and classified advertisements, search engines and directories, email, chat rooms, bulletin boards and personal home pages, and access to information, such as news headlines, stock market prices, weather forecasts and so on (Eisenmann 2002). Often portals cater for a broad spectrum of interests (known as *horizontal portals*) whereas others tailor their services towards a specific interest group (called *vertical portals*).

Marketplaces or hubs

The main purpose of the marketplace or hub is to facilitate transactions between external parties, often between businesses, and hence many of these marketplaces are known as *B2B marketplaces* or *market makers* (Philipson 2001). Like the auction model, marketplaces do not usually temporarily own goods and services. Rather they provide the technical infrastructure to enable a buyer and seller to trade online, and in some cases they provide the value and services to attract and retain buyers and sellers. The success of marketplaces is typically dependent on the number of completed transactions, and hence to be successful marketplaces need to attract large numbers of buyers and sellers.

Buyers appreciate the ease of sourcing desired goods and services and the ability to compare prices and availability easily. The attractiveness of the marketplace model for suppliers (sellers) is less obvious as markets tend to commoditise goods, and suppliers tend to lose control over both their goods and services and their relationship with the customer. Consequently they can end up in a situation in which competition is based on price alone (Philipson 2001). Hence there have been many failures in B2B marketplaces in recent times (Laseter, Long & Capers 2001; Wise & Morrison 2000).

Components of the business model framework

Having considered these four variants on the basic Intermediary business model, we shall now consider each of the six components of the business model framework (see figure 2.1) in turn.

▶ Customer management

Again, the Intermediary model needs to identify a potential customer base clearly. Does the organisation intend to offer what is essentially an infrastructure for anyone to use (such as eBay), or is the organisation serving a narrow or specialised community of interests (such as ChemUnity.com)?

The customer value proposition is also essential to the Intermediary model. Understanding those aspects of the range of services offered to customers (both buyers and sellers) and then ensuring the delivery of those services is vital to the success of this model. For example, it could be that customers value the services of an Intermediary in helping them to navigate through the complexity of the Internet. Likewise, a marketplace might be valued for the ease of comparison of prices and availability. To others, the Intermediary model may be attractive because of the size of the 'network' of potentially connected buyers and sellers that it offers.

An issue for the Intermediary model, however, is that different participants will value different aspects of the services offered, and at times these might be in conflict. Take, for example, a marketplace that attracted buyers because of the ability to compare on price and which allows purchase on the basis of cost. Such a marketplace might become decidedly unattractive to suppliers, who start to compete primarily on the basis of price and find that the differentiating features of their products and services are overlooked. Failure to offer a value proposition to both buyers and sellers will almost certainly lead to the demise of organisations adopting this model.

▶ Product and service portfolio

In some situations, the notion of goods and services in the Intermediary business model is easy to think about. Typically the Intermediary business model consists only of a service: that of acting as some type of intermediary in facilitating trade between cohorts of buyers and sellers. What is essential is that a case can clearly be established to demonstrate that there is a need and a demand for such a service and that that way of generating a stable source of revenue can be achieved (see the section Financial Viability opposite).

Processes and activities

Unlike the Direct-to-Customer business model, the Intermediary business model rarely requires an organisation to develop processes for managing inventory and delivery. However, success will be contingent on its knowledge of a particular industry in some cases, or on its ability to appreciate buyers' and sellers' requirements in marketplaces generally. Also, in many cases, the Intermediary survives on the quality of the information it gathers (think of the insurance broker previously discussed). Hence processes and activities associated with the gathering and management of information and knowledge management need to be exemplary.

Another factor that must be considered is the fact that the business processes of the Intermediary might well stretch into other organisations. Therefore the processes of the Intermediary would need to integrate with the processes of sellers and buyers. Such integration is often difficult to achieve as it involves working and operating across the traditional boundaries of organisations.

Resources, capabilities and assets

In many cases, the Intermediary business model revolves around providing infrastructure to enable electronic trading between parties. Hence its IT resources, capabilities and assets are pivotal to its success. It must offer stable, reliable systems that take account of appropriate requirements for security and privacy. The systems must also be such that the Intermediary retains control of any transactions facilitated.

In as much as the difficulty of integrating processes was mentioned in the previous section, information systems might well need to be integrated across organisational boundaries. Even if the activity of the Intermediary is limited to one industry, few industries have been willing or able to dictate common standards and processes by which trading over computer networks can take place (Philipson 2001). Clearly, this becomes much more complex when multiple industries are involved.

Suppliers and business networks

The extent to which organisations adopting the Intermediary business model rely on strategic business networks vary widely according to the suite of services offered to their clients. For example, where portals offer email, news and search facilities to customers, it could well be that these services are sourced from specialists and that an alliance has been entered into for the service. Some portals, for example, rely on specialised search engines to provide the search facilities on their site or specialised news services to provide the news headlines posted on their site. Other Intermediaries use specialist services to oversee and manage the Internet-based payment to complete a transaction for example. Hence the Intermediary business model, like the Direct-to-Customer business model, relies on decisions being made about which services are provided by building internal capabilities and which are provided by relying on specialist external providers.

▶ Financial viability

There are a number of ways in which the Intermediary business model can generate revenue streams. Some sort of commission or transaction fee is relatively common. Hence the payment from either the seller or buyer might be levied on each successfully completed transaction. Alternatively, organisations adopting one of the variants of the Intermediary business model might generate revenues from subscription fees. For example, organisations wishing to place job advertisements on an online employment service would pay some sort of subscription (fee per month or per job advertisement). In other circumstances, fees might be charged per use. Some publishers provide online content, and a fee is charged for each download of that content.

It is also often the case that substantial revenues can be generated from advertising. Popular Intermediaries often attract an enormous volume of traffic and thus become attractive locations for advertisers. Intermediaries that are geared towards a specific interest group can also generate advertising revenues from other organisations who provide goods and services to a similar cohort.

The major cost associated with the Intermediary business model stems from building and maintaining a robust technological infrastructure capable of delivering the services offered to customers. Marketing activities and building a brand name have also proved to be costly with this type of business model.

The major challenges for Intermediaries have been building the required infrastructure and attracting and maintaining a critical mass of customers so that the resultant transaction volume and resultant revenue generation enables the organisation to be profitable and viable in future. This has proved a substantial challenge for many Intermediaries.

The Content Provider model

Some researchers recognise the Content Provider business model (Weill & Vitale 2001) or the Content model (Philipson 2001). Essentially the **Content Provider model** does just that: it develops content based on its expertise, which it then sells to other parties or makes available free of charge to consumers. For example, some companies produce content about regional weather forecasts, or financial and investment information, which they sell on to other interested parties. Thus weather forecasts, which are commonly found on general portals, are likely to have been produced by a specialist Content Provider and then provided by that Content Provider to the portal, most likely for an appropriate fee. This variant of the Content Provider model is not a unique business model but rather an example of the Direct-to-Customer business model, whereby the product or service being sold is information.

Another variant is the Content Provider who generates content but apparently makes it freely available to consumers over the Internet. Many newspapers (such as the *Daily Telegraph*, the *New York Times* and *The Australian*) and commercial TV stations (such as CNN) allow Internet users to read content quite freely. However, such sites typically rely on generating traffic, thus attracting advertisers, and revenues are generated from selling advertising space rather than selling content.

However, the trend is for many of these sites to sell some of their content. Some provide some content free but require payment for detailed reports or higher-quality content. Currency of information sometimes increases its value, and hence up-to-date material is sold whereas older material is made freely available. In contrast, some newspapers (such as the *Australian Financial Review*) require payment from customers who wish to access their excellent archive facility. As this type of arrangement with the Content Provider model could arguably be seen as a variation on the Direct-to-Customer business model, we shall not deal with it in any more depth at this stage.

Implications for managers

This chapter has discussed in detail the components of a business model and has tried to illustrate the basic business model architecture of three common Internet business models. The literature often presents business models as being enormously complex and having many variants (see Applegate 2001, Weill & Vitale 2001, Philipson 2001 and Eisenmann 2002 in Suggested Reading, for example). Rappa (2002) presents more than thirty discrete business models, many of which could be argued to be variants of the two business models present in this chapter. Maybe such a refinement is necessary in certain circumstances, but we argue that the main purpose of the business model is to enhance understanding among the members of an organisation of the driving blueprint for an organisation's operations, as a way of aligning employees to the organisation's mission. The framework presented here provides ample scope for analysis, discussion and learning, and we believe it is therefore more helpful than focusing on minutiae. Those interested are encouraged to read in more detail about business models. For many, however, the business model architecture presented here will be adequate for learning and understanding.

It must be stressed that a sound, coherent and articulated business model is vital for any business. But on its own a good business model will not guarantee success. The business model must be complemented by a strategy that takes account of the nature of competition and industry factors, among other things. Thus, whereas the business model provides a framework or model of how the business will operate, and particularly includes careful considerations about how the organisation will achieve probability, the business model on its own cannot deliver success. Rather the business model must be viewed as a blueprint for the organisation, implemented via a set of strategies by which the organisation articulates how it will achieve its goals and objectives. Whereas the business model defines *what* the organisation is, its strategies describe *how* the organisation will achieve its targets. (Business strategies are the subject of the next chapter.)

Magretta (2002) proposes two sample tests for business models: what she calls 'the narrative test' and 'the numbers test'. To pass the narrative test, a business model must tell a coherent and logical story about customers, about the customer value proposition and about how that value proposition is to be delivered to the customer. In addition, a business model must also pass the numbers test: it must be based on sound and realistic economic reasoning. Managers are encouraged to use the business model architecture to challenge their assumptions and must develop models that will pass both the narrative and the numbers tests.

Conclusion

The business model of an organisation is a blueprint for how the particular organisation operates as a business. The business model describes the target market of customers and how the business will earn revenues and profits by delivering value to them. The business model is a statement that defines what the organisation is, whereas the strategy of an organisation essentially defines the specific goals and objectives of an organisation and how the organisation will achieve them.

A good articulation of a business model will include a description of the following elements:

- the customer segments that the organisation intends to serve
- the mix of goods and services offered by the organisation
- the major or core processes and activities of the organisation
- the internal resources and capabilities required by the organisation
- a consideration of the organisation's suppliers and the types of relationships it needs to develop with those suppliers and other trading partners
- a consideration of the sources and magnitude of revenues, costs and profits.

A careful consideration of the above elements should provide a good reality check on the sustainability and profitability of a business or proposed business. This could be helpful for any business or business initiative. However, it is likely to be particularly helpful for an e-business initiative, whether it concerns a stand-alone Internet-based business or the integration of e-commerce and other Internet-based innovations into an existing traditional enterprise. This is because the nature of successful Internet-based businesses is less well known than the nature of successful traditional businesses.

For Internet-based businesses or e-businesses it is helpful to consider the elements of common or generic business models. Three important generic models are the Direct-to-Customer model, the Intermediary model and the Content Provider model. These three models give a guide to the nature of important kinds of Internet-based businesses. The more elaborate taxonomies of the business models given in some books and articles are often more confusing than helpful.

Although having a good business model for planned Internet-based business initiatives is vital, a good business model does not guarantee success. A good business model must be complemented by a well-crafted and well-implemented business strategy.

key terms

business models	Intermediary model
Content Provider model	reintermediation
Direct-to-Customer business model	strategic business networks
disintermediation	value proposition

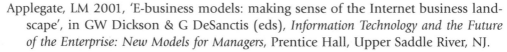

discussion questions

1. An *application service provider* (or ASP) promises information systems applications 'on tap' delivered across the Internet. An organisation that has determined what portfolio of information systems applications it requires can thus pay a fee for access to the required software from the ASP and then run the applications on the ASP's computers across the Internet. Use the business model architecture described in this chapter to identify the key elements of the business model for a successful ASP.

2. An *Internet service provider* (or ISP) provides consumers or businesses with connectivity to the Internet, allowing them to receive and send online information, such as web pages, emails, MP3 music files, and business transaction data (Eisenmann 2002). Use the business model architecture described in this chapter to identify the key elements of the business model for a successful ISP.

3. Consider the following interrelated terms:
   (a) business model
   (b) mission and vision
   (c) strategy.
   Discuss your understanding of each term and ascribe the interrelationships between these terms. (Mission, vision and strategy will be discussed more thoroughly in chapter 3. At this stage, just attempt to articulate what you think they mean and the major difference between them.)

4. Is a good business model alone enough to guarantee success in e-business? If not, specify what other elements are necessary for e-business success.

5. Discuss whether the core competencies of an organisation are the same as the capabilities determined as part of the organisation's business model.

6. A business model is a blueprint for the appropriate activities, processes, structures, capabilities and resources, and values of the organisation. Discuss whether the advent of the Internet has fundamentally influenced the nature of business models.

suggested reading

Applegate, LM 2001, 'E-business models: making sense of the Internet business landscape', in GW Dickson & G DeSanctis (eds), *Information Technology and the Future of the Enterprise: New Models for Managers*, Prentice Hall, Upper Saddle River, NJ.

Dubosson-Torbay, M, Osterwalder, A & Pigneur, Y 2002, 'E-business model design, classification and measurement', *Thunderbird International Business Review*, vol. 44, no. 1, pp. 5–23.

Eisenmann, TR 2002, *Internet Business Models: Text and Cases*, McGraw-Hill/Irwin, Boston.

Linder, J & Cantrell, S 2000, 'Changing business models: surveying the landscape', *Accenture Institute for Strategic Change*.

Philipson, G (ed.) 2001, *Australian E-business Guide*, 1st edn, CCH Australia, Sydney.

Weill, P & Vitale, MR 2001, *Place to Space: Migrating to E-business Models*, Harvard Business School Press, Boston.

Wise, R & Morrison, D 2000, 'Beyond the exchange: the future of B2B', *Harvard Business Review*, November–December.

references

Applegate, LM 2001, 'E-business models: making sense of the Internet business landscape', in GW Dickson & G DeSanctis (eds), *Information Technology and the Future of the Enterprise: New Models for Managers*, Prentice Hall, Upper Saddle River, NJ.

Chesborough, HW & Teece, DJ 1996, 'When is virtual virtuous?', *Harvard Business Review*, vol. 74, no. 1, pp. 65–73.

Dubosson-Torbay, M, Osterwalder, A & Pigneur, Y 2002, 'E-business model design, classification and measurement', *Thunderbird International Business Review*, vol. 44, no. 1, pp. 5–23.

Eisenmann, TR 2002, *Internet Business Models: Text and Cases*, McGraw-Hill/Irwin, Boston.

Gulati, R, Nohria, N & Zaheer, A 2000, 'Strategic networks', *Strategic Management Journal*, vol. 21, issue 3, pp. 203–15.

Hamel, G & Prahalad, CK 1994, *Competing for the Future*, Harvard Business School Press.

Laseter, T, Long, B & Capers, C 2001, 'B2B benchmark: the state of electronic exchanges', *Strategy and Competition*, Fourth Quarter 2001, www.strategy-business.com

Linder, J & Cantrell, S 2000, 'Changing business models: surveying the landscape', *Accenture Institute for Strategic Change*.

Magretta, J 2002, *Why Business Models Matter*, HBR Onpoint, Harvard Business School Publishing, Boston.

Marshall, P, McKay, J & Burn, J 2001, 'Structure, strategy and success factors for the virtual organization', in S Barnes & B Hunt, *E-commerce and V-business: Business Models for Global Success*, chapter 10, pp. 171–92.

McKay, J & Marshall, P 2001, 'Conceptualising information systems planning across strategic business networks', *Journal of Global Information Management*, vol. 9, no. 2, pp. 23–33.

Philipson, G (ed.) 2001, *Australian E-business Guide*, 1st edn, CCH Australia, Sydney.

Rappa, M 2002, 'Managing the digital enterprise: business models on the web', http://digitalenterprise.org/models/models.html, accessed 8 August 2002.

Sandberg, KD 2002, 'Is it time to trade in your business model?', *Harvard Management Update*, Harvard Business School Publishing.

Tapscott, D, Ticoll, D & Lowry, A 2000, *Digital Capital: Harnessing the Power of Business Webs*, Nicholas Brealey Publishing, London.

Taylor, D & Terhune, AD 2001, *Doing E-business: Strategies for Thriving in an Electronic Marketplace*, John Wiley & Sons, New York.

Turban, E, King, D, Lee, J, Warkentin, M & Chung, HM 2002, *Electronic Commerce: A Managerial Perspective*, Pearson Education, Upper Saddle River, NJ.

Ward, J & Peppard, J 2002, *Strategic Planning for Information Systems*, 3rd edn, John Wiley & Sons, Chichester.

Weill, P & Vitale, MR 2001, *Place to Space: Migrating to E-business Models*, Harvard Business School Press, Boston.

Wise, R & Morrison, D 2000, 'Beyond the exchange: the future of B2B', *Harvard Business Review*, November–December.

case study

Stories from the Bush and Surf — an e-business adventure

Stories from the Surf and Bush (SB&S) is an old and successful Australian company based in Melbourne. The company has been the leading supplier of comics and books to Australian children of primary school age (5–12 years old) for more than thirty years. Until 1996 comics and books were sold mainly to bookshops, news agencies and school libraries. Some of their material was also sold to TV and film production companies and became the basis of children's serials. SB&S had no direct contact with the children who avidly consumed their products but assumed that strong sales figures reflected customer satisfaction with their products.

A network of fifty-two writers and graphic artists create and illustrate stories and comics with an Australian background and culture. Fifteen of these writers or illustrators are contracted exclusively to SB&S, and the rest are freelance. The company has developed close, family-like ties with many of the writers and illustrators, and staff turnover has been unusually slow.

The printing of SB&S's products is carried out by Australian Printed Products Limited, a medium-sized printing company in Melbourne. In the last ten years SB&S's comics and books have been sold not only in Australia but also in New Zealand, South Africa and Europe (mainly in the UK). Distribution and promotion of comics and books beyond Australia is handled by Empire Entertainments Limited (EEL), which is based in London and also has offices in Sydney and throughout Europe. EEL has recently withdrawn from the South African market, and SB&S is worried about successfully negotiating with an alternative distributor for South Africa.

Revenues for the company are approximately $60 million per year, giving profits of about $5 million for 1995. However, although SB&S remains profitable, revenues in profits are slowly declining. The European and South African markets are showing rapid declines in demand. The cultural relevance of the material produced by SB&S is questioned for those markets, although management are also concerned about reports of sales over the Internet by their major competitors as contributing to this decline.

A head office staff of fifteen dealt with administrative and management matters. The senior management team of CEO, production director, marketing director and finance director all had extensive experience relating to the creation and sale of books and comics although, despite the creative nature of their business, they were a moderately conservative group.

The advent of the Internet and its apparent consequences surprised and shocked SB&S management. The head office team watched as a few competitors and a significant number of new entrants in comics established themselves on the Web and began advertising in selling comics and books online. Comics were being sold by allowing customers either to order the comics and have them delivered or, if they wished, to download the comics. Downloads obviously save the customer distribution costs and save the producer the printing costs. Books were also being sold online by some very high-profile organisations, such as Amazon.com.

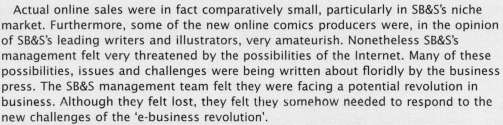

Actual online sales were in fact comparatively small, particularly in SB&S's niche market. Furthermore, some of the new online comics producers were, in the opinion of SB&S's leading writers and illustrators, very amateurish. Nonetheless SB&S's management felt very threatened by the possibilities of the Internet. Many of these possibilities, issues and challenges were being written about floridly by the business press. The SB&S management team felt they were facing a potential revolution in business. Although they felt lost, they felt they somehow needed to respond to the new challenges of the 'e-business revolution'.

SB&S had in fact very little experience or maturity with respect to the use of IT in business. They had a server and several PCs networked together for basic accounting. These were located at head office in Melbourne. The organisation's capability and maturity in IT was thus very low. Hence the management called in IT Connect, a Melbourne-based group of consultants specialising in e-business and the effective utilisation of IT in business.

Question

At this point in the case, stop reading and reflect on the situation. What would you recommend that SB&S management do? Explain your reasons and justify your conclusions.

IT Connect reports

IT Connect prided themselves in being competent and up-to-date in e-business strategy and technology, and in providing clients with excellent advice about the Internet and its likely impact on a particular organisation. Furthermore the consultancy also prided itself on giving a total business perspective on problems, not just a myopic IT perspective. After a thorough examination and analysis of SB&S's business and its use of IT, IT Connect not only suggested that SB&S respond to the challenge of e-commerce but also indicated that SB&S could profitably utilise IT within its business more extensively. They also made some broad suggestions about new business directions for SB&S in the light of the 'new interconnected world of business'.

IT Connect suggested that SB&S should develop a website both to advertise its content and to sell its books and comics. The books and comics were to be available by download as well as by delivery to customers' homes. The web page, IT Connect argued, should be lively and attractive to children, and should reassure parents that only content and materials suitable for children would be available on that site. Hence it suggested that the web page would perhaps have some games, puzzles and crosswords as well as featuring some celebrity content from their popular, best-selling characters such as Camellia Koala, and the adventures of Louis Philippe. They also felt that some animation effects on the web page would be desirable.

IT Connect recommended that SB&S utilise its website to create a community of SB&S clients, a community of children positive about SB&S's characters and stories who would share their experiences with each other. SB&S had an opportunity, IT Connect felt, to begin to manage the children's relationships with them positively. This, according to IT Connect, would be an excellent opportunity for IT-enabled customer relationship management (CRM). Children could register on the website, giving appropriate details, such as their age, gender and address as well as SB&S likes and dislikes. Children who had registered could join an SB&S chat room, and they could also upload comments on SB&S books and comics. Other children could then read moderated comments on books and comics. Thus SB&S would receive valuable feedback on its products. IT Connect also suggested a collaborative filtering application that enabled recommendations to be made to children (or their parents) on the basis of their web searches and their web-based purchases. They suggested that SB&S look towards building an Amazon.com-style wish-list capability such that each child could easily construct a wish-list of items for birthday and Christmas presents.

IT Connect suggested that a computer network or extranet linking writers and illustrators with each other and with SB&S head office would be valuable in enabling communication and workflow in the product creation process. To assist this process, IT Connect felt SB&S should motivate and assist its head office staff and its writers and illustrators to become computer literate and competent. Only 40 per cent of the writers and illustrators and three of the head office staff rated themselves as computer literate and competent at this time.

Specifically, IT Connect suggested that SB&S provide appropriate training courses for staff at suitable times and locations so that the dispersed network of writers and illustrators could attend. The courses should be free to the writers and illustrators, and assistance with any travel required should be made available. Computers and broadband connections should be provided for the writers and illustrators contracted exclusively to SB&S, and some help and inducements should be provided to the freelance workers to encourage them to become part of a productive and efficient collaborative network connected via the SB&S extranet. Furthermore SB&S should make available to its contract workers copies of the sophisticated graphics package, the Artist's Palette. Again, more encouragement, perhaps in the form of discounts arranged by SB&S, should be given to the freelance writers and illustrators.

IT Connect also believed that increased efficiencies and effectiveness could be achieved by the indexed electronic storage of all products (content, graphics, comics and books) in an 'electronic warehouse' of all products, which would be accessible via the Internet by all artists and illustrators. Previously the storage of master copies of all products was quite a time-consuming task, and the process of writers and illustrators retrieving and reusing illustrations and text was also time-consuming. The electronic warehouse was believed to be a way of improving the situation markedly.

IT Connect asserted that the new IT infrastructure required for its plans plus the hiring of a new CIO and three IT specialists could largely be paid for by online sales and online advertising. Online sales, IT Connect predicted, would grow from zero to 15 per cent of sales in three years and would yield revenues of $9 million. Thus, borrowing for IT infrastructure and to build IT capability would be funded in a short time by revenues from Internet-based business.

IT Connect mentioned that the Internet had made the world a smaller place. Businesses were much more interconnected and interdependent than before. Collaboration was much more possible and much more appealing. SB&S could now look to some of the companies in the USA, for example, that produced children's comics and/or books both as sources of material for SB&S to on-sell and as distributors of Australian goods. With their network of contacts in the US markets, Marvel and King Features would be excellent partners for the creation and distribution of comics. The Internet now made such collaboration a possibility. Material could be sent between SB&S and its US companies as quickly as the click of a mouse.

SB&S implements the recommendations

SB&S management, after taking a deep breath and reflecting on IT Connect's report, decided to go ahead with the recommendations. SB&S thought that the new business model for their Internet-based activities, as outlined by IT Connect, looked logical and complete. They therefore moved to begin implementation of the recommendations.

The first issue they tackled was that of their IT capabilities. They recruited and appointed a new CIO. They felt very comfortable and secure with their new appointment, a young highflyer who was an expert in the business technology and in the technical security aspects of e-commerce. He recruited a bright young team to join him, each of whom was capable in various aspects of e-business technology. With this team in place, SB&S's management's move towards e-business began with a sense of optimism.

Five years later SB&S are scaling down their Internet-based business. The website has generated revenues of only $100 000, and Internet-based advertising has been returning close to zero. Relations between the IT team and the rest of the business are very tense. The management team and many of the writers and illustrators felt that the IT team's understanding of the children's book and comic business is very questionable. Indeed some of the SB&S 'old-timers' felt that the IT team had a problem understanding people. Because of this poor relationship there had been problems with the website design. Many in the business and indeed the industry felt that the design of the website was poor and was not attractive or even user-friendly to children. Furthermore, despite the long, successful history of the company, they have never had direct relationships with the children who love their products, a fact clearly evident in the way they designed their website.

The development of IT projects within the business was also believed to be problematic. Most projects were over budget and were not finished on time. The development of the network and the electronic warehouse was punctuated by upsetting disagreements between the IT team on the one hand and the head office workers and writers and illustrators on the other. An investigation of the situation by IT Connect concluded that there was not as much wrong technically as those outside the IT team felt, but that the problems related to the IT team's rather offhand approach to people and their insensitivity to important aspects of the children's books and comics business. Although IT Connect advised against doing anything precipitous, the management team was considering dismissing the IT team and outsourcing the IT activities of the company.

Questions

1. Assess the business model proposed by IT Connect. Was it as complete and logical as SB&S thought? What problems do you think were inherent in the business model proposed by IT Connect? Use the business model architecture put forward in this chapter to consider its strengths and limitations.

2. Explain what you think were the major causes of the failure of the SB&S e-business model together with SB&S's associated e-business implementation.

3. IT Connect knew that SB&S was a conservative company with little IT infrastructure and capability, yet recommended a sophisticated IT solution for the company with respect to the Internet. In retrospect, would you consider this advice to be appropriate? (You might like to refer back to the Stages of Growth for e-Business model introduced in chapter 1.)

4. SB&S must now decide on how to proceed in future. They are aware of some of the shortcomings of their first foray into e-commerce, but recognise that the Internet is an important technology that could contribute substantially to their business.

5. Recommend a suitable business model for SB&S. In particular, comment on the business model architecture that you think would be necessary for SB&S to be successful and profitable as a clicks and mortar company.

chapter 3

E-business strategy formulation

learning objectives

After reading this chapter, you should understand:

- the need for high-level thinking about business and IT before making decisions about IT and e-commerce investments
- the importance of developing sound IT and e-business strategies
- the nature and objectives of strategic information systems planning (SISP) and the influence of e-commerce, e-business and the Internet on SISP
- the problems associated with a lack of planning
- alignment, its implications for business, and the importance of achieving strategic alignment
- the application of tools and techniques for the analysis of IT and e-commerce requirements, and appreciation of the different emphases of each tool
- the complementarity and contrast between the portfolio approach to planning and the resource-based view of planning.

chapter overview

E-business strategy formulation involves a review of the way information, information systems and information technology (I/IS/IT) are used in a business to create business value and to enable the achievement of strategic business objectives. It also involves a search for opportunities to utilise new opportunities profitably for the application of information systems and information technology in the course of creating value and supporting the business strategy. Hence one of the results of formulating an e-business strategy is a new portfolio of application systems as well as the building of a suitable IT infrastructure.

Central to the formulation of an e-business strategy are several key decisions that shape the approach to the delivery of IT in an organisation. These decisions involve the role of IT and e-commerce in the organisation, the sourcing of IT, the structure of the IT organisation and the view of the IT infrastructure of the organisation. To guide this decision-making, the strategic context of the firm must be well understood and the strategic intent of the firm formulated and expressed. Business and IT maxims are formulated to help express and communicate the strategic intent of the business and

enabling role of IT. The analysis undertaken as part of SISP leads to a new and po:
enhanced **application systems portfolio** and possibly also to some new
infrastructure investments. Informing these decisions is an analysis of the internal and
external business environments together with an analysis of the external and internal
information systems and information technology environments.

Why focus on planning for e-business?

It might be tempting to think that, in times of extreme turbulence, uncertainty and
rapid technological change, planning is impossible: that in such circumstances the
best an organisation can do is to react and respond as rapidly as it can. However, an
alternative perspective would suggest that in environments of great uncertainty and
change, planning becomes a vital component in managing and responding to such
complexity. Planning in this context is not thought of as a ponderous, bureaucratic
process that takes place annually and results in elaborate written documents, which
are then seldom referred to. Rather, the term *planning* is used in the sense of day-to-
day thinking, recognising and responding. It is almost akin to an incessant 'worrying'
about the organisation and what it wants to achieve, what obstacles it is likely to
encounter (or is currently encountering), how the objectives of the organisation can
be better realised and, in the context of IT, how information, information systems and
information technology can be deployed to help the organisation achieve its goals. It
is as if the management of the company maintains a 'strategic conversation' within
the company corridors. Formal planning sessions can give more focus and intensity to
this process. However, they need to do so without stifling the creativity and energy of
the 'strategic conversation'. Generally speaking, the emphasis is on the strategic
thinking rather than on the planning (Masifern & Vila 1998).

Planning for e-commerce, e-business and IT aims to consider the major trends
occurring in the utilisation of IT in business, and thus equip the organisation to take
advantage of appropriate technologically driven opportunities. The potential strategic
importance of IT and the Internet has been noted by many writers (Porter 2001; Feeny
2001). To realise strategic value, the authors believe that organisations need to devote
some of their senior managers' time to strategic analysis of the possibilities inherent
in IT and the Internet.

Trends enabled by information technology

Already in this textbook a number of critical trends enabled by IT and the Internet
have been identified, all of which could be argued to emphasise the need for careful
planning of the utilisation of IT and the Internet as critical organisational resources.
Other important trends include:

- the ability to use IT and the Internet to re-engineer the organisation's supply chain,
  to use information to smooth out inefficiencies and bottlenecks in the supply
  chain, and thus to achieve significant efficiency and effectiveness gains

- the ability to use IT and the Internet to re-engineer the organisation's relationships with its customers, manipulating the large amounts of data about customers that can be obtained to identify purchasing habits, trends and preferences, and then use this to make better decisions regarding production of goods and services, and thus add value from the customer's perspective
- the ability to use IT and the Internet to gather, store, manipulate and disseminate vital corporate information to decision-makers throughout the organisation and to support greater efficiency of internal processes.

Hence formulating careful strategies and planning for the appropriate use of IT and the Internet is vital as IT adopts a more strategic role in organisations. For most organisations, the last decade or so has seen a move from the use of IT primarily to support core business to the use of IT and Internet technologies to enable, drive and enhance core business operations. Thus the stakes are higher now with proposed investments in IT. Many of these investments are very costly, and as IT is used more and more to create strategic business networks, the organisation's reputation and credibility can be at risk in a much more public sense if such investments in IT are poorly thought out and poorly implemented (Nixon, Hitt & Ricart i Costa 1998).

For many organisations, IT is now the fastest growing area of capital expenditure and, in some industries, it now represents more than 50 per cent of capital expenditure. Hence for most organisations, IT represents a very substantial investment. However, at the same time as companies are investing more and more in IT and Internet technologies, senior managers are also expressing concerns about whether these investments are delivering value to the organisation: questions regarding the return on investments in IT are prevalent among some business leaders. This is of concern at a time when many business leaders are also acknowledging that the future of their organisation is now inextricably linked to IT, and hence the successful and appropriate deployment of IT is essential to the future health of their enterprises.

The view adopted in this chapter is that e-commerce and the Internet must be regarded as important, pervasive technologies that should be included in the thinking and planning of all organisations. Cognisance of the role of the Internet in affecting an organisation's industry, its basis for competition, the goods and services it produces and markets, and the way relationships with customers can be established are essential (as was illustrated in chapter 2 in the discussion of formulating business models). In this chapter, the assumption is made that the Internet is also central to considerations of the importance and contribution of technology to an organisation and hence is included in the formulation of IT strategy.

Defining strategic information systems planning and e-business planning

In the information systems field, a classic definition of strategic information systems planning (SISP) is offered by Ward and Griffiths (1996, p. 6), who write that SISP involves 'planning for the effective long-term management and optimal impact of information, information systems, and information technology'. Despite the fact that this definition was written several years before the wide-scale adoption of the Internet by business, it remains a useful definition. The specific technologies that organisations now need to manage and use might have changed, but planning for the IT resource, now embracing the Internet and associated technologies, remains concerned with achieving optimal benefits, in terms of the achievement of business goals and objectives, for that organisation.

If an organisation is to manage its IT capability effectively and achieve excellent results from it, then it must identify what information and systems are required and what technology is needed to deliver the required information and systems. The organisation must also identify and determine appropriate levels of resourcing for IT over a two- to three-year time frame and develop a realistic implementation plan.

There are likely to be a number of objectives when planning an organisation's IS, IT and e-commerce resources, and some of these will be discussed later. However, there are three overarching objectives that need to inform and guide all the planning activity and the formulation of strategies. First, the main aim is to ensure that the focus of all IT investments (Internet-based technologies included) is squarely on the delivery of core business goals and objectives. Second, an important objective of planning and strategy formulation is to ensure that all stakeholders, but especially the senior management team, understand what IT and the Internet can achieve within their organisation and become committed to the deployment of technology to enable the achievement of key business objectives. The third overarching objective is to develop appropriate levels of resourcing for IT and e-commerce and, in so doing, to establish priorities for IT investments.

The relationship between business strategy, IT strategy and e-commerce strategy

A **business strategy** can be thought of as a plan that integrates an organisation's major goals, policies and action into a coherent coordinated whole (Quinn 1996). Quinn (1996, p. 3) goes on to argue:

> a well formulated strategy helps to marshal and allocate an organisation's resources into a unique and viable posture based on its relative internal competencies and shortcomings, anticipated changes in the environment, and contingent moves by intelligent opponents.

Strategy can be thought of therefore as the direction that an organisation takes so that it can compete effectively in a particular marketplace and ultimately meet the expectations of stakeholders in the organisation (Johnson & Scholes 1999). In order to do this, it needs to harness its capabilities and resources effectively. A key component of strategy is to identify goals and objectives that state precisely what it is that the organisation aims to achieve in a particular time frame. Organisations will usually have multiple goals, and an important task for senior management is to ensure the alignment of those goals and to establish a hierarchy of goals (Quinn 1996).

Other important concepts in the context of business strategy are vision and mission. These terms are similar but by no means identical. A **vision** is a challenging statement that articulates the desired future state of the organisation. The **mission** of an organisation refers to its overriding purpose, its reason for existence (Johnson & Scholes 1999).

The traditional relationship between business strategy and IT strategy is captured in figure 3.1. In essence, it was argued that an **IS strategy** (concerned with the information and systems needs of an organisation) should grow out of a business strategy or, in other words, once an organisation's direction and its objectives have been established, then a need for information, systems and technology might well be apparent in supporting the accomplishment of those goals and objectives. The IS strategy focuses on articulating the information requirements of the organisation and the systems that would be required for the delivery of that information. Having identified a required suite of applications, an organisation could then articulate its **IT strategy** and in doing so identify the technology required to deliver the required systems. In figure 3.1, note the heavy downward pointing arrows representing the direction of these relationships.

However, it is also recognised that the existing technological infrastructure of an organisation could limit its ability to build systems and deliver information and hence could, at a particular time, restrict the types of strategies adopted by an organisation. This is represented by the dotted, upward pointing arrows in figure 3.1.

In addition, it was recognised that from time to time a technological breakthrough would fundamentally affect the way organisations do business and compete. The Internet is in fact a very good example of such a technological development. Hence, in formulating strategy, businesses must be aware of technological developments that potentially affect the way they do business and the nature of competition in an industry.

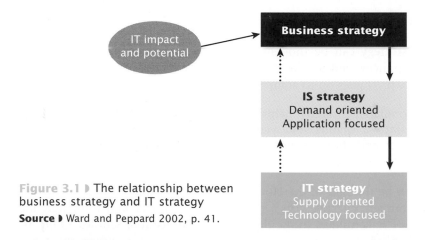

Figure 3.1 ▶ The relationship between business strategy and IT strategy
Source ▶ Ward and Peppard 2002, p. 41.

The question that needs to be posed here, however, is whether this model still applies in the era of the Internet and e-commerce. Are new models needed to guide planning activities in the post-Internet era? Some authorities suggest that that new models are needed. Take, for example, the model presented in figure 3.2. The author of this model elevates e-commerce above IT strategy, perhaps to emphasise the criticality of the Internet in many modern organisations.

Figure 3.2 ▶ An alternative perspective of e-commerce strategy formulation
Source ▶ Turban et al. 2002, p. 678.

However, for the purposes of this chapter, it is argued that the advent of the Internet requires or imposes only a small change on the original model presented in figure 3.1. One effect of the Internet is to expand the thinking of managers and to elevate strategic thinking about a form of technology to the level of business strategy. At the level of business strategy formulation, managers need to take into account the potential of the Internet to affect fundamentally the way they interact with suppliers and customers and to change the basis for competition in their industry. Likewise at the level of IT strategy, managers need to think carefully about the effect of Internet-based technologies to support the capture, storage and provision of information resources and to influence the need for sound information systems given new business realities. In terms of technology, managers need to consider the potential of the Internet and associated technologies to affect their infrastructure and their delivery mechanisms for required information systems. Hence, the preferred model of the relationship between business planning, IT planning and e-commerce planning is one that sees thinking about and planning for the Internet as being subsumed into each of the three levels of planning, but therefore necessarily expanding the types of thinking that need to be undertaken at each stage.

Figure 3.3 ▶
The Internet expanding planning horizons
Source ▶ Ward and Peppard 2002.

In developing an e-business strategy, it is important that managers are clear on how organisations can leverage the connectivity, speed and accessibility created by the Internet and associated technologies to extend, enhance and/or enable business vision and strategy. Essentially there needs to be a clear picture of how IT (including the Internet) can be exploited to deliver value to customers profitably.

Objectives of e-business planning

A number of key objectives can be identified for any planning exercise related to the use of IT in business. The major objectives are:

- to help ensure that IT and e-commerce support the achievement of business objectives and help ensure business competitiveness and the delivery of the customer value proposition
- to achieve cost-effective investment in IT and e-commerce for measured business benefits, thus controlling expenditures and ensuring the delivery of value for money
- to protect existing technology and information assets and to reduce maintenance costs for the organisation
- to prioritise the application of limited financial resources towards IT investments that meet important business needs
- to gain the commitment to and understanding of senior executives to the role of IT and e-commerce in the organisation.

If the planning exercise is to meet its objectives, it is important that the right people be involved. Planning the IS, IT and e-commerce requirements of an organisation should not be regarded as a technical activity: indeed, it would be preferable for e-business planning to be regarded as a business activity in which senior IT executives were involved along with other senior managers. It is also important that in developing strategies for e-business, planners are cognisant of the prevailing management view of technology and the level of organisational maturity with respect to IT. Are the senior management team generally supportive of IT, and do they view IT as integral to the future success of their enterprise? Does IT have a significant but minor role in improving business processes by reducing costs and/or increasing the speed at which tasks and activities are done? Or are management not yet persuaded that IT has such a central role to play in the achievement of business goals? Is the overall organisation quite sophisticated with respect to its adoption and use of IT, or is it still at a relatively immature stage? Understanding the answers to these key questions enables the articulation of a technology vision and strategy that is appropriate for the current state of the organisation.

Organisations that fail to plan effectively put themselves at risk from a number of perspectives. First, they run the risk of becoming uncompetitive and, in some circumstances business goals can become unachievable owing to limitations of the deployment of technology throughout the organisation. There might be a lack of commitment on the part of senior executives and a failure to appreciate the important role that IT and the Internet are playing in most modern organisations. (This is particularly the case in the post dotcom crash era.) Problems can occur because systems are not well integrated, resulting in a duplication or replication of effort across the organisation, inaccuracy in corporate data and poor information being supplied to decision-makers. In addition, new systems can fail to deliver business benefits because of a lack of focus on business needs. In extreme cases of poor planning and strategy formulation, IT can actually become a constraint on the business. Another issue with respect to inadequate planning is that there is no sound means by which resources are allocated to IT projects, nor are IT investment projects well prioritised. These problems were issues for organisations before the advent of the Internet. However, it is fair to say that the rapid uptake of the Internet and associated technologies might have exacerbated these problems in many cases.

Framework for e-business strategy formulation

Formulating strategy for the e-business for many organisations is a complex process. For that reason a framework to guide and structure thinking might be helpful (see figure 3.4). Such a framework is not intended to be used as a step-by-step approach that is doggedly followed from start to finish. Rather, it is intended as a way of structuring the world and attempting to highlight salient features that in the view of the authors might be vital in formulating a coherent, appropriate strategy. The sections that follow will consider sections of this framework in turn.

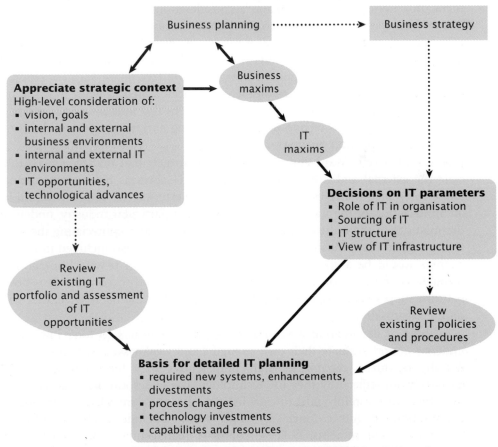

Figure 3.4 ▶ A framework to support the formulation of strategy for IS, IT and e-commerce
Source ▶ concepts from Hirschheim and Sabherwal 2001 and Broadbent and Weill 1997.

Appreciate strategic context: high-level strategic thinking and visioning about IT and the Internet

There can be little argument that thinking about and planning the entire IT resource (including the Internet) in an organisation is a major and complex task. For large organisations, there are all the challenges of effectively utilising new technologies, but there is often also a substantial legacy of systems that have been developed and/or acquired over decades. How to produce a coherent vision and plan in the face of both this complexity and the competing demands for IT resources throughout the organisation is not always obvious. In this section, a framework based on the work of Broadbent and Weill (1997) and Hirschheim and Sabherwal (2001) will be presented and discussed.

Broadbent and Weill (1997) suggest that, in order to produce effective strategies, it is essential for senior managers to understand and appreciate what they call the 'strategic context'. Included in this notion is an understanding of the long-term goals of and vision for the organisation, what the organisation sees itself doing or, in their words, 'its strategic intent' (Broadbent & Weill 1997, p. 81). Along with an appreciation of the external business environment and the firm's position in that environment, this notion also encapsulates a consideration of some internal factors. Such factors include the extent to which similarities exist between business units (in terms of customers, suppliers, goods and/or services delivered and business culture) within the organisation and hence whether opportunities exist for synergies and economies of scale to be achieved throughout the organisation (see figure 3.5). For emphasis, an appreciation of the context of e-commerce has been added to figure 3.5. The purpose is to emphasise the need to consider specifically the influence and effects of the Internet and associated technologies in examining and understanding the context in which the organisation operates.

In a similar vein, Ward and Peppard (2002) suggest that managers need to appreciate the external and internal business and IS/IT contexts before formulating IS/IT and e-commerce strategies. Consideration of the external environment would include an appreciation of the nature of competition in a particular industry, understanding the maturity of the industry and key industry trends, and appreciating the impact of technology in that industry, particularly IT for example. Also included in the external analysis would be a consideration of the potential for a new technological breakthrough to affect the organisation and the industry and to consider also how competitors, suppliers and customers are deploying IT and the likely effect that will have on the organisation.

Analysis of the internal environment requires managers to look inwards and to understand and evaluate their own strengths and weaknesses, in terms of what they do, the resources, capabilities and competencies they have access to, and how effectively and efficiently they use technology. The IT resources in particular need to be subject to a careful audit to establish whether they are adequate for serving the organisation in future. Such an audit would include both IT infrastructure, information requirements, IS/IT skills and IT management. (Note that subsequent sections will consider tools and techniques suitable for supporting this type of analysis.)

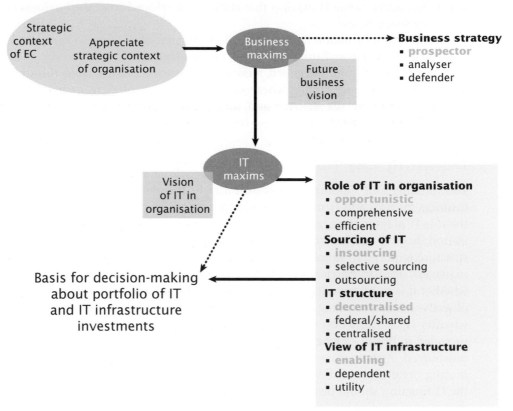

Figure 3.5 ▶ High-level strategic thinking and visioning

Source ▶ concepts from Broadbent and Weill 1997 and Hirschheim and Sabherwal 2001.

Articulating business and IT maxims

Once an understanding of the strategic context, including the external and internal business environments, has been achieved, Broadbent and Weill (1997) argue for the articulation of business maxims, high-level statements that express simply and clearly an organisation's competitive position, the way it creates value for customers, its intentions regarding growth, flexibility and agility, its stance towards the use and value of resources, its approach to management and so on. Examples of business maxims for a service-based organisation might include such statements as:

• Set the highest possible one-stop service standards from a low-cost base.
• Develop products and services that are driven by customer needs.
• Develop the cross-selling of services.

From such statements of intent regarding the business strategies and focus, it is then possible to articulate 'IT maxims' or statements about the way IT will be deployed in an organisation. These statements would summarise thinking about the use of IT for the purposes of storing and disseminating information and promoting the sharing of information resources, the way IT services will be provided, the role of IT in the achievement of business objectives, and the centrality of IT resources in the competitive stance of the organisation. This might indicate appropriate levels of resourcing for IT. Some IT maxims that could be developed from the business maxims above are listed below:

- Centralised information flow should allow all parts of the firm to spot trends more easily and quickly and use them to the firm's advantage.
- IT must provide one integrated view of the customer and enable the immediate delivery of customer profiles wherever in the organisation they are needed.
- IT must facilitate the delivery and monitoring of low-cost service of acceptable quality to customers.

Defining key parameters for IT

The thinking and visioning that contributes to the ability of managers to articulate business maxims and IT maxims should mean that the organisation becomes clear on the role IT plays in the organisation, how IT services will be sourced within that organisation, how IT will be structured throughout the organisation and the type of infrastructure required to support the provision of IT services (see figure 3.5). For example managers need to be clear on whether IT is viewed primarily as a support tool or whether it is to be regarded as fundamental to the achievement of business goals and objectives. Understanding the role that IT is to play could then inform decisions about whether IT as a function should be regarded as a key corporate resource, and hence provided in-house, or whether it is regarded more as a commodity and hence could be outsourced. Appreciating the role of IT in supporting decision-making and in promoting organisational flexibility and responsiveness also provides insights into how the IT function should be structured in an organisation. Hence decisions regarding the degree of centralisation can be appropriately reached. Finally, understanding the role, sourcing arrangements and structure allows informed choices to be made regarding the nature of the infrastructure that needs to be developed so that IT can be utilised according to the role defined for it.

▶ Strategic alignment

At this point another important consideration involves the notion of **strategic alignment**, or 'the extent to which the IS mission, objectives and plans support and are supported by the business mission, objectives and plans' (Hirschheim & Sabherwal 2001, p. 88). Alignment of business and IT resources and activities requires that IT decisions and investments contribute in the desired way to the achievement of business goals and objectives.

In figure 3.6, three broad types of business strategy are identified: the prospector, the analyser and the defender. Drawing on the work of Miles and Snow (1978), Hirschheim and Sabherwal (2001) suggest that organisations orient themselves strategically around one of three broad stances. The prospector is an entrepreneurial, somewhat aggressive position, constantly seeking new opportunities, both embracing and causing change in an industry. By contrast, the defender establishes itself usually in some sort of niche market competing on the basis of quality and price, and rarely initiates or seeks change. The analyser adopts a position midway between the two, being much more cautious and careful to manage risk than the prospector when seeking out new opportunities but being more entrepreneurial than the defender.

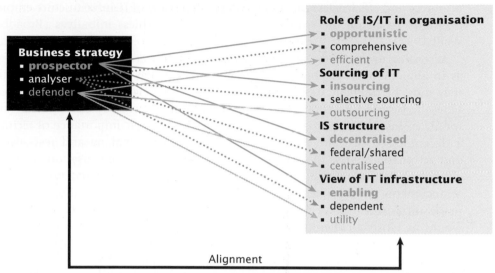

Figure 3.6 ▶ Aligning IT profiles with business strategy

Source ▶ adapted from Hirschheim and Sabherwal 2001.

Hirschheim and Sabherwal (2001) then extend these ideas to formulating strategies and making investment decisions with respect to IT. Thus, in considering a role for IT in the organisation, managers can see IT as playing an opportunistic role (IT is exploited to support the pursuit of business opportunities and thus supports flexibility and rapid decision-making), or IT can be seen primarily as a driver of organisational efficiencies via process improvements and efficient transaction processing. The comprehensive role for IT would be positioned somewhat between these extremes, seeking efficiencies but also providing accurate information to support careful decisions regarding business expansion opportunities.

In terms of the sourcing of the IT resource, Hirschheim and Sabherwal (2001) identify an insourcing approach when IT is regarded as inextricably linked to the future success of the organisation and is regarded as a critical differentiator. An outsourcing approach is one that regards IT primarily as a commodity in the organisation, and a selective sourcing approach is when an organisation sees IT as more important than a commodity but do not yet view IT as fundamental to business success. The structure of the provision of IT resources reflects the role of IT in supporting decision-making throughout the organisation. Thus, a centralised structure enhances control and the determination of central policies and procedures, and avoids duplication of data and systems, whereas a decentralised structure offers greater local flexibility, autonomy and responsiveness to the requirements of business units. A federal structure, part centralised and part decentralised, attempts to maintain the strengths of both the centralised and decentralised approaches (Hirschheim & Sabherwal 2001).

Finally, consideration must be given to the approach to building IT infrastructure. Hence, an enabling IT infrastructure represents one designed to allow for future expansion and growth and therefore must offer flexibility; a utility view of infrastructure is oriented towards achieving economies of scale, sharing of information resources and efficiencies; whereas the dependent view of IT infrastructure emphasises decisions based on the requirements of current business initiatives (Broadbent & Weill 1997).

According to the model presented in figure 3.6, for an organisation to be regarded as in alignment, its business strategy and its IT strategy must be consonant; that is, they must be mutually supportive and aiming to achieve the same sort of objectives. Thus the prospector organisation might well be best served by an opportunistic role for IT, an insourced approach that recognises the strategic importance of technology, a decentralised structure that promotes local decision-making and responsiveness, and an enabling view of IT infrastructure. The defender organisation would be in alignment if it adopted an efficiency-oriented role for IT, entered into outsourcing arrangements reflecting its commodity view of IT, adopted a centralised structure and made infrastructure investments based on a utility view. The analyser organisation would be closer to alignment if it adopted a comprehensive role for IT, a selective sourcing approach to the delivery of IT services and a federal structure to support decision-making, and if it took a dependent view of infrastructure.

The combined content of figures 3.4, 3.5 and 3.6 provides a sound basis for high-level thinking and visioning with respect to IT deployment in an organisation. The prospector, defender and analyser organisational types are clearly 'ideal types', and they might not find exact replication in the real world. However, they do form a basis on which strategic thinking and subsequent decisions can be taken. Understanding strategic alignment at a high level can inform more detailed discussion and decisions taken in the formulation and articulation of specific IS, IT and e-commerce strategies and plans.

In much of this discussion, there have been few mentions of e-commerce and the role of the Internet. This is not because it is not important or not to be considered here: nothing could be further from our intentions. It is because we are assuming their interpretation into any discussion of IT.

Complementary views of strategic thinking about e-business

Business strategy has typically been articulated in terms of what an organisation can do (in terms of its internal resources) when faced with what it might like to do (in terms of external opportunities and threats) (Collis & Montgomery 1995). Seminal writers including Michael Porter developed a view of strategy (and supporting tools and techniques) that concentrated primarily on positioning in response to external factors, seeking to understand the structure and nature of competition within an industry, which then served as a basis from which an organisation could identify strategies that it could adopt in order to create a sustainable competitive advantage over its industry rivals (de Kluyver 2000). This became known as the 'industry structure' view of strategy or sometimes the 'industrial economics' view of strategy (de Kluyver 2000; Collis & Montgomery 1995).

This view was subsequently challenged by such writers as Hamel and Prahalad (1994), who urged that strategic thinking shift from competitive positioning given the dictates of the business environment to a focus more on a distinctive blend of internal resources, competencies and capabilities, which could then be harnessed and exploited as a source of competitive advantage. This resourced-based view of strategy argues that strategy should be developed in accordance with an organisation's resources, competencies and capabilities, that resources and capabilities ultimately act as a constraint on the type of strategy and initiatives that can be adopted, and that a resource-based strategy offers potentially a much more sustainable source of competitive advantage than do products and services positioned within a particular market. Resources and competencies are seen as much more robust, longer lasting and harder to imitate than specific products or services in dynamic, turbulent business environments.

In terms of e-business, the **resource-based view** of strategy focuses on developing IT resources and capabilities, the effective deployment of which can arguably lead to sustainable competitive advantage. Bharadwaj (2000) classifies firm-specific IT resources into IT infrastructure, human IT resources and IT-enabled intangibles. After a study of IT capability and firm performance he concluded that firms with high IT capability tend to outperform firms with lower IT capabilities.

Mata, Fuerst and Barney (1995) mention proprietary technology, technical IT skills, managerial IT skills and the financial capability to acquire the necessary capital to make risky but strategic IT investments as resources or capabilities that have the potential to generate a sustained competitive advantage for firms. A study by Armstrong and Sambamurthy (1999) found that the quality of senior leadership and the sophistication of IT infrastructures among other things affected the ability of firms to leverage the potential of IT in their business activities and strategies.

Peppard, Lambert and Edwards (2000) point out that the effective deployment and exploitation of information in companies should be viewed as a strategic asset. They go on to make the important point that organisations must recognise and develop information competencies and that the elements of these competencies are distributed throughout the organisation and not solely resident in the IS function.

It can be seen therefore that there is a growing body of literature supporting the notion that the resource-based view of strategy is an important perspective on the role of IT in supporting the business strategy of firms and in supporting the creation of competitive advantage for firms.

Not all writers see the **strategic positioning view** and the resource-based view of strategy as complementary, arguing for the supremacy of one over the other. This is not the position adopted in this chapter. Rather, it is argued that each perspective offers invaluable insights into the direction an organisation can adopt and that this is particularly important when considering the priorities for IT investments because investments that help an organisation to manage competitive forces are just as vital as investments that help to build the sorts of capabilities and competencies that an organisation requires. Both views will be considered in discussing various approaches to planning in the sections that follow.

thinking strategically

Carnivale: using IT to achieve business goals and objectives?

Read the following case and then discuss the questions that follow.

Carnivale is famous for its design and manufacture of exclusive silk ties and silk scarves. Although the firm does produce some lines for sale through upmarket department stores world-wide, it pitches its designs to and sells mainly through exclusive boutiques. Hence most of their items have very small production runs.

Carnivale is a very conservative company. All its sourcing of the finest silk fabrics is done through personal contacts. Its sales staff travel around to the boutiques with glossy brochures that illustrate the next season's ties and scarves. They accept orders on paper forms, often promising delivery dates and availability to make the sale, but tend to collect a number of orders before faxing them through to head office. All invoices, despatch notes and the like can now be generated by computer systems, but there is little integration of these systems, and often sales staff can accept orders and promise delivery dates without knowing or being informed that some items might be out of stock or out of production. Many of the boutiques like to retain the glossy brochure, as some of their customers like to browse through it and place special orders to suit their personal preferences. Carnivale's purchasing system (obtaining silk required for production) is also unreliable, meaning that product lines advertised in the brochure are not always available owing to problems in obtaining the right fabric of the right quality in the right quantities.

All the retail outlets that stock Carnivale's products like to offer outstanding service to their discerning customers, and they are becoming increasingly frustrated by accepting special orders that cannot be fulfilled, by placing orders with sales people that do not arrive on schedule, and so on.

Carnivale is concerned about any drop in market share or in perceptions of the quality of their product and service. They are therefore undertaking a major business and IT planning exercise. Major IT investments are being considered to help achieve business objectives and to ensure prosperity for the company in future.

Questions

1. How might a strategic information systems planning (SISP) exercise assist Carnivale with its current problems?
2. What might be the vision for Carnivale? Discuss some of the key internal and external factors that affect the company.
3. Draw up three to five business maxims for Carnivale. On the basis of these maxims, draw up appropriate IT maxims.

Undertaking detailed planning for e-business

Once the high-level directions have been clearly and coherently established, then the process of detailed planning for the IT resource in an organisation becomes much simpler. Clearly the process needs to be informed by reviewing the existing IT portfolio as a suite of systems to see the extent to which levels of service and information provision are regarded as being adequate currently and in the future. Identifying gaps in what is required as opposed to what is provided is important at this stage, as is a detailed assessment of existing IT opportunities within the organisation. Technological developments and business change (such as changes in strategy) all suggest that there might be opportunities to exploit IT and the Internet in ways that were not previously possible or practicable. Hence the review of the existing portfolio needs to identify weaknesses in current levels of service as well as opportunities for deployment of IT resources in creative, beneficial ways that had not previously been considered.

At this stage it is also appropriate to review existing IS, IT and e-commerce policies, procedures and governance to identify areas of weakness. Deriving improved business value from IT might not just imply future investment: it might also result from a need for better management of the existing resource and therefore the development of better policies, procedures and processes through which this management could be achieved.

Tools and techniques to support the strategy formulation process

A number of tools and techniques can be used to help managers better appreciate the strategic context of the organisation, the role of IT, the strengths and weaknesses of the existing IT function, and so on. Some of these will be briefly described and indications of their applicability and use will be given. The tools and techniques discussed here are not intended to be complete; they are representative only. There will be many other possibilities, which might prove to be equally effective. Neither are they intended to limit or straightjacket thinking. It is intended that they be used as ways of stimulating and structuring thinking, rather than limiting thinking. It is also not the intention that they are considered suitable for use only at one stage in the strategy formulation framework. Many of these tools are such that the insights they provide could inform thinking at nearly every stage of the framework, and therefore potential users are encouraged to 'mix and match' them to find their own best ways of using these approaches.

SWOT analysis

SWOT (strengths, weaknesses, opportunities, threats) is a simple technique, often used for strategic planning (Hubbard 2000; Johnson & Scholes 1999). As the name implies, it involves identification of the strengths and weaknesses of an organisation as well as opportunities and threats. Consideration of strengths and weaknesses typically focuses on the internal capabilities, resources and skills of an organisation, thus identifying those areas in which the organisation possesses strengths that could and should be exploited for advantage, and those areas where potentially the organisation needs to build or access skills and resources to avoid putting itself at a disadvantage. By contrast, thinking about opportunities and threats requires a consideration of the external environment and an identification of the opportunities and threats that exist. In considering whether an opportunity should be exploited, or in considering how to counter a threat, an organisation's internal capabilities and competencies, and/or its ability to access desired skills, capabilities and resources externally through some sort of outsourcing arrangement, will obviously impact on its ability to respond to opportunities and threats.

SWOT analysis can be directly applied to the IT resource in an organisation. Thus, in terms of its information, IS and IT resources, an organisation needs to understand those areas of strengths and those areas of weaknesses and to be aware of the implications of not rectifying weaknesses. Also, an organisation must be aware of the external IT opportunities and threats. In considering its e-business strategy, for example, an organisation might find that it has excellent back office skills, resources and capabilities but that it is weak in terms of the skills and capabilities it needs to develop appropriate front office systems. Likewise, it would be essential to consider the influence of the Internet, both as a potential threat to the organisation and as an opportunity. In thinking of the Internet as a potential threat one could ask: how are our competitors using the Internet and with what success? Are our suppliers insisting that we adopt the Internet? However, one would also look for opportunities, via the Internet, to enter new marketplaces, develop closer relationships with customers and suppliers, and even to develop new Internet-delivered products and services. Being cognisant of the strengths and weaknesses of an organisation with respect to IT, and of the opportunities and threats posed by IT is an essential consideration in the overall planning process.

Revisit the Carnivale case presented earlier. Do a SWOT analysis on Carnivale. What can we learn about the internal (strengths and weaknesses) and external (opportunities and threats) views of Carnivale? What ideas could we derive from a SWOT analysis that we would then contribute to the formulation of IS/IT/e-business strategy?

Product and service lifecycles

The notion of a product or service lifecycle is premised on the idea that products (or services) have a finite life. In other words, they pass through stages of emergence, growth and maturity before decline (see figure 3.7). The product lifecycle is not regarded as some inevitable course; rather, managerial decision-making might be able to influence the rate at which a product passes through each stage. Some products pass through the entire lifecycle in a matter of months (such as some children's toys, fashion items or new music DVDs), whereas others remain in the mature phase for many decades (such as Coca Cola, Guinness or Cadbury's Dairy Milk Chocolate).

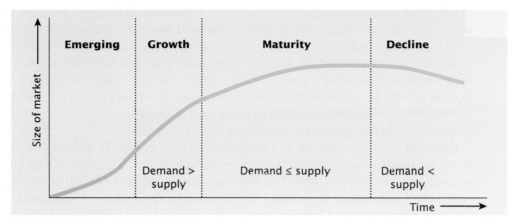

Figure 3.7 ▶ The product lifecycle
Source ▶ Ward and Peppard 2002, p. 88.

An associated concept is that of the product portfolio, shown in figure 3.8 (Ward & Peppard 2002). Innovative ideas start as wildcats, which require a lot of investment (for relatively small return) to turn them into rising stars. Stars enjoy high market growth yet still require high investment to ensure their position in the marketplace. It is hoped that they will then become cash cows, mature products or services that generate good returns for the organisation with comparatively little investment. When the market share declines, the product or service becomes a dog, and eventually management must decide on the fate of that product or service. Sometimes great ideas can fail, and hence the wildcat will be viewed as a problem child and go into immediate decline without having ever been much of a success for the organisation.

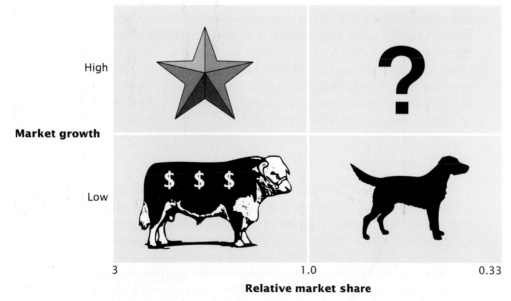

Figure 3.8 ▶ Product portfolio
Source ▶ Ward and Peppard 2002, p. 89, from Boston Consulting Group.

What are the implications of this tool for e-business planning? Think about the nature and type of information that managers need about products or services in each of the quadrants in figure 3.8. What do managers need to know about these products or services in order to manage them effectively and make good decisions about them?

For wildcats (emerging), demand is uncertain and the market ill-defined. Information needed by management would be supplied by market research to establish a market and see whether demand is there and thus enable product development focused on meeting demand from perceived market niches.

For rising stars (growth), major investments to meet growth in demand are needed. Such investment will include investment in marketing, production and product refinement, and it might mean that the organisation needs to revise its relationship with suppliers to ensure its supplies for the growing demand for this product or service. Information needed by managers at this stage would be the type of information that enabled them to make good decisions to support the growth. Systems that tied your suppliers to you would also be appropriate at this stage.

During the cash cow stage (maturity), competition increases and the organisation must fight to retain market share. This means managers need information that enables them to increase their productivity and produce goods more efficiently, they need to better manage supply and distribution channels, they need to build up customer loyalty and to build customer switching costs, and they might need to adopt a defensive strategy with respect to their competitors.

Dogs (decline) will survive only while an organisation can produce them and serve a market cost effectively. Therefore managers need accurate information about the profitability of the products or services concerned and about the profitability of their customers. They need information to assist in cost control, and they need accurate demand forecasts. These things together enable decisions to be made about when a product or service should be terminated.

In terms of formulating strategies for e-business, using the product lifecycle and the product portfolio can help managers to think creatively about whether they have the information they need to manage their wildcats, their rising stars, their cash cows and their dogs. For each quadrant, the tool is used to identify information needs and to consider how quickly that information must be received and how accurate it must be. It is also important to assess the current provision of information and to identify gaps in what is needed and what is provided.

PEST analysis

PEST (political/legal, environmental, sociocultural, technological) analysis, as the name implies, involves considering a number of key environmental influences on the organisation (Johnson & Scholes 1999). Consideration is given not just to the current situation but also to how these influences might change (weaken or strengthen) in future. Specifically in terms of planning for e-business, it is essential to consider whether, and indeed how, technological change and innovations are driving changes in these other arenas. In contemporary business environments, this would clearly imply a need to consider the effects of the Internet and the e-commerce 'evolution' and whether they are driving change elsewhere.

The political/legal dimension involves a consideration of such factors as government legislation with respect to business and trade, taxation, industrial relations and employment legislation, environmental protection requirements, privacy and telecommunications, all of which are political factors that could affect the way an organisation can compete. These factors should be taken into account as they influence not only the current environment but also the potential for change (such as a change of government and the effect that would have on the legislative process).

The economic factors revolve around the state of the economy and therefore include such things as the stage of the economic cycle, rates of unemployment and inflation, interest rates, the relative affluence of a society (i.e. levels of disposable income), world trends and so on.

Sociocultural factors refer to lifestyle changes that can affect organisations. Included here are such things as demographic characteristics, social mobility, attitudes to work and leisure, materialism and income distribution, consumer preferences and changing lifestyles.

Technological factors include the rate and amount of technological innovation, rates of infusion and diffusion with respect to technology, and government support for technology investments (Johnson & Scholes 1999).

PEST analysis is used in business planning to understand the business environment in which an organisation operates and to establish the key drivers of change and the likely effect of changes on an organisation. PEST analysis is a deliberate strategy for avoiding surprises in the business environment. In terms of formulating an e-business strategy, this tool is important for identifying likely environmental changes and from this to consider the role of IT in helping to mitigate the potential negative effects of those changes and to exploit other changes to the organisation's advantage. Change in the business environment might imply a need for investments in IT, and identifying such required investment would be a major output of this technique. Another important consideration here would be the influence of the Internet as a driver of change itself.

Competitive forces analysis

Understanding an organisation's competitive position is also another way of thinking about the information needed to manage effectively and the types of systems needed to deliver that required information and to help mitigate competitive forces in the business environment. Competitive forces analysis assumes that, at any given time, an organisation is subject to a number of different forces from its environment, springing from existing competition and rivalry in the industry, the power that suppliers and buyers are able to exert over the organisation, the threat of customers changing to another product or service and the likelihood that new players will enter the industry (Porter 1980) (see figure 3.9).

The aim in formulating strategies for IT should be to invest in systems and technology that will help protect and improve the competitive position within a particular marketplace. Each of the forces is examined in the light of IT ameliorating or improving the effect of the force on the organisation. It is assumed that in considering each of these forces, modern organisations must necessarily consider the influence of the Internet in changing (positively or negatively) the effect of these forces within an industry.

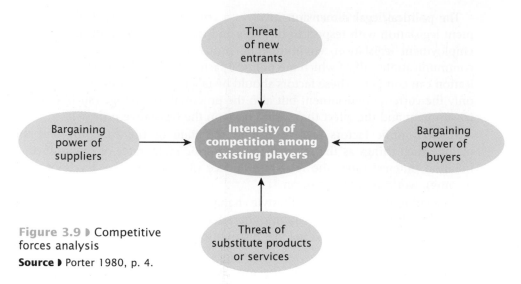

Figure 3.9 ▶ Competitive forces analysis
Source ▶ Porter 1980, p. 4.

Think about each of the five forces depicted in figure 3.9. What affects the strength (or weakness) of each of these forces? How might you use IS/IT to counteract some of these forces? Apply this analysis to the Carnivale case mentioned earlier.

▶ Threat of new entrants

New entrants to an industry can mean additional capacity, reduced prices and a new basis for competition. IS/IT and the Internet can be deployed to make it more difficult for new entrants and thus reduce the likelihood of new entrants in the following ways:

- reduce costs through greater efficiencies in production, for example
- increase rate of production and/or service innovation and development
- obtain better control of distribution and supply channels (and thus make it much more difficult for new entrants)
- help achieve a better match between products or services and customer needs and wants, through careful analysis of customer and sales trend data.

Each of the above points can make it much more difficult for a new entrant to be competitive.

▶ Bargaining power of suppliers

Supplier power over an organisation will be high when there are few suppliers, when the brand of the supplier is powerful, when there is the possibility of the supplier integrating forwards (i.e. buying out the organisation that buys from it) and when the supplier is in the privileged position of not caring too much about its customers. When supplier power is high, prices and costs tend to be higher, the quality of supply might well be lower, and there will tend to be a reduced availability of supply. IT and the Internet can help to reduce supplier power in the following ways:

- extending quality control into suppliers
- developing supplier sourcing systems
- enabling forward planning with suppliers through the use of interorganisational systems that link inventory and production systems with those of the suppliers.

▶ Bargaining power of buyers

The bargaining power of buyers will tend to be high when there are relatively few buyers or when there are alternative sources of supply. If this occurs, then prices tend to be forced down, higher quality can be demanded by the buyers, service requirements can be higher, and there can be more competition in the industry. Should this be the case, the IS/IT and the Internet can assist an organisation in the following ways:

- differentiating products or services
- helping to improve the price:performance ratio
- increasing the switching costs of buyers
- facilitating the buyer product selection process.

▶ Threat of substitution

Threat of substitution takes on a number of forms. Customers can substitute one product for another, or they can chose to do without something. Remember too that a new process of production, for example, might actually render a particular product or service superfluous, thus representing a form of substitution. When the threat of substitution is high, typically the potential market and profits are limited. This means there tends to be a ceiling on the price that can be charged without causing customers to substitute something for that product or service. E-business can help to reduce these effects by helping to:

- improve the price:performance ratio
- enhance products or services and thus increase their value
- improve an organisation's rate of innovation
- identify new customer needs and wants.

▶ Rivalry within industry

When competitive rivalry is high, there tends to be intense competition on price, there is competition with respect to product or service innovation and development, distribution and service become critical factors in customer choice, and there is a need for an organisation to build up customer loyalty. E-business can help an organisation if industry competition is high in the following ways:

- helping to improve the price:performance ratio
- differentiating products or services
- improving the rate of innovation
- helping an organisation to better understand the needs and wants of its customers.

    Using competitive forces analysis to think creatively about an organisation and its place in the competitive forces existing within an industry can help to identify areas of possible investment for IT and thus help managers to prioritise spending on IT so that it directly supports business initiatives. Competitive force analysis allows managers to identify and analyse significant players within each force and, from that, to determine the nature and strength of the influence that each player can exert on the organisation. Understanding this enables strategies to be devised to exploit, defend or neutralise such influence, and this entails that there will be opportunities for IT to support and manage these strategies.

Internal and external value chain analysis

❱ Internal value chain

The concept of the internal value chain is another important tool for considering the role of IT and e-commerce technologies in an organisation and in identifying opportunities for IT investments. Value chain analysis enables a consideration of the internal activities of the organisation and thus an understanding of where in the organisation value is being added to the product or service (see figure 3.10). The value chain breaks an organisation's activities into primary (or core) activities and support activities. Figure 3.10 details the types of activities that are classified as primary and support. The difference between overall costs and the selling price represents the margin or profit for an organisation.

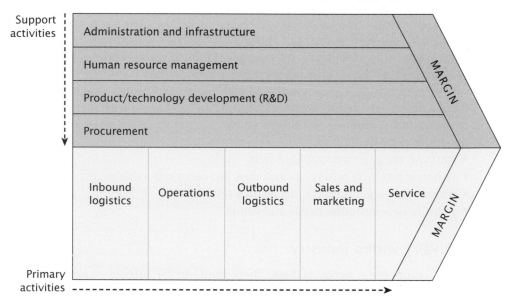

Figure 3.10 ❱ Internal value chain

Source ❱ Porter 1985, p. 37.

Typically in the past a lot of IT investment was in support activities, such as payroll, financial systems and so on. These are of course important. But a lot of current thinking says that IT and e-commerce investments will only ever be really useful to the organisation and deliver substantial returns on investment if investments go beyond support activities. For strategic applications of IT, one needs to look at investing directly in the primary value chain or, in other words, in the core business of the organisation. The value chain provides a simple and graphic illustration of where the priorities for IT investment have been in the past and makes it easier for managers to think creatively about investing more directly in core business.

Figure 3.11 provides an idea of how the value chain can be used. IT might well have been used already to achieve efficiencies in support activities. But there might be plenty of opportunity to improve information flows through the core activities or to improve efficiency within each core activity. With the advent of the Internet, opportunities could arise to seek efficiency and effectiveness gains through linking the organisation backwards to its network of suppliers and forwards to its network of customers. (See the discussion of the external value chain below.) Furthermore, the Internet and e-commerce might have changed the importance of the respective primary activities relative to one another. For example, a traditional bookshop does not have to be concerned with outbound logistics as customers typically carry their purchases out of the store with them. Yet for online bookshops, developing an efficient and effective logistics capability could be essential to their success.

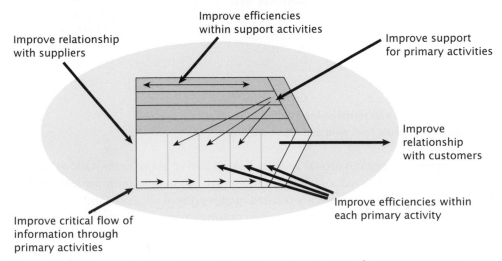

Figure 3.11 ▶ Internal value chain — identifying opportunities for IT investment

Think of your organisation. Divide the various functions and activities into core and support. Use the value chain to analyse the use of IT in the past. Use the value chain to identify areas, particularly to do with the primary activities, where your organisation could benefit greatly from further investments. What might the effect of these new investments be? In particular consider the role of the Internet in changing the use of technology for both core and support activities. Does the Internet change the relative importance of any of these activities?

▶ External value chain

External value chain analysis extends the internal value chain analysis to consider an organisation's entire supply chain. Hence the issue to be considered now is how IT and e-commerce might be deployed to improve the relationships and seek efficiencies with suppliers, with various distribution channels and with customers. These might have the effect of building in switching costs for suppliers' customers. Remember also that the competitive forces analysis might have indicated that investments that tied an organisation to its customers and/or suppliers might have been an appropriate strategy to adopt.

External value chain analysis might reveal several types of IT investment that reach beyond the traditional boundaries of the organisation and which might be worthwhile for an organisation to consider (discussed in more detail in chapters 6 and 7). For

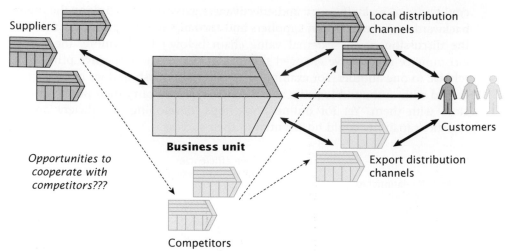

Suppliers

Business unit

Opportunities to
cooperate with
competitors???

Competitors

Local distribution
channels

Customers

Export distribution
channels

Figure 3.12 ▶ External value chain analysis
Source ▶ adapted from Ward and Peppard 2002, p. 247.

example, interorganisational systems linking two or more organisations can help both buyer and seller to reduce administrative costs, can help to optimise inventory levels for both, can be used to implement shared quality control measures and can help to support joint new product development and to optimise payments between the two parties.

The internal and external value chains are simple devices that managers can use to clarify their thinking about the use of IT and e-commerce in their organisation and to gain better insights into how IT can be used to gain a strategic advantage. While using these analytical tools, it is imperative to bear in mind the company's mission and objectives and to refer back to them regularly. This will help to ensure that business objectives are always in the forefront when making decisions about potential investments in IT and e-commerce.

Critical success factor analysis

Critical success factors (CSFs) are an important device for ensuring that managers receive the information they need to ensure the achievement of corporate goals and objectives. CSFs are those areas that must go well in order for an organisation to achieve its objectives. Typically, CSFs can be identified for each business objective. These CSFs can then be consolidated across all the business objectives. In order for managers to monitor these CSFs and thus achieve their business objectives, they will need information that they might or might not currently receive. Thus, CSFs are a useful way of determining the information needs of managers in key result areas for the business. Meeting these information needs might mean that new systems need to be built or purchased or that existing systems need to be enhanced in order to provide these information needs (see figure 3.13).

Many managers are quite surprised to find that they do not have the information they need to monitor CSFs. This means that they might not have been well informed about the progress an organisation was making in achieving its business objectives.

The idea of CSFs can also be used in conjunction with the external value chain to see whether creative and innovative use of IT can help to tie suppliers and customers to the organisation.

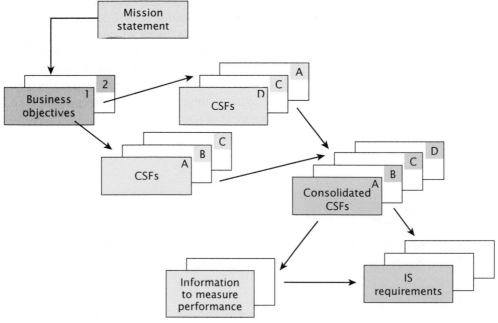

Figure 3.13 ▶ Critical success factor analysis

Source ▶ Edwards, Ward and Bytheway *The Essence of Information Systems*, 2nd edn. Pearson Education Limited. © Prentice Hall International (UK) Ltd, 1991, 1995, p. 79.

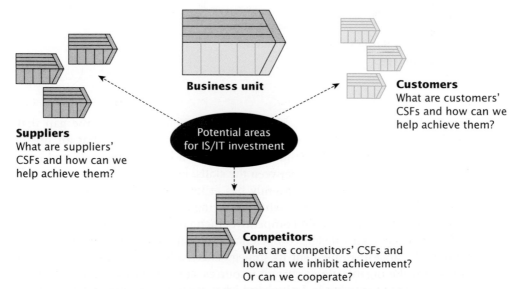

Figure 3.14 ▶ Combining CSF analysis and external value chain analysis

Source ▶ Edwards, Ward and Bytheway *The Essence of Information Systems*, 2nd edn. Pearson Education Limited. © Prentice Hall International (UK) Ltd, 1991, 1995, p. 81.

The business technology audit

A simple but effective tool for supporting discussions at this point is the business technology audit (see figure 3.15). This enables managers to provide an assessment of the business value of particular systems while also allowing the IT staff to assess the technical health of such systems. The business value is a judgement about the contribution a particular system makes to the achievement of business goals and objectives and how well it is perceived to be meeting the needs of its user groups. The technical quality is an assessment based on the age of the system, the amount spent on maintenance each year, the ease of maintaining and enhancing the system, the infrastructure required to run the system, the available documentation, the risk of failure (and hence the risk to the business of such failure) and such like (Ward 1990). These assessments can then be plotted on the matrix shown in figure 3.15.

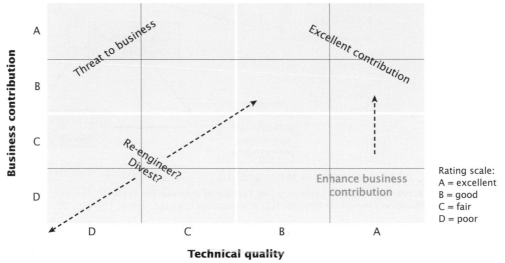

Figure 3.15 ▶ Business technology audit
Source ▶ Ward 1990.

Gap analysis

Gap analysis is based on first identifying and then remedying the gap that exists between the skills, knowledge, competencies and capabilities that an organisation requires to adopt strategies so that it can do what it both wants to do and feels that it must do to be successful, and between the skills, knowledge, competencies and capabilities that the organisation currently has at its disposal. Thus, as it becomes clear what the organisation's vision is, what it is trying to accomplish and how it is going to achieve objectives and remain competitive, then consideration also needs to be given to what resources, knowledge, competencies and capabilities the organisation requires if it is to be able to implement its strategy effectively. This in turn needs to be compared with the organisation's current resources, competencies and capabilities, and if a gap exists between what is desired and what exists, to consider whether all strategies can be implemented without building the required resources. Figure 3.16 is an attempt to illustrate the concept of gap analysis.

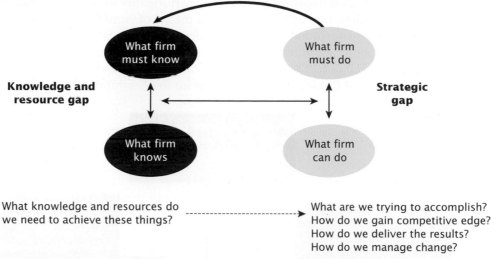

What knowledge and resources do   What are we trying to accomplish?
we need to achieve these things? - - - - - - - - - →   How do we gain competitive edge?
                                          How do we deliver the results?
                                          How do we manage change?

Figure 3.16 ▶ Gap analysis for skills, knowledge and capabilities
Source ▶ adapted from Zack 1999 and Bellinger 2002, p. 5.

This tool has clear implications for the formulation of strategy for e-business. IT becomes a vital component in the implementation of strategy but also serves as a means of internally storing and distributing knowledge and intellectual assets and capabilities throughout the organisation.

Combining the tools

The tools and techniques that might be helpful in supporting the e-business strategy formulation process have thus far been presented in a linear fashion, perhaps implying that there are few interdependencies between the tools. This is not the case. Rather, it is intended that managers appreciate that the tools offer different 'views' of the organisation and its information, IS and IT requirements. A key aspect of the planning activity, then, is to look at all tools and techniques employed to understand the overall picture of requirements that emerges. The essence of the tools presented in this chapter is captured in figure 3.17.

The product or service portfolio is excellent for helping managers to recognise that the information required to manage the product portfolio is different at each of the stages in the lifecycle and thus identify gaps in their IT requirements. PEST and competitive forces, in contrast, focus externally to the organisation and help managers to identify the environmental factors and competitive forces buffeting their organisation. In terms of IT, they help managers to recognise that IT can be deployed to help mitigate or exploit those forces. The value chain supports examination of the internal strengths and weaknesses of an organisation, identifying where and how IT is being used effectively and enabling managers to identify key areas where IT could be employed to increase efficiencies, improve effectiveness and/or increase the flexibility and responsiveness of the organisation. Critical success factors help to identify key areas that affect the ability of the organisation to achieve its goals and objectives. Typically the achievement of CSFs is measured by KPIs (key performance indicators), which require accurate information. Gap analysis provides a means of considering whether internal resources are adequate for future growth and development, and hence provides a basis for making decisions about required resources and capabilities. SWOT likewise looks primarily at internal factors and considers internal strengths and weaknesses while also considering external threats and opportunities for the organisation.

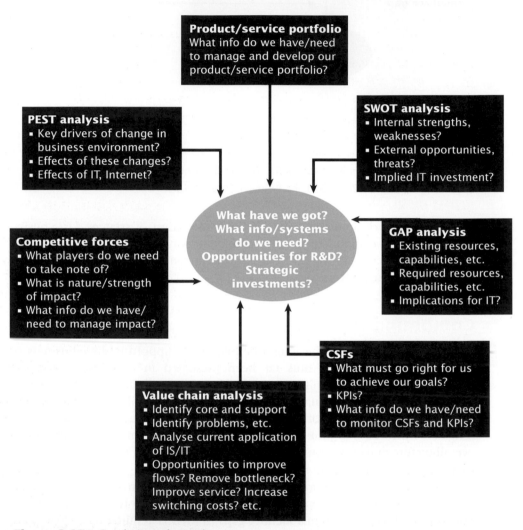

Figure 3.17 ▶ Combining the tools

Using the tools in combination this way provides a much more holistic and coherent view of the opportunities for the organisation to exploit IT effectively and to identify R&D opportunities for potential future strategic investments in IT.

There is no suggestion that these are the only tools and techniques suitable for use. There are many others that could be and are used to support the e-business planning process. These tools are simply ones that support a range of views and thinking about the technology needs of an organisation.

Portfolio of systems

At the end of the planning and strategy formulation process, the organisation should be clear on its business goals and objectives, on its e-business goals and objectives and, in particular, on how IT is being deployed directly to support the achievement of business goals and objectives. It should also be clear on the state of its existing portfolio of IT and, in particular, on where its strengths and weaknesses lie. This suggests that it should be apparent which systems might need upgrade or enhancement and which need to be critically reviewed with a view to major refurbishment, replacement or divestment. It also suggests that there is established a prioritised 'list' or 'set' of required IT investments that might need more detailed analysis and investigation before investment.

Use of the notion of a portfolio of applications and mapping existing IS (and the need for changes to those systems) and required and desired future investments using an application portfolio could help to clarify the managers' thinking about IT requirements. The use of application portfolio analysis could also ensure that an appropriate balance of new investments and maintenance of existing investments has been achieved. An example of one means of categorising the application portfolio is given in figure 3.18.

From figure 3.18 it can be seen that one way of categorising systems is in terms of their role in the organisation. Thus, systems can be deemed to be: strategic, if they fundamentally affect the way the business competes and directly support the achievement of key strategic objectives; key operational, if they are essential to the efficient running of the operations of an organisation; support, if they are primarily directed at support activities in the organisation

STRATEGIC	HIGH POTENTIAL
Applications that are **critical** to achieving future business strategy	Applications that might be **important** in achieving future business success
KEY OPERATIONAL	**SUPPORT**
Applications on which the organisation **currently depends** for success	Applications that are **valuable** but not critical to business success

Figure 3.18 ▶ Application portfolio analysis
Source ▶ Ward and Peppard 2002, p. 42.

such as email, payroll and basic accounting systems; or high potential, if they are experimental, representing possibilities that an organisation is testing before deciding whether they could take on a strategic role in future. The key to using application portfolio analysis is not to say that strategic systems are good, for example, and therefore the more investment in that quadrant the better. Rather, the key is to ensure that the balance of the portfolio reflects the strategic objectives of the organisation. Figure 3.19 (p. 84) attempts to illustrate this point.

An organisation adopting a prospector stance typically sees IT as vital to taking advantage of opportunities and thus contributing to its competitive advantage. Therefore it would be expected that the prospector portfolio has heavy emphasis on strategic investments, that there is a commitment to some R&D investments (high potential), with sound key operational and support systems required to build in flexibility and responsiveness throughout the organisation. By contrast, the defender adopts IT primarily as

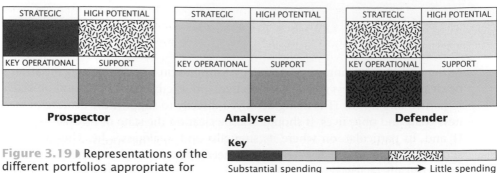

Figure 3.19 ▶ Representations of the different portfolios appropriate for different strategies

Key

Substantial spending ────────▶ Little spending

a driver of efficiency, and thus it would be expected to see major emphases on key operational and support systems and some strategic systems, such as supply chain management, which could increase efficiencies throughout the entire supply chain, resulting in competitiveness based on an efficient supply chain, for example. The analyser adopts somewhat of a mid-position, which places importance on efficiency but also uses some strategic initiatives to explore and take advantage of other possibilities.

Look at the application portfolios in figure 3.20. These represent the same organisation, one snapshot in 1994 (pre-Internet hype) and one in 2000 (during the Internet hype). What can you infer from these portfolios? How might a knowledge of their intended strategies in 1994 and 2000 affect your inferences? What advice would you give to management?

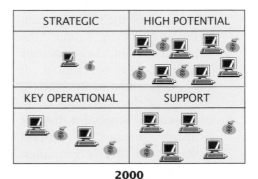

Figure 3.20 ▶ Application portfolios in 1994 and 2000

Summary

Before formulation of e-business strategy can begin, it is essential to understand an organisation's business strategy. It is helpful also to review the firm's broad strategic context. A high-level appreciation of the vision for the future organisation as well as its major goals needs to be gained. A high-level review of the internal and external business environments and the internal and external IS, IT and e-commerce environments is also required, together with an idea of major new IT opportunities.

It is helpful to use the understanding of the organisation's strategic context to articulate some business and IT maxims that succinctly and vividly express the firm's strategic intent in terms of both business and the supporting information systems and information technology. The maxims are used to guide some key decisions on some fundamental IT parameters: namely the role of IT in the organisation, the sourcing of IT, the structure of the information systems organisation and the view of the IT infrastructure.

Once these high-level decisions have been made, the existing portfolio of information systems is reviewed and assessed along with the appropriateness of the supporting information technology infrastructure. This review is followed by detailed IT and e-commerce planning for new systems, system enhancements and divestments, and new information technology investments. Included in this detailed planning is a review of the capabilities and resources of the firm's IS organisation together with a review of existing IT policies and procedures.

There are a number of tools and techniques that are helpful both in high-level and in more detailed IT planning and strategy formulation. These include SWOT analysis, product and service lifecycle analysis (including the product portfolio analysis), PEST analysis, competitive forces analysis, internal and external value chain analysis, critical success factor analysis, the business technology audit and gap analysis. These tools and techniques can be combined and utilised where appropriate, depending on the type of strategic analysis required, the context of the analysis, and the skills and predilections of those doing the analysis.

key terms

applications systems portfolio

business strategy

IS strategy

IT strategy

mission

resource-based view

strategic alignment

strategic positioning view

vision

discussion questions

1. In the late 1990s many organisations formed e-business or e-commerce teams to take charge of e-business strategy or e-commerce strategy. These teams examined e-commerce opportunities provided by the advent of the Internet, and they also considered through the opportunities offered in forming electronic linkages with suppliers and customers, thus achieving supply chain efficiency and effectiveness. The teams were also responsible, in many cases, for implementing their ideas.

   At the same time more traditional (non-Internet) IT planning continued. Thus there were two areas in the organisation looking after the planning of information, information systems and information technology, arguably of course with different emphases. Discuss the issues, benefits and problems involved in such an approach to e-business strategy.

2. The CEO of a large organisation reflecting on the relationship between business strategy, IS strategy and IT strategy argues that all IS strategy should be formulated within business strategy formulation sessions, leaving only some technical details for the IT planners. The CIO differs, saying that the focus and intensity of the IS strategy sessions will be lost if this activity becomes part of a general business strategy formulation. He also argues that the presence of various technical specialists in such areas as database and telecommunications will be lost, and this will mean that plans lack informed technical input.

    Discuss these two opposing views, giving the benefits as well as the challenges and problems inherent in each.

3. The CIO of a medium-sized business argues that there is no need for IS/IT strategy formulation in her organisation. She argues that the organisation is implementing an enterprise resource planning (ERP) package with modules and systems in every function of the organisation. 'This package has a rich functionality that embodies best business practice for our industry. The package has software systems that efficiently support all of our core business processes and then some. All we need to do is implement this state-of-the-art package. We do not need an information systems strategy — it all comes down to ERP package implementation!'

    Critically discuss the CIO's viewpoint on IT strategy formulation. Is e-business strategy formulation satisfactorily accomplished through purchasing and implementing large software packages?

4. Discuss the relationship between:
    (a) determining an appropriate business model for an organisation
    (b) formulating a business and IT strategy for an organisation.
    In your answer outline the differences between the inputs, processes and outputs of business model formulation and business and IT strategy formulation.

5. Discuss the differences between:
    (a) the industry structure or strategic positioning view of strategy
    (b) the resource-based view of strategy
    as they apply to IT strategy formulation.
    Why is it important to have resource-based emphasis for IT strategy formulation along with the strategic positioning view? (You might need to do some additional reading to answer this question thoroughly.)

suggested reading

Armstrong, CP & Sambamurthy, V 1999, 'Information technology assimilation in firms: the influence of senior leadership and IT infrastructures', *Information Systems Research*, vol. 10, no. 4, December, pp. 304–27.

Broadbent, M & Weill, P 1997, 'Management by maxim: how business and IT managers can create IT infrastructures', *Sloan Management Review*, Spring, pp. 77–92.

Collis, DJ & Montgomery, CA 1995, 'Competing on resources: strategy in the 1990s', *Harvard Business Review*, July–August, pp. 118–28.

Hirschheim, R & Sabherwal, R 2001, 'Detours in the path toward strategic information systems alignment', *California Management Review*, vol. 44, no. 1, Fall, pp. 87–108.

Mata, FJ, Fuerst, WL & Barney, J 1995, 'Information technology and sustained competitive advantage: a resource-based analysis', *MIS Quarterly*, December, pp. 487–505.

Peppard, J, Lambert, R & Edwards, C 2000, 'Whose job is it anyway? Organisational information competencies for value creation', *Information Systems Journal*, vol. 10, pp. 291–322.

Porter, ME 2001, 'Strategy and the Internet', *Harvard Business Review*, March, pp. 63–78.

Ward, J & Griffiths, P 1996, *Strategic Planning for Information Systems*, 2nd edn, John Wiley & Sons, Chichester.

references

Armstrong, CP & Sambamurthy, V 1999, 'Information technology assimilation in firms: the influence of senior leadership and IT infrastructures', *Information Systems Research*, vol. 10, no. 4, December, pp. 304–27.

Bellinger, G 2002, 'Knowledge management — emerging perspectives', http://www.outsights.com/systems/kmgmt/kmgmt.htm, accessed 13 September 2002.

Bharadwaj, AS 2000, 'A resource-based perspective on information technology capability and firm performance: an empirical investigation', *MIS Quarterly*, vol. 24, no. 1, March, pp. 169–96.

Broadbent, M & Weill, P 1997, 'Management by maxim: how business and IT managers can create IT infrastructures', *Sloan Management Review*, Spring, pp. 77–92.

Collis, DJ & Montgomery, CA 1995, 'Competing on resources: strategy in the 1990s', *Harvard Business Review*, July–August, pp. 118–28.

De Kluyver, CA 2000, *Strategic Thinking: An Executive Perspective*, Prentice Hall, London.

Edwards, C, Ward, J & Bytheway, A 1995, *The Essence of Information Systems*, 2nd edn, Prentice Hall, London.

Feeny, D 2001, 'Making business sense of the new opportunity', *Sloan Management Review*, Winter, pp. 41–51.

Hamel, G & Prahalad, CK 1994, *Competing for the Future*, Harvard Business School Press, Boston.

Hirschheim, R & Sabherwal, R 2001, 'Detours in the path toward strategic information systems alignment', *California Management Review*, vol. 44, no. 1, Fall, pp. 87–108.

Hubbard, G 2000, *Strategic Management: Thinking, Analysis and Action*, Prentice Hall, London.

Johnson, G & Scholes, K 1999, *Exploring Corporate Strategy: Text and Cases*, 5th edn, Prentice Hall, London.

Masifern, E & Vila, J 1998, 'Interconnected mindsets: strategic thinking and the strategy concept', in MA Hitt, JE Ricart i Costa & RD Nixon (eds), *New Managerial Mindsets: Organizational Transformation and Strategy Implementation*, John Wiley & Sons, Chichester.

Mata, FJ, Fuerst, WL & Barney, J 1995, 'Information technology and sustained competitive advantage: a resource-based analysis', *MIS Quarterly*, December, pp 487–505.

Nixon, RD, Hitt, MA, Ricart i Costa, JE 1998, 'New managerial mindsets and strategic change in the new frontier', in MA Hitt, JE Ricart i Costa & RD Nixon (eds), *New Managerial Mindsets: Organizational Transformation and Strategy Implementation*, John Wiley & Sons, Chichester.

Peppard, J, Lambert, R & Edwards, C 2000, 'Whose job is it anyway? Organisational information competencies for value creation', *Information Systems Journal*, vol. 10, pp. 291–322.

Porter, ME 1980, *Competitive Strategy: Techniques for Analyzing Industries and Competitors*, Free Press, New York.

—1985, *Competitive Advantage: Creating and Sustaining Superior Performance*, Free Press, New York.

—2001, 'Strategy and the Internet', *Harvard Business Review*, March, pp. 63–78.

Quinn, JB 1996, 'Strategies for change', in H Mintzberg & JB Quinn (eds), *The Strategy Process: Concepts, Contexts and Cases*, 3rd edn, Prentice Hall, Upper Saddle River, NJ.

Turban, E, King, D, Lee, J, Warkentin, M & Chung, HM 2002, *Electronic Commerce: A Managerial Perspective*, Prentice Hall, Upper Saddle River, NJ.

Ward, BK 1990, 'Planning for profit', in T Lincoln (ed.), *Managing Information Systems for Profit*, John Wiley & Sons, Chichester.

Ward, J & Griffiths, P 1996, *Strategic Planning for Information Systems*, 2nd edn, John Wiley & Sons, Chichester.

Ward, J & Peppard, J 2002, *Strategic Planning for Information Systems*, 3rd edn, John Wiley & Sons, Chichester.

case study

SouthWest Furniture

SouthWest Furniture manufactures chairs, tables and benches from pine and from eucalypt hardwoods, such as jarrah, karri and marri. The company was founded in 1921, and it had a long period of largely slow but steady growth until the late 1990s.

In 1998 its revenues stood at approximately $80 million per year, on which it earned profits of $7 million. It had 125 employees, of whom twenty-eight worked in its office, five worked in sales and the rest worked in the factory. Many old-time employees felt that the office and administrative section of the company was growing too fast and was impeding company earnings.

The product line comprised tables, chairs and benches for garden and outdoor settings. All of the company's products were coated with approved finishes for the outdoors. The product range also included a number of accessories for the garden and outdoors, including planter boxes and large umbrellas.

Since 1980, SouthWest Furniture has sold its products packed in cardboard containers ready for the customer to assemble. Assembly was advertised as easy and quick, and much care and attention was given to making sure this promise to customers was fulfilled.

SouthWest Furniture promised to provide the customer with pleasant, well-designed and long-lasting outdoor furniture at a price that would not 'empty your wallet'. The company strove to keep manufacturing and administrative costs to a minimum while not compromising its manufacturing quality or its design quality.

The company had a good relationship with several timber supply companies in the south-west of Western Australia. These well-managed relationships meant that SouthWest Furniture had access to reliable and regular supplies of quality Western Australian hardwood at reasonable prices.

The company factory was bright and modernised. The production equipment was generally the latest and best. This was the result of a recent modernisation campaign in which SouthWest Furniture had invested in new machinery and a new factory layout to enable it to reduce production costs markedly through automation. Although its production machinery was thus state of the art, the same could not be said for the company's information systems.

Generally, the company could be said to lack a coherent vision for IS/IT. It had a set of fragmentary systems that were technically troublesome and did not give a good coverage of the company's core business processes. Systems had generally been pushed by local departmental champions who often teamed up with one of the IT department to promote a particular system. The development and delivery of information systems had historically been a lengthy and costly process, and the promised business benefits of the systems had often not materialised. The company's mid-range computer supported a network of dumb terminals that dated from the 1980s. The reliability of this network was not up to contemporary IT standards. The IT department, which consisted of a manager and two other people, seemed to spend a lot of their time tending to technical issues and firefighting technical problems.

The manufacturing manager was quite proud of the jobcode production scheduling system that had been developed by the joint efforts of himself and a local university professor. It was quite an ingenious, if technically unreliable system that scheduled production while taking account of each work centre's production capacity constraints. It also scheduled the required materials along with the specific production operations. It thus gave the production personnel a good idea of whether, given machine or work centre capacity constraints and material availability constraints, the work orders could be manufactured on time to meet sales or customer order requirements. Hence, the basic logic of the production and materials scheduling system was very well suited to the needs of SouthWest.

Unfortunately customer orders had to be manually broken down into a number of works orders and these individually tracked to find out whether customer due dates could be met. Also any bill of materials processing necessary to determine the required subassemblies and raw materials and their quantities inherent in customer orders either had to be done manually or obtained through the use of another system that was not integrated with the jobcode system. The local university professor, working from some specifications given to him by the manufacturing manager, was working on the system to program some upgrades to cater for these matters. The professor had assigned a PhD student to help him part-time with his task.

Some time ago, a local software sales representative had sold the estimating department a bill of materials costing program. After some enhancements by the local IT section, this program could take a customer order, break it down into subassemblies and raw materials, and then cost the order on the basis of budgeted manufacturing costs provided by the accountants. However, not only were there technical and reliability problems with this package but also it had become the focus of political problems between sales, accounting and manufacturing personnel. The people in manufacturing claimed that the package was 'worse than useless' since they regarded its costings as unrealistic and unrelated to the capacity constraints of the factory and the current work loadings of the production schedule. The production manager complained, 'If we have a light workload or production schedule I can easily make those costs, but if I have a full workload plus overtime — as I often do lately — then there's no way!'

Other systems in the company consisted of a simple inventory control system, a sales statistics system and several accounting and financial reporting systems. All of the systems apart from the accounting system had been developed by the IT department. Unfortunately, the inventory control system was not integrated with the production scheduling system so that the appropriate raw materials and work in process had to be checked to see whether there was sufficient inventory in stock to proceed with the production schedule. The sales statistics system presented sales statistics broken down by product, region and sales rep. However, when it was being written, the IT department had promised that sales order processing would be included in the system to help the sales and manufacturing departments track manufacturing performance against customer orders. Sales forecasting had also been promised as part of the sales statistics system to help the manufacturing department gauge the size of its winter make-to-stock activities. Both of these aspects of the sales statistics system had been cut by the general manager when the sales statistics system's development had been 50 per cent over budget.

The financial reporting and accounting systems were generally thought to be helpful and relevant systems for the accounting clerks, but they were not linked to the production scheduling, inventory control or sales statistics systems despite the fact that these systems contained much of the basic data needed. Hence much of the sales and production data had to be rekeyed into the accounting and financial systems, which caused errors and inaccuracies as well as consuming considerable clerical labour.

In keeping with the previous history of SouthWest Furniture responding to 'local champions' where IS/IT was concerned, the current situation had three new 'champions': the purchasing manager, the accounting manager and a sales manager, who were all lobbying for rather expensive new information systems. All the new systems ideas, as usual, had some merits.

The purchasing manager wished to have some interorganisational systems developed that would enable communications with the several timber supply companies that were suppliers to SouthWest Furniture. He wished these systems to have capabilities for electronic EDI-based purchasing. Order data and data on the supply of goods would flow automatically into the appropriate in-house systems, such as inventory control in the accounting systems.

The sales manager had been reading about the revolution in business brought about by the Internet and e-commerce. Two competitors, Furniture Yard and Patio Life, had established websites that offered company and product information as well as the capability for customers to order and pay for goods online. Reacting to this initiative by the competition, the sales manager had been talking with e-Connect, an e-commerce consulting group based in Western Australia who were preparing a report for him on the implications of e-commerce for SouthWest Furniture. He had in mind the development of an attractive, easy-to-use website with full e-commerce transactional capabilities, and he had encouraged the consultants to 'see the potential in this innovative application — a natural development and part of the e-commerce revolution in business!'

Even more worrying than the issue of business-to-consumer e-commerce for the sales manager, however, was the fact that SouthWest Furniture's biggest business customers — Target, Kmart and Outdoor Megastore — were all pressing SouthWest Furniture to develop Internet-based EDI links so as to deliver a vendor-managed inventory (VMI) service to them. Under VMI, suppliers of these companies would be given access to the retailer's inventory and sales data and would then manage the inventories for them. SouthWest Furniture would thus be responsible not only for ensuring that minimum but adequate stocks were on the shelves in Target, Kmart and Outdoor but also be responsible for spotting trends in sales and responding appropriately with respect to stock levels, product mix and new product designs. Hence the development of a VMI capability was also being enthusiastically pushed by the sales manager.

The accounting manager had for some time been frustrated by the rekeying of data between the manufacturing systems and the accounting systems. He was very keen for SouthWest Furniture to develop an integrated suite of systems. He had been impressed by the reports of ERP systems that promised a totally integrated package solution to a business's information system needs. He had been talking to EpiSystems, a supplier of ERP systems to medium-sized companies. According to EpiSystems' sales representative, EpiSystems would provide a total IT solution for SouthWest Furniture's information needs, and all systems would be totally integrated. Furthermore, all the systems were professionally developed to run efficiently and reliably, and EpiSystems' IT staff would maintain the systems. However, the manufacturing manager argued that EpiSystems' manufacturing module lacked a suitable production scheduling package — particularly one that dealt adequately with production capacity constraints. He felt that SouthWest's manufacturing department would be better sticking to the system development plans of the local university professor. He also felt that SouthWest Furniture, and in particular the manufacturing department, would become very dependent on EpiSystems — too dependent in his view — for all their system needs, including upgrades, new reporting needs and so on.

The general manager had for some time been concerned about coherence and the benefits of SouthWest Furniture's investments in IT. These concerns had been intensified by the last three proposals by the purchasing, sales and accounting managers. The general manager's view of IT was that it should help the company achieve its mission of being a moderate quality low-cost producer of furniture. He felt that, properly applied, IT would enable SouthWest Furniture to drive costs down even further, without sacrificing its reputation for quality manufactured goods. A weekend session that focused on strategic IT planning was arranged by the general manager. Liz Bentleigh, a consultant with an excellent reputation for facilitating strategic IT plans, was engaged to help SouthWest's management team to review its business plan and formulate a strategic IT plan. The general manager thought that even if it was not possible to come up with a fully formulated and detailed IT plan in a weekend, at least his management team could formulate a strategic IT vision in that time. The details of the planning effort could then be finished in the next month or so.

Questions

1. Formulate some business maxims and some related IT maxims for SouthWest Furniture. Do you consider that the maxims you have developed would help to develop a business vision and an IT vision for the company? Would the maxims help to guide IT and e-business strategy formulation? Give your views on the usefulness of maxims for guiding and facilitating business and e-business strategy formulation.

2. Give your views on the key IT parameters for SouthWest Furniture (i.e. consider appropriate decisions regarding the role, sourcing arrangements, structure and infrastructure for IT at SouthWest). Is the profile you have decided on one of the profiles suggested by Hirschheim and Sabherwal?

3. Carry out a SWOT analysis for the business and the IT capability at SouthWest Furniture. What are the conclusions of your analysis for the business and for IT?
   Do you feel the SWOT analysis technique is sufficient for IT strategy formulation, or do you need to complement it with other techniques and approaches?

4. Carry out a competitive forces (or five forces) analysis for the business and for IT in SouthWest Furniture. What are the conclusions of your analysis for the business and for IT?
   What are the strengths and weaknesses of competitive forces analysis for e-business strategy formulation?

5. Carry out the internal and external value chain analysis for SouthWest Furniture. What are the conclusions of your analysis for e-business strategy formulation for the company?
   What are the strengths and weaknesses of internal and external value chain analysis for e-business strategy formulation?

6. Using the business and IT maxims formulated in question 1, together with the outputs from the various techniques used in questions 2 through 5, formulate a strategic vision and a strategic IT plan for SouthWest Furniture.

chapter 4

E-business strategy for small and medium-sized enterprises

learning objectives

After reading this chapter,[1] you should be able to:

- appreciate the contribution and importance of small and medium-sized enterprises (SMEs) to a healthy national economy
- appreciate the nature and distinguishing characteristics of SMEs, their use and adoption of IT, and the attitude of the owner-manager to IT innovation
- understand the risks if SMEs do not adopt e-business and some of the reasons why SMEs have been comparatively slow to adopt e-business
- understand some of the problems associated with a lack of planning of e-business requirements and initiatives in SMEs
- understand the need for SMEs to undertake careful planning and strategising before adopting e-business
- understand a framework presented to support visioning and thinking about e-business strategy for SMEs.

chapter overview

In the previous chapter, a range of tools and techniques suitable for IT planning and strategy formulation were considered. The extension of these tools and techniques to embrace e-business and e-business environments was discussed and a framework put forward to support the entire process of strategy formulation. However, these tools have all been developed to support the needs and requirements of larger enterprises, and although some could migrate to a small business environment, generally speaking, these tools are too heavy for use in small and micro businesses. Hence, additional tools and frameworks are required to support the process of e-business strategy formulation in SMEs.

This is particularly important given the key contribution that SMEs make to national, regional and local economies: they are critical to the overall health and prosperity of the nation. However, studies have suggested that SMEs in general have been relatively slow to adopt e-business and associated technologies and that many SME owner-managers have yet to be persuaded of the benefits of e-business adoption. Research suggests that many e-business ventures have not been successful and delivered the expected business benefits, and some common factors of poor planning and poor strategising seem to lie at the heart of the problem. Hence, a framework to support e-business strategy formulation for SMEs is developed and discussed in detail in this chapter. It attempts to present and embrace a holistic view of the issues that SME owner-managers must carefully think through if they are to embrace new technologies successfully and benefit from the e-business revolution.

Introduction

In previous chapters of this book, there has been discussion of the influence of e-business and, despite concerns about the hype associated with e-commerce and e-business, there can be little doubt that e-business and the Internet have had, and will continue to have, an enormous impact on the commercial, social and economic fabric of society. The past decade has seen exponential growth rates in most metrics of e-business (US Department of Commerce 1999; Andersen Consulting 1998; DOCITA 2000), and generally speaking, most forecasts predict that this growth will continue over the next few years (DOCITA 2000; Ernst & Young 2000a). Some sources suggest, however, that the rate of growth might slow somewhat (ABS 2003).

This rise in the importance of the Internet as a source of both information exchange and commerce leads us inexorably closer to a truly global community, and hence such notions as globalisation and a global economy increasingly manifest themselves in commercial and information exchanges. For business, e-business, the Internet and a trend towards a global economy offer the prospect of access to worldwide market-places and hence exciting opportunities for cost-effective expansion, operating free of time and location constraints ($24 \times 7 \times 365$), and potentially building and leveraging communities of interest (Rayport & Jaworski 2001).

Operating globally, however, poses challenges and threats in addition to these opportunities. For example, it exposes businesses to increased competition as foreign operators lure local consumers with a range of goods and services offered over the Internet. Thus organisations and those with whom they trade (customers and suppliers) cross physical, temporal and legal boundaries in a manner that has no precedent. In so doing, an organisation must manage a range of policy, regulatory and social issues, including consumer privacy, security, fair trading, taxation, intellectual property rights, conflicts of international law, the status and enforceability of electronic contracts, international liability, establishing trust and cross-cultural communication issues (Jarvenpaa & Tiller 1999; APEC 1999; Currie 2000; Bidgoli 2002). The 'new economy' might present opportunities to organisations, but to be successful businesses must rise to meet the challenges identified above.

For **small and medium-sized enterprises (SMEs)**, the Internet has much to offer as a business vehicle as it can serve as a relatively efficient and effective channel for information provision and exchange, collaboration, advertising and publicity, marketing, completing transactions, and in some cases facilitating or directly supporting the distribution of goods and services to global trading partners and customers (Mehrtens, Cragg & Mills 2001; Czerniawska & Potter 1998; Ernst & Young 2000b; OECD 1998; Baldwin, Lymer & Johnson 2001). However, SMEs do not always seem to appreciate that ignoring e-business because the current level of transactions is relatively low and few short-term benefits are being derived (Poon & Swatman 1999) puts them at risk of becoming uncompetitive in the medium and long term, and hence of failing in the future (Crawford 1998), perhaps succumbing to more aware and aggressive international operators. Combined with reports that SMEs owner-managers often lack the requisite technological knowledge and skills, are unsure of whether their businesses are suited to e-business, and are fearful of alienating vital intermediaries and so on (NOIE 2000; Baldwin, Lymer & Johnson 2001), this failure to achieve substantial benefits in the short term does not serve to motivate SME owner-managers. This is particularly so given current media interest in organisations, both large and small, that have failed in terms of their e-business initiatives (Bryant 2001; Hughes & Needham 2001), which only serves to undermine confidence in e-business initiatives.

The authors have conducted a deal of research into the adoption of e-business by SMEs and the barriers they experience in moving towards operating more electronically. This research suggests that success with e-business seems to depend on determining an appropriate blend of an e-business vision, strategy and technology, coupled with a knowledge of industry and marketplace pressures and trends, and concepts of value creation for customers, both traditional and online interactions and dealings. It is argued therefore that what is required to support the decision-making of SME owner-managers as they grapple with the challenges of a move into e-business is a more structured, holistic approach to planning the adoption and implementation of e-business in SMEs. Such an approach must be cognisant of and sensitive to a range of business changes and issues that must be addressed if e-business and the Internet are to be successfully embedded in the business activity of SMEs. This approach does not need to be as thorough or 'heavy' as strategy formulation needs to be for large enterprises. It can be less costly, less formal, less bureaucratic and much simpler, and can be completed quickly without consuming many resources. But it does need to be done. Despite the concerns that some owner-managers have about planning, there is evidence to suggest that an absence of planning with respect to e-business and the adoption of Internet technologies is deleterious to the business outcomes achieved (McKay & Marshall 2002).

Developing and managing e-business strategies is clearly vital to any successful e-business venture (Venkatraman 2000; Lientz & Rea 2000; Willcocks & Sauer 2000; Chen 2001). But underpinning and influencing the strategy are a range of issues, including developing an appropriate e-vision for the organisation, marketing in the new media and adequately managing customer relationships, acquiring and managing a range of resources and skills, redesigning existing business processes to accommodate new arrangements and activities, and acquiring and developing an appropriate IT infrastructure on which to build the e-business initiative. Emphasis and concern must also be placed on managing organisational knowledge resources and intellectual capital, and successful implementation will also require a carefully planned program of change management. The aim of the holistic framework articulated in this chapter is to work with SMEs to develop appropriate business models tailored to individual needs with respect to e-business rather than imposing 'one-size fits all' solutions on them.

Why focus on SMEs?

Many attempts have been made to define precisely what is meant by an SME, and most national governments have developed their own standards, based on industry type, number of employees, ownership and annual turnover, for example. For the purposes of this chapter, a more general definition of an SME will be used, which uses characteristics of the SME as defining features. An SME will be defined as a business that, first, has a relatively small share of the market and, second, is managed in a personal and idiosyncratic way directly by the owners of the business (hence the concept of owner-manager) in an independent way, free from external influence or control over decision-making (Mitev & Marsh 1998). Australia and many countries in the region are heavily dependent on SMEs for their wealth, growth and prosperity. For example, 96 per cent of non-agricultural businesses in the private sector in Australia have fewer than twenty employees, and 75 per cent of these are in the service sector. In 2000, SMEs in Australia employed more than half of the workforce and contributed about 33 per cent of the gross non-agricultural production (ABS 2001).

Thus, it is clear that SMEs make a significant contribution to social cohesion, employment and production throughout the region, and to some extent the health of national and regional economies is linked to the health of the small business sector (Scupola 2002). The SME sector generally is considered to be crucial to a nation's economic renewal and competitive development and its ability to innovate and to create wealth (Barry & Milner 2002). Arguably, continued and sustained development within the SME sector is important to the economy as a whole, and the success of SMEs is contingent on their remaining competitive and efficient and responding to changing customer demands and needs and to changing competitive pressures. Adopting appropriate technologies is often argued to be essential to their continuing ability to be competitive, and e-business is often touted as one means by which SMEs can remain competitive and responsive to changing consumer demands and, indeed, expand market opportunities (Turban et al. 2000).

However, concerns have been voiced about the relatively slow adoption of e-business by SMEs (Brown 2002; Van Beveren & Thomson 2002) and the proficiency with which these new technologies have been applied (Barry & Milner 2002). Underlying this concern is the notion that if SMEs ignore e-business, or are relatively slower in their adoption of e-business, then there is always the risk that they will become uncompetitive in the long term, that they might fail to avail themselves of opportunities to develop and expand their business into truly global marketplaces, and that they run the risk of losing market share to global competitors moving into their historic customer base. The consequences would be grave indeed.

However, there are suggestions that SME owner-managers have yet to be persuaded of the benefits of e-business, although they are adopting some e-business and/or Internet technologies (McKay & Marshall 2002). A key factor is the attitude of the owner-manager to technology, as owner-managers are typically very keen to retain control of their businesses and shun those elements (such as IT) that they feel they do not understand and hence cannot control (Mitev & Marsh 1998). Owner-managers who are innovative, are comfortable with IT and have a positive attitude towards it are more likely to adopt technological innovations such as the Internet than others (Mehrtens, Cragg & Mills 2001). Some SMEs struggle to show a return on their investment in e-business, despite the conceptual arguments as to its benefits and its attractiveness from the customers' perspective (Barry & Milner 2002). This is significant, as Fuller (1996) has argued that SME owner-managers tend to implement IT and other new technologies according to their own assessments of the impact of that technology on the bottom line of their business. If they do not perceive a significant cost saving for the business, they are less likely to embrace the new technology. If SMEs are to be encouraged to adopt e-business, then it is clearly important that potential e-business initiatives and applications are carefully identified and explicated such that the benefits can clearly be demonstrated (with the implication that if no clear business benefit can be identified, it might well be unwise to pursue the investment).

Most SMEs have already adopted email and have access to the Internet for browsing, obtaining information and competitive intelligence, and the like (Dun & Bradstreet 2002). Of the 75 per cent who now have access to the Internet, about 50 per cent have their own corporate website (Dun & Bradstreet 2002). Approximately 50 per cent are using electronic banking and are accessing government services online. However, when it comes to core business activities such as procurement and purchasing, receiving orders from customers, tracking orders and so on, fewer than 20 per cent of SMEs have adopted such applications of e-business (Small Business Research 2000). If Fuller's (1996) contentions are correct, then we can infer that whereas most SMEs see the benefits of email and having Internet access (bearing in mind that these are typically low-cost strategies), relatively few are yet persuaded that the additional costs and risks associated with major changes to supply chain operation and capabilities are worthwhile. This inference is supported by other research, which found that non-adoption even after trial usage was driven by difficulties in seeing business value and returns associated with uptake of e-business (Mehrtens, Cragg & Mills 2001).

Before moving to more detailed discussion of the framework developed to support the strategising and planning activities of SMEs, it is proposed to describe in detail some of the thirty cases investigated as part of the research. These cases were selected as together they serve to illustrate a majority of the issues and problems that emerged in all thirty cases. They encapsulate and hence represent the types of experiences we encountered in so many of the SMEs investigated.

thinking strategically

Read cases 1 and 2 below, and then discuss the questions that follow.

Case 1 — Metro Cars
Case 1 involves a medium-sized, new and used car dealership. It is a well-established business, has enjoyed considerable growth over the past decade, has diversified in terms of the number of makes of car being sold, and now operates from a number of different locations across the city. The owner-manager (CEO) of

Metro Cars has many years experience in the car retailing industry. At the time of the interview with researchers early in 2000, he was familiar with the concept of the Internet, but was uncertain and sceptical about the role and effects of e-business on car retailing. The CEO had already made a foray into e-business, developing an amateurish, publish-only website, which had apparently generated little interest among potential customers. His own line managers had certainly paid little attention to it.

The CEO was approached by an external IT consultant (one of many approaches, in fact), who argued that involvement in an Internet-based, online buying service (along the lines of autobytel.com or carsales.com.au for example) would be an effective strategy for the dealership to adopt, preferable to 'going it alone' and developing its own website with linkages only to the car manufacturers. The potential and functionality of such a service was discussed and viewed through the use of a prototype system. (The suggested system was to include detailed and varied search capabilities, information about each car and a photograph of the car, features that aimed to provide potential customers with more information and more attractive information than was typical in traditional marketing channels such as weekend newspapers.) The prototype system enabled the CEO to try out the search function using different parameters such as vehicle make and model, features and attributes of the car (price, age, automatic/manual transmission, air-conditioning and so on), and to view photographs. The CEO believed the system provided an excellent overview of how his vehicles would be presented to prospective customers via the final system. He was concerned: cooperating with previous 'enemies' (other car dealerships in direct competition with him) by joint listings on an online buying service seemed to be an anathema to him, but he was aware of the dangers of not being prominently represented on such an online buying service. He thus contracted with the IT consultant to develop a website and listing as demonstrated.

The entire management team, comprising the CEO, the financial manager and the sales manager, was very enthusiastic at the prospect of increased sales initiated and motivated by its presence in the online buying service. In addition, they believed that substantial cost savings would accrue through a reduction in advertising and marketing costs. Previously most advertising had been done through television and expensive newspaper and other print media advertisements, and the Internet option promised to reduce that.

What happened after the system was implemented? Quite simply, almost nothing, as indicated by this quote from the CEO: 'New car enquiries...zero June, zero July, zero August, zero September, October to November seven [enquiries], December zero, January one of [enquiry]...so it's zero, zero, zero...' When the researchers worked with the CEO and senior managers to reflect on and analyse their disappointment at their first attempt to embrace electronic business, some interesting issues arose that were viewed, if not as the only cause of failure or disappointment, then as major contributing factors to the less than successful outcomes.

First, it emerged clearly that the e-business initiative had been viewed and treated almost as an independent, stand-alone 'project'. This has been shown to be problematic if the stand-alone initiative indicates a technology-led approach decoupled from strategy (Venkatraman 2000) rather than arising from a carefully thought-out business vision and mission. Such approaches are thus argued to result in diminished business benefits (Feeny 1997; Willcocks & Sauer 2000). In the case of Metro Cars, there was no business strategy to cover the web-based activity. Their actions and decisions reflected what Feeny et al. (1997) would describe as a technology-led approach to strategy formulation. In other words, the availability and potential of the technology (the online buying service as already designed by the consultant) pre-empted the CEO's decision to invest, rather than the decision being driven by carefully articulated business principles and vision.

Second, perhaps as a result of having no articulated strategy in place, the company had made no attempt to review and re-engineer their business processes in light of changing business realities. So, although the car dealership had clearly defined processes by which it handled telephone and walk-in enquiries, it had not developed parallel processes for handling email enquiries, nor did it have any information as to whether the website had influenced any of the walk-in or telephone customers. The managers had failed to revisit existing business practices and processes to accommodate the new channel, and while proclaiming that their involvement in the online buying service had not been successful, they had no concrete information on which to base this claim. They simply had no knowledge of whether walk-in customers had been influenced by the Internet.

Third, closely allied to this second issue was the issue of reward mechanisms and structures. There had been no review of and no change to the performance measurement for sales staff. On reflection, the managers of the car dealership could see it was hardly surprising that none of the sales staff had changed their behaviour in terms of embracing the Internet as a potential sales channel: there was little incentive for them to do so. Furthermore, none of the managers had been explicitly allocated responsibility for the web-based initiatives and activity, and none of them was specifically and actively managing this component of the business.

Case 2 — Cool Books Co.

Case 2 involves a small bookshop, located in an up-market, trendy area of town. For about seven years the bookshop had operated successfully as a 'bricks and mortar' enterprise, loosely specialising in philosophy, literature, culture and feminist thinkers. In 1999, on the advice of her spouse who was a technical e-business consultant (otherwise not involved in the bookshop), the owner-manager (CEO) was encouraged to make a foray into e-business. Her husband persuaded her of the enormous potential of e-business and used the example of other online bookstores as indicative of how suited books were to being sold online. It is fair to say that, at the outset, the CEO was extremely optimistic about the prospects of success in e-business.

The husband developed the website and organised all required infrastructure arrangements but provided the CEO with minimal training on how to download Internet orders and so on. The CEO assumed an unchanging market on the Internet, believing that she was still serving the same marketplace. Thus, she considered no change in stocked items, which also meant that she saw no reason to reassess supplier relationships. She also assumed unchanging customer value creation, arguing that her specialist knowledge and personalised service would likewise be viewed as sources of value creation for web-based customers. In interviews, she frequently asserted that she had expected her existing clientele would be the main users of the website.

What happened? In short, the website was closed after nine months in operation, after rapidly escalating costs and a disappointing level of trade over the Internet started to threaten the existence of the bricks and mortar business. Once again, it proved instructive to reflect on and analyse this unfortunate outcome with the CEO. She admitted comparatively little knowledge of e-business and felt that, as a result, she had acquired a simplistic, technical view of all that would be required for online trading. She admitted that no time had been devoted to strategy development, competitive analysis and the like. Once again, some interesting issues arose that the CEO accepted might have been contributing factors to the failure of her online venture.

First, there had been no consideration of the e-marketplace and its implications for the e-business initiative. So, in deciding to trade online, the bookshop (somewhat inadvertently) entered into a global marketplace, and a very competitive one at that, with significant, more established players such as Amazon.com and BarnesandNoble.com and a host of other, smaller players. Her previous belief that her existing customers would become her online customers also proved to be largely incorrect, meaning that she had never conducted any real analysis of what market she was selling to, who her customers were or what the potential source of competitive advantage might prove to be. Although local people who shared her passion for American philosophy, literature, and so on might become loyal customers of the bookshop, this seems less obviously true in a global, Internet market space.[2]

Second, marketing planning was almost non-existent. Very little consideration and effort had been devoted to publicising her presence online, other than telling some of her existing customers.

Third, very little attempt had been made to analyse and understand the nature of the e-competition. Thus, whereas the bookshop had successfully competed against the larger, national book chains partly through specialisation and partly through selecting an ideal location, the move online had put the business in competition with the large online players such as Amazon.com, global Internet start-ups and so on. Her source of differentiation was largely annulled over the Internet.

Questions

1. Analyse what went wrong in each case. How would you advise the owner-managers of these SMEs to do things differently?

2. Would you agree with the decision to close down the e-business initiatives in case 2? Why or why not?

3. If we accept that the owner-managers and their organisations exhibited all the typical characteristics of SMEs (relatively small market share, absence of formalised processes and structures, lack of time, financial resources and technological capabilities, opposition to excessive growth because of a fear of losing control, and personal and idiosyncratic managerial behaviour by the CEO), how might a consultant approach these CEOs and what advice would he/she offer with respect to their e-business initiatives?

Lessons learned about e-business needs of SMEs

The issues and problems illustrated in these cases indicate the types of issues and problems that seem to have contributed to less than satisfactory outcomes with respect to e-business in most cases included in our sample. Not every case displayed all the problems, but subsets of these problems were noticed in a number of the cases where either a real failure had occurred with respect to e-business (the website had been closed or web-based activity had been dramatically scaled back) or in cases where results had been disappointing (trade and/or revenues at much lower levels than anticipated).

However, it is also fair to say that in cases where owner-managers were satisfied with their e-business initiatives, it was felt that some of the issues had been overcome by trial and error or serendipity, rather than through careful analysis and planning.

The major issues or problems that were repeatedly identified in our research were as follows:

- inadequate knowledge of e-business (potential, risks, benefits and so on) leading to inadequate decision-making
- no clear business vision with respect to e-business
- limited or no clear strategy development with respect to e-business
- limited or no integration of e-business business vision and strategy with existing organisational vision and strategy (in the case of existing bricks and mortar enterprises) or no consideration of the impact of one (e-business vision and strategy) on the other (existing business vision, strategy and activities)
- little or no consideration of the appropriateness of existing business processes and practices in light of the requirements of e-business
- little or no consideration of the requirement for changes to performance measurement systems (HR, customer satisfaction, finance etc.)
- little or no consideration of the possible effects on key relationships with suppliers or inadequate fostering of appropriate supplier relationships
- little or no attention paid to the logistics capabilities required to support the e-business activity
- little or no understanding of the nature of e-competition and the implications of potentially entering into a global e-marketplace
- little or no attention to understanding and effectively managing customer relationships in the e-business environment
- little or no attention paid to developing a marketing plan for the e-enterprise
- inadequate consideration of required resources, such as IT expertise, financial backing and so on
- insufficient consideration of the need for organisational change management.

In the sections that follow, the development of a framework to help support the small and medium-size enterprise owner-manager in thinking through these issues is articulated and explained.

Towards a framework to support the development of an e-business strategy

Given these recurring problems with the adoption of e-business by SMEs, clearly there was a need for some kind of device to help structure and integrate managers' thinking about the many and diverse elements of e-business. A relatively simple framework to support **e-business strategy development** and to help guide the thinking and decision-making of managers was required. Such a framework, it was felt, would support a systematic and holistic approach to e-business and would help SME owner-managers to develop an effective e-business mindset.

In developing the framework, issues that need to be considered included appropriate investment or sourcing of IIT; appropriate analysis, re-engineering and redesign of appropriate core business processes, such as procurement, order fulfilment and the like; effective marketing and customer relationship management; effective sourcing, acquisition and management of resources and relationships; and the development and management of effective logistics or distribution capabilities.

However, before these issues are reviewed there needs to be a broad strategy formulation effort that decides on what is to be done, the drivers and rationale of this 'what' and, in very broad organisational terms, how it is to be done. This we have called the e-vision.

A framework for e-business strategy formulation

Strategy development is envisaged taking place in two broad steps. A forward-looking vision is articulated that paints an overall informing picture of the e-business future. This future (or e-vision) is concerned with the e-business aspects of an organisation's operations, but is highly likely to influence and be influenced by the organisation's existing vision and mission.[3] The e-vision informs and guides the second step, which is the detailed **e-business strategy formulation**. Each of these steps will be considered in more detail.

In suggesting that strategy development comprises two broad steps, there might be a tendency to view them as discrete and sequential. This was not our intention. So a relatively unconstrained free flow both within and between the steps was envisaged. The actual process anticipated is much more iterative and messy than can be easily captured in a diagram. But our aim was to provide points of focus for managers, which are important issues to be considered and analysed (and possibly rejected) among relatively circular discussions about e-business directions and strategies.

Step 1: e-vision

The broad general vision of e-business is formed from a number of considerations. Normally these considerations would include the following:

- **environmental analysis**, including the e-environment
- **competitive analysis**
- **market analysis**, including considerations of brand and e-brand
- customer needs and wants
- business and IT governance
- current and future needed capabilities.

The above considerations form and develop the e-vision, as shown in figure 4.1.

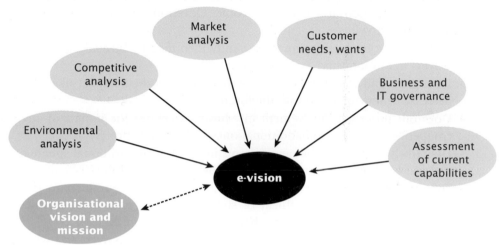

Figure 4.1 ▶ Articulating an e-vision
Source ▶ Marshall and McKay 2002.

▶ Environmental analysis

In carrying out an analysis of the firm's business environment, an attempt is being made to ascertain the major forces affecting a 'clicks and mortar' SME that has both a traditional business and an e-business-based business. Thus, environmental analysis includes an analysis of the major political, economic, social and technical influences in the environment and an assessment of their significance for the future of the business. (Refer back to the discussion in chapter 3.) The e-environment, or the environment of the Internet, also needs to be considered in terms of these influences, with awareness gained of the major driving forces or influences affecting a possible e-business venture. Thus, the types of questions to be considered include the following:

What are the major political, economic, social, legal and technological influences affecting our organisation currently?

- How significant or important are these influences?
- How stable and/or certain are these influences likely to be in the future?
- How does a move into e-business affect or impact these influences?
- Does involvement in e-business raise the spectre of other influences not experienced in our traditional business environment? (Marshall & McKay 2002)

Competitive analysis

The competitive analysis is performed for both the traditional business and the e-business initiative. This would include consideration of industry factors and sources of competition, competitive influences exerted along the supply chain, the stability of demand, and the likelihood of new entrants in both traditional and e-business spheres of operation (Johnson & Scholes 1999). The aim is to derive a complete picture of future competition for the firm that is adding an e-business capability or that is starting on the Web. The traditional non-Internet competitors might for example be local firms only. However, the Internet-based competitors might include global rivals. Thus a downtown bookstore for example would have local and national book chains as competitors, but its Internet-based competitors would include global players like Amazon and Barnes & Noble. Questions and issues of concern might include the following:

- What are the competitive forces currently identified by buyers? Suppliers? Existing players in our industry?
- How great and how significant is their impact? Is their impact likely to increase, decrease or remain stable into the future?
- Does our proposed involvement in e-business change the impact of any of these competitive forces or add additional ones? With what effect(s)?
- How likely are there to be new entrants into both our traditional sphere of activity and our e-business activity? What might be the impact of this?
- To what extent might demand for our goods/services be influenced by changing customer preferences, the threat of substitute products or services and the like? Does involvement in e-business change this to any great degree?
- What/who are the industry benchmarks and/or prime movers, and what are they doing with respect to e-business?
- How will e-business change the marketplace and the way we do things?
- How do we ensure we retain (and increase) our current competitive positioning? (Marshall & McKay 2002)

Market analysis

A broad marketing analysis should influence and inform the future e-vision for the firm about to undertake an e-business initiative. A traditional broad review of markets for the firm is in order to bring knowledge about markets up to date. An analysis of possible markets that could be reached via the e-business or Internet-based channel is then completed and a picture formed of the markets to be targeted by the future 'clicks and mortar' business. Further, the brand image of the firm and its major products is reviewed, and considerations and efforts regarding branding for the traditional part of the future business are noted. The e-branding issues are then considered. These considerations would include developing an awareness of the website name and the products or services in Internet-based markets (Kleindl 2001). Issues to be considered by management include the following:

- What is the current value of our image and branding?
- How will e-business affect our image and branding?

- Have we considered issues associated with operating in a potentially global marketplace?
- Do we understand our current markets?
- How does a move into e-business affect our current markets? Does it open new markets? With what implications? (Marshall & McKay 2002)

▶ Customer needs and wants

The value that the firm provides to its current customers is then considered and reviewed. Then this value proposition is considered in terms of the e-business initiative. Consideration needs to be given to issues such as the fit between the needs and wants of customers and traditional business activity first and e-business activity second. It appears important to establish that both existing and potential new customers value the proposed e-business initiative and to consider carefully the issues associated with delivering value to the organisation's Internet-based customers. The overall view of the customer value proposition inherent in the 'clicks and mortar' business consisting of the e-business initiative and traditional business needs to be clearly articulated (Deise et al. 2000). Hence the types of questions to be considered include the following:

- What is it about our existing activities that adds value from the perspective of our customers?
- How well do we understand the needs, wants and preferences of our existing customers?
- Will existing and potential customers see value in the proposed e-business services we are planning to offer?
- What are the issues involved in delivering value to the organisation's Internet-based customers?
- How will we build an ongoing loyal and personal relationship with customers through our clicks and mortar activities and initiatives? (Marshall & McKay 2002)

▶ Business and IT governance

There are also some high-level issues of governance to be considered. Prime among these is the issue of how closely coupled the Internet-based business and traditional business should be. They can be seamlessly integrated, sharing staff skills and business processes, although they could be quite separate, even to the point of having separate financing and shareholders. This latter possibility constitutes the e-business 'spin-off' option. Other possibilities exist between seamless integration and spin-off.

There are also some IT governance issues to consider. IT governance issues are concerned with whether to develop IT-based e-business capabilities, such as whether the website development, operation and maintenance should be undertaken in-house or whether these concerns should be outsourced. The broad conclusions on governance will quite deeply affect the formulation of the e-vision (Venkatraman 2000). Management perhaps need to consider questions associated with the governance issue such as those listed below:

- Should the e-business initiative be closely integrated into existing business structures and procedures, or should it be spun off into a relatively independent entity?

- Will changes be required to our organisational structure?
- Is our administrative infrastructure adequate to support the e-business initiative?
- Is our IT infrastructure adequate to support the e-business initiative?
- Do we require external assistance to develop our business?
- How do we finance this e-business initiative?
- How does our proposed e-business initiative fit with the overall strategic direction of the business?
- Do we have appropriate governance structures and processes in place, so that risk is minimised and value will be delivered on the investment? (Marshall & McKay 2002)

Assessment of current capabilities

A related issue to that of IT governance is a review and assessment of current capabilities or core competencies. The organisation needs to ensure that it has adequate capabilities to perform its core business processes at an acceptable level. Further it must also ensure that its current capabilities match what is required for the successful pursuit of its e-business initiative. Understanding the correct blend of capability building and outsourcing will permit the e-business initiative to go forward successfully, as shown below:

- What are our core/distinctive competencies? Are these the competencies required for the proposed e-business operation?
- What are our core/distinctive IT competencies? Are these the competencies required for the proposed e-business operation?
- Are our current levels of skills and capabilities (both business and IT) adequate? Will they remain so into the future? Will the proposed e-business initiative imply a need for a different set of skills and capabilities?
- Which skills and capabilities might need to be fostered in-house, and which might be accessed through outsourcing or contracting arrangements? (Marshall & McKay 2002)

Having articulated an e-vision, the organisation must then proceed to actualise that vision by formulating a detailed set of strategic intentions informed by that vision.

Step 2: strategy development

Once the vision and broad thrust of the strategy has been decided, the organisation must then consider a number of issues to ensure successful adoption of e-business. These issues include the following:

- investment in suitable information systems and technology
- appropriate re-engineering and redesign of business processes
- effective marketing and customer relationship management
- efficient and effective acquisition and management of resources and relationships
- the development and management of an efficient and effective logistics or distribution capability.

Figure 4.2 draws these issues together into a cohesive and integrative framework. There follows a brief review and analysis of each of these issues for the planning of an e-business initiative.

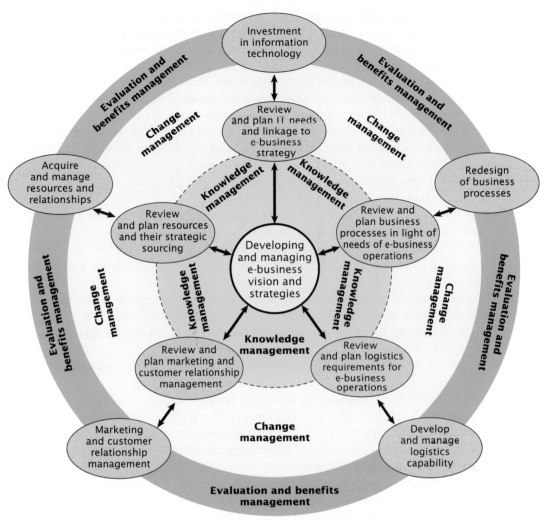

Figure 4.2 ▶ A framework to support e-business strategy development
Source ▶ Marshall and McKay 2002.

▶ Investment in appropriate information systems and technology

The adoption of an e-business capability requires investing in or sourcing the appropriate systems and technology to carry out the planned Internet-based initiative. Planning this investment in IT requires the strategy formulation exercise to be accompanied by information systems planning (IS planning) and information technology planning (IT planning) respectively.

Planning for e-business is so central to strategic planning that the coupling between strategic planning, IS planning and IT planning is likely to be very close. Business issues and issues regarding IT are much more likely to converge when e-business is being discussed than when, in years past, IT issues tended to focus on support for the back office systems of finance, accounting, manufacturing and the like. Hence IT played more of a support role for the activities of the enterprise than an enabling one, as is the case with e-business (refer back to figure 3.1 in chapter 3).

Having identified the required IT functionality for the organisation's e-business undertakings, the issues surrounding the sourcing of that functionality must be considered. Although it could be argued that such a strategic initiative might be more appropriately handled internally (Lacity et al., in Willcocks et al. 1997), external expertise and resources in the form of Internet service providers (ISPs) and application service providers (ASPs), along with the usual IT outsourcing vendors, might well provide quite viable alternatives. Since most SMEs do not have substantial IT resources, increased demand for IT resources and expertise is likely to involve planning and managing outsourcing contracts of one kind or another. The kinds of questions and issues that might need to be addressed here include the following:

- What information do we need to support the e-business operation? Do we currently have that information?
- Are our proposed investments directly linked to and closely aligned with business and e-business directions and strategies?
- What hardware, software and telecommunications do we require to enable the proposed e-business initiative? Will this be adequate as our business grows into the future?
- Do we need to integrate existing IT investments with e-business investments? How do we achieve this?
- Have we considered the potential of the Internet to facilitate re-engineering of our supply chain?
- Are management equipped to deal with the increased technology? What training might be required?
- What disaster recovery planning is in place for the e-business initiative?
- Should we source all our IT requirements internally, or should we rely on the services of ISPs, ASPs and/or IT outsourcing vendors?
- Have we considered the strategic use of corporate data to enhance our competitiveness and/or our service to customers?
- Do we have the IT expertise and resources to support the e-business infrastructure adequately for continuous operation ($24 \times 7 \times 365$)?
- Are we exposing our organisation to acceptable levels of risk?
- Have we paid adequate attention to security issues, such as contractual liability, intellectual property, privacy, system security and integrity? Can we assure customers that web-based transactions will remain secure?
- Are we prepared to manage the change that will be required for the successful transformation of our organisation?
- What knowledge management issues and opportunities need to be considered? Can IT support the knowledge management process? (Marshall & McKay 2002)

▌ Appropriate re-engineering and redesign of business processes

An e-business capability, particularly one that involves a change in the way an organisation interacts with its customers and/or suppliers, might well require the design of new business processes. Handling online queries, managing inventories, selling and processing online payments, and organising packaging and delivery could all imply that existing business processes need to be reviewed and revised and that new processes need to be developed.

The nature and extent of this re-engineering effort will depend on some fundamental strategic decisions made by the organisation at the early stage of strategy formulation mentioned above. If the organisation decides to integrate physical and virtual operations closely, and/or to enter at a more advanced stage of e-business, then extensive re-engineering of business processes could be needed. However, if the organisation decides to keep its e-business operations separate or relatively basic, then perhaps comparatively little re-engineering of existing processes will be necessary. Issues to be considered at this stage include the following:

- How efficient and effective are our existing core business processes?
- Do additional, new business processes need to be designed for the e-business initiative? How will these business processes affect the operation of the existing ones?
- Are information flows adequate to facilitate management control of existing and new business processes?
- Are existing support processes adequate? Will they remain adequate to support the e-business operation?
- Does the e-business initiative offer the potential for even greater efficiencies to be achieved to core business processes?
- Do reward mechanisms for staff need to be changed or modified to reflect changes to core business processes?
- Do performance measures need to be changed or modified to reflect changes to core business processes? (Marshall & McKay 2002)

▶ Development and management of an efficient and effective logistics capability

With the exception of digitisable goods and services that can be delivered remotely over the Internet, frequently customers expect physical goods and personal services to be delivered to their homes or businesses. Hence a very important consideration in a B2C e-business initiative is the development of an efficient and effective logistics capability. In some cases, such as the selling of whitegoods, this capability might already be part of the organisation's current services, and the logistics capability might not need much development. However, a review of such a capability in the light of the e-business initiative would be wise. A number of issues might need attention. Distribution planning could need to be improved if delivery is going to be promised within tighter time windows. The time period over which deliveries are being planned for the e-business initiative might be different from that which holds at present. On entering the world of e-business prices for delivery might be altered for competitive reasons. Thus the review, in fact, should range over all distribution and warehousing issues, including the handling and packaging of goods. Any necessary changes in warehousing and distribution should then have been anticipated. Furthermore, developing a capability to deliver ordered goods in a timely manner also implies receiving goods from suppliers in an efficient and orderly manner. The planning for a logistics capability must therefore consider both flows into and out of the organisation.

In the case of organisations like bookstores, which do not have a distribution capability but are considering B2C e-business, this capability must be developed within the firm or obtained via an alliance or outsourcing arrangement. Again, an assessment of needs should range over all distribution and warehousing issues. Dealing with the delivery peaks, such as Christmas, should be included in such deliberations. The logistics capability, including warehousing, packing and distribution, is such an important capability in e-business ventures that it merits thinking through carefully in the above manner. The types of questions and issues that might need to be addressed include the following:

• Are we satisfied with existing logistics arrangement and capabilities?
• Will the e-business initiative imply a need for additional, different and/or improved logistics capabilities?
• Should the logistics capability be developed in-house, or could we rely on external vendors to provide this service? At what level of risk?
• Is our logistics capability expandable to cater for seasonal peaks in our business? (Marshall & McKay 2002)

◗ Effective marketing and customer relationship management

An organisation that is planning an e-business capability is likely to need to review its marketing and customer relationship management activities. Consideration of the Internet in terms of marketing, sales and support activities includes considering the potential role of the Internet in expanding and improving market research and market testing, in product/market extension, in market exposure, in prospect generation and contact, in sales channel support and in post-sale customer support (Stroud 1998). Among other things, this might involve a consideration of the potential of the Internet for gathering feedback from a large and geographically distributed audience of people and the capacity of the Internet to change and extend the nature of an organisation's products and markets.

There is also a need to consider the Internet as a channel for advertising the organisation and its products. The organisation might also need to determine a policy for prospective customer contacts achieved through the website. For example, in what ways and with what expenditure are such leads to be followed up? Should a website be equipped with facilities to enable a customer-controlled dialogue to be established? Such questions need consideration, as does the use of the Web to support the organisation's traditional lead generation campaigns that would be based on advertising, mailshots and the like.

Opportunities to use the Internet as a channel to sell directly to the end-user, as well as a support mechanism to selling via a direct sales force or via intermediaries such as agents, distributors, wholesalers and the like, need also to be reviewed. So too should the potential to use the Internet to serve customers better with pre- and post-sales information and to help maintain a continuing dialogue with customers who might decide to make further purchases. Questions and issues that need to be considered include the following:

• Are we using data gathered from traditional and e-business activities to enhance our relationship with our customers?
• Do we understand the value proposition from the perspective of the customer?
• Have we considered the potential of the Internet to change or enhance markets, products and/or services?

- Does the e-business initiative provide opportunities for one-to-one marketing, mass customisation, etc.?
- Does e-business give us the opportunity to exploit online community concepts to create value for our customers? (Marshall & McKay 2002)

▶ Effective and efficient acquisition and management of resources

An e-business initiative on the part of an SME is likely to stretch resources and require the integration and use of a number of capabilities, both human and technological. Additional financial resources might also need to be accessed. Those investigating such initiatives need to assess the resource requirements for such an initiative and then look at how best to acquire and manage such resources. This has already been determined for IT. However, one now needs to look at the financial, human resources and physical asset implications of the e-business initiative. The requirements for each resource type need to be carefully determined and set out in a feasible and realisable time-phased plan.

It might be found that the best, or perhaps the only, way of building an e-business capability in a reasonable period is by building and managing alliances with business partners and/or entering into relationships with outsourcing vendors of various types (Grenier & Metes 1995; Impact Programme 1998; Chesborough & Teece 1996). This could be done to obtain specialist consulting services such as strategic planning, IT management and the like or it could be done to achieve various functional capabilities such as IT services, warehousing and distribution. Therefore the resource requirements, as well as their mode of procurement and management, are planned and costed, thus ensuring that the overall e-business strategy is feasible. Management might like to consider issues like the following:

- Where do we source the required skills, capabilities and competencies to support the e-business initiative?
- Does the e-business venture change our relationship with our suppliers or imply a need to develop a relationship with additional or alternative supplier(s)?
- How certain are we of being able to guarantee supply in the new trading environment ($24 \times 7 \times 365$)?
- Do we need to consider forming alliances with business partners in order to be more competitive, flexible and/or responsive in the new environment? Would such an alliance allow us to better focus energies on developing and exploiting core competencies? (Marshall & McKay 2002)

E-visioning and e-business strategy development

The relationship between **e-visioning** and e-business strategy development is shown in figure 4.3 (p. 112). Arguably, the main influence is as depicted by the thick arrow, but the process of analysis and learning that takes place during strategy development might itself influence an organisation's e-vision.

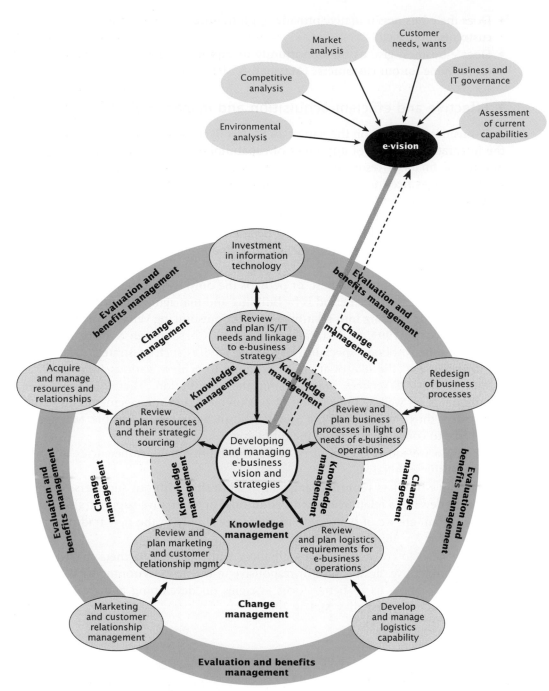

Figure 4.3 ▶ E-visioning and e-business strategy formulation
Source ▶ Marshall and McKay 2002.

Managers are also urged to consider some more generalised, important issues: included here would be issues to do with knowledge management, change management, and the evaluation and proactive realisation of benefits from their e-business initiatives. For example, it might be that knowledge and information are the fundamental building blocks of continuing organisational success. Raising awareness of this, and considering the role of knowledge management processes in organisations to enhance and protect this asset, seems an important consideration (see chapter 8). Likewise, any move into e-business is likely to involve substantial change in an organisation. Being equipped and planning appropriate change management initiatives will improve the chances that such a transformation can be effected successfully. Finally, managers are urged to consider the need to evaluate their investments. The notion that benefits will automatically flow from carefully thought-out investments needs to be challenged, and instead discussions encouraged as to how to manage the organisation proactively such that changes needed to fully exploit and support the potential of IT are made.

Summary

This chapter has considered the importance of SMEs in national, regional and local economies, and has concluded that SMEs play a vital role in supporting social cohesion, economic development and growth, employment opportunities, innovation and so on. A healthy SME sector is vital for a healthy national economy. This implies that SMEs need to become involved in e-business to remain competitive, responsive to changing customer needs and wants, and flexible enough to respond to increased competition in global marketplaces. However, concerns have been expressed that SMEs have been relatively slow to adopt e-business and the Internet. Although many have email and access to the Internet for information searching and the like, far fewer SMEs have made the more expensive and riskier investments in using e-business and associated technologies to fundamentally alter core business processes and relationships with major suppliers and customers.

One of the problems is that most tools and techniques to support the articulation of strategy have been developed for larger corporations and, as such, could be too cumbersome for SMEs to apply. Furthermore, as some SME owner-managers do not readily embrace the notion of innovation and growth, a simpler, less threatening framework needs to be developed so that moves into e-business, when they are made, are done in a coherent, coordinated approach with clear objectives and expected returns in mind. Such a framework is presented and discussed in this chapter. It has been expressly designed for the use of small groups of managers or individuals to help them to reflect on key issues of concern for their businesses.

key terms

competitive analysis

e-business strategy development

e-business strategy formulation

environmental analysis

e-visioning

market analysis

small and medium-sized enterprise
   (SME)

discussion questions

1. In what ways is the ideal approach and method for IT and e-business strategy formulation different for large organisations and small organisations? Do you think the differences are very significant?

   Comment on the viewpoint that SMEs do not need to formulate business strategy or IS strategy. Further, comment on the viewpoint that SMEs do not have the resources to carry out business strategy formulation or IS strategy formulation.

2. Describe the risks of SMEs not adopting e-business. Should all SMEs adopt e-business? Under what circumstances should SMEs not adopt e-business?

   Describe how SMEs should go about deciding whether to adopt e-business. Furthermore, how should an SME decide whether to have a website, perhaps without e-business functionality?

3. Explain how an SME should go about measuring and evaluating the performance of its e-business activity. Be careful to include the possibility of 'cannibalisation' in your analysis, i.e. the possibility of the e-business channel attracting a number of customers away from the other channels, such as face-to-face, telephone and catalogue selling.

   Consider both the case of full e-business transactional capability and a case of Internet information provision and advertising via a company website.

4. Describe a process for determining a vision for e-business for a firm. Describe the major elements of a vision for e-business. How does a vision for e-business differ from a strategy for e-business?

5. Are SMEs more likely than large companies to outsource their IT and e-business technologies? If so, why?

   Are the risks, difficulties and challenges of outsourcing the same for large and small companies? Are the principles for evaluating IT and e-business outsourcing arrangements the same for SMEs and large companies?

   Do the above considerations apply to outsourcing e-business related distribution and logistics? What are the risks, challenges and difficulties of outsourcing e-business-related distribution and logistics for SMEs? Describe a process for planning and evaluating the outsourcing e-business distribution and logistics for SMEs.

notes

1. This chapter is heavily based on P Marshall & J McKay 2002, 'An emergent framework to support visioning and strategy formulation for electronic commerce', *Information Systems and Operational Research* (INFOR), vol. 40, no. 1, February, pp. 3–22.

2. Indeed, research indicates that small online book retailers in Australia seem to do better by specialising in Australian literature or Australiana (see Valli & Marshall 2001).

3. Much of the discussion that follows will assume a traditional business (a 'bricks and mortar' organisation) as it migrates towards an Internet presence of some sort in addition to existing operations (a 'clicks and mortar' organisation). However, it is argued that by omitting the references to the traditional business activities or domain, this framework is equally applicable to an Internet start-up enterprise.

suggested reading

Baldwin, A, Lymer, A & Johnson, R 2001, 'Business impacts of the Internet for small and medium-sized enterprises', in S Barnes & B Hunt (eds), *E-commerce and V-business: Business Models for Global Success*, Butterworth Heinemann, Oxford.

Chen, S 2001, *Strategic Management of E-business*, John Wiley & Sons, Chichester.

McKay, J & Marshall, P 2002, 'Current approaches to realising the benefits from e-commerce investments amongst SMEs', *Australian Journal of Information Systems*, vol. 9, no. 2, pp. 135–47.

Mehrtens, J, Cragg, PB & Mills, AM 2001, 'A model of Internet adoption by SMEs', *Information & Management*, 39(2001), pp. 165–76.

Poon, S & Swatman, PMC 1999, 'An exploratory study of small business Internet commerce issues', *Information & Management*, 35(1999), pp. 9–18.

Van Beveren, J & Thomson, H 2002, 'The use of electronic commerce by SMEs in Victoria, Australia', *Journal of Small Business Management*, vol. 40, no. 3, pp. 250–3.

references

Anderson Consulting 1998, 'E-commerce: our future today', http://www.ac.com accessed 12 May 2000.

Asia Pacific Economic Cooperation (APEC) 1999, *SME Electronic Commerce Study*, (TEL05/97T) Final Report.

Australian Bureau of Statistics 2001, *Small Business in Australia* (Cat. No. 1321.0), ABS, Canberra.

—2003, 'Business adoption of information technology slows', media release 2 April 2003 (8129.0), ABS, Canberra.

Baldwin, A, Lymer, A & Johnson, R 2001, 'Business impacts of the Internet for small and medium-sized enterprises', in S Barnes & B Hunt (eds), *E-commerce and V-business: Business Models for Global Success*, Butterworth Heinemann, Oxford.

Barry, H & Milner, B 2002, 'SMEs and electronic commerce: a departure from the traditional provision of training?', *Journal of European Industrial Training*, vol. 26, no. 7, pp. 316–26.

Bidgoli, H 2002, *Electronic Commerce Principles and Practice*, Academic Press, San Diego.

Brown, E 2002, 'Accelerating the up-take of e-commerce by small and medium enterprises. A report and action plan by the SME e-commerce Forum Taskforce, July 2002', available online at http://www.setel.com.au/smeforum2002.

Bryant, G 2001, 'After the hype, the hard work', *Business Review Weekly*, vol. 23, no. 40 (11–17 October), p. 64.

Chen, S 2001, *Strategic Management of E-business*, John Wiley & Sons, Chichester.

Chesborough, HW & Teece, DJ 1998, 'When is virtual virtuous?', *Harvard Business Review*, vol. 74, no. 1, pp. 65–73.

Crawford, J 1998, NEWS: *A Project to Get Smaller Enterprises On-line*, Department of Industry, Science and Tourism, Ultimo, NSW, and Tradegate ECA, Sydney.

Currie, W 2000, *The Global Information Society: A New Paradigm for the 21st Century Corporation*, John Wiley & Sons, Chichester.

Czerniawska, F and Potter, G 1998, *Business in a Virtual World: Exploiting Information for Competitive Advantage*, Macmillan Press, London.

Deise, MV, Nowikow, C, King, P & Wright, A 2000, *Executive Guide to E-business*, John Wiley & Sons, New York.

DOCITA (Australian Department of Communications, Information Technology and the Arts) 2000, 'Australia's e-commerce report card', http://www.noie.gov.au/ReportCard.

Dun & Bradstreet 2002, 'Small business survey Australia 2002. Summary report', available online at http://www.dnb.com/pdfs/about/press/SBS_Summary_0402.pdf, accessed 15 June 2003.

Ernst & Young 2000a, 'Global on-line retailing', http://www.ey.com.au, accessed May 2001.

—2000b, 'Virtual shopping in Australia', http://www.ey.com.au, accessed June 2001.

Feeny, D 1997, 'Introduction-information management: lasting ideas within turbulent technology', in L Willcocks, D Feeny & G Islei (eds), *Managing IT as a Strategic Resource*, McGraw-Hill, London.

Fuller, T 1996, 'Fulfilling IT needs in small business: a recursive learning model', *International Small Business Journal*, vol. 14, no. 4, pp. 25–44.

Grenier, R & Metes, G (1995) *Going Virtual: Moving Your Organization into the 21st Century*, Prentice Hall, Upper Saddle River, NJ.

Hughes, A & Needham, K 2001, 'Flatline.com', *The Age*, 13 October 2001.

Impact Programme 1998, 'Exploiting the wired-up world: best practice in managing virtual organisations', http://www.achieve.ch.

Jarvenpaa, S and Tiller, EH 1999, 'Integrating market, technology and policy opportunities in e-business strategy', *Journal of Strategic Information Systems*, vol. 8(1999): pp. 235–49.

Johnson, G & Scholes, K 1999, *Exploring Corporate Strategy: Text and Cases*, 5th edn, Prentice Hall, London.

Kleindl, BA 2001, *Strategic Electronic Marketing: Managing E-business*, South Western, Melbourne.

Lacity, MC, Willcocks, LP & Feeny, DF 1997, 'The value of selective sourcing', in L Willcocks, D Feeny, & G Islei (eds), *Managing IT as a Strategic Resource*, McGraw-Hill, London.

Lientz, BP & Rea, KP 2000, *Start Right in E-business*, Academic Press, San Diego.

Marshall, P & McKay, J 2002, 'An emergent framework to support visioning and strategy formulation for electronic commerce', *Information Systems and Operational Research*, vol. 40, no. 1, February, pp. 3–22.

McKay, J & Marshall, P 2002, 'Current approaches to realising the benefits from e-commerce investments amongst SMEs', *Australian Journal of Information Systems*, vol. 9, no. 2, pp. 135–47.

Mehrtens, J, Cragg, PB & Mills, AM 2001, 'A model of Internet adoption by SMEs', *Information & Management*, 39(2001): pp. 165–76.

Mitev, NM & Marsh, AE 1998, 'Small business and information technology: risk, planning and change', *Journal of Small Business and Enterprise Development*, vol. 5, no. 3, pp. 228–45.

National Office of the Information Economy 2000, *Small Businesses Index: Survey of Computer Technology and E-commerce in Australian Small and Medium Business*, NOIE, Canberra.

OECD 1998, *SMEs and Electronic Commerce*, Working Party on Small and Medium-sized Enterprises, Directorate for Science, Technology and Industry, Organization for Economic Co-operation and Development.

Poon, S & Swatman, PMC 1999, 'An exploratory study of small business Internet commerce issues', *Information & Management*, 35(1999): pp. 9–18.

Rayport, JF & Jaworski, BI 2001, *E-commerce*, McGraw-Hill/Irwin, Boston.

Scupola, A 2002, 'Adoption issues of business-to-business Internet commerce in European SMEs', *Proceedings of the 35th Hawaii International Conference on Systems Sciences.*

Small Business Research 2000, 'Small business opinion survey: summary of results. November 2000', available online at www.smallbusinessresearch.com.au/survey/november 2000.htm, accessed 25 June 2003.

Stroud, D 1998, *Internet Strategies: A Corporate Guide to Exploiting the Internet,* Macmillan, Basingstoke, UK.

Turban, E, Lee, J, King, D & Chung, M 2000, *Electronic Commerce: A Managerial Perspective,* Prentice Hall, Englewood Cliffs, NJ.

US Department of Commerce 1998, 'The emerging digital economy II', available online at http://www.e-commerce.gov/emerging.htm.

Valli, C & Marshall, P 2001, 'An initial study of Australian on-line bookstores', paper accepted for presentation at 2nd Annual Global Information Technology Management 2001 World Conference, Dallas, Texas, 10–12 June 2001.

Van Beveren, J & Thomson, H 2002, 'The use of electronic commerce by SMEs in Victoria, Australia', *Journal of Small Business Management,* vol. 40, no. 3, pp. 250–3.

Venkatraman, N 2000, 'Five steps to a dotcom strategy: how to find your footing on the web', *Sloan Management Review,* Spring, 2000.

Willcocks, L, Feeney, D & Islei, G (eds) 1997, *Managing IT as a Strategic Resource,* McGraw-Hill, London.

Willcocks, L & Sauer, C 2000, *Moving to e-Business,* Random House, London.

case study

Black Swan Books: an innovative bookshop

Black Swan Books was established in 1871, just several blocks west of the central business district of Perth. The bookstore had three floors, two of which were filled with books with an Australian focus. These books covered Australian novels as well as collections of Australian short stories and poetry. Other specialist sections included Australian history and culture, art, wildlife, plants and wildflowers, geography, travel and the like. There was also a well-stocked section for children, which again focused on Australian books, including old-time favourites *The Complete Adventures of Blinky Bill*, *The Magic Pudding*, *The Complete Adventures of Snugglepot and Cuddlepie* and *Seven Little Australians*.

One floor was devoted to non-Australian titles in literature, business, travel, culture and science. In general these were quality books for the educated book-lover. Thirty per cent of sales came from this floor.

Recently, Black Swan Books had began to open until 11 pm. It had been an experiment at first, but had led to markedly increased sales, which easily paid for the two extra staff that had been required for these extended hours. In keeping with the late hours, an inviting and comfortable ambience had been achieved, with chairs and some tables provided for reading and reflection. Prints of famous Australian paintings were hung on the walls, particularly around the reading sections where the chairs and tables were placed.

Another innovation had been to invite authors to give talks about their books. Black Swan Books had featured such authors as Tim Winton, Peter Carey and David Malouf. These talks had been given in the evening, when part of the third floor had been converted temporarily into a lecture presentation space. Lectures had been well advertised and attracted a number of international tourists and visitors to Perth from the Australian countryside, along with the Perth city dwellers.

In 1997, Black Swan Books had continued its innovative approach to selling books. In this year the bookshop established an online presence. A website with full transactional capability had been constructed by the E-Business Professionals, a local group specialising in e-commerce websites. The website was to include a brief description and review of each book on sale. Godfrey Harold Hardy, the owner and general manager of Black Swan Books, wished to keep the initial venture into e-commerce as a 'pilot' or experimental initiative.

'If it doesn't prove itself, we are closing the e-business venture down and going back to the traditional basics of being a quality Australian books bookseller,' he told his staff, just before the website opened.

However, he did caution his staff that this was not a cavalier venture. Speaking to his staff in December 1998, Godfrey Hardy said, 'We have done our market research on this. We know from an Australian Bureau of Statistics survey that 18 per cent of Australian households had Internet access in July this year. The ABS calculated that 1.25 million households had Internet access, up from 971 000 in May, and up from 154 000 in February, totalling a 46 per cent increase.

'The ABS also estimated that 4.2 million adults used the Internet between August 1997 and August 1998, representing more than 23 per cent of the population. A total of 1.9 million users — 45 per cent — access the Internet from home and a further 1.9 million at work [NUA 2003]. These figures are compelling and indicate business opportunity. At least we believe so.

'Regarding e-commerce, an IDC report mentions that revenues are projected to grow from $127.3 million last year to $16 billion in 2002. In IDC's report, entitled "Internet commerce and usage in Australia, 1997–2002", it is reported that the individual online shopper in the business, education and government sectors will increase their spending to $7600 by the year 2002. For the same period, IDC say shopping from home will show spectacular growth, as confidence in secure transactions increases. An increase of 300 per cent to the year 2002 is forecast. Meanwhile the first Australian Netbuyers Report shows that of the 650 buyers surveyed, 96 per cent had bought from Australian websites [NUA 2003]. And indeed we have more detail like this. There is enough here to indicate that this might indeed be a business opportunity for us.

'Some weeks ago I gave this general data plus our own market research to Pierre Laplace, our management accountant, and he has modelled future e-commerce take-up in our industry. We have been a lot more conservative than the ABS, IDC and some of the forecasts of the major consultancies. We believe that the take-up of e-commerce in Australia will be much slower than many industry watchers predict. People will take time to feel comfortable and secure about buying online. So we predict a slow but steady growth in e-commerce over the next ten years. Our estimates, although very approximate, are that we should be able to achieve 15 per cent of our revenues from e-commerce by 2003. Pierre thinks that I am being very optimistic with its estimates. He, I feel I must tell you (since many of you respect

Pierre's rather sober forecasting), predicts that we will reach only 7 or 8 per cent of revenues from e-commerce by 2003. However, based on my particular implementation of e-commerce, I believe we will reach 15 per cent. The basis of my optimism is my belief that we should provide very good e-commerce customer service.

'Our e-commerce customer service will include a generous returns policy, good packing and packaging of the books, and efficient and timely delivery of the books. We will, of course, have a well-designed and easy-to-navigate website. Indeed, we will try to make the website interesting, informative and even educational with respect to Australian books. For example, we will feature articles by well-known Australian authors and literary critics.

'To keep the cost of our new Internet venture low, we will try to manage the e-commerce activities with only one new additional staff member who will be dedicated to e-commerce activities. All other staff members will help out, as needed, with the e-commerce activities, including answering emails, packaging the books for transport and so on. I will go further into this later with each of you individually. Hopefully, in the future, when the e-commerce venture succeeds, there should be more senior positions opening up for some of you in that part of our company. We are keen for everyone to grow, develop and eventually profit from this new initiative.'

From 1998 onwards, the e-commerce activities of Black Swan Books grew slowly but positively. By 2003, revenues from e-commerce were between 9 and 10 per cent, somewhat more than Pierre Laplace had predicted, but much less than the revenues expected by Godfrey Hardy.

During the last few years, as e-commerce activity grew larger, some problems had begun to be evident. Some large orders (such as thirty to forty copies of a particular book) had been received from North American, European and Asian universities that were studying Australian literature. However, the people doing the ordering often wanted substantial amounts of advice and information on various books and authors and often requested telephone support. The hours that were convenient to them for direct dialogue were not covered by Black Swan Books, despite some advertising on the website that indicated quality service, including advice for customers. Furthermore some universities ordering books were interested in inspecting information on a large range of books in a particular time period and speciality, such as late nineteenth-century children's books. To make their choice of texts and references for their students they wished to have a larger range of books available than Black Swan Books kept. They had also asked for more reviews and critiques. Indeed, some universities had indicated that deeper and more informative reviews would be appreciated. (They had also intended asking students to use websites like Black Swan's for browsing and gathering information for research.) Enquiries such as those from overseas universities reminded Godfrey Hardy and his staff that they were now dealing in a global marketplace where substantial ordering could come from small niche markets.

In the last year or so, the informal arrangements for e-commerce had come under some strain. Ingrid Daubechies, who was the e-commerce specialist for Black Swan Books, was now occupied full-time on answering emails and in dealing with accounting and financial information for the e-commerce activity. (A very elementary invoicing and accounting system was used for e-commerce, and all information

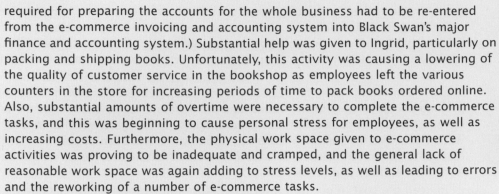

required for preparing the accounts for the whole business had to be re-entered from the e-commerce invoicing and accounting system into Black Swan's major finance and accounting system.) Substantial help was given to Ingrid, particularly on packing and shipping books. Unfortunately, this activity was causing a lowering of the quality of customer service in the bookshop as employees left the various counters in the store for increasing periods of time to pack books ordered online. Also, substantial amounts of overtime were necessary to complete the e-commerce tasks, and this was beginning to cause personal stress for employees, as well as increasing costs. Furthermore, the physical work space given to e-commerce activities was proving to be inadequate and cramped, and the general lack of reasonable work space was again adding to stress levels, as well as leading to errors and the reworking of a number of e-commerce tasks.

'Isn't it about time we became more professional about our e-commerce business processes — both financial and operational — and integrated them with all the rest of the business?' Pierre Laplace was always muttering something like this during the past year.

A number of employees agreed with him, but until now Godfrey Hardy had been extremely sensitive about e-commerce costs. 'This is not going to be another dotcom waste of money,' he used to say in a threatening kind of way. 'This is a very careful and prudent business initiative.'

Pierre Laplace had been doing more than getting irritated about the lack of professionalism with respect to e-commerce. He had sought and obtained Godfrey Hardy's support to employ a local information systems academic, David Hilbert, to investigate Black Swan's business, with a particular focus on the e-commerce activities, and he was asked to recommend improvements to the e-commerce operations. Pierre had warned David that given Godfrey Hardy's views on e-commerce, the improvement should be economically justified.

David Hilbert had made it clear that he wanted to do a broad analysis first. Then, after discussions with Godfrey, Pierre and Ingrid, this broad analysis would form the basis for more detailed and complete analysis later. After two weeks of investigation, David had prepared an initial analysis of the issues, problems and challenges regarding the e-commerce venture.

David presented his initial report sitting across the table from Godfrey Hardy, Pierre Laplace and Ingrid Daubechies in the now crowded and cramped lecture area on the third floor. Books ordered via the website and now ready for packing and shipping were stacked in all sorts of places around this area.

David began his presentation. 'You really need a clear vision for your e-commerce activity. One possibility is a positive and significant commitment to e-commerce as an important sales channel for your business. Other visions are possible, such as a website functioning as a sales catalogue only. Such a vision, of course, would involve a phase-down of the current e-commerce activities.

'An issue bound up with your vision for e-commerce is whether to continue with your general books on the third floor. One future for you is one where you focus on becoming a specialist Australian literature, culture, travel etc. bookshop, catering for the West Australian market face-to-face and a global market via e-commerce. With this option, I think you should seriously consider closing your general books area and putting the resources into improving the Australian books specialisation — both face-to-face and online.

'Of course, you need to do a marketing analysis regarding this vision, particularly of the online aspect. This marketing analysis needs to assess the prospects for you in the Australian books specialisation, both face-to-face and online. The marketing analysis of the face-to-face aspects would be a routine marketing analysis. Many consultancies could carry this out for you. With regard to your prospects online, the marketing analysis might include a general survey and analysis of online buying, particularly of Australian books. It may also include some focus groups of your current customers to provide a more in-depth analysis of online buying behaviour, particularly of your customer group.

'The whole area of market analysis (including the analysis of online buying behaviour and online buying trends) is a new one for information systems academics like myself. I think you should go to a marketing specialist for help with this. Dr Hendrik Lorentz, in the marketing department at my university, might be an appropriate person to help you, since he is a marketing academic who has specialised in Internet-based business. I know that he has been involved in considerable consulting regarding online retailing. For my part, however, I would simply note that e-commerce seems to be marching slowly but surely onwards and upwards, and will probably peak in five to ten years from now at . . . well . . . most experts would be guessing . . . but let's suppose at between 10 per cent to 15 per cent of retail — depending to some extent on what you are selling. Books may be near 15 per cent in ten years.

'So the broad trend of e-commerce looks good, and this is a positive if your business in the future is to depend heavily on e-commerce. I would add further that a quick intuitive examination of the competitive space also looks good for you. Of the three other well-known online bookstores, Aussie Bookshop (www.aussiebookshop.com), Aussie Books (www.Aussiebooks.com.au) and the Australian Online Bookshop (www.bookworm.com.au), only the Australian Online Bookshop specialises in Australian books and includes the categories of Australian adult and children's literature as well as Australian history and culture. The Aussie Bookshop has a travel/environment focus, whereas it is difficult to discern the focus of Aussie Books. The few reviews (as distinct from fairly bland "descriptions" of books' contents) that are on the Australian Online Bookshop are done by the owner and his family, rather than professional literary critics, so there is a place for a "quality" literary approach using professional critics and authors to be taken up by Black Swan Books.

'Another area of concern and potential improvement is your website. At present, it is well designed, functional and, indeed, attractively presented. However, you wish to gain and hold the quality end of the Australian books market, both online and offline. Now, if you are to compare your online business with world's best practice, then the exemplar is Amazon.com. Amazon has a number of features that you ought to consider in a careful cost/benefit analysis. Overall, Amazon.com has a personalised and relationship approach to online selling. For example, customers can establish "Wish Lists" of books, so that relatives and friends can see the books the customer is keen to get and perhaps purchase one of them for a birthday or Christmas present. These "Wish Lists" also record details of the customer's desired books as a convenient small database of favourite titles for future purchase.

'Another excellent personalisation and relationship feature of Amazon.com's website is "Recommended Books". Based on an analysis of a customer's purchase behaviour, "Wish List" creation and website viewing behaviour generally, recommendations of books for purchase are made to customers. These recommended books are displayed in a part of the website that is easy to access, and new recommendations generally appear each time the customer enters the website. Amazon.com has an excellent reputation for making very shrewd recommendations that are very close to customers' interests. Amazon.com does this through an approach called "collaborative filtering", which bases a person's recommendations on the purchases of customers with a similar online profile. Of course, this approach requires a database of customers that includes their purchase behaviour and details of website behaviour as well. This is a very sophisticated technique, but it is also a very powerful technique in establishing a relationship with online customers. In addition to personalised recommendations, when a customer is viewing a book, there is a part of the screen indicating that "Customers who bought this book also bought..." Thus, as a customer is searching through various book titles, they are also offered other titles that are likely to be of interest. This is more than a simple sales tactic if those other titles really help the customer to find books of interest.

'Yet another feature that is valued by customers of Amazon.com is the "Customer Reviews". Customers can rate the books they have read from one star to five stars and can upload reviews. If you visit Amazon.com, you'll find that many of these reviews are very good guides to the content, style etc. of the book. The "Customer Reviews" are in addition to, not in place of, the editorial and other reviews provided by the book publishers and other experts.

'Amazon.com has also gone some distance to recreating online some of the activities that customers value in browsing in bookshops. For example, in the feature called "Look Inside", a customer can view the front cover of the book, the table of contents, portions of the text, and the index and back cover. Given the personalised book recommendations, the customer reviews, and the "Look Inside" features, Amazon.com could be argued to present a customer with a better "bookshop experience" than many traditional bricks and mortar bookshops offer. Given that this experience is consistently available twenty-four hours a day and seven days a week, no wonder Amazon.com has a large number of dedicated customers.

'So there are a number of website features that I think you need to examine in detail. You need to determine how the particular feature fits with your vision and hence what benefits the feature would have for your business. Of course, the benefits will be somewhat intangible and hence your analysis will have to cope with that. You then have to match the costs of establishing the feature with those benefits that you estimate you will receive from having the feature, and then make a decision. I suspect that such a decision needs a lot of intuition and qualitative judgements. It is not going to simply fall out of a lot of accounting numbers!

'Further to this, I think you also need to revisit both your e-commerce business processes and your e-commerce logistics. With respect to your e-commerce business processes, you need to think through the issues of establishing efficient processes as well as the issues of integrating those processes with the rest of the business, where it is sensible and effective to do so. I suspect you need to integrate e-commerce with the rest of your business and integrate the e-commerce processes with the traditional business processes, right through from purchasing stock to invoicing and accounting. With respect to logistics, you need to audit the performance of your outsourced distribution activities. Perhaps in doing so you could even look at outsourcing the packing of the books before transport.

'What I have reported here, really, is some general considerations, including the need for a clear and vivid vision of the future. What I think you need to do now is to use my report as a framework for a more detailed analysis.'

Godfrey Hardy thanked David Hilbert for his broad-based analysis of the e-commerce opportunity. There was, however, quite a lot more work to do before an implementable strategy for the future could be established.

Questions

1. Visit Amazon.com's website and review the features mentioned in the case. Which features do you think would help Black Swan Books? In your answer be sure to consider (at least) the following:
   - Wish Lists
   - Recommended Books
   - customer rating and reviewing
   - Look Inside.

   Are the above features necessary for Black Swan Books' success as an online retailer?

2. Describe, review and critique David Hilbert's analysis of the future for Black Swan Books. Do you think his approach is adequate? Are there any issues, problems or challenges he has neglected?

3. Use the framework for e-commerce described in the chapter to identify the major issues, problems and challenges for Black Swan's e-commerce venture.

   Does the set of issues, problems and challenges from this analysis match with the concerns identified by David Hilbert?

4. If you were Godfrey Hardy, would you go ahead with axing the general books part of Black Swan Books? Why or why not?

   Would you go ahead with the online opportunity? How thoroughly and vigorously would you pursue the online opportunity?

5. Suppose Godfrey Hardy decides to pursue the online opportunity vigorously with a view to obtaining 20 per cent of Black Swan Books' revenues from e-commerce within five years. Should Godfrey plan to build and develop some internal IT capability? If so, would it be appropriate to leave the IT outsourced to the e-Business Professionals (or some other outsourcing vendor)?

chapter 5

Organisational transformation enabled by information technology and the Internet

learning objectives

After reading this chapter, you should be able to:

- understand how IT, the Internet and associated technologies are driving change and transformation in contemporary organisations
- understand the nature and importance of organisational transformation, and success factors in implementing change
- appreciate and apply a framework to support organisational transformation
- appreciate the benefits of a process view of organisations and the role of information technology in supporting processes
- understand the role of enterprise resource planning systems as drivers of change
- appreciate the need to take a holistic approach to the implementation of enterprise resource planning systems.

chapter overview

This chapter considers the nature of substantial organisational change (or organisational transformation) and provides a framework to support the process of designing and integrating a diverse range of elements required for any successful organisational transformation. The framework is based on the idea that successful and productive organisational transformations will be based on the elements of strategy, people and culture, processes, technology, and structure and systems. Organisational transformation will not be therefore limited to an overly rationalistic focus on, say, technology and/or process.

This chapter outlines the value of an IT-enabled process focus — provided, of course, that it is part of a balanced approach, as mentioned above. The advantages of a process view of an organisation are examined. These advantages include a focus on the customer as the end point of processes, the attainment of a 'single view of the customer' and a strategic clarity of working with core process maps.

The chapter then examines the phenomenon of enterprise resource planning (ERP) systems and the organisational transformations brought about by the adoption and implementation of such enterprise-wide systems. A plea is again made for a balanced and holistic approach to such transformations.

ERP systems are seen to redesign the 'back office' or internal information systems that enable and power the internal operations of an enterprise. Furthermore, ERP systems are becoming web-enabled, and this, together with their reliable and comprehensive 'back office' functionality, makes them an excellent basis from which to launch interorganisational systems, such as supply chain management and customer relationship management systems, that are appropriately integrated with the 'back office' systems, such as accounting, purchasing, manufacturing and so on.

Introduction

Information technology, together with the Internet and associated technologies, is facilitating and/or driving some quite profound changes in organisations. Many of those changes affect core operational **business processes** and therefore the way work is done within an organisation. In this chapter, some of those changes and transformations are explored. The argument is developed that if an organisation is to utilise Internet technologies effectively, to avail itself of the many advantages of e-business and to exploit these IT investments to their full extent, then they are likely to have to change or transform some of their existing business processes and activities, both internal and external to the organisation.

Consider a simple example. Previously, if you wanted to buy a new car, you might phone a car dealership and speak to a salesperson, or you might simply walk in and deal with sales staff in person. Business processes were designed to handle these scenarios. Once the car dealership goes online, however, you have the additional option of contacting the organisation via email. Possibilities do not change only for the customer, however. The organisation must also develop new processes and hence new reward mechanisms and structures to encourage sales staff to deal with incoming email enquiries in an appropriate manner. Furthermore, there is no historical basis on which to do this: no one has years of experience to draw on in defining such processes and rewarding appropriate behaviour.

This situation is being repeated throughout organisations in a variety of contexts. Procurement and purchasing activities in organisations can now be partly or completely performed via the Internet in some circumstances. There have been important changes to the way in which knowledge workers, particularly professional case-based workers, such as consultants and social workers, are able to store, retrieve and share information relevant to their jobs. The main point to consider in this chapter is that it is IT and the Internet that are facilitating and driving these changes. If organisations are to utilise the potential of these technologies effectively, then understanding the nature and process of transformation is important in developing an understanding of how to leverage the power of available technology.

Transformation defined

Before proceeding, it is important to ensure that there is a shared understanding of the notion of 'transformation'. Consider the following definitions:

> The process of transformation is ongoing, permeates the entire organization, and represents a sharp break from the past. The break is a major difference between transformation and simple reform. While reform is an attempt to go

down the same path more efficiently, transformation involves the development or discovery of entirely new paths. (Garfield 1992)

Garfield (1992) associates the size or scope of the change as a distinguishing feature of transformation. Transformation is therefore not just about seeking efficiencies, although clearly greater efficiency could be an outcome of transformation. It is about seeing and doing things differently or seizing new opportunities. Arguably, the Internet offers possibilities for new ways of working and operating and, at times, of repositioning an organisation in terms of its industry position and the nature of its operations, and hence might facilitate organisational change in an organisation.

> While the goal of all transformation is to improve performance, many efforts to improve performance are not transformational...to qualify as corporate transformation, a majority of individuals in an organization must change their behavior...the difference is palpable. (Blumenthal & Haspeslagh 1994, p. 101)

Blumenthal and Haspeslagh (1994) take a slightly different perspective from Garfield (1992) in their definition. They stress the importance of behavioural change in organisational transformation. Thus transformation must involve not only new ways of acting and discovering new opportunities. It must also result in a change in the ways of thinking, doing and behaving for a majority of the organisation's members.

> Transformation implies a change in form, not function. Transformation is therefore not a problem-solving experience, it is a process of creating a new context of existence. Transformational change demands change in both context and content...The content of any business includes the legacy systems, structures, practices and physical configurations that dictate how processes function ...Context comprises the deeply embedded business models and mindsets that drive organizations...The transformation of any business comes face-to-face with the enormous barrier of contextual change. (Wentz 2000, p. 27)

The concepts included in the first two definitions seem to come together in the ideas of Wentz (2000). Thus Wentz (2000) would assert that transformation involves more than relatively superficial changes to processes and procedures, or bottom-up, evolutionary changes to content involving re-engineering or innovation in terms of business processes, by relying on new technologies. It should also embrace fundamental changes to the ways of thinking and the vision of the organisation, or top-down, revolutionary changes to context involving creating a new organisational vision and rethinking business models and business strategy (Dutta & Manzoni 1999).

The key points to think of, then, in understanding **organisational transformation** are that:

- The change must involve a substantial break from previous ways of acting. It will likely involve discovering and developing new opportunities and new ways of doing things.
- The change must permeate through and impact on the behaviour of a majority of organisational members.
- The change will involve creating new systems, procedures and structures that not only enable and dictate how new processes function but will also impact on the deeply embedded business models and understandings that drive the organisation.

It is the contention of the authors that IT and the Internet are at the heart of corporate transformation in current business contexts. IT and the Internet are driving and enabling changes to both the content and the context of modern organisations; or perhaps, to de-emphasise the role of technology a little, we could say that IT and the Internet form a significant part of the mix of ingredients causing the impetus to change, particularly in operationally based organisational transformations. These concepts will be further explored throughout this chapter.

Types of transformation

Three major types of transformation can be identified (Blumenthal & Haspeslagh 1994). These are strategic transformation, operational transformation and corporate self-renewal. Each will be briefly considered.

▶ Strategic transformation

Strategic transformation is essentially concerned with large-scale change with a view to retaining or achieving a significant competitive advantage. Such change might have been necessitated by changes in customer demand, the hyper-competitiveness of contemporary business environments or technological advances. Strategic transformation is likely to involve redefining the vision and mission of the organisation, which in itself will imply a need to reassess organisational goals and objectives. This type of transformation is also likely to imply a need to develop or obtain new competencies and capabilities, which must then be harnessed to the achievement of corporate objectives and to taking advantage of perceived opportunities in the marketplace.

In many senses, this type of transformation could be the most profound and disruptive for organisations. In circumstances where the Internet has brought about rethinking of an organisation's vision and/or mission, where organisational goals and objectives are reassessed and so on, then it could be argued that the Internet and IT are enabling strategic transformation. Merrill Lynch and Charles Schwab are both companies that in recent times could be said to have undergone a strategic transformation, enabled by the advent of the Internet. Australia Post is another organisation that has dramatically transformed itself in the past few years, moving from a bureaucratic government instrumentality concerned with the delivery of mail to a truly innovative e-business, with strengths in mail and parcel delivery, courier services, logistics and warehousing, and bill payment.

▶ Operational transformation

IT and, particularly in recent years, Internet technologies can often bring about a transformation in the operations of an organisation. Appropriate and skilful application of technology can result in substantially reduced operating costs, can reduce the time to market and increase throughput, and can increase quality and service levels; all of which contribute to dramatic improvements in efficiency. These improvements are often achieved through re-engineering or innovation in terms of business processes, supporting or enabling these processes with appropriate IT, and accompanying these changes with carefully redefined roles and responsibilities, which implies a need for new competencies and capabilities. Performance standards and measures are also redefined so that the new required behaviours are fostered and developed.

It is likely that changes to business strategy might well be driving such operational transformations. As many of these transformations to operations result in cross-functional business processes, then an important aspect of this type of change could well be the development and use of effective cross-functional teams supported by IT. Many banks, for example, are using the Internet and IT to achieve operational efficiencies and substantial cost reductions.

⟩ Corporate self-renewal

It might be tempting to think from the previous two types of transformation that large-scale, one-off transformations are all that is required to reposition an organisation and/or to seek improved operational efficiencies. However, in this era of rapid change and uncertainty, long-term success requires the ability to change and adapt continuously. The objective of corporate self-renewal is to create an organisational environment that is always anticipating, making sense of and responding to environmental and techno-logical change and therefore is able to embrace change on an on-going basis. Toyota is an example of a company that excels at continuously being able to adapt to changing business environments and to learn from experience of adaptation.

Framework for transformation

It is fair to say that these three types of transformation might well differ in terms of the time required to achieve results, the difficulty and challenges of implementing the type of change required, and the type of leadership desirable. However, they are similar in a number of important ways. They are all motivated by a desire to improve organisational performance continuously over time and therefore accept that trans-formation might be a necessity. They all acknowledge that organisations operate in increasingly competitive, turbulent and uncertain environments and that transform-ation might be required to respond effectively to such pressures. They all acknowledge that business success ultimately depends on understanding and delivering on the cus-tomer value proposition and, in modern contexts, recognise that technological advance might be a key component in ultimately delivering value to customers.

The process of transformation, irrespective of type, shares many similarities and could be said to be characterised by a relentless focus on rethinking and renewing aspects of the organisation with the express aim of making substantial overall improvements to organisational performance. Transformation involves questioning the vision of the organisation and, in many cases, of redefining that vision in light of existing or anticipated changes in environment. This might also be accompanied by a questioning and examination of the values that guide organisational behaviour, with a view to reassessing the type of organisation that is desired and required to be com-petitive and effective. At times, it could also involve considering whether the nature of the business in which the organisation is involved has changed. This is particularly the case since the advent of the Internet, which has enabled organisations to repo-sition themselves in terms of what business they are in in quite fundamental ways at times. Transformation will also likely involve a revisiting of organisational mission, goals and objectives, to ensure that all individuals, teams and business units are united around a common theme or themes.

The process of transformation must also be supported by a sound knowledge of what constitutes the core business of an organisation. That knowledge is composed of two types. *Domain knowledge* refers to the knowledge an organisation has about its business environment, industry trends, the effects of technological change and so on. *Process knowledge* refers to a knowledge an organisation has about its inventory of core processes: where strengths, weaknesses and opportunities for improvement currently lie, for example. For transformation to be successful and effective, both domain and process knowledge needs to be excellent, and managerial thinking needs to be focused on opportunities for change and improvement.

The following framework is offered to support the process of transformation in organisations (see figure 5.1). The framework is premised on the view that organisations are composed of interconnected dimensions from which synergies will be accrued only if they are kept in balance with one another. If a need for transformational change is recognised, then it is vital to acknowledge and balance the multiple dimensions of organisations. In other words, a change in strategy, for example, will imply a need for a change in the structure and systems of an organisation, a change in processes and in the technological support for those structures and systems, and a change in competencies and capabilities (i.e. the people) and the culture of the organisation. Elements in this framework will be considered in more detail.

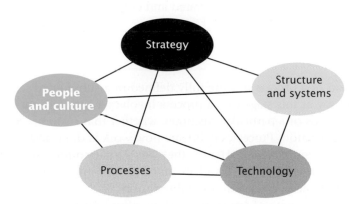

Figure 5.1 ▶ A framework for organisational transformation

Source ▶ derived from Dutta and Manzoni 1999, pp. 6, 14.

▶ Strategy

As strategy has been the subject of the previous two chapters, readers should now be familiar with the concept. What is implied in thinking about transformational change is establishing a customer-oriented vision and mission that will engender and support long-term success, and articulating strategies by which this can be achieved. Clearly, this affects and is affected by an understanding of the external business environment in which the organisation operates. In addition, it must be influenced by an appreciation of the internal resources, competencies and capabilities an organisation has at its disposal. From an e-business perspective, understanding and evaluating the IT infrastructure is essential in understanding internal capabilities. It seems fair to assert that most transformational changes will involve a significant change to organisational vision, mission and/or strategies.

People and culture

This dimension of the framework considers the organisation's human resources and its culture. Its inclusion in this framework suggests that when organisational transformation is undertaken, it is likely that changes in the organisation's skill sets and knowledge might be required, as well as a change in culture to adopt new practices, procedures and processes and to become more customer-centric in orientation and behaviour. Included here would be a consideration of the shared values, experiences and common goals of organisational members and the lessons that have accrued throughout the organisation through surviving and competing in the external environment and from dealing with issues of internal integration.

Transformation is often required so that there is a widespread recognition of the need for flexibility and adaptability, there is acceptance of the need to adopt and implement corporate goals, and there is appreciation of the importance of change in dynamic and turbulent business environments. A recognition of the importance of knowledge and learning to corporate survival and sustained competitive advantage is also important.

A key component in achieving the desired changes in behaviour might involve revisiting corporate reward systems and incentive programs, so that desired behaviour is rewarded and people feel motivated and empowered to succeed in the transformed enterprise.

Processes

The notion of a process is more fully defined in a subsequent section of this chapter: suffice to say at this stage that a process involves a sequence of activities designed to fulfil the needs of a particular customer, whether that customer is external or internal to the organisation. Processes delineate how work is done and how and when action needs to be implemented. Hence, they are a vital component of implementing an organisation's strategic vision and are an essential component in ensuring the efficient and effective use of all organisational resources.

Part of the activity of transformation involves identifying core business processes, those that are central to the delivery of the customer value proposition, as often those are the processes from which maximum leverage can be achieved through change. This might involve streamlining or innovation or becoming more customer focused, often through the application of information technology and Internet-based technologies. Desired outcomes might also be achieved through a consideration of and change to the administration and management of these processes.

Technology

Technology plays a vital role in most organisations. It is pivotal to the generation, transfer, management and use of information and knowledge in most modern organisations. It supports and enables key business processes, and it provides tools that support the activities of most of the workforce. More recently, IT and the Internet have been applied directly to support and enhance key relationships with suppliers and customers. Hence, technology in general, but IT in particular, is often at the heart of most corporate transformations.

In considering the transformation that might be required to the technology component, it is essential that IT requirements be driven by business objectives and requirements. IT solutions must support organisational goals and change initiatives. This will often be achieved if a successful and effective partnership can be developed between the business and IT staff. Integration of existing fragmented systems might be essential to make full use of the capability of IT and to leverage the capabilities of new technologies like the Internet, particularly so when leveraging the capability of creating electronic interorganisational linkages.

▶ Structure and systems

It is not unusual for substantial changes to be required to **organisational structures** and systems when a major change effort is undertaken. Organisational structures and systems (both formal and informal) give an indication of reporting lines and therefore of responsibilities and accountabilities. They also offer insights into the way decision-making is conducted in an organisation and into patterns of communication among members of the organisation, and hence are a vital component in the implementation of organisational strategy. Structures and systems are vital in enabling the necessary communication and knowledge transfer to occur for strategy to be implemented, for appropriate service to be offered to customers and generally for the realisation of the customer value proposition. Dysfunctional structures and systems, however, can and sometimes do exactly the opposite.

In recent years, it has often been the case that organisational transformation has been accompanied by a move towards flatter organisational structures, which implies a need to change lines of communication and reporting structures. In addition, however, such flatter structures are often accompanied by the introduction of cross-functional, team-based approaches to work. Such teams often support and take responsibility for a core business process in its entirety, irrespective of where it crosses functional boundaries. Team-based approaches to the organisation of work can result in matrix structures, whereby individual members report both to their process owner and to their functional manager. Inevitably, this means that jobs must be redefined, and it might imply a need for additional education or training. It often requires managers willing to both empower and delegate to their subordinates, it requires a need for excellent and open communication, and it certainly requires the commitment of management if the new structures and systems are to prove successful.

Successful transformation

These elements — strategy, people and culture, processes, technology, and structures and systems — do not operate in isolation from one another. Changes made in one area necessarily influence all the others, and a key to successful transformation is recognising the scale of the change involved and in making the appropriate changes to all elements in this framework to maintain balance in the organisation. For transformation to be successful, however, there must be a degree of skill and accuracy in identifying why and where the organisation perceived a need to change. Radical change in response to the 'wrong' problem will not help an organisation accomplish its objectives. Not only must the right changes in all elements be identified, but success is also contingent on implementing and institutionalising the desired changes in all dimensions. The changes must suit the organisation's vision, mission and objectives, and must result in the outcomes desired by senior management. This is not a simple undertaking, and hence an organisation needs managers with skill in leading and implementing change. Part of that skill will be the ability to create conditions that motivate others to change and behave in desired new ways.

In a post-Internet world, many organisations have been forced to undertake substantial change programs in order to equip themselves with the flexibility and responsiveness required to be competitive in this new networked environment. IT has been at the heart of these transformations, and the implementation of this technology has required a critical review of core organisational processes. Obviously the other elements in the transformation framework require consideration and are also changing. It is difficult to think of the implementation of IT without realising that a change in strategy might have driven the investment, and in also recognising that the skills and culture might change, and the structure and systems are also likely to change to accommodate new ways of working and interacting with trading partners, and so on. In the sections that follow, however, it is proposed to focus on the types of internal transformations that IT is bringing about in organisations. Before doing so, it is important to understand the notion of a process and the importance of process innovation or re-engineering.

Process innovation and re-engineering

Processes take on an important dimension when it is realised that without effective and innovative business processes, IT innovation is unlikely to deliver all the potential benefits of that investment. Replicating a manual process within a modern computer-based information system will rarely produce the types of results that could be made possible by a more thorough understanding of the best way to exploit the potential of the technology. The reason for this is quite simple. Many existing business processes developed in a somewhat ad hoc way before the introduction of large-scale introduction of computers. Furthermore, they might well have originated at a time of stability and growth in the business environment. By contrast, organisations today are faced with hyper-competition, turbulence and uncertainty, and managers increasingly recognise that the successful exploitation of modern technologies driving innovative business processes is essential to their future growth and development. This is echoed in the following quote from Hammer and Champy (1993, p. 24), who argue: 'Companies created to thrive on mass production, stability and growth need to be re-engineered to succeed in a world where customers, competition and change demand flexibility and quick response.'

Consider the following definitions of a business process or processes:

- 'groups of logically related decisions and activities required to manage the resources of a business' (Turban, McLean & Wetherbe 2002, p. 343)
- 'a set of interrelated work activities characterised by specific inputs and value-added tasks that produce customer-focused outputs. Business processes consist of horizontal work flows that cut across several departments or functions.' (Sethi & King 1998, p. 4)
- 'activities which contribute to the delivering of a final product or service and creation of a satisfied customer' (Sadler 1995, p. 111)
- 'an activity carried out as a series of steps, which produces a specific result... processes are groups of actions that have a common purpose, and that purpose advances the business in some way' (Morris & Brandon 1994, p. 38)
- 'any activity, or group of activities, that takes an input, adds value to it, and provides an output to an external or internal customer' (Obeng & Crainer 1994).

Essentially these definitions agree that a process consists of a series of purposeful activities, which contribute to the delivery of a product or service to a customer, whether that customer is an external customer purchasing a good or service from the organisation or an internal customer (for example, a colleague who relies on another worker to produce something in order that he/she can do their job). Information technology not only often implies a change in the type and nature of activities performed, but it might also now remove the need for the physical and temporal collocation of workers in order for a good to be adequately produced or a service to be adequately performed.

Recently Hammer (2001, p. 85) has emphasised the potential interorganisational nature of business processes: 'Companies are starting to see business processes — and manage them — as they truly are: chains of activities that are performed by different organizations.' Hammer (2001, p. 82) clearly thinks that the interorganisational view of business processes is important. To quote him further: 'You've cut the waste out of your own operations. Now, you face an even tougher challenge: streamlining the processes you share with other companies.'

Why focus on processes?

An organisation's long-term survival is contingent on its ability to deliver value to its customers. It may do so by means of innovations in terms of the products and services it offers its customers, and it can also do so by means of innovation in terms of its core business processes, which enable the organisation to achieve efficiency and effectiveness gains. A simple example can help illustrate this point.

Many banks, for example, organise themselves around the products and services they offer. In the example in figure 5.2 (p. 134), the same customer might have a home loan, one or more credit cards and one or more insurance policies all organised by the same bank. Potentially in future that same customer might purchase other services, such as travel, financial planning, retirement planning, and so on. Such a situation might be organisationally very neat and convenient for the bank itself. However, from the customer's perspective, it could be problematic, because it is sometimes difficult to talk to one person about *all* aspects of his/her business with the bank. And even from the bank's perspective, when they attempt to find out everything about a particular customer, or to capture a single view of the customer, they often find that

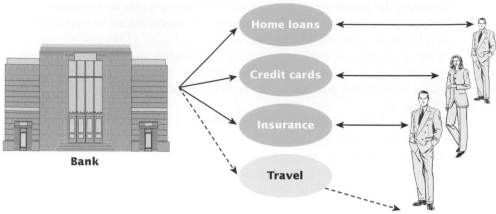

Figure 5.2 ▶ A product view of a bank

their information systems have become a constraint on their ability to do so. Systems, structures, processes and technology have all been designed around a product view rather than a process or customer-centric view. Banks are not the only examples: many organisations that organise themselves and their systems around product or service lines can experience difficulties of this sort. Taking a product view can seem very logical from an internal perspective, but it can mean that it is much more difficult to focus on the end customer.

Relying solely on product improvement and innovation can also become exhausting for a company. It requires a tremendous amount of creativity to constantly come up with innovative ideas that are also marketable! The other major problem with focusing on products is that they are typically easy to copy, and hence any source of competitive advantage gained through the launch of a new product or service lasts a comparatively short time. (Think of some instances in your daily life when products or services have been quickly copied by a competitor organisation. TV ads are a great source of information for this!)

There are two reasons why a process focus could be a better option for an organisation. First, a process has a customer as its end point. This means that it is entirely natural for a process focus to focus on your end customer. From the customer's perspective, this should result in better service. From an organisation's perspective, it offers opportunities to understand clearly the needs, wants and preferences of its customers, and it gives the organisation a better opportunity of accurately identifying who its profitable and important customers are. In previous chapters, it has been argued that becoming more customer-centric is essential if an organisation is to cope with the competitive pressures and uncertainties in modern business environments.

Second, because processes are largely internal to the organisation, they are much more difficult to copy than products or services, and therefore might provide a more sustainable source of competitive advantage. From a management perspective, a process view emphasises how an organisation satisfies customers across functional boundaries, and hence it provides an understanding of how different sections of an organisation operate in conjunction with one another in creating value for customers. This is emphasised by Cats-Baril and Thompson (1997, p. 265), who write: 'The key

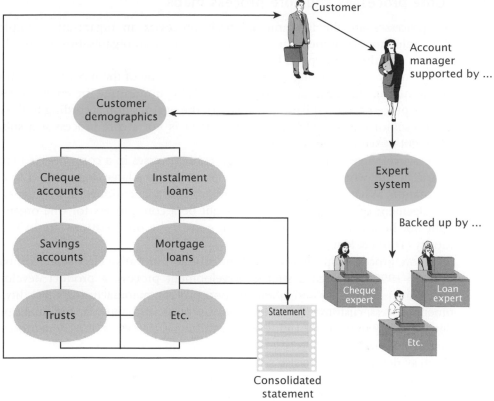

Figure 5.3 ▶ A process view of a bank

Source ▶ Turban, McLean and Wetherbe 2002, p. 370.

to long term organizational success is to identify a set of processes that deliver an output that is needed by a given customer, and then to implement those processes in the most efficient way possible.'

Why re-engineer processes?

Laudon and Laudon (1999, p. 339) write: 'Re-engineering involves radically rethinking the flow of work and the business processes used to produce goods and services with a mind to radically reduce the costs of business. Using IT, organizations can rethink and streamline their business processes to improve speed, service and quality.' Perhaps the most famous definition of **business process re-engineering** (BPR) is that of Hammer and Champy (1993, p. 32): 'the fundamental rethinking and radical redesign of business processes to achieve dramatic improvements in critical measures of performance such as cost, quality, service, and speed.'

From these definitions, it can be seen that re-engineering is all about rethinking business processes and implementing those processes with the support of the latest IT to achieve business objectives. Most importantly, however, re-engineering processes can allow organisations effectively to use the latest in IT, including the Internet, to improve quality, improve efficiency and reduce cost (with no reduction in output or quality), to improve customer service and responsiveness, and to improve competitiveness.

Core processes and core process maps

Core processes are the fundamental basic processes an organisation employs to deliver value to a customer. The core process map of an organisation shows the core processes and their conceptual linkages.

In a process re-engineering or redesign initiative, one of the most important things a senior management team can do is design and communicate the core process map. The core process map is the process vision of the organisation according to the organisation's senior management. Hence what is or is not a core process is a subjective judgement of senior management.

In practice, there is usually five to eight core processes in a core process map. This tends to be true whether the core process map refers to a large organisation or a small organisation. What turns out to be a core process, as mentioned above, depends on the judgement of management. What might be a core process for one organisation might not be a core process for another, even if the organisations are in the same industry (Dutta & Manzoni 1999).

The core process map for Texas Instruments, an innovative electronics company, in the early 1990s included a strategy development process, a product development process, a customisation design and support process, manufacturing capability development process, customer communications process, and an order fulfilment process. A large brewery in the early 1990s had the following processes in its core process map (see figure 5.4):

- strategy development process
- customer interface process
- integrated supply chain process
- order fulfilment process
- infrastructure and capacity development process (Dutta & Manzoni 1999).

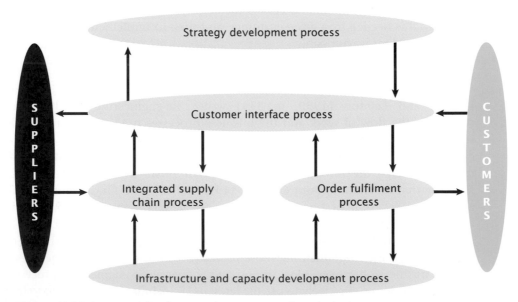

Figure 5.4 ▶ An example of a core process map for a brewery
Source ▶ Dutta and Manzoni 1999, p. 66.

Business process re-engineering

When business process re-engineering (BPR) first emerged in the early 1990s, it was accompanied by phrases like 'fundamental, radical, dramatic change' (Hammer 1990; Davenport 1993; Hammer & Champy 1993). It was very much about challenging assumptions about the nature and type of organisation, the business it was in, the efficacy of existing processes in delivering customer value and so on. It was also very much about becoming more customer-centric and in becoming cross-functional in organisation, and it emphasised the need to exploit the potentialities of modern IT in the achievement of transformational objectives.

In its practical outworkings in organisations, however, re-engineering gained a tarnished reputation in many places, such ambitious change projects were accompanied by high rates of failure, a loss of key employees, a destruction of staff morale, increased stress levels among remaining staff and the like. Hence the radical dramatic change sometimes became known as the 'slash and burn' approach (Mumford & Hendricks 1996), or shorthand for getting rid of every person and activity that was at all possible. However, there have been important lessons and learning from those early days of re-engineering. Peppard (1998) documents many of those lessons, and these are summarised below.

From rhetoric to reality

In practice, re-engineering is nearly always performed on existing business processes, and so the ability to start completely anew is very limited. Nor can the business be closed down for months while the re-engineering activity takes place. Thus, the radical change has tended to be more evolutionary and incremental in implementation, particularly so when confronted with all the political, cultural, organisational and resource constraints of the real world.

From IT as a driver to IT as an enabler

Early writings suggested that IT was driving the re-engineering transformation. History suggests that IT, on its own, is rarely a source of sustainable competitive advantage (Clemens & Row 1991; Mata, Fuerst & Barney, 1995; Powell & Dent-Micallef 1997; Peppard, Lambert & Edwards 2000). Furthermore, as the framework for transformation would suggest (see figure 5.1 and the surrounding discussion), IT on its own cannot bring about successful transformation without significant changes elsewhere. The advent of the Internet and e-commerce, however, brings with it a recognition that new technologies can bring about new ways of working and that both efficiency and effectiveness gains can be achieved by means of carefully implemented IT and other business changes.

From an analytic to a holistic process

As suggested by the framework for transformation (see figure 5.1), simply designing and implementing new processes is unlikely to bring about sustainable transformation. The human, cultural and political dimensions of change must be considered;

so too must the need for new strategies, systems and structures, and innovative uses of technology. The holistic nature of the change process must acknowledge the constraints on change and must also acknowledge the resource constraints in undertakings of this type. Hence, any notions of a quick fix need to be replaced by thinking through the implications of large-scale transformation of all interrelated elements in an organisation.

From an internal process to external networked processes

The advent of e-commerce and e-business have demonstrated clearly to most organisations that they are not islands but rather must view themselves as part of an integrated, mutually advantageous trading network. Competition becomes more focused around one supply chain versus other supply chains in the same industry, and therefore an organisation's competitiveness is derived partly from its internal strategy, skills, structures, processes and technology. However, it is also partly derived from the performance of and interactions with other trading partners in the network (Gulati, Nohria & Zaheer 2000). Notions of organisational boundaries become much more porous and challenge many of the previously held assumptions about organisational structures. IT and the Internet are vital elements in this move to supply chain integration (which is the subject of the following chapter).

From re-engineering an organisation to re-engineering its business

IT and the Internet are also driving quite profound changes in many industries, and contemporary managers must address the issue of how technology could affect the nature, content and context of their business. This simultaneously poses threats and offers opportunities to organisations. Using the Internet for e-commerce, for example, offers opportunities for growth and development, new markets and new channels to customers, among other things. But it also poses threats of disintermediation, new global competition and so on. Re-engineering an organisation might not help if technological change is rendering it obsolete. Hence, re-engineering activities need not only to focus on the organisation level but also to appreciate the role of the organisation in a dynamic trading network, with a view to repositioning if necessary (Gulati, Nohria & Zaheer 2000).

From re-engineering projects to re-engineering capability

The final lesson about re-engineering is that it is folly to conceive of it as a one-off project. The challenge of modern organisations demands an ability to question incessantly, to challenge assumptions, to learn, to adapt and to change, often radically. Organisations need to develop mechanisms that encourage learning and value the need for constant renewal and development. Management, planning and control thus all become activities that promote organisational learning, which is the cornerstone of successful organisational transformation.

ERP systems and organisational transformation

In recent years there has been the growth of another type of IT-driven organisational transformation. It has come about because of the availability of computer software packages offering enterprise-wide suites of integrated systems. These packages of **integrated systems**, offering IS/IT support for business processes right across an enterprise, are known as **enterprise resource planning systems** (ERP) systems.

More than thirty years ago, Dearden wrote against the notion of such a totally integrated supersystem as an ERP system, mainly owing to the limited power and reliability of IS/IT in those days, and owing to the limitations of the systems analysis, design and programming capabilities at that time. Indeed, in 1972, he wrote: 'The notion that a company can and ought to have an expert (or group of experts) create for it a single completely integrated supersystem — an "MIS" — to help it govern every aspect of its activity is absurd' (Dearden 1972, p. 101). Today such integrated supersystems are available in the form of ERP systems.

The promise and attractivity of ERP systems to business is that they offer an integrated IS/IT capability across the whole enterprise. This has long been the dream of CIOs and IT managers. A suite of integrated systems means that information systems can share information and transaction capability across system applications. Thus basic accounting information and transaction capability is directly available to the production planning and scheduling system, which can share information with the inventory system. In turn the inventory system can share information with the sales and purchasing systems. All these systems can share information with the financial evaluation and reporting systems, and so on. There is no rekeying of data to produce management reports. All information necessary for management to carry out evaluation, monitoring and control, forecasting and planning, and so on is up to date and potentially immediately available. Thus, ERP systems provide a fast, reliable, integrated enterprise-wide information architecture for a business, often replacing a set of badly documented, fragmentary legacy systems that are expensive to maintain.

Holistic approach to ERP implementation

Despite the potential of ERP systems to deliver substantial business benefits, the history of ERP implementation efforts is littered with disappointing results (Davenport 1998). Such results, however, are in line with the previous history of disappointing results from IT-driven business projects. If the ERP implementation project is recognised and thought through as an organisational transformation, the prospects of success will increase. Such an approach will involve carefully establishing the objectives of the ERP implementation and how these objectives fit into IS/IT strategy and the business strategy. A holistic approach will also consider the human resource elements of the ERP implementation and the implications for organisational culture. Indeed, integration of the elements of strategy, structure, process and, most importantly, people or human resource management aspects with the implementation project or program will, the authors believe, alleviate many of the problems associated with ERP implementations (Markus & Tanis 2000; Davenport 1998; Adam & O'Doherty 2000).

ERP systems and process re-engineering

ERP systems contain within them an inherent discipline for business processes. They define, to some extent, the manner in which business processes are carried out. Indeed, the vendors of ERP systems assert that their systems embody best practice for the various business processes they support. The ERP systems, it is claimed, have been tried, tested and adapted to the business processes of the world-class companies into which they have previously been implemented. Thus they are designed to enable and support efficient and effective processes, and an advantage a company gains from implementing ERP is the opportunity to re-engineer its processes to embody world's best practice. That at least is the argument of the ERP vendors. Although there is some truth to this argument, the benefits achieved by companies implementing ERP systems depend very largely on the quality of the implementation process and how that process fits with or is aligned to the strategy of the company.

Whether or not world's best practice is available to an organisation implementing an ERP system, there is a need to re-engineer business processes to an extent to fit the enabling software and to develop a business process that can leverage the capabilities of modern IT to a great extent and thus deliver good outcomes for the organisation. There is in fact, in each case, some flexibility in the precise way of carrying out a process in line with the dictates of the software, but the software very broadly shapes the business process. Overall companies implementing ERP software need to consider carefully the way their business processes will work with the software, and plan and carry out such re-engineering as necessary. Of course, it is an excellent opportunity to re-examine processes and to consider their appropriateness to current and future business.

ERP systems and web enablement

Connecting the ERP system to the Internet and Internet-enabling or web-enabling the ERP applications systems can make an ERP system truly enterprise-wide. Employees can access all the information and transaction support that they need via the window of a web browser. The corporate intranet can service all the information needs of employees and blend with the company extranet, which contains links to suppliers and business partners. With appropriate security controls, then, employees have a truly extended enterprise that links processes and transactions seamlessly across organisational boundaries. Beyond the extranet, employees then have access to information worldwide via the Internet. All of this functionality can be available via the Internet-enabled PC on the desktops of employees.

Typical functionality available globally from intranet-enabled ERP systems includes the following:
• the potentially global availability of EIS (executive information systems), DSS (decision support systems) applications and BI (business intelligence) applications

- employee self-service HR applications showing employee pension and benefit information and the like
- communication, distance learning and knowledge management applications, including the ability to share best practices, possibly globally, via streaming video and accompanying detailed graphic and text documents
- collaboration and work flow management applications enabling the creation and communication of new and improved process support applications (Nolan, Porter & Akers 2001).

Typical functionality available globally and from extranet-enabled ERP applications would include the following:

- extranet-based supply chain management including the selection and monitoring of suppliers, Internet-based and value-added network EDI-based purchasing, applications to help with the phasing out of old supply parts and phasing in newly developed supply parts, applications to support collaborative product design and development, and the like
- customer self-help and self-service through the website including such information as how to care for and maintain the company's products, how to repair the company's products, and so on
- e-commerce applications
- marketing via the Internet
- support for sales teams by the Internet (Nolan, Porter & Akers 2001).

The potential and need for these applications are potentially beneficial for all companies, but particularly for global companies.

thinking strategically

GEEC seeks advice in implementing an ERP system

The Global Elevator and Escalator Company (GEEC) is considering implementing an ERP system. It has a presence in fifty-five countries in Europe, North America and Asia. Each country has its own set of information systems and technology. Some systems are common to several countries, but there are many idiosyncrasies and differences. This means that there is a need for IT specialists in each country. GEEC wishes to move to a common IT architecture of software and hardware in each country, with a common set of business processes being supported by a common set of systems. The company intends to have several global IT centres staffed with IT specialists who could, if need be, move between the global centres, working efficiently and effectively in any of the centres. There are tentative plans for three IT centres: one in Europe, one in Asia and the other in North America.

Three experienced IT specialists from Europe have been chosen to plan the ERP system implementation. They have identified two major issues. One issue is that the data in the legacy systems of GEEC is not of the quality needed for the ERP system. In fact, the quality of the data in the legacy systems is poor. Since the legacy systems are, in the main, not integrated, this poor-quality data stays in the

local systems and does not in general permeate other systems, so it currently does not create an insurmountable problem. Furthermore, the local users are very knowledgeable about their local systems and the data, and can deal with and work around the difficulties caused by the bad quality data. However, the situation will not be tenable for the highly integrated enterprise-wide ERP system.

The other major issue the three IT specialists have identified is the need to re-engineer business processes to fit the ERP package so as to avoid modifying the ERP system's source code, a task that they believe will be complex and costly. After several meetings they believe they have established an approach to deal with the process re-engineering difficulties.

The IT specialists believe that the two major issues are the only main issues. They believe that another relevant issue, which they regard as secondary, is end-user training on the relevant screens of the package. Another secondary issue they have identified is the choice of a standard hardware configuration to support the ERP system in each country.

Believing they have identified the major and secondary issues involved in the ERP implementation, they call on you to check their thinking and approach before moving to more detailed planning.

Questions

1. In what ways will an ERP system improve efficiencies for GEEC globally? In your opinion, will the efficiency gains be worth the disruption associated with such a large-scale change initiative?

2. Think about the framework for organisational transformation introduced in figure 5.1. Discuss its implications for managing the introduction of the ERP system at GEEC.

3. GEEC is planning a staged implementation of the ERP, rolling out module by module in one region before moving on to the next region. Which ERP applications or modules offer greater potential to GEEC globally, and therefore which ones would you recommend they focus on in the first instance?

4. What advice would you give them regarding the implementation of an ERP system? Why?

ERP systems and business, and IT strategy

The adoption and implementation of an ERP system is a large and expensive undertaking for a company. Hence it is best for a company to have a clear view of the objectives of such an undertaking. Indeed, it is desirable that the project or program of adopting and implementing an ERP system fits with and is part of the IT strategy of the company, which in turn is aligned with the business strategy.

It is also important to articulate clear objectives for the ERP project or program. It could be that the overall aim is to reduce costs, particularly the cost of maintaining what could be, at present, a fragmentary group of legacy systems. On the other hand, the overall objective could be to establish an enabling IT architecture for future customer relationship management (CRM) and supply chain systems together with other strategic information systems initiatives. A lack of clear objectives will lead to difficulties in planning, designing and carrying out the ERP implementation project in such a way as to achieve measurable success. Clear objectives, backed by appropriate performance measures, together with good evaluation and benefit realisation processes, are essential to motivating and achieving optimal benefits from an ERP implementation project or program.

Given that ERP systems are commercial software packages that are purchased rather than conceived, designed and programmed in-house, the development lifecycle is different. The main tasks become mapping the information and transaction requirements of the organisation on to the processes that are defined and enabled by the software package. The ERP vendors have provided alternatives for the basic business processes and implementing companies can configure the package by choosing the alternative (setting the parameter 'switch') for a particular process that most suits their purposes.

Even when the software package has been optimally configured for the organisation, some re-engineering of the business processes will inevitably be necessary. In total, this re-engineering effort can be considerable. Indeed, this effort often amounts to an organisational transformation, at least at an operational level.

An alternative to re-engineering a company's business processes to fit the ERP system is to reprogram the source code of the ERP system. This is a risky procedure and can, if not planned and considered very carefully, lead to negative and costly consequences (Markus & Tanis 2000; Brehm, Heinzl & Markus 2001). Partly this is owing to the complexity and interconnectedness of ERP systems, and partly this has been attributed to difficulties created with the relationship between a company and the ERP system vendor. When a company purchases and implements an ERP system, of necessity they enter a potentially long-term relationship with the vendor. This is because not only are ERP systems often maintained by the vendor but also they are evolving systems. The vendor develops the system to take advantage of new technological developments, to remedy problems and to give new functionality in terms of the depth and breadth of the business processes and business process options that they support. If a company has altered the source code, they will experience real difficulties and costs when the ERP vendor brings out its new version and begins to lower the support offered to the old package. To avoid these problems, most companies now, after configuring the software appropriately, re-engineer the business processes to fit the configured package, leaving the source code for the ERP vendor to maintain and evolve. Some ERP users groups, of course, pressure ERP vendors into evolving the software in certain directions, adding particular process options and functionality. In this way, organisations can gain some control over the ERP source code and development.

ERP and change management

The overall ERP implementation initiative involves a considerable change management effort. Indeed, given that all functions and areas of the organisation, from marketing and sales to production to accounting and purchasing and so on, will likely be involved in the effort of re-engineering processes and procedures and implementing the new interconnected systems, the company will be involved in what amounts to an organisational transformation, at least at the operational level. Effective executive leadership and management of the human resource elements of the ERP project are most important.

Members of the organisation need an understanding of the rationale and reason for the implementation and its accompanying changes. They need leadership to help design and deal with the re-engineering changes. They also need an understanding of and anticipated involvement with the process of change. Adequate and well-timed training will be necessary, as will careful documentation of the new system procedures. Such considerations are vital to a successful ERP implementation program. Indeed, we can conclude that an ERP implementation program that is, in essence, a well-planned and executed people-oriented change management program alongside the more technical IT elements will very likely be much more successful than a program that is centred on the IT elements alone.

Arguably, ERP systems offer the promise of integration (data being able to flow seamlessly between modules in different functional areas of the organisation), sound business processes, and all the benefits and conveniences that these entail. However, it remains extremely challenging to implement these systems effectively, and it is not uncommon for reports of failures, substantial financial losses and degraded organisational performance to be reported as a result of a failed ERP implementation. The complexity of these systems should not be underrated, as they attempt to integrate many disparate activities and processes within the organisation. They are complex too in the sense that successful implementations will need to find a balance between technology, re-engineered processes, new systems, procedures and organisational structures, business strategy and, perhaps most importantly, between the many different people with a stake in the outcomes of the implementation, the political context of the organisation, and the culture of the organisation. Failures of ERP systems are seldom a failure of the technology itself but rather a failure to take into account the full extent of the complexity of the undertaking when implementing these systems.

Summary

The business possibilities in IT and the Internet often drive or lead to organisational transformation. Indeed such translations may be referred to as e-business transformations. Often in such transformations there is a process focus, and much of the designed change in an organisation is concentrated around the redesign or re-engineering of the business processes of the organisation. Much of the business process re-engineering (BPR) initiatives of the early 1990s were of this type of process-focused transformation.

An overly rationalistic focus on process and IT can lead to the failure of efforts to bring about successful and productive change. Transformation should include the elements of strategy, structure and people in addition to the process and technology elements. These aspects are critically important, particularly the focus on the human resource management elements of change.

Organisational transformation, as mentioned above, can be enabled by Internet technologies and the possibilities therein, such as e-commerce and IT-enabled supply chain management. It can also be enabled by powerful integrated back office software in the form of ERP systems. Such systems are commercially available packages that can replace the possibly fragmentary legacy systems with seamlessly integrated and reliable systems that give comprehensive back office functionality. Such systems not only enable and power the internal business operations of a company but also today are becoming web-enabled, and thus can form the basis of good interorganisational systems, such as supply chain and customer relationship management systems.

In planning and executing the organisational transformations that result from the adoption and implementation of ERP systems, the same broad principles apply to transformations based on re-engineering. One needs to balance the technology emphasis with the elements of strategy, structure, process and people.

key terms

business process	integrated system
business process re-engineering	organisational structures
enterprise resource planning system	organisational transformation

discussion questions

1. In the early 1990s, the dominant approach to organisational transformation was business process re-engineering (BPR), an approach introduced and championed by Michael Hammer, James Champy, Tom Davenport and other academics and consultants. One of the business drivers for the BPR initiatives of the early 1990s was the increased competitiveness of the emerging global business environment of the times. Another was the increasing power and availability of modern information technology. Indeed early BPR was characterised by a focus on process redesign through information technology.

   Many of the early BPR attempts were unsuccessful or at least failed to deliver the business benefits that were planned and expected from them. Describe the reasons for these disappointing results, and then go on to outline the major principles for an approach to organisational transformation through process redesign that you believe would be more successful.

2. As mentioned in question 1, the organisational transformation efforts of the early 1990s — the BPR initiatives — had a focus on process redesign to information technology. Thus IT was a key driver in many of these initiatives. As also mentioned in question 1, many of these initiatives had disappointing results. Indeed many were criticised as having an overly logical, rationalistic view of organisational transformation.

   In the light of the above comments, discuss the appropriate role of IT and process redesign in organisational transformation.

3. Describe the role and importance of the human resource management aspects of organisational transformation, such as motivation, reward systems, organisational culture, learning and knowledge management etc. How can IT help in these matters?

4. One of the effects of the process re-engineering-oriented organisational transformations of the early 1990s was the reduction of organisational hierarchy. In other words, the number of layers of management was reduced and, in consequence, there was an increase in the empowerment, responsibility and accountability of employees. Describe the important issues and challenges in making such a delayering of an organisation a success. What is the role of IT in such changes?

5. The process re-engineering approach to organisational transformation focuses on redesigning the business processes of an organisation, beginning with the customer value proposition: delivering value to the customer. The process redesign effort works back from this crucial point of satisfying the customer. It is hoped that the redesign effort, when implemented, will result in an organisation having 'one view of the customer'. Explain why one view of the customer is a desirable process redesign objective. Describe the benefits of attaining one view of the customer. Explain the challenges organisations face in attaining this business process redesign objective. Make sure that you include the IT aspects of attaining one view of the customer.

6. Your company is planning to adopt and implement an ERP system. You recognise that the adoption and implementation of the ERP system will transform the process and technology basis of your company. What principles will you apply to the planning and execution of the upcoming organisational transformation? Aside from the general principles of organisational transformation, what particular challenges and issues are raised by the ERP system adoption and implementation?

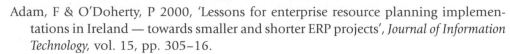

suggested reading

Adam, F & O'Doherty, P 2000, 'Lessons for enterprise resource planning implementations in Ireland — towards smaller and shorter ERP projects', *Journal of Information Technology*, vol. 15, pp. 305–16.

Brehm, L, Heinzl, A & Markus, L 2001, 'Tailoring ERP systems: a spectrum of choices and their implications', *Proceedings of the 34th Hawaii International Conference on Systems Sciences*, 3–6 January 2001, pp. 2946–54.

Davenport, TH 1998, 'Putting the enterprise into the enterprise system', *Harvard Business Review*, vol. 76, issue 4, pp. 121–31.

Hammer, M 2001, 'The superefficient company', *Harvard Business Review*, September, vol. 79, issue 8, pp. 82–91.

Markus, LM & Tanis C 2000, 'The enterprise system experience — from adoption to success', in R Zmud (ed.), *Framing the Domains of IT Management: Projecting the Future Through the Past*, Pinnaflex Educational Resources, Cincinnati, OH, pp. 173–207.

references

Adam, F & O'Doherty, P 2000, 'Lessons for enterprise resource planning implementations in Ireland — towards smaller and shorter ERP projects', *Journal of Information Technology*, vol. 15, pp. 305–16.

Blumenthal, B & Haspeslagh, P 1994, 'Toward the definition of corporate transformation', *Sloan Management Review*, Spring, vol. 35, issue 3, pp. 101–6.

Brehm, L, Heinzl, A & Markus, L 2001, 'Tailoring ERP systems: a spectrum of choices and their implications', *Proceedings of the 34th Hawaii International Conference on Systems Sciences*, 3–6 January 2001, pp. 2946–54.

Cats-Baril, W & Thompson, R 1997, *Information Technology and Management*, Irwin, Chicago.

Clemens, EK & Row, MC 1991, 'Sustaining IT advantage: the role of structural differences', *MIS Quarterly*, vol. 15, issue 3, September, pp. 275–92.

Davenport, TH 1993, *Process Innovation: Re-engineering Work Through Information Technology*, Harvard Business School Press, Boston.

—1998, 'Putting the enterprise into the enterprise system', *Harvard Business Review*, vol. 76, issue 4, pp. 121–31.

Dearden, J 1972, 'MIS is a mirage', *Harvard Business Review*, vol. 50, issue 1, January–February, pp. 90–9.

Dutta, S & Manzoni, JF 1999, *Process Re-engineering, Organisational Change and Performance Improvement*, McGraw-Hill, London.

Garfield, C 1992, *Second to None: How Our Smartest Companies Put Profit First*, Business One, Irwin.

Gulati, R, Nohria, N & Zaheer, A 2000, 'Strategic networks', *Strategic Management Journal*, vol. 21, pp. 203–15.

Hammer, M 1990, 'Re-engineering work: don't automate, obliterate', *Harvard Business Review*, vol. 68, issue 4, July and August, pp. 104–12.

—2001, 'The superefficient company', *Harvard Business Review*, September, vol. 79, issue 8, pp. 82–91.

Hammer, M & Champy, J 1993, *Re-engineering the Corporation: A Manifesto to Business Revolution*, Nicholas Brealey Publishing, London.

Laudon, KC & Laudon, JP 2000, *Management Information Systems: Organisation and Technology in the Networked Enterprise*, 6th edn, Prentice Hall, Upper Saddle River, NJ.

Markus, LM & Tanis C 2000, 'The enterprise system experience — from adoption to success', in R Zmud (ed.), *Framing the Domains of IT Management: Projecting the Future through the Past*, Pinnaflex Educational Resources, Cincinnati, OH, pp. 173–207.

Mata, FJ, Fuerst, WL and Barney, JB 1995, 'Information technology and sustained competitive advantage: a resource-based analysis', *MIS Quarterly*, vol. 19, issue 4, December, pp. 487–505.

Morris, D & Brandon, J 1993, *Re-engineering Your Business*, McGraw-Hill, USA.

Mumford, E & Hendricks, R 1996, 'Business process re-engineering RIP', *People Management*, vol. 2, issue 9, May, pp. 22–9.

Nolan, RL, Porter, KA & Akers, C 2001, *Cisco Systems Architecture: ERP and Web-enabled IT*, Harvard Business School Case Study No. 9-301-099, Harvard Business School Publishing, Boston, MA.

Obeng, E & Crainer, S 1994, *Making Re-engineering Happen*, Pitman Publishing, Great Britain.

Peppard, J 1998, 'Broadening visions of business process re-engineering', in V Sethi & WR King (eds), *Organizational Transformation Through Business Process Re-engineering: Applying the Lessons Learned*, Prentice Hall, Upper Saddle River, NJ.

Peppard, J, Lambert, A & Edwards, C 2000, 'Whose job is it anyway? Organisational information competencies for value creation', *Information Systems Journal*, vol. 10, pp. 291–322.

Powell, TC & Dent-Micallef, A 1997, 'Information technology as competitive advantage: the role of human, business, and technology resources', *Strategic Management Journal*, vol. 18, issue 5, May, pp. 375–405.

Sadler, P 1995, *Managing Change*, Kogan Page, London.

Sethi, V & King, WR 1998, *Organisational Transformation Through Business Process Re-engineering: Applying the Lessons Learned*, Prentice Hall, Upper Saddle River, NJ.

Turban, E, McLean, E & Wetherbe, J 2002, *Information Technology for Management: Transforming Business in the Digital Economy*, 3rd edn, John Wiley & Sons, New York.

Wentz, TK 2000, 'Beyond the barrier of context', *IIE Solutions*, January, vol. 32, issue 1, pp. 26–30.

case study

Organisational transformation at Australian Glass Manufacturers

With its headquarters in Sydney, and factories in Sydney, Melbourne and Adelaide, Australian Glass Manufacturers Ltd (AGM) had been Australia's only glass producer in the early years of the twentieth century. The company manufactured sheet or plate glass made via float, drawing and rolled processes. It also manufactured toughened glass doors suitable for security doors. Car windows and windscreens were another major product line. These products, manufactured to high standards, were sold to the Australian market and had provided AGM with good profits and a leading market position since the 1960s.

AGM operated on technical licences from Pilkington Glass (UK) and had established float glass manufacturing under licence in the 1960s. In the 1970s, however, Pilkington's themselves set up float glass plants in Sydney and Melbourne and began to compete directly with AGM for the Australian float glass market. AGM also faced competition from imported flat glass produced by such global companies as St Gobain and Pittsburg Plate Glass. AGM's competitors were soon offering products similar to AGM's at lower prices. By the late 1990s, this situation had become critical for AGM as it was losing market share at the rate of several percentage points per year. By 2000, its overall market share of flat glass products had dropped from 60 per cent to 45 per cent of the Australian market.

Manufacturing

Although AGM had a considerable distribution and sales organisation throughout Australia, it was essentially a manufacturing company with a very production and product-centred culture. It was essentially organised along production and product lines. Even its sales organisation was led by product sales managers.

AGM's production centres were in Sydney, Melbourne and Adelaide. Sydney had production facilities for float glass, sheet glass, rolled plate glass and toughened glass products. Melbourne had production facilities for float glass, toughened glass, and vehicle windows and windscreens. Adelaide had production facilities for float, sheet and toughened glass. Each factory or production centre was managed separately with its own distribution and logistics capabilities along with its manufacturing capability.

Sales and distribution

The sales and distribution organisation was coordinated nationally by national product sales managers for float glass, sheet glass, rolled plate, toughened glass and automotive products (windows, windscreens, headlight and tail light covers etc). These managers and their sales teams worked closely with both technical and production management teams.

In each Australian state there was one stock depot located in the capital city. These depots played important roles in the sales and distribution organisation of AGM. The depots supplied glass merchants in each state with the flat glass products that they required. Each depot was responsible for ordering its requirements from one of the production centres or factories and for establishing its own inventory control.

The depots were the central stock repositories in each state. Also established in each state, however, were sales centres. There were several of these in each state: five in the larger states of Victoria and New South Wales and three in each of the smallest states. One sales centre in each state was in the capital city, and the others were in large regional cities. Along with their sales responsibilities, the centres also tended to hold stocks of flat glass products, which they ordered from the depots or from the factories, depending on stock availability and convenience. They often held more stock than needed, since they regarded the depots as well as the factories as slow and unresponsive to sales needs.

Suppliers

Companies producing silica sand, soda ash and lime or limestone of suitable quality for glass production were located in all states. By far the cheapest and most efficient producers were in Western Australia. The production facilities were raw material crushing and basic processing plants situated next to the quarries from which the raw material was extracted.

AGM had good relations with the suppliers, and supplies were generally reliable in regard to timing, but there were often problems with batches of raw material with respect to levels of impurities, particularly for inputs to the sensitive float glass process. There was a steady flow of technical information moving between technical and manufacturing management at the various factories and the suppliers. The factories felt that a number of suppliers were slow in reacting to concerns about quality and impurity and felt that both the technical education of suppliers and the communications between suppliers and factories needed to be improved.

In many cases when a truck left a particular supplier's premises loaded with an unacceptable batch of raw material it was some time before the problem was discovered and communicated so that corrective action could be taken. Thus, before the situation was corrected, a number of trucks loaded with the unacceptable batch might have left the supplier's premises. This meant that in addition to lost production at the factory and the wasted trips by the trucks, a lot of negotiation and clerical work resulted from settling the issue of who was responsible for the losses and who indeed paid for the bad batches and the wasted logistics expenses.

In addition to the raw material impurities problem, there was a general feeling that raw material stocks were far too high and that better scheduling of the deliveries of the various raw materials could lead to better balanced stocks as well as significant reductions overall in total raw material stocks. Factory management at many locations throughout Australia felt that this significant reduction could be achieved without risking highly costly stock-outs at glass manufacturing sites. Better communication of needs between factories and suppliers would permit much better scheduling of supplies, which in turn, together with good planning, could lead to lower stock levels. Indeed some managers at AGM felt that better information flows from glass merchants to sales centres to stock depots to manufacturing plants and thence to suppliers would enable stockholding economies right along the glass products supply chain. As it was, factory managements had moderately uncertain information about truck dispatching from the suppliers, and given both these uncertainties, together with the high cost of having no raw material feed for the factory glass tanks, factory managements felt comfortable with relatively large raw material stocks. This also suited the suppliers, who, being paid monthly, often over-delivered late in the month so as to increase their sales revenue for the month. These factors generally led to high raw material stock levels.

The problem and beginnings of a solution

The CEO, Les Johnson, had been told very firmly by the board that they believed that substantial cost reductions had to take place at AGM, so that the locally produced glass products could sell at prices lower than the European and US manufactured glass that was being shipped to Australia. They also believed that the organisation had to improve its marketing and sales operations, becoming much more service-oriented and market-driven. The board was quite critical of the product-centred perspective of sales and marketing, and suggested that the company should be organised around the major markets of building products and automotive products instead of being organised around the various product lines. Overall, however, the board would leave the details of the necessary changes to Les Johnson, but they left the CEO in no doubt that costs had to be significantly reduced and that the company had to be much more market-driven and customer-centred.

Les Johnson felt that he needed some help in dealing with the complexity of the problem he was facing. The board was very keen on AGM becoming more customer-centred and -focused. However, Johnson was close enough to business operations to know that there were many significant problems with business processes and the associated information transactions and flows in addition to the issue of whether AGM was a customer-centred or a product-centred organisation. A simple restructure, he felt, would not solve some of these fundamental problems. He believed that a business process re-engineering approach that looked at the fundamental business processes from the viewpoint of increasing the customers' (glass merchants') value proposition would be the most helpful. Therefore he contacted BRIT Solutions (Business Re-engineering and IT Solutions), a consulting firm well known for creative business solutions that included the innovative use of IT as an enabler of better business processes.

The BRIT consultants began their task by spending several weeks intensively reviewing AGM's business with a particular emphasis on customer satisfaction through good business processes, possibly enabled by the use of contemporary IT. The first output from BRIT's investigations was a core process map for debate with Les Johnson and the senior management team. When Les Johnson and his team began to debate the core process map and its implications, Les began to feel that his faith in BRIT as creative problem-solvers with a holistic approach to business problem-solving was justified.

Questions

1. Create a core process map that you believe would represent the fundamentally important processes for AGM viewed as a customer-centric organisation.
2. Outline the broad process redesign improvements that you feel would be important for AGM. In each case, describe the role of IS/IT in the new processes.
3. Outline an implementation plan for your business process redesign plan in question 2. Mention the principles of change management that you feel it is important to build into any implementation.
4. Comment on the role and importance of empowered cross-functional teams to a business process re-engineering or redesign effort such as the one you are recommending for AGM.

chapter 6

Transforming external relationships with suppliers

learning objectives

After reading this chapter, you should be able to:

- understand the importance of logistics and supply chain management in contemporary organisations
- identify the issues and challenges in logistics and supply chain management and how, if well managed, these can be used as a source of competitive advantage
- understand the changing nature of trading relationships along the supply chain
- understand the role of IT and the Internet in transforming logistics and supply chain management
- enumerate and discuss the benefits associated with re-engineered supply chains.

chapter overview

This chapter describes supply chain management and, in particular, the role of information, information flows, information systems, information technology (IT) and the Internet in efficient and effective supply chain management. Supply chain management is defined, and basic principles of supply chain management are outlined. The distinction is made between the efficiency-oriented supply chain required for functional or commodity products and the market-responsive supply chain required for innovative products, such as fashion or high-technology items.

The potential and significance of information systems and technology, including the Internet, for supply chain management is examined. Such IT-enabled innovations as demand-driven supply chains and vendor-managed inventory (VMI) are discussed along with the role of EDI. An outline of the role and significance of decision support systems (DSS) for supply chain management is also presented.

Introduction

In the previous chapter, some of the internal transformations affecting organisations were discussed. In particular, the changes brought about through a focus on processes and the notion of business process re-engineering were outlined. IT and the Internet are playing a role in these internal transformations, particularly through the implementation of enterprise-wide systems, known as ERP systems. The more recent versions of these systems are web-enabled (Nolan 2001; Lee & Whang 2001; Johnston, Mak & Kurnia 2001).

This chapter continues the theme of transformation but looks outside the organisation. It focuses on the major changes taking place with respect to suppliers, the types of relationships that organisations can now enter into with suppliers and other trading partners in the supply chain, such as distributors, retailers and indeed even end consumers, and logistics and supply chain management. Of particular interest are the role of IT and the Internet in making substantial changes to the operations and hence to the efficiency and effectiveness of the supply chain processes. These changes are seen as important, and indeed there are those who now argue that improvements along the **supply chain** can prove to be a source of competitive advantage for an organisation (Gelinas, Sutton & Fedorowicz 2004; Lee, Padmanabhan & Whang 1997).

Before examining the nature and extent of these external transformations, it is necessary to define the concepts of logistics and the supply chain and to understand how they worked before recent technologically enabled changes.

Supply chain and logistics defined

In chapter 3, the notions of an internal and an external value chain (Porter 1985; Ward & Peppard 2002) were introduced. The internal value chain divided the internal activities of an organisation in order to understand where costs were added, where value was added, where problems occurred, where improvements could be made, and therefore the manner in which an organisation differentiated itself from its competitors. The notion was that in order to be competitive and gain an advantage over competitors, an organisation either had to be able to perform required activities at a lower cost than its competitors or had to find a way of differentiating itself (and thus adding customer value) through the performance of these activities. The external value chain continued this idea along the entire supply chain. Hence the supply chain is composed of the complex interconnections and relationships between all organisations involved in the progression from raw materials to the delivery of goods and services to a customer. A simple supply chain for some sort of manufacturing supply chain is illustrated below (see figure 6.1).

Figure 6.1 ▶ A simple supply chain

However, few modern manufacturing companies would enjoy an idealised supply chain such as this. Their reality would involve multiple suppliers, multiple distributors, multiple retailers and so on (see figure 6.2), and hence it could be referred to perhaps more accurately as a supply network or b-web (Tapscott, Ticoll & Lowry 2000).

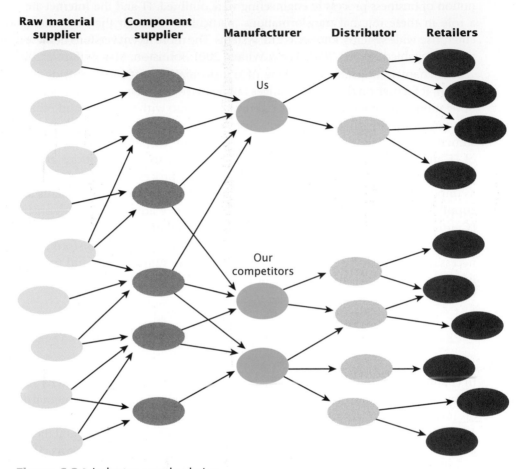

Figure 6.2 ❯ Industry supply chains

Gaining access to quality suppliers, seeking efficiencies in the distribution of goods, services and information throughout the supply chain, and looking for ways to add value from the perspective of the consumer are all ways in which an organisation's supply chain can be a source of differentiation and hence competitive advantage. Thus, supply chain management can be defined as 'the management of upstream and downstream relationships with suppliers and customers to deliver superior customer value at less cost to the supply chain as a whole' (Christopher 1998, p. 18).

In attempting to emphasise the interconnectedness of supply chains and to stress the need for integration along the supply chain Aitken (1998) stresses that supply chain management now needs to encompass the notion of an interconnected and interdependent network of organisations operating cooperatively to manage and improve the flow of goods, services and information among members of the supply chain network for the benefit of all players. A major focus for this chapter includes a consideration of the role that IT and the Internet can play in integrating the supply chain and facilitating the flows of goods and information among members of the supply chain network.

Christopher (1998, p. 4) defines logistics as a

> process of strategically managing the procurement, movement and storage of materials, parts and finished inventory (and the related information flows) through the organization and its marketing channels in such a way that current and future profitability are maximised through the cost-effective fulfilment of orders.

The emphasis of logistics shifts to the movement and storage of goods and services, but it seems that an efficient and effective logistics capability is an essential component of an effective and efficient supply chain.

It has been argued that effective supply chains and logistics capabilities offer an organisation (and its trading partners) a source of competitive advantage. This claim is based on two potential benefits of supply chains. First, a supply chain can offer opportunities to add value from the customers' perspective and thus provide participating organisations with opportunities to differentiate themselves from their competitors. Information about customer preferences and needs is one key factor here in being able to differentiate one organisation's products and services from those of another. Second, benefits can accrue if one supply chain operates with greater efficiency than another and therefore offers lower prices to customers and/or a source of additional profitability.

Before considering how IT and the Internet are driving and facilitating transformations to external relationships and the operations of the supply chain, it is proposed to consider briefly how traditional supply chains have worked.

Traditional supply chains

The simple supply chain offers an opportunity to examine the various flows within the supply chain to understand how they operate and how the supply chain functions. Products and services typically flow from left to right, although flows from right to left are possible when faulty or inappropriate goods and services are returned by customers. Information about customer needs, wants and preferences flows from right to left, as does the money associated with payment for a good or service. Information flows in both directions along the supply chain. Managing these flows of goods, services, information and money is an essential component of managing the supply chain (see figure 6.3 on p. 156).

The operation of the simple supply chain of the type illustrated in figure 6.3 typically relied on forecasting demand. For example, retailers needed to think ahead and forecast (or guesstimate) how much of a particular item they might sell for a given time period. They might have historical data on which to base their forecasts (i.e. how much of this item did we sell in the same period last year?), and their local business knowledge would also be called into play (what does my intuition based on my experience and my knowledge of my customers tell me about the likely sales of this item in future?). But essentially an educated guess would be made as to their requirements. These figures would be handed back to the distributors (or agents), who would aggregate orders from a variety of such sources, and then hand back a larger order to the manufacturer. The manufacturer can then place orders for raw materials and components to their suppliers, based on an aggregation of all the orders received for particular items.

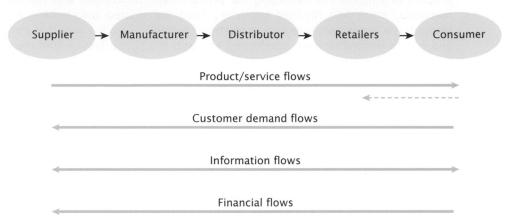

Figure 6.3 ▶ The flows in a typical supply chain

The manufacturer's ability to start producing required items is thus dependent on the timely receipt of raw materials and components. Any delays to these supplies can cause substantial delays to the manufacturing process, which can then affect the rest of the supply chain. Once produced, stocks of various items can be distributed to distributors who break the order into smaller numbers and distribute them to the various retailers. As consumers, we are very dependent on this complex process to function effectively if the goods and services we desire are to be available for purchase. Given the abundant choice of goods available, it is tempting to think that this type of supply chain works efficiently. However, a look at the number of instances of stock not being available, say on local supermarkets shelves, where consumers are forced to select another brand or a similar item, or to go without, suggests that there is the potential for problems to occur with many of the forecast-driven supply chains.

What are the implications of relying on forecast-driven supply chains? First, a number of 'problems' can occur. At just about any stage along the supply chain, an organisation can (and often does) choose to batch orders. In other words, they do not reorder very frequently (as there are administrative overheads associated with ordering and additional transportation costs with lots of small orders) but batch their orders and place a larger order less frequently. For the recipient of that order (the organisation upstream), this results in spikes in ordering, with great variability in demand for goods. The further upstream one goes along the supply chain, the greater this variability tends to be, contributing to what is known as the 'bullwhip effect' (Lee, Padmanabhan & Whang 1997).

Second, the phenomenon known as 'forward buying' can contribute to the bullwhip effect. Consumers would recognise this phenomenon immediately: forward buying occurs when consumers buy products in large quantities, which they then hold before consuming them, which is exactly what occurs when people buy additional quantities during promotions, sales or 'specials'. Indeed in the 1980s branded consumer goods manufacturers, such as Procter & Gamble, were involved in such a promotions frenzy that it caused massive variability and inefficiency in supply chains. In the early 1990s Procter & Gamble carried out an IT-enabled organisational transformation that re-engineered its supply chain to create a more efficient and less variable system that delivered more value to consumers (McKenney & Clark 1995). In response to promotional activities, retailers might order in larger quantities than usual, anticipating this surge in demand, or might push manufacturers to produce large quantities utilising overtime to meet surges in demand. This type of behaviour can cause significant problems upstream and could result in increased costs throughout the supply chain.

The third problem can be associated with human behaviour caused by the fear of missing out, a phenomenon that seems to occur nearly every Christmas with toy demand, for example. Estimates might suggest that demand for the 'hot' toy for children could exceed supply and hence might be rationed by the manufacturer, on the assumption that it is better to meet, say, 50 per cent of a retailer's order than none. This encourages retailers to overstate their requirements and inflate their order, which creates a false demand with subsequent amplification all along the supply chain. The net effect of these forecast-driven supply chains is that due in part to such behaviour as batching of orders and forward buying, the potential exists for inefficiencies to occur all along the supply chain, with dissatisfied customers and organisations with too little or too much inventory at every point. It seems apparent that cooperating organisations that manage to coordinate their requirements better and to gain efficiencies throughout the supply chain have the potential to gain a competitive advantage over those who do not.

The right supply chain for your product?

In a classic article on supply chains, Fisher (1997) writes about the critical differences between the correctly designed supply chain for functional products and innovative products. The differences in demand pattern, and hence the differences in supply chain designed, can be quite marked and fundamental for different categories of products (see table 6.1). A company producing functional products, such as groceries and petrol, faces a predictable demand situation and should plan for an efficient low-cost supply chain. In such a situation of predictable demand, the correct statistical analysis and forecasting, together with good logistics management and efficient information flows enabled by IT, can result in a very good match between supply and demand. On the other hand, a company with innovative products, such as fashion or high-technology items, where today's sale is tomorrow's markdown, requires a market-responsive supply chain (see table 6.2). In this case, where products have short lifecycles and there is considerable risk of shortages or excess supplies, suppliers should be chosen for speed and flexibility and the supply chain designed with these factors in mind. In subsequent sections of this chapter it will be considered how supply chains can be smoothed and the role of IT in supporting some of these initiatives.

Table 6.1 ▶ Differences in demand: functional versus innovative products

	Functional (predictable demand)	Innovative (unpredictable demand)
Functional versus innovative products: differences in demand		
Aspects of demand		
Product lifecycle	>2 years	3 months–1 year
Contribution margin*	5%–20%	20%–60%
Product variety	Low (10–20 variants per category)	High (often millions of variants per category)
Average margin of error in the forecast at the time production is committed	10%	40%–100%
Average stockout rate	1%–2%	10%–40%
Average forced end-of-season markdown as percentage of full price	0%	10%–25%
Lead time required for made-to-order products	6 months–1 year	1 day–2 weeks

* The contribution margin equals price minus variable cost divided by price and is expressed as a percentage.

Source ▶ Fisher 1997, p. 107.

Table 6.2 ▶ Physically efficient versus market-responsive supply chains

	Physically efficient process	**Market responsive process**
Primary purpose	Supply predictable demand efficiently at the lowest possible cost	Respond quickly to unpredictable demand in order to minimise stockouts, forced markdowns and obsolete inventory
Manufacturing focus	Maintain high average utilisation rate	Deploy excess buffer capacity
Inventory strategy	Generate high turnover and minimise inventory throughout the supply chain	Deploy significant buffer stocks of parts or finished goods
Lead-time focus	Shorten lead time as long as it doesn't increase cost	Invest aggressively in ways to reduce lead time
Approach to choosing suppliers	Select primarily for cost and quality	Select primarily for speed, flexibility and quality
Product-design strategy	Maximise performance and minimise costs	Use modular design in order to postpone product differentiation for as long as possible

Source ▶ Fisher 1997, p. 108.

Interorganisational systems and the supply chain

Amid the hype surrounding e-commerce and e-business the picture was painted that suggested that the use of IT to facilitate the flows of goods, services and information along industry supply chains was a new phenomenon, which emerged alongside the advent of the Internet. This, however, was not the case, and the concept of using IT to support core business processes, including interorganisational processes, is not new; it has been important in organisations since the late 1960s. Indeed, using IT to improve the interorganisational supply chain was a central feature of the celebrated American Hospital Supply Company (AHSC) case study (Vitale 1988; Vitale & Konsynski 1991; Applegate, McFarlan & McKenney 1999), which is still used as an exemplar of the use of IT for competitive advantage.[1]

In this section, it is proposed to focus on pre-Internet concepts and developments in this area and then, in subsequent sections, the impact of the Internet on the supply chain and logistics will be considered. Two concepts are essential to the discussion here: interorganisational systems (IOS) and electronic data interchange (EDI). **Interorganisational systems** are literally information systems that reach beyond typical organisational boundaries and electronically link two or more organisations. Haag, Cummings and Dawkins (1998, p. 68) define IOS in the following way: 'an IOS automates the flow of information between organisations to support the planning, design development, production, and delivery of products and services'. A different emphasis is offered by Applegate, McFarlan and McKenney (1999, p. 88), who write that an IOS consists of 'networked computers that enable companies to share information and information processing across organizational boundaries'.

Thus, from figure 6.4, it can be seen that IOS are systems that span organisations. Pre-Internet, all IOS ran on private networks (and were sometimes known as dedicated IOS), and since the advent of the Internet, some IOS now also run over this public network (Johnston, Mak & Kurnia 2001).

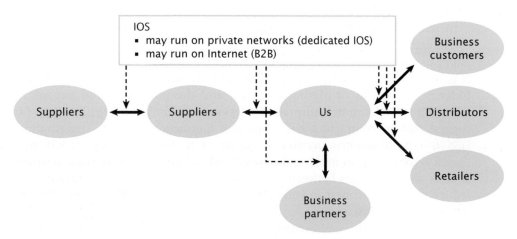

Figure 6.4 ▶ IOS illustrated

For IOS to work effectively, computers in different organisations must be able to 'communicate' with one another. **Electronic data interchange** is software that enables this communication. Specifically, EDI is the suite of software and protocols that enables this computer-to-computer communication or transfer of information and electronic documents. Thus EDI enables the electronic transmission of common business documents (such as a purchase order for example) between trading organisations. EDI systems relied on the adoption and use of communication and document standards so that computers at either end of the transaction could interpret and enact the digital signals being received. Thus organisations at either end of the transaction must adopt the same standards, and business documents could not be easily changed without consultation with trading partners.

Figure 6.5 provides an example of the potential of EDI. It depicts a simple transaction between a buyer and a supplier. Thus, the potential purchaser might send out a request for a quote, the potential supplier sends a response to that request for a quote. If the terms of their quotation are acceptable to the purchaser, then they can send a purchase order to the supplier. Receipt of this purchase order may be acknowledged by the supplier. When some delays occur in fulfilling the order, then the supplier might send a status response, informing the purchaser of information about the state of their order. When the desired goods are finally shipped, the supplier would send a shipping notice and an invoice. Once the goods are received by the purchaser, then a receiving notice might be sent, followed by a payment notice when the goods are paid for.

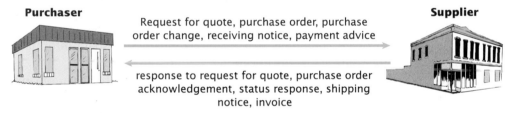

Figure 6.5 ▶ Interorganisational information flows in a basic transaction
Source ▶ Senn 1990, p. 612.

In manual (i.e. paper-based) systems, most of these forms exist in triplicate, and considerable administrative overheads are associated with getting various bits of paper to the right person at the right time. Business rules are often premised on this (e.g. 'We do not pay invoices until all forms have been received in accounts payable'). Indeed, the process of placing an order, and the processing and storage of information involved, can be a surprisingly expensive business for organisations. Estimates suggest that to complete a basic business transaction costs an organisation about US$70 in administrative overheads (Turban et al. 2002). The aim of IOS and EDI is therefore very clear: to increase the speed and reduce the costs of basic business transactions and exchanges between organisations, to reduce the administrative costs, to reduce the time involved in completing transactions, and thus to result in improved levels of customer service.

All the flows, forms and exchanges outlined in figure 6.5 can be translated into EDI and automated, resulting in substantial reduction in costs — some estimates put the figure at about US$4 for exactly the same transaction conducted electronically via EDI (Turban, McLean & Wetherbe 2002). The human inputs can be substantially reduced, meaning that data is not rekeyed into different systems, resulting in fewer data input errors. In sophisticated EDI systems, many of the electronic forms exchanged should be able to be 'interpreted' by and acted on by the recipient's computer, which will then forward and enter the required information into the appropriate systems, say the production, inventory and/or accounting systems for example, thus reducing substantially the amount of human intervention in the systems.

A reduction in data entry errors is just one benefit of EDI-based IOS. Other benefits include a massive reduction in paperwork and all the human activities associated with sorting, filing, reconciling and mailing documents. This generally results in improved quality and consistency in interorganisational exchanges, which decreases the time spent auditing transactions and tracing errors. But there are other substantial benefits that accrue along the supply chain. Typically, systems of this type result in substantial reductions in the costs. As the costs of placing an order have reduced many times (from US$70 to US$4), organisations tend to start placing smaller orders much more frequently, smoothing out the supply chain and helping to dampen the bullwhip effect referred to earlier. Suppliers find it easier to meet smaller orders placed more frequently and hence stock-outs tend to decrease, as does bulking up orders when shortages are suspected. However, not only do direct costs reduce but also many organisations report substantial reductions both in the time taken to complete transactions and in the number of staff required to manage the purchasing activities.

Customer service is often seen to improve, as customers receive better information about the status of their orders, shipping schedules are more accurate, and lead times between the placement of an order and the receipt of the required goods decrease, assisting in internal production planning and scheduling activities. As audit trails of transactions are more accurate, there is often a reduction in the time before payment is received. All these benefits result in improved trading relationships between trading partners, and more time can be devoted to managing the trading relationship rather than sorting out problems.

EDI-based IOS are very fast and relatively secure, and support just-in-time (JIT) operations, which tends to result in re-engineered supply chains, all of which have positive effects among trading partners. What are the problems associated with systems of this type? First, the issue of standards and integration with existing corporate information systems has always been problematic with IOS. To work effectively, these EDI systems must be directly usable by the recipient's computer systems without rekeying, and hence agreements must be reached on standards and formats in advance of the development of the system. Changes are thus not as easily accommodated as in a paper-based system. Effective use also requires that the EDI systems be integrated with internal corporate systems such as the ERP systems described in the previous chapter, yet integration has not always proved easy to accomplish.

Second, traditional EDI systems tend to be very expensive, and although they have been substantially adopted among large organisations, generally speaking they are too expensive to be adopted by small and medium enterprises. Furthermore, the technical issues involved in installing and maintaining EDI systems are often beyond the capabilities and IT maturity of SMEs. Given the role of SMEs in many economies (see chapter 4), this can limit the effectiveness of EDIs, as most supply chains will involve SMEs somewhere along the chain. Some estimates suggest that only about 15–20 per cent of the trading network of an organisation is likely to have invested in EDI, and therefore other arrangements have to be in place to service the remaining 80 per cent. Having two systems operating in parallel clearly reduces many of the advantages of the EDI systems.

Moving EDI to the Internet

In recent years, EDI technologies have become available over the Internet. This means that organisations do not have to invest in private networks but can rely on the public network of the Internet, and their web browser thus becomes the interface with these EDI-based IOS. The major advantage of this is cost: it is a much cheaper proposition for most organisations to consider adopting web-based EDI systems. There are a number of reasons for this. One is associated with the pervasiveness of the Internet: it is readily available, it is relatively cheap, training costs are much lower as most users have familiarity with browser technologies, and the public network (via an ISP) is much cheaper than a private network. A number of standards have been agreed over the Internet, and therefore it is easier to achieve worldwide connectivity. Furthermore, it is much quicker to implement in most cases. It is fair to say that reducing the cost barriers has enabled and encouraged many organisations to adopt these systems, even small and medium enterprises.

There are some disadvantages with EDI over the Internet. First, it is slower, and the speed is somewhat dependent on the amount of traffic on the public network at any time. The speed is largely outside the control of any of the trading partners. Because it uses a public network security is generally less and, once again, no one player in the trading network can completely control the security of the system. Thus, arguably there is an increased risk of attack, fraud and damage to sensitive corporate data. For very high volumes of transactions between trading partners requiring utmost security, the Internet might not prove to be the best solution. However, for many organisations, putting adequate security measures in place will be sufficient, and they can then enjoy the benefits of Internet-based EDI at much lower costs than would otherwise be possible. Another issue is that, although telecommunications standards are generally well established on the Internet, there are as yet no agreed standards for B2B payments, which somewhat reduces the usefulness of Internet-based technologies at this stage.

Re-engineering supply chains using IT

The aim of re-engineering the supply chain and enabling and supporting the flows of goods, services and information along the supply chain via IT is to establish an integrated supply chain. An integrated supply chain offers participating trading organisations a number of benefits, but it has two requirements before benefits can be realised. First, an integrated supply chain must be responsive to customer needs and demands. It must support real-time integrated checks of the entire supply chain to check availability, price, quality, delivery schedules and the like. In other words, quick checks can be made along the supply chain so that it can be established whether a customer order can be met (i.e. can supply of this good or service be promised at a particular price for a given quantity?). Second, integrated supply chains need to be both dynamic and robust. In other words, partners in the trading network must understand and allow for the need to reconfigure rapidly when trading and business conditions and customer requirements change. Hence, supply chains are not static but rather must be fine-tuned regularly in response to drivers of demand and preference. Not only do they need to be dynamic but also they must be robust, forming and reforming to strengthen any weak links. Integrated supply chains require thinking outside the organisational 'box' and instead need organisations to cooperate in end-to-end process thinking about the way(s) in which value is delivered to the end customer (Lee & Whang 2001; Deise et al. 2000; Kalakota & Robinson 2000).

If integration of the supply chain and the supporting logistics capability can be achieved, then participating organisations should achieve a number of benefits. First, there is expected to be an increase in customer satisfaction, as orders are received in a timely manner. The challenge then comes in building loyalty from that satisfaction. Second, organisations can generally reduce their inventory levels and increase throughput, thus reducing operating costs for the business. Other outcomes of supply chain integration are reduced lead times (i.e the length of time between the placing of an order and the receipt of the goods or services ordered) and reduced payment cycles (i.e. the time between delivering a good or service to a customer and receiving payment for that good or service).

These are substantial benefits, and it is no surprise to learn that many organisations regard exploiting supply chain integration as a key plank of their strategy and hence as contributing to their competitive advantage. Strategic thinking about competition is therefore shifting from us versus them to thinking about the relative merits of our integrated supply chain as opposed to our competitors' integrated supply chains (Gulati, Nohria & Zaheer 2001). Thus, in contemporary business, competition needs to be thought of as occurring between supply chains or networks of integrated businesses rather than individual firm versus individual firm. In the section that follows, we will consider the types of systems that are emerging and the ways in which IT is being used to support decision-making with respect to a number of elements within the supply chain.

IT-enabled supply chains

A number of areas associated with the supply chain and managerial decision-making with respect to the supply chain are now well supported by IT. A number of these aspects will be considered, although in no sense is this list intended to be exhaustive. Nor are these aspects or types intended to be mutually exclusive. A good deal of overlap is involved and intended. They are illustrative of the types of IT-driven initiatives that are being adopted by organisations and causing substantial re-engineering of industry supply chains.

Management of suppliers and supplier networks

Integral to the success of a supply chain is involvement of the right partners. What is meant by 'right' in this context? This is somewhat contingent on the type of organisation and the types of industry being considered, but what is right has a lot to do with a supplier's ability to deliver consistently at agreed to dates and times, a supplier's ability to supply goods of a consistent quality and a reasonable price, and so on. Consider this example.

Supplier A and B both produce glass windows used for the construction of new homes. Supplier A can sometimes deliver an order within twenty-four hours of receipt of the order, but has been known to take up to thirteen working days. When builders place their orders, however, supplier A cannot give them a definite delivery date. Foremen of the construction site do not like dealing with supplier A, as they never know when the goods will be delivered. If they come very quickly, before the home is ready to have the windows installed, the goods must be stored and this increases the risk of damage or theft. If the windows are delivered late, however, teams of tradespeople might be left waiting with no work to do, as progress is contingent on the windows first being installed. Supplier B, by contrast, always delivers five days from placement of the order. This makes planning and scheduling for the customer (in this case, the foreman at the home building site) much simpler. On the surface, this makes supplier B a much more attractive proposition than supplier A. But what are supplier B's prices like? Are supplier B's windows of comparable or better quality than supplier A? Supplier B could probably charge a premium over supplier A on the basis of their consistency of delivery if their quality is comparable.

Organisations differ in their need for quality, price and punctual, consistent delivery schedules. Organisations also vary enormously in the complexity of their procurement decisions. Some organisations might deal with a handful of suppliers whereas others must contend with thousands (Ford Motor Company in the USA was dealing with several thousand suppliers before restructuring their procurement activities (Austin 2001)). Information systems are now available to support some of the decision-making related to sourcing and managing suppliers. Such systems can be configured to suit a particular organisation's requirements, and can easily identify the best and worst performing suppliers, given those parameters. Furthermore, indications of the types of risk associated with suppliers can be given, thus facilitating the management of that risk. Finally, such systems can also help organisations consider what information they need to share with their suppliers, when it is required and so on. This will be discussed further in the next section.

Supply chain planning

To understand the concepts associated with supply chain planning, it is perhaps easiest first to consider an example.

Consider the trading relationship that exists between WalMart (or any other large variety store) and companies like Procter & Gamble (P&G) (or other large companies involved in the manufacture and distribution of consumer packaged goods or the like). If the traditional model of the supply chain was still in operation, then WalMart would be checking shelf stocks, checking inventory levels in warehouses, checking point-of-sale data and then forecasting demand. Only after this would large orders be placed with P&G. In discussing traditional supply chains earlier in this chapter, some of the problems associated with this way of working would undoubtedly have arisen, even if WalMart had possessed very accurate internal systems controlling goods. This approach is labour-intensive and hence costly for WalMart.

Heavy investment in IOS enables WalMart and P&G (and other trading partners) to make fundamental changes to the way the supply chain works. Instead of WalMart taking responsibility for all goods in their stores, it adopts an approach called vendor managed inventory (VMI) (Kulp 2002; Waller & Johnson 1999; Haavik 2000; McFarlan & Dailey 1998), in which control of P&G's goods is handed back to P&G, even when the goods are physically in WalMart's stores. Thus, P&G are able to look into WalMart's database and to obtain highly specific information about what goods are selling where, what stock levels exist at various store locations, the effect of specific item promotions and so on. P&G can then take responsibility for restocking WalMart stores, adjusting WalMart's inventory levels to reflect the additional stock and sending invoices.

This sounds as if WalMart has shifted work that it historically did back to P&G, which might sound like a good outcome for WalMart but not so good for P&G and other suppliers. However, there are important benefits from the suppliers' perspective. First, P&G is able to obtain raw sales data from WalMart, which it can use to analyse for sales trends, and early indicators of successful products and failures. This data is then used to adjust the manufacturing and distribution scheduling within P&G, to minimise the likelihood of stock-outs in any WalMart store and to maximise the opportunity to ensure that stocks of items are on shelves in stores where they are selling well. This then enables P&G to better plan their requirements in terms of raw materials and component parts, thus helping to smooth out the entire supply chain.

This example underscores some important principles in IT-enabled supply chains. First, there is the important concept of just-in-time inventory. Retailers (and those downstream in the supply chain) do not want excess stock sitting in warehouses for long periods, at risk of spoiling or getting damaged and tying up large amounts of capital. Second is the concept of VMI — vendors (suppliers) are increasingly being encouraged to take responsibility for their inventory downstream in the supply chain. This can be accomplished through the use of sophisticated IT, and it offers the benefit to suppliers of receiving better and more timely information about sales and trends, which is then fed into their own production and distribution scheduling. This third concept, of adjusting production and distribution scheduling according to consumer demand and preferences, thus shifting the emphasis from supply-driven to **demand-driven supply chain** management, is also an important change in supply chain management. IT-enabled supply chain planning has enabled the supplier to:

- track stock levels of the buyer (at multiple locations if necessary) or those downstream in the supply chain
- ship supplies according to the requirements of the buyer
- adjust the buyer's inventory levels
- invoice the buyer accurately for stock delivered
- gain better insights into customers' behaviour and preferences
- schedule their production and distribution to meet the requirements of the buyer (or downstream party).

From the buyer's perspective, the benefits include the ability to:

- monitor the performance of the suppliers, such as checking that there is no deliberate overstocking and that there are no stock-outs
- make electronic payments
- understand the behaviour and preferences of end consumers and thus to work collaboratively with the suppliers on new product development, product enhancement and the like
- monitor production scheduling, quality control systems and distribution scheduling to ensure the smooth flow of goods and services.

Implementation of these systems is not simple or cheap. A culture of openness must be developed between trading partners as most firms are unaccustomed to opening their databases and corporate information to anyone, and certainly not to suppliers. There must be a willingness to build the relationship, as a genuine sense of trust tends to be at the heart of these systems when they are successful. They must be able to accept some risk as inevitably with major IT innovation there is risk involved. In a sense, the effect of these systems is to link data and information residing within internal ERP systems and to share that information with trading partners who might benefit from it and provide better service as a result. There is evidence to suggest that superior integration along the supply chain is potentially a source of competitive advantage for trading partners.

Order management and fulfilment

The types of concepts important here are again perhaps best illustrated by means of a couple of examples.

Take a small business, involved in selling ready-made curtains, curtain fabrics and accessories, and in producing made-to-measure curtains. The business relies on targeted advertising and marketing, but their mobile sales staff are also vital in clinching their most profitable sales: made-to-measure curtains. Sales staff, equipped with a large number of swatches of fabric, travel to people's homes to advise on curtain selection, styles and fabric choices. Householders can see and feel most of the fabrics available. Management has noticed that often a special event (such as a forthcoming wedding in the family, Christmas, a wedding anniversary or a twenty-first birthday party) is often the trigger to buy new curtains. However, this inevitably means that there is a finite lead time between the decision to purchase and the need to have the new curtains hung. Sales staff offer advice, take window measurements, calculate costs of both the fabric selected and the cost of making the curtains, and offer fixed price contracts to householders who decide to proceed with the purchase. Sales staff phone through orders at the end of each day, and call into the business for a weekly meeting every Monday, when they are briefed on the arrival of new fabrics, the availability of fabrics and the production schedule (i.e. the waiting time for making the curtains).

Almost inevitably, sales staff will face a dilemma. Current schedules for the factory suggest a twenty-one-day wait, but suppose the householder is insistent that the curtains must be ready in nineteen days time. What should the salesperson do: refuse the order; take the order and have a word with the factory supervisor to ensure that this particular order is completed in time; or take the order with no intention of delivering in nineteen days? None of the sales staff (paid by commission) like the first option. Experience suggests that the third option is not a good strategy in the long term. So their behaviour is typically to go for the second option. On many occasions, a slight change to production schedules can accommodate their request. But there are always some cases in which either an order is not fulfilled on the date promised or, if it is, to the detriment of a different order. Another issue surrounds fabric availability. At the Monday meeting, they are told about the availability of fabrics (how much is available, how long it takes to reorder if additional fabric is required), but this situation might have changed substantially, say, by the Friday afternoon, depending on the sales made by other staff.

The net effects of these problems are customers becoming upset at not having their needs adequately met and sales staff becoming upset at accepting orders in good faith that for one reason or another cannot be delivered.

Some investment in IT could help to alleviate these problems. If the sales staff were equipped with mobile phones and laptop computers, enabling them to dial into corporate databases, then they could check the availability of curtain fabrics, reorder times (if a fabric is not available), prices, when an order of a particular size could be scheduled and so on, and thus could make accurate promises to the customer. The types of commitments they need to be able to make include:

- Is inventory available for us to be able to fulfil this order (or if not, when will inventory become available)?
- Does our current manufacturing capacity allow us to accept this order and commit to a particular delivery date?
- Is it profitable for us to accept an order at a particular price that is being offered by the buyer (especially the case when dealing with items that are subject to rapid fluctuations in price) (Kalakota & Robinson 2000; Lee & Billington 1992)?

The importance of this sort of information does vary from industry to industry and business to business. But irrespective of the organisation, having accurate and timely information available can lead to increased customer satisfaction and a much more efficient supply chain. For instance, it can help to eradicate or reduce some of the potential problems associated with traditional forecast-driven supply chains. Achieving this level of service, however, depends on the application of IT throughout the supply chain. Hence, the traditional, forecast-driven supply chain must be re-engineered to become demand-focused. With a demand-focused supply chain, when an enquiry is received from a potential customer, real-time online checks can be made along the supply chain to check the availability of raw materials, component parts, manufacturing capability, production and shipping dates, and costing so that accurate promises can be made and an order confirmed together with the specifics of costs and delivery dates.

Another example might be helpful at this juncture. Consider figure 6.6 (on p. 168). Imagine a scenario in which an end consumer goes to a local retailer to buy a pair of jeans. The sales assistant scans the bar code on the jeans, which displays the price and facilitates the completion of the purchase transaction. But less visible systems are managing and facilitating a lot of the back office functionality. Hence, a completed transaction will trigger the system to decrease store inventory levels by 1,

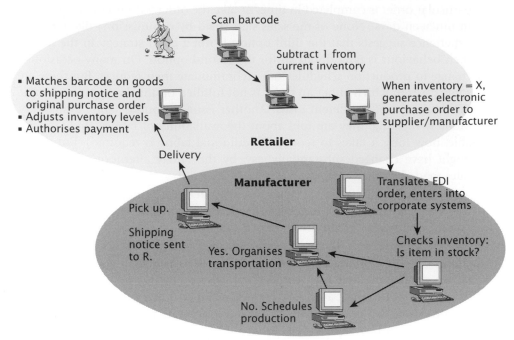

Scan barcode

Subtract 1 from
current inventory

- Matches barcode on goods
  to shipping notice and
  original purchase order
- Adjusts inventory levels
- Authorises payment

When inventory = X,
generates electronic
purchase order to
supplier/manufacturer

Retailer

Delivery

Manufacturer

Translates EDI
order, enters into
corporate systems

Pick up.

Shipping
notice sent
to R.

Yes. Organises
transportation

Checks inventory:
Is item in stock?

No. Schedules
production

Figure 6.6 ▶ The use of IT in order management and fulfilment

thus keeping accurate and timely information about inventory levels of all stock items. The system will also have business rules embedded in software, to place orders for additional stock once the store's inventory gets down to a certain point. So, for example, there might be a rule that says: 'When the number of jeans in stock equals 6, generate a new electronic purchase order to the supplier/manufacturer for 50 new pairs of jeans.' This purchase order is sent via EDI (perhaps over the Internet or possibly over private networks) to the manufacturer's computer systems, which can interpret and enact some of the instructions contained in that order. The manufacturer's systems can first check their stock levels, to see whether enough of the desired items are available in their finished goods inventory. If they are, the system can arrange for those stock items to be taken from inventory and shipped to the retailer, with a shipping notice and an electronic invoice. The manufacturer's inventory level will then be adjusted downwards to recognise that stock has been sold and shipped, while on receipt, the retailer's inventory will be increased to recognise the receipt of the new goods, provided the bar code on the received goods matches that on the original purchase order. If all is satisfactory, the retailer's systems can then authorise electronic payment for the goods. If checks of the manufacturer's stock levels indicate that there is not enough stock to meet the order, then the computer systems can actually schedule production of the required items and advise the retailer of a scheduled delivery date.

Figure 6.6 illustrates a simple example of the potential of IT in modern automated warehousing and order management and fulfilment. Nonetheless, this example illustrates what is possible and the direction that IT innovations are taking.

Decision support systems

For the IOS just described above to work effectively, decision support systems and tools will be embedded throughout that system. For example, how does the retailer set a particular reorder trigger point, expressed in the business rule 'When the number of items in stock equals X, generate a new electronic purchase order to the supplier/ manufacturer for quantity Y of new items'? A number of factors must be considered here. The retailer's supplier management systems will provide information about how quickly a particular manufacturer can replenish stock, how consistently this is accomplished and so on. Other data from point of sale (POS) systems can provide insights into what styles, colours and sizes are selling at what rate. A combination of these two bits of information enables a reorder point to be established. If an item takes one week to be restocked, then one week's worth of stock must still be available at the point of reorder. In cases where the retailer can look forward into the manufacturer's systems to check inventory levels at the manufacturer, then this information can set two reorder points (i.e. if the manufacturer has items in stock that can be received in twenty-four hours, the reorder point can be set much lower than if the manufacturer must produce those items). But sophisticated decision support systems (DSS) are often able to work with more data than this and to perform more challenging analyses. So, for example, information about such matters as the following can be considered in addition to the POS and supplier information, to provide quite accurate forecasts of demand for a particular product or service:

- the seasonality of the item: is it an item that will sell only in summer?
- the known and the expected product lifecycle information: is this a new, fad item with increasing interest and demand, or are sales starting to fall off, or is demand for this item relatively stable over time?
- macroeconomic data: is the economy booming and consumer confidence high, or is there a downturn, which is dampening consumer spending?
- industry trends: how are others in a similar industry performing at this time?

This is only one example of a DSS. The manufacturer of jeans in our earlier example might also rely on DSS to help establish production levels and so on. Essentially DSS are systems that can gather vast amounts of data, often from a variety of internal and external sources, and perform analyses on that data. The aim of such analysis is to support the decision-making activities of managers through the detailed manipulation of a range of relevant data. Hence, DSS are essentially viewed as systems that bring together the analysis of a range of reasonably objective data, which can then be used as a support to human judgement and decision-making (Turban et al. 2002). Many DSS are equipped with the capacity to perform sensitivity analyses, whereby suggested solutions can be tested to see how robust a particular solution might be. Sensitivity analysis helps managers to consider how readily a suggested solution could change according to changing conditions and assumptions that have been incorporated into the DSS.

The intention here is not to give a complete coverage of the capabilities of DSS. The intention was to suggest that DSS have a very important role to play in helping to smooth out the operation of an industry supply chain and in supporting the decision-making of trading partners so that decisions taken that affect the entire supply chain are as sound as possible and are based on as much objective data as possible.

Logistics

Much of this chapter has focused on an important shift in emphasis in supply chains. Essentially, the shift is summarised in figure 6.7, in which the orientation and organisation of activities along the supply chain are shifting from a product push notion (whereby lots of goods are made and then pushed long the supply chain to the end consumer) ideally towards a demand pull notion (whereby goods are produced in response to more certain customer demand and hence pulled down the supply chain).

This shift in emphasis has profound implications for the logistics function, which was previously defined as involving the procurement, movement and management of materials and inventory. The new strategies for managing the supply chain now imply the need for smaller, quicker batches to be moved and stored, rather than efficient batches. Hence modern logistics is heavily reliant on IT to help plan small, more rapid movements of raw materials and inventory, to track inventory using bar coding technology, and to plan carefully and optimise the mix of transport options (small versus large trucks, routing decisions and so on).

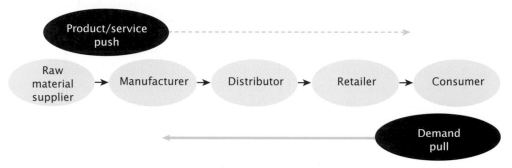

Figure 6.7 ▷ Changes in emphasis in contemporary supply chains

Collaborative new product development

An interesting development that seems to have evolved from greater interconnectivity and greater access to and sharing of information comes in the area of product design and development. It was previously argued that one of the benefits of e-commerce-enabled integrated supply chains was that organisations upstream in the supply chain (such as the manufacturer in our example above) receive a more detailed and accurate picture of customer needs, preferences and values and therefore gain insights into desirable product modifications, enhancements and new product developments. However, more and more organisations are relying on others to produce component parts and subsystems of the final product. Thus OEMs (original equipment manufacturers) do not make an entire product but design and develop some parts while relying on other manufacturers (usually more specialised) to produce other components. The extent to which this happens varies from industry to industry, but it is not uncommon for more than 60 per cent of an item to be produced by organisations operating in some sort of trading relationship with the OEM.

For example, car manufacturers rely on manufacturers outside their organisation to produce car subassemblies. Companies specialising in brake systems or suspension systems will design braking and suspension systems to meet specifications set by the car manufacturer to suit a particular model of vehicle. Computer manufacturers (such as Dell) do not produce every component part of their computers but rather rely on specialists to design, develop and often produce components. They do so simply because of the complexity of many modern products and the attendant difficulty of becoming and remaining a world-class expert in every component, the administrative and managerial costs associated with trying to do so, and because there would be a much greater risk of becoming uncompetitive if they were faced with a challenge from smaller, more agile experts in a narrowly defined field. But when there are heavy interdependencies in component parts produced by a number of different organisations, then it is essential for information, knowledge and expertise to be shared among the cooperating players. Being willing to share and collaborate in this way can result in substantial time and cost savings, arguably resulting in better products and services being offered to customers in a shorter space of time (McIvor & McHugh 2000; McGinnis & Mele Vallopra 1999; Croxton et al. 2001).

IT plays an important role in facilitating this. Sharing of knowledge and expertise via knowledge management systems, collaborative design programs such as CAD/CAM, virtual workspace tools, collaborative work flow and project management tools are all essential to coordinating the activities of disparate experts working collaboratively. Successful integration of the supply chain in many industries will be enhanced through collaborative product development.

thinking strategically

Can GEA's bullwhip effect problems be smoothed with IT?

Grasshopper Engineering Australia (GEA) specialises in making bearings, bushings, blades and drive parts for several manufacturers of lawnmowers and other lawn-, edge- and hedge-cutting products. The manufacturers sell their lawn- and hedge-cutting products to several national chains of outdoor and garden stores as well as to smaller gardening stores in the capital cities and regions. GEA obtains its raw material supplies of alloy steel rod, bar and plate from several alloy steel producers. The GEA supply chain through to the retailers is shown in figure 6.8 (on p. 172).

GEA management likes to have large and stable production runs of the products it is manufacturing. However, owing partly to seasonal factors, partly to promotions run by the lawnmower and gardening tools manufacturers, and partly to the introduction of new products, demand on the GEA factories varies considerably, causing instability in finished goods stock levels. The variable demand also leads to a large number of small-sized production runs and costly production changeovers.

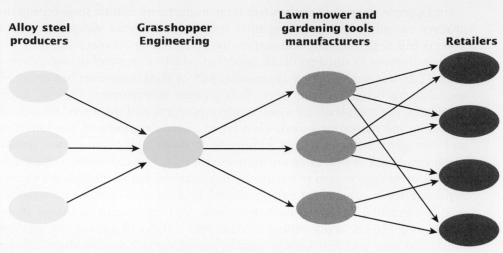

Alloy steel producers   Grasshopper Engineering   Lawn mower and gardening tools manufacturers   Retailers

Figure 6.8 ▶ Grasshopper Engineering's supply chain

GEA wishes to improve its predictions of demand. Recently GEA had hired Decision Sciences Inc. (DSI) to help it forecast demand more accurately and thus to stabilise its production schedules and reduce the amount of finished goods stocks that it holds. GEA had also hoped that with better demand forecasting it could then also give more stable and longer-term orders to its own suppliers, thus increasing the reliability of suppliers and possibly reducing the cost of supplies.

DSI had examined the time series of demand placed on GEA from the lawnmower and gardening tools manufacturers and developed some sophisticated forecasting methods for GEA. However, the sophisticated forecasting algorithms that DSI had developed had helped only marginally.

David Hewitt, the manufacturing manager of GEA, reflected on the supply chain problem, sharing his thoughts with his middle managers. 'The problem is that right down the supply chain, we — and all the other companies — do our own forecasting on the stream of demand coming at us. The retailers, for example, watch their stock levels very carefully. As they reach a certain safety level of stock, the retailers reorder a certain quantity of product — usually an economic batch quantity — a quantity calculated to trade off ordering costs: the smaller the order, the more often you order, thus the greater the ordering cost per order, and the stockholding cost: the larger the order, the larger the stockholding over time, and hence the larger the stockholding cost. Thus demand becomes very chunky, variable and uncertain. As this chunky demand works its way down the supply chain it becomes less and less related to the current trends in the sales data of the retailers and becomes more chunky, more variable and more uncertain.

'The lawnmower and gardening tool manufacturers have to meet this very chunky and inaccurate set of demands. But because of the uncertainty of demand on them and the larger batches demanded of them, they manufacture even larger batches for safety and hold quite large quantities of finished goods stock.

'A similar effect happens right down the supply chain. This results in small movements in demand at the retailer's end, which results in large changes at the manufacturing and raw materials end of the supply chain. Thus small movements in

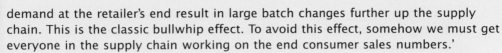

demand at the retailer's end result in large batch changes further up the supply chain. This is the classic bullwhip effect. To avoid this effect, somehow we must get everyone in the supply chain working on the end consumer sales numbers.'

'I think you have the beginnings of a solution there. Yes! I think in your clear description of the problem there lies the beginnings of a solution,' said Don Hamilton, GEA's production scheduling manager.

Questions

1. Describe a possible solution to the GEA supply chain problem along the lines suggested by David Hewitt.
2. How might IT (including the Internet) be used to help minimise the bullwhip effect described by David Hewitt?
3. Discuss the benefits to each of the organisations in GEA's supply chain (see figure 6.8) that could be achieved through appropriate applications of IT and the Internet.

The benefits of re-engineered supply chains

It is fair to say that among the most dramatic organisational changes occurring with the advent of e-commerce/e-business are the transformations that are occurring in thinking about and implementing supply chain management. The problems that plagued supply chains previously (inventory levels were either too high or too low, or inventory was not in the right place, forecasting of demand was unreliable and erratic, leading to a lack of trust and poor customer service, and little agreement of what/when/where products are required) can be, not solved, but certainly ameliorated through the application of IT and the appropriate use of the Internet.

For illustrative purposes, the type of supply chain referred to in this chapter has typically been a retail supply chain. The nature, complexity, and precise configuration of alternative industry supply chains may vary somewhat but the principles discussed in this chapter remain. Benefits can be derived through the re-engineering of supply chains and the application of IT, but essentially managers must consider a number of issues if they wish to design effective supply chains.

Business strategy affects supply chain strategy, or the type of supply chain which suits a particular organisation. But a key question to consider is 'What type of supply chain strategy is going to add value from the customers' perspective, and help to maintain and create a profitable enterprise?' Arguably, organisations could aim for efficiencies and effectiveness gains, but need to be aware of the sorts of circumstances in which these two objectives may be in conflict. For example, if the organisation produces functional or commodity products then a lean, efficient supply chain will be appropriate, whereas for an organisation producing innovative products, a flexible market-responsive supply chain would be appropriate (Fisher 1997). Second, an organisation potentially will participate at the same time in multiple supply chains, and to integrate one without the others may create more problems than it solves. As multiple players are likely to be involved in and affected by any transformation of the supply chain, another key question to consider is how agreement is going to be reached on the sorts of changes that may be necessary along the supply chain. How is ownership of the supply chain to be apportioned? How is the cooperation of trading partners to be sought and managed?

Key decisions must be made about the infrastructure required to support an integrated supply chain. How compatible are the infrastructures of trading partners (including the ERP systems adopted internally), are the infrastructures and business processes in alignment with the proposed changes, and how easy or difficult will it be to integrate the proposed IT investments for the integrated supply chain into existing internal IT infrastructures? In the previous chapter, the need to balance various dimensions in an organisation was mentioned. In re-engineering the supply chain effectively, these dimensions or competing forces need to be balanced through an entire trading network (see figure 6.9), which may prove a challenging thing to achieve.

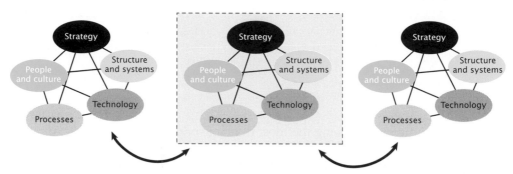

Figure 6.9 ▶ Balancing organisational dimensions along the entire supply chain
Source ▶ adapted with amendments from Dutta and Manzoni 1999.

Another issue to do with supply chain re-engineering is particularly pertinent in countries like Australia and much of the Asian region, in which a substantial proportion of the economy is made up of small and medium-sized enterprises. The full efficiency and effectiveness gains of transformed supply chains are not achieved unless most if not all of the supply chain participates. Yet in economies based on SMEs, there is a likelihood that somewhere along the supply chain an SME will be encountered. In itself this might not be problematic, but SMEs sometimes lack IT maturity and expertise, they might lack the necessary infrastructure, and there might be challenges in integrating supply chain systems with existing internal systems. Therefore the readiness of all partners, their ability and willingness to participate, particularly in terms of the skills, knowledge, resources and culture needed, is a factor in accomplishing supply chain integration (Johnston, Mak & Kurnia 2001).

As mentioned in the previous chapter, the management of change is essential for the success of these ventures. Supply chain improvement initiatives could suffer from unclear objectives or objectives that are not shared among all trading partners. There might be a lack of senior executive support and sponsorship and hence an attendant risk of supply chain integration being regarded as an IT initiative (and therefore the preserve of the IT staff) rather than a business initiative.

Summary

Supply chain management can be defined as the management of upstream and downstream relationships with suppliers to deliver superior customer value at an acceptably low cost to the supply chain as a whole. An important part of supply chain management is logistics management, which is the process of strategically managing the procurement, movement and storage of materials, parts and finished inventory (and the related information flows) for the organisation and its marketing channels in such a way as to maximise current and future profitability through the cost-effective fulfilment of orders.

In the supply chain, products and services flow from suppliers via manufacturers, distributors and retailers down to end consumers. Finance and information, including information regarding customer demand, flow in the opposite direction. Optimal and integrated management of all these flows is the essence of supply chain management.

A fundamental distinction is made in the performance objectives for supply chains of functional or commodity products and supply chains of essentially innovative products, such as fashion or high-technology items. Functional or commodity products require efficient supply chains whereas the major concern for innovative products is a market-responsive and flexible supply chain.

Information systems and technology have great potential significance for supply chain management as they can markedly improve information flows in the supply chain. Electronic data interchange (EDI) based on fast private computer networks or on the cheaper, more widespread but slower Internet can speed up the basic transactions surrounding purchases and payment in supply chains. More elaborate interorganisational systems, together with interorganisational process redesign, can enable supply chains to change fundamentally, from supply-push systems to demand-driven or demand-pull systems. Marketplace information is enabled to flow quickly through the whole supply chain, and this, together with good forecasting and other decision support tools, enables much better decision-making, monitoring and control of the supply chain, with benefits flowing both to organisations and to consumers.

key terms

demand-driven supply chain

electronic data interchange (EDI)

interorganisational system

supply chain

discussion questions

1. Discuss the role and importance of information systems and technology in supply chain management. In particular, discuss the role of the Internet.

2. Discuss the significance of personal and organisational relationships in supply chain management. In particular, discuss the role and importance of trust, collaboration, negotiation and win–win scenarios in supply chain management.

3. Discuss the role and importance of trust, collaboration and negotiation in the planning, design and implementation of interorganisational systems (IOS) for supply chain management.

4. Describe the role and importance of business process re-engineering to supply chain management. In particular be sure to describe the major problems and issues involved in establishing efficient and effective interorganisational business processes.

5. Describe the role and importance of good and appropriate decision support systems (DSS) to efficient and effective supply chain management.

note

1. This case is described in detail in Applegate, McFarlan & McKenney 1999.

suggested reading

Fisher, ML 1997, 'What is the right supply chain for your product?', *Harvard Business Review*, vol. 75, issue 2, March–April, pp. 105–16.

Johnston, RB, Mak, HC & Kurnia, S 2001, 'The contribution of Internet electronic commerce to advanced supply chain reform — a case study', in S Barnes & B Hunt (eds), *E-commerce and V-business: Business Models for Global Success*, Butterworth Heinemann, Oxford.

Lee, HL & Billington, C 1992, 'Managing supply chain inventory: pitfalls and opportunities', *Sloan Management Review*, vol. 33, issue 3, Spring, pp. 65–73.

Lee, HL, Padmanabhan, V & Whang, S 1997, 'The bullwhip effect in supply chains', *Sloan Management Review*, Spring 1997, pp. 93–102.

Lee, HL & Whang, S 2001, 'E-business and supply chain integration', Stanford Global Supply Chain Management paper no. SGSCMF-W2-2001, November, http://www.stanford.edu/group/scforum/

references

Aitken, J 1998, 'Supply chain integration within the context of a supplier association', PhD thesis, Cranfield University, UK.

Applegate, LM, McFarlan, FW & McKenney, JL 1999, *Corporate Information Systems Management: Text and Cases*, 5th edn, McGraw-Hill/Irwin, Boston.

Austin, RD 2001, *Ford Motor Company: Supply Chain Strategy*, Harvard Business School Case No. 9-669-198, Harvard Business School Publishing, Boston.

Christopher, M 1998, *Logistics and Supply Chain Management: Strategies for Reducing Costs and Improving Service*, 2nd edn, Financial Times/Prentice Hall, London.

Christopher, M & Towill, DR 2002, 'Developing market specific supply chain strategies', *International Journal of Logistics Management*, vol. 13, no. 1, pp. 1–14.

Croxton, KL, Garcia-Dastugue, SJ, Lambert, DM & Rogers, DS 2001, 'The supply chain management processes', *International Journal of Logistics Management*, vol. 12, no. 2, pp. 13–36.

Deise, MV, Nowikow, C, King, P & Wright, A 2000, *Executive's Guide to the Business: From Tactics to Strategy*, John Wiley & Sons, New York.

Fisher, ML 1997, 'What is the right supply chain for your product?', *Harvard Business Review*, vol. 75, issue 2, March–April, pp. 105–16.

Gelinas, UJ, Sutton, SG and Fedorowicz, J 2004, *Business Processes and Information Technology*, Thomson South Western, Mason, OH.

Gulati, R, Nohria, N & Zaheer, A 2001, 'Strategic networks', *Strategic Management Journal*, vol. 21, pp. 203–15.

Haag, S, Cummings, M & Dawkins, J 1998, *Management Information Systems for the Information Age*, McGraw-Hill/Irwin, Boston.

Haavik, S 2000, 'Building a demand-driven vendor-managed supply chain', *Healthcare Financial Management*, vol. 54, issue 2, February, pp. 56–60.

Hammer, M 2001, 'The superefficient company', *Harvard Business Review*, vol. 79, no. 8, pp. 82–91.

Johnston, RB, Mak, HC & Kurnia, S 2001, 'The contribution of Internet electronic commerce to advanced supply chain reform — a case study', in S Barnes & B Hunt (eds), *E-commerce and V-business: Business Models for Global Success*, Butterworth Heinemann, Oxford.

Kalakota, R & Robinson, M (2000) *E-business 2.0: Roadmap for Success*, Addison-Wesley, Boston.

Kulp, SC 2002, 'The effect of information precision and information reliability on manufacturer–retailer relationships', *Accounting Review*, vol. 77, no. 3, July, pp. 653–77.

Lee, HL & Billington, C 1992, 'Managing supply chain inventory: pitfalls and opportunities', *Sloan Management Review*, vol. 33, issue 3, Spring, pp. 65–73.

Lee, HL, Padmanabhan, V & Whang, S 1997, 'The bullwhip effect in supply chains', *Sloan Management Review*, Spring 1997, pp. 93–102.

Lee, HL and Whang, S 2001, *E business and Supply Chain Integration*, Stanford Global Supply Chain Management Paper No. SGSCMF-W2-2001, November, http://www.stanford.edu/group/scforum/

McAfee, A 2001, *Syncra Systems*, Harvard Business School Case Study No. 9-601-035, Harvard Business School Publishing, Boston.

McFarlan, FW and Dailey, M 1998, *www.springs.com*. Harvard Business School Case Study No. 9-398-091, Harvard Business School Publishing, Boston.

McGinnis, MA and Mele Vallopra, R 1999, 'Purchasing and supplier involvement: issues and insights regarding new products success', *Journal of Supply Chain Management*, vol. 35, issue 3, Summer, pp. 4–15.

McIvor, R & McHugh, M 2000, 'Partnership sourcing: an organisation change management perspective', *Journal of Supply Chain Management*, vol. 36, issue 3, Summer, pp. 12–20.

McKenney, JL & Clark, TH 1995, *Procter & Gamble: Improving Consumer Value Through Processor Redesign*, Harvard Business School Case Study No. 9-195-126, Harvard Business School Publishing, Boston.

Nolan, RL 2001, *Cisco Systems Architecture: ERP and Web-enabled IT*, Harvard Business School Case No. 9-301-099, October.

Porter, ME 1985, *Competitive Advantage: Creating and Sustaining Superior Performance*, Free Press, New York.

Senn, JA 1990, *Information Systems Management*, 4th edn, Wadsworth Publishing Co., Belmont, CA.

Tapscott, D, Ticoll, D & Lowy, A 2000, *Digital Capital: Harnessing the Power of Business Webs*, Harvard Business School Press, Boston.

Turban, E, McLean, E & Wetherbe, J 2002, *Information Technology for Management: Transforming Business in Digital Economy*, 3rd edn, John Wiley & Sons, New York.

Vitale, M 1988, *American Hospital Supply Corporation: The ASAP system (A)*, Harvard Business School Case Study No. 9-186-005, Harvard Business School Publishing, Boston.

Vitale, M & Konsynski, B 1991, *Baxter Healthcare Corporation: ASAP Express*, Harvard Business School Case Study No 9-186005, Harvard Business School Publishing, Boston.

Waller, M & Johnson, ME 1999, 'Vendor-managed inventory in the retail supply chain', *Journal of Business Logistics*, vol. 20, no. 1, pp. 183–203.

Ward, J & Peppard, J 2002, *Strategic Planning for Information Systems*, 3rd edn, John Wiley & Sons, Chichester.

case study

BizElegance: a supply chain story

Elegant Fashions was an Australian company founded in the nineteenth century in Melbourne, Australia, to cater to the women's fashion market, primarily designing and selling women's suits, dresses, blouses and skirts. In the 1960s the company had begun to specialise in designing work and evening wear for the business and professional woman, and in the process it had changed its name to BizElegance. The company currently has revenues of $170 million per year and has 135 employees, among whom are seven well-known and highly skilled designers of women's fashion wear.

Although the business had been profitable up to and throughout the 1990s, intense competition for the career women's dollar in all sectors had meant that the company had lost several per cent market share. Kate Clench, the current CEO, was convinced that her designers needed to come up with four collections a year instead of the two (Autumn–Winter and Spring–Summer) releases of previous years. Kate also felt that better inventory management would help BizElegance by having production and the supply chain focus on what the market was actually buying, rather than on what the market was forecast to buy, resulting in better sales and reduced losses or wastage from 'markdowns' or unsold items. In short, a more market-responsive or agile supply chain was needed.

To sell its clothing, BizElegance has its own set of boutiques. It has fourteen stores in all, ten in Australia and four in New Zealand. In Australia there are four stores in Sydney, four in Melbourne and two in Perth. In New Zealand there are stores in Auckland, Wellington, Christchurch and Dunedin.

The established practice was for the company's designers to design two collections a year for release in Autumn–Winter and Spring–Summer. The fully specified designs were sent to an appropriate manufacturer, who contracted to supply samples in a given time for a given cost. On the return of the samples, they were test-modelled within BizElegance and alterations were made. Then a contract was established, often with the manufacturer who had produced the samples, for a production run of the items.

BizElegance has an association or relationship with five manufacturers that it usually uses to make garments according to its design specifications. Two of these are in Jakarta, one is in Kuala Lumpur and two are in Bangkok. Initially, the joint lead times for the manufacture of samples and finished items together varied between these manufacturing companies. The best of them achieved a lead time of seven weeks, whereas the longest lead time had been around twelve to thirteen weeks. After some negotiation with each company, the lead times for the manufacture of samples and a corresponding production run had been reduced to about five weeks in total for each company. The lead time for sample manufacture was two weeks (including delivering the finished samples to Australia) and the lead time for production runs of around a hundred items of each design was about three weeks.

The fabrics used in BizElegance garments included wool, silk, silk–wool blends, cashmere, cashmere–wool blends, cotton and cotton–polyester blends. The highest quality of fabric was chosen for both appearance and wear characteristics. The fabric was sourced by BizElegance for the garment manufacturers. The garment manufacturers would assist BizElegance with this choice, but the final say was with BizElegance. Nonetheless the manufacturers knew the Asia–Pacific fabric producers well, and BizElegance valued their advice. The process of choosing fabric involved a lot of communication, which was conducted by telephone, fax and post.

Yarn for BizElegance's garment production was sourced by the fabric manufacturers in accordance with BizElegance's specifications. It was sourced from a wide variety of locations throughout the Asia–Pacific region from cashmere yarn producers in Japan, China and India to woollen mills in Australia. The selection of yarn markers by the manufacturers was often based on the criterion of lowest cost. Because this sometimes led to unsatisfactory results, BizElegance occasionally intervened in the choice of yarn, stipulating a particular yarn manufacturer's yarn or the particular type and quality of yarn to be used. Again this process required a lot of communication and could be lengthy.

The supply chain and information flows for the clothing are shown in figure 6.10.

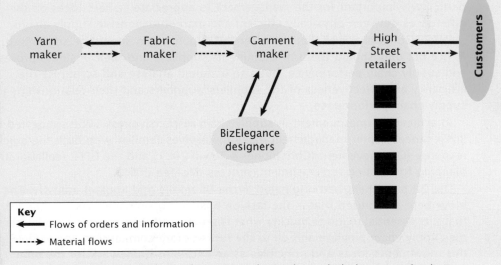

Key
← Flows of orders and information
----→ Material flows

Figure 6.10 ▶ BizElegance's involvement in the traditional clothing supply chain
Source ▶ adapted from Christopher and Towill 2002, p. 3.

In human and cultural terms, BizElegance was a somewhat paradoxical company. Although very contemporary and trendy with respect to fashion and design, it was a very conservative company in other ways, especially in respect of business innovation. Its business processes had evolved slowly around the needs of its designers and had never been the subject of analysis. The company's transactions were manual and paper-based. Apart from the use of a fax machine and telephones, the company's communications were also paper-based. Computerisation was restricted to the financial and accounting systems run on a small computer in the accounting department. The culture of the firm was based on the notion of the designer as the 'centre of the universe'. The designers thus had excellent support and assistance. They were also provided with the latest education and training in fashion and design, and were generally helped to keep up with the latest trends. However, very little attention was given to other developments in contemporary business.

Kate Clench, concerned about the plateauing and downward trend of sales as well as the proportion of markdowns in sales figures, contacted the strategy consultants Strategic Visioning and Planning (SV&P) to advise her on ways to improve the problematic situation. SV&P had made a report after a few weeks study of BizElegance and its supply chain.

SV&P's overall recommendation was for BizElegance to keep and indeed foster its excellence in creative design and to move from two collections a year to four. At the same time they advised the company to increase the speed and responsiveness of its supply chain, since in fashion 'today's style is tomorrow's markdown' (Christopher & Towill 2002). SV&P also felt that, along with increased responsiveness, cost savings could be made in the supply chain as well. However, they strongly emphasised that for any innovative fashion company these economies in the supply chain should be secondary to increased responsiveness. Indeed, to make sure that senior management at BizElegance understood the differences in supply chain design between functional and innovative products, they recommended that all senior managers make themselves familiar with Marshall L. Fisher's (1997) paper, 'What is the right supply chain for your product?'. They thought it would be particularly important for the management to appreciate Fisher's ideas on the differences between physically efficient and market-responsive supply chains.

SV&P also emphasised that the extended supply chain should be scrutinised. Hence not only should the firm examine its suppliers and their business processes and supply chain performance, but also it should analyse and scrutinise the efficiency and effectiveness of the suppliers' suppliers and their relationships to supply chain performance.

To achieve an improvement in supply chain responsiveness SV&P suggested that BizElegance's senior management make themselves familiar with both the quick response (QR) movement (Christopher & Towill 2001) and the CPFR (collaborative planning forecasting replenishment) process (McAfee 2001).

The QR movement had originated in the US textile and apparel industry. The QR movement recognised that in the fashion business responsiveness was the key and that it is essential to judge quickly what is selling and then move it speedily through the supply chain pipeline and on to the racks before competitors do so. SV&P saw this movement's ideas and principles as an excellent framework for the time compressing of the BizElegance supply chain and the increasing of its responsiveness. They also applauded the QR emphasis on cooperative efforts among all members of the extended supply chain from basic raw material suppliers right through to the end customer (Christopher & Towill 2002). SV&P thus recommended both close and careful analysis of the QR movement concepts and principles and the application of such principles to the BizElegance supply chain.

CPFR was developed jointly by the VICS Association (Voluntary Interindustry and Commerce Standards Association) of the USA and some leading US consultants in the mid to late 1990s. The basic CPFR process is outlined in figure 6.11. As its name suggests, CPFR is a framework that aims to provide companies with a common approach to sharing demand, forecast and planning information with the aim of the companies concerned gaining the benefits of those collaborative processes (McAfee 2001).

Collaborative planning

YEARLY

Step 1: Develop front-end agreement: participating companies identify sponsors, agree to confidentiality and dispute resolution processes, develop a scorecard to track key supply chain metrics relative to success criteria and establish any financial incentives or penalties.

QTRLY

Step 2: Create joint business plan: the project teams develop plans for promotions, inventory policy changes, store openings/closings and product changes for each product category.

Collaborative forecasting

QUARTERLY

Retailers and suppliers share consumer demand forecasts and identify exceptions that occur when partners' plans do not match or when they change dramatically. They resolve exceptions by determining causal factors, adjusting plans where necessary.
Step 3: Create sales forecast.
Step 4: Identify exceptions for sales forecast.
Step 5: Resolve/collaborate on exception items.

Collaborative replenishment

WEEKLY

Step 6: Create order forecast.
Step 7: Identify exceptions for sales forecast.
Step 8: Resolve/collaborate on exception items.

Step 9: Order generation/delivery exception: result data (POS, orders, shipments, on-hand inventory) is shared and forecast accuracy problems, overstock/understock conditions, and execution issues are identified and resolved.

Figure 6.11 The nine-step CPFR process
Source McAfee 2002, p. 14.

SV&P felt that CPFR could reduce the 'bullwhip effect' (Lee, Padmanabhan & Whang 1997), which was causing highly negative effects in the BizElegance supply chain. Order fluctuation, for example, went from approximately 5 per cent variability at the customer–retailer interface to approximately 40 per cent variability at the yarn maker–fabric maker interface, i.e. 8 times greater than marketplace variability (see figure 6.12).

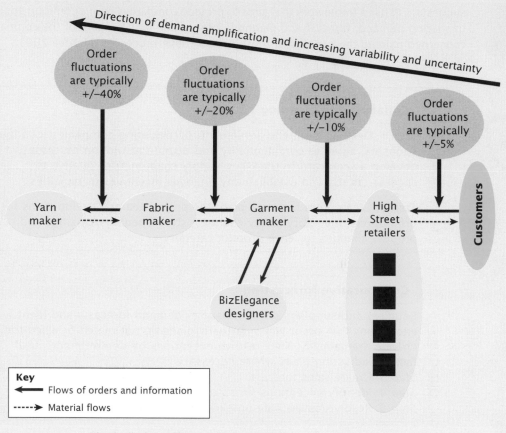

Figure 6.12 ▶ The bullwhip effect in BizElegance's supply chain

Source ▶ adapted from Christopher and Towill 2002, p. 3.

The above two approaches, SV&P thought, would enable BizElegance to negotiate win–win processes for supply chain management with its supply chain partners. To sharpen their ideas on interorganisational process design, SV&P suggested that BizElegance's senior management take the time to study Michael Hammer's paper, 'The superefficient company' (Hammer 2001). SV&P suggested that in approaching interorganisational process redesign, BizElegance should consider establishing IT-enabled interorganisational processes. Indeed, some of these interorganisational processes could be improved further by establishing some IT-enabled intra-organisational processes. SV&P cautioned BizElegance that people-oriented change management would be a particular concern here and that establishing a sophisticated IT infrastructure and application portfolio would probably be too much change too quickly. However, perhaps such IT-enablement of intra-company and business processes should perhaps be envisaged and planned for in the longer term.

Although SV&P cautioned on too much change too quickly, it did feel that IT could help with cumbersome telephone, fax and postal communications. They therefore suggested some investigation of electronic mail and systems based on electronic data interchange (EDI). SV&P also suggested that the BizElegance management investigate the potential of computer-aided design and computer-aided manufacture (CAD/CAM) software as an internal tool for enabling efficiencies in the design process and as a tool for electronically transmitting designs quickly to supply chain partners. If adopted, the CAD/CAM software would also allow supply chain partners to enter the design details of a garment efficiently into their production systems. Potential savings could come from reducing omissions and errors in the designs and in reducing errors in reading and interpreting the designs. The CAD/CAM software, with its standards and conventions for designs, could thus create a set of understood conventions between designers and manufacturers.

After a brief reading of the SV&P report, and a presentation by the consultants to Kate Clench and her operations manager and chief financial officer, Kate Clench's initial response was that the report was comprehensive and well informed. It contained, she thought, some very worthwhile suggestions and recommendations. After studying the SV&P report in detail, she outlined the major recommendations to her senior management team and then circulated the report to them for further study. She also presented the findings and major recommendations to the BizElegance staff, pointing out that although the company needed to look carefully at the recommendations given the downward sales trend, the report was only a set of recommendations at this stage.

Kate then requested that her senior management team study the report and investigate the issues and challenges of implementing its major recommendations. She mentioned that, in carrying out this investigation, consultation with staff was of the utmost importance. Kate then allocated particular responsibilities to her operations manager, Heather McClintock, and McClintock's deputy, Don McDermid. Heather was to investigate in some detail the readiness of supply chain partners to consider some of the recommended changes. McDermid was asked to look into possible internal changes within BizElegance.

McDermid was the first to report back to Clench. He had found very quickly that the SV&P report had caused considerable consternation among the staff. Most of the staff had very little knowledge of computers, and most had no experience of using them. They were very concerned about potential job losses as well as about their ability to learn how to use computers. The concern among the purchasing department team, for example, was only heightened by McDermid's explanation of EDI as 'computer to computer purchase order placement' — a notion that seemed to spell redundancy for many of the purchasing team. The general concern among staff was expressed as a high degree of irritation among the designers, who felt that their skills would be diminished and the creative design process 'corrupted' by the process of utilising CAD/CAM software.

Don McDermid took these concerns back to Kate Clench, who was somewhat alarmed by the reaction, particularly that of her first-class design team. However, Heather McClintock was faring no better in her talks with the supply chain partners.

Heather McClintock had spent considerable time both with each of the five garment manufacturers and with a number of the most prominent fabric and yarn makers that BizElegance had dealt with in the past. The garment manufacturers, without exception, were focused on cost minimisation. McClintock found that although each of them said they would strive to meet contractual quality and time specifications, the real motivation was to keep their costs as low as possible. Furthermore, they were not innovative in their business processes, and they made little use of information technology. McClintock felt that although the manufacturers' management teams were polite with her, they seemed reluctant to enter into a collaborative planning forecasting and replenishment process, and even more reluctant to invest in IT and the concomitant training that introducing IT systems would involve.

Another issue that arose indirectly was the fact that these manufacturers not only served BizElegance but also a number of other important fashion houses in Europe and the USA. Hence any new developments, new IT or business systems introduced would have to suit their other customers as well — particularly if they were introduced enterprise-wide. McClintock found that the fabric makers and the yarn makers, similarly to the garment manufacturers, had cost minimisation strategies and little or no utilisation of IT. They also had a number of important customers aside from BizElegance and generally felt that any new systems introduced would have to suit their other customers as well.

As Heather McClintock prepared to fly back to Australia with rather grim, or at least challenging, news for Kate Clench, she reflected that she did have some news that could turn out to be good news. On her trip McClintock had visited a number of other garment manufacturers to gain further information on the industry in the Asia–Pacific region. Two of those garment manufacturers, one in Shanghai and the other in Jakarta, had shown a particular interest in BizElegance. They had heard of the company and were keen to win a large proportion of its orders. Both the manufacturers were medium-sized only and therefore would regard BizElegance as a large and important client. Both the Jakarta manufacturer and the Shanghai manufacturer were surrounded by a cluster of fabric and yarn makers, and seemed to have good relationships with a few of these companies. It was true that, in common with the other manufacturers, these two were cost minimisers, but in the conversations that McClintock had with them, they seemed keen to form a relationship with BizElegance. Indeed, several of the management team in each of these companies had been to university in Australia and had some understanding of Australian business and culture. Both the Jakarta and the Shanghai producer had begun to implement basic IT systems and seemed to be able and willing to innovate. McClintock began to reflect on whether the two companies could possibly make close and responsive supply chain partners of the type the new BizElegance of the future would need.

When Kate Clench had an opportunity to discuss all the issues with McClintock and McDermid, she felt that the investigations the two had carried out had led to a lot of important issues concerning the future of the company. She felt that the full senior management team should think through the possibilities and challenges facing the company. She proposed a weekend retreat at Mount Eliza, by the sea outside Melbourne, as a perfect place to work quietly and determinedly through all the issues and come up with an executable plan.

Questions

1. Describe what you believe is the most serious and important challenge facing Kate Clench; that is, clearly describe what you see as the problematic situation facing BizElegance.

2. Outline the main elements of a possible way forward for the company; that is, outline the main elements of the solution to BizElegance's difficulties.

3. An IT consulting firm, hearing of BizElegance's problems, suggests that the first move the company makes should be to create a basic intra-company IT infrastructure to enable the proper development of interorganisational systems. Without such a basic infrastructure, the consulting firm argues, it will be impossible to implement a reliable and robust IT-enabled system of supply chain management. Furthermore, the consulting firm argues, the best way to create a good fundamental IT infrastructure is to implement the manufacturing, purchasing and financial modules of its own ERP system.

   Kate Clench asks you to assess this proposal. What would be your advice?

chapter 7

Transforming external relationships with customers

learning objectives

After reading this chapter, you should be able to:

- understand the concept of and issues surrounding a demand chain
- appreciate the importance of switching emphasis from a supply chain to a demand chain
- appreciate the importance of a customer focus in contemporary organisations and the implications of increasing customer satisfaction and loyalty
- describe the capabilities of IT-enabled demand chains
- grasp the significance and benefits of customer relationship management
- appreciate the role and contribution of IT in customer relationship management
- understand the steps and success factors in implementing customer relationship management.

chapter overview

This chapter moves its focus towards customers and considers how IT, e-commerce and e-business are contributing, even causing, major transformations in the ways organisations interact with their customers. The chapter begins with a consideration of the importance of customers to the long-term profitability and sustainability of organisations, and argues that modest increases in customer loyalty can have substantial effects on profitability. This implies a need to become a customer-centric organisation, one that takes customers, their needs, wants and preferences, and the business processes by which customer value is delivered, as the starting point for organisational activity. Hence, the concept of a customer-driven supply chain, or demand chain, is discussed.

IT plays a vital role in this reorientation towards a demand chain. The notions of electronic catalogues, online customer self-service, channel management and business intelligence tools and techniques (including data warehousing and data mining) are all vital to the organisation achieving the required transformation. Thus IT has enabled new ways of building relationships with customers, and the whole philosophy of customer centredness enabled by IT is called customer relationship management (CRM). These ideas are explored, and the significance, benefits and challenges of CRM are examined. The role of IT and some critical success factors to ensure the viability of these initiatives are explored. The chapter concludes with a discussion of some of the issues and ethics associated with CRM in organisations.

Introduction

In chapter 5 of this book, the importance of focusing on customers was briefly introduced. At that stage, the interest was on arguing the case for a process focus or orientation,
with its end point of a customer, and on adopting IT to support efficient and effective
process flows throughout an organisation. In chapter 6, the idea of efficient and effective
processes as being a way to deliver value to customers and hence to ensure viability and
sustainability for an organisation was extended beyond the boundaries of an organisation
to include all those processes and systems that link an organisation and its trading partners. A similar concept of electronic linkages between sellers and buyers is explored and
developed in this chapter, but instead the focus in this chapter is specifically on why an
organisation should pay attention to the needs, wants, preferences and values of its
customers and the ways an organisation can reach out to and interact with its customers.

The importance of customers

Sam Walton, founder and celebrated CEO of Wal-Mart, is supposed to have made the
following comment: 'There is only one boss. The customer. And he can fire every-
body in the company, from the chairman on down, simply by spending his money
somewhere else' (AT Kearney 2001:1).

Walton was referring to a simple but important homily in business: in times of
hyper-competition, when for most goods and services supply outstrips demand, if
customers do not value the goods and/or services an organisation offers, that business
is likely to fail. Hence, many organisations attempt to understand what it is about the
bundle of goods and services of a particular quality for a particular price offered to its
customers that those customers value. This renewed emphasis on the customer is an
attempt to improve the goods and services offered and to tailor or modify them in
accordance with customer needs and wants. In this way an organisation can aim to
increase customer satisfaction and loyalty, and therefore to retain existing customers
and to win new customers. Converting a satisfied customer into a satisfied and loyal
customer has the effect of increasing the customer lifetime value (i.e. the value that a
customer contributes to the profitability of an organisation over his/her lifetime),
which is a potentially important source of increasing profitability for an organisation.

Consider these statistics on how many average companies perform on this score.
Every five years, the average corporation in the United States loses about 50 per cent
of its customers. Cutting this figure to just a 45 per cent loss over the same period can
lead to a doubling of company profits. Furthermore, Reichheld (1996a) asserts that a
5 per cent increase in customer retention can increase the average lifetime value of a
customer from between 35 and 95 per cent, depending on the industry and the
specifics of a particular organisation (Ryals & Knox 2001). The impact of increases in
customer retention on profits is, of course, equally dramatic. A 5 per cent increase in
customer retention leads to improved profits of between 25 and 80 per cent
(Reichheld 1996b; Reichheld & Kenny 1990). Hence, one of the obvious reasons for a
focus on and orientation towards customer satisfaction and loyalty is simply that

retaining more customers increases their average lifetime value, which in turn can have a significant positive effect on corporate performance.

Figure 7.1 offers another indication of why this focus is particularly important in the contemporary business environment. A typical organisation incurs costs on its customers potentially for a much longer period than it enjoys (financial) benefit. It bears the cost of trying to attract and win a potential customer in the first place, there are still costs associated with providing service to existing and loyal customers and, if it attempts to win back a former or dissatisfied customer, then this is a source of cost as well. By contrast, it enjoys benefits from customers only when they are purchasing goods and services. If it is accepted that by achieving customer loyalty and hence retaining a greater proportion of customers over time substantially affects an organisation, then clearly an organisation needs to know its costs with respect to each customer, which customer or customer segment is profitable, and how much profit is contributed by respective customer segments.

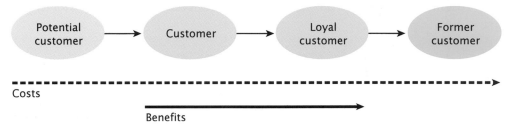

Figure 7.1 ▶ The relative period of accruing costs of and benefits from customers

An example from the Service Management Interest Group, Harvard Business School, might help to clarify some of these concepts. Figure 7.2 gives an indication of the profit per customer for an average credit card company. Notice that in the first year the company makes a substantial loss, which is attributable to the costs involved in attracting and winning over the customer, but thereafter it starts to make modest profits (although it should be noted that these seem to stagnate after about the third year).

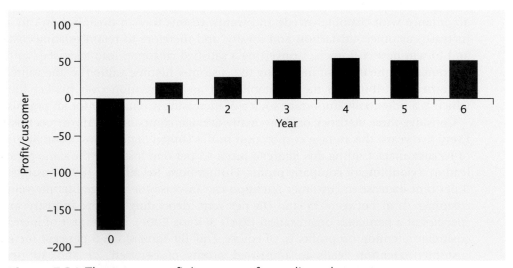

Figure 7.2 ▶ The average profit/customer of a credit card company
Source ▶ Cash 1999.

However, if the cumulative profit/customer is considered, then a different picture emerges (see figure 7.3). Given the substantial size of the loss in the first trading year, the company actually does not recoup that loss and start to make a profit on the customer until the sixth year of their trading relationship. This, then, provides a clear picture of why and how increasing customer loyalty (the length of the period a customer does business with a company) can make a dramatic impact on the overall profitability of that customer or customer segment.

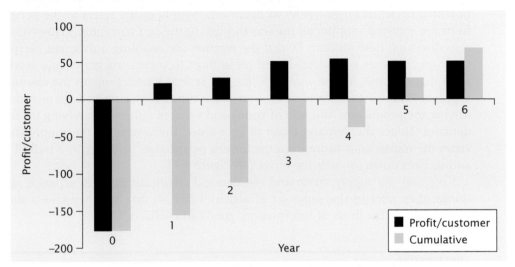

Figure 7.3 ▶ Cumulative versus net profit/customer for a credit card company
Source ▶ Cash 1999.

Why do customers become more profitable the longer they remain loyal to an organisation? Remember that the acquisition costs, although a sizeable loss, are incurred once only. The additional benefits that start to accrue from loyal customers include the following:
• Loyal customers refer other, new customers to the organisation, and do this increasingly over time, thus substantially reducing the acquisition costs of those additional customers.
• Loyal customers tend to purchase more and more goods and services over time.
• Loyal customers are less price-sensitive, and hence can be charged premium prices without deserting the organisation.
• Loyal customers typically incur fewer administrative costs over time (Cash 1999).

In as much as the benefits of loyal customers increase over time, the damage done by dissatisfied customers can also escalate. Let's imagine that a customer has a bad dining experience at a particular restaurant. It is unlikely that the customer will readily return to this restaurant, and therefore the business has lost the opportunity to create a loyal customer from this first time customer. Not only does the organisation lose on that customer's loyalty, however, but also dissatisfied customers tend to tell others of their bad experiences, and so there develops a pool of potential customers who will never try the restaurant: they have been scared off by their friend's stories of dissatisfaction. Hence the losses to that business actually compound over time. It is therefore not hard to realise why there has been an upsurge in interest in understanding the preferences and needs of customers.

The concept of a demand chain

In the previous chapter, the notion or concept of a supply chain was discussed. Essentially, the supply chain is the concept of suppliers of materials, components, goods and services selling these items to parties further down the supply chain who have a need for such items. The perspective adopted is essentially that of supplier to potential or actual buyer. (Refer to figure 6.1. 'Supply chain' refers to the perspective from raw material supplier all the way through to the end consumer.) However, it was also discussed how modern IT and the Internet are enabling a different perspective, i.e. from customer wants, needs and preferences to producing goods and services to meet that demand, all the way back through several transactions to the raw material suppliers. One of the effects of IT is to move much closer towards known demand driving the production and sale of goods and services rather than relying on forecast demand. Hence the demand chain is, in a sense, the reverse of the supply chain. It views the transactions more from the buyer's perspective, resulting in a pull of goods and services down towards the buyer (see figure 7.4).

Note that the supply chain and the demand chain are not two separate, discrete things: they refer to the same set of activities and so on, but they take a different perspective on the flows of information, goods and services.

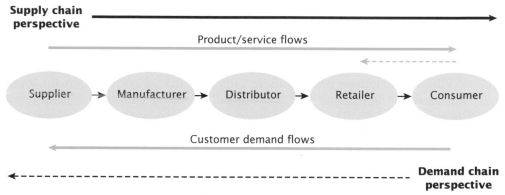

Figure 7.4 ▶ Differences in perspective between the supply chain and the demand chain

IT-enabled demand chains

On the one hand it could be said that these two concepts — the supply chain and the demand chain — are essentially the same thing from a different perspective. However, IT and the Internet are offering new systems that enable the customer to interact with the organisation in new ways, and it is these new systems and IT applications that will be the focus of our attention in this chapter. It is fair to say that the broad aims of these types of systems are to improve customer satisfaction and hence loyalty. In light of the preceding discussion about the importance of maintaining satisfied customers, it is fair to say that these systems represent significant investments for organisations, but if they do support the maintenance of a satisfied customer, then they offer potentially enormous business benefits to organisations.

One of the concerns for many organisations that was introduced in chapter 5 was the difficulty for some organisations in obtaining a single 'snapshot' of any particular customer or customer segment. At that time, it was argued that moving from an orientation towards product lines (goods and services) and towards a process view (which inevitably has a customer as the end point of a process) was an important source of greater efficiency and effectiveness and therefore is appropriate for many organisations. If the new information about the behaviour of customers is added to that, then it becomes clear that an orientation towards customers is vital in achieving success in the long term. Not only do organisations need to keep a holistic view of their customers but they also recognise a need to present themselves in a consistent manner to their customers, i.e. they want to present a single face to the customer. From a customer's perspective it is helpful to find that one branch of the bank is essentially the same as all others. As customers move into electronic interactions with the bank (for example), then it is helpful if the organisation presents a consistent face to the customer no matter what channel the customer chooses by which to interact with the organisation.

Electronic catalogues

One aim of business is to facilitate the process by which customers can do business (obtain information and transact) with them. Fundamental to this is providing accurate, complete, relevant and accessible information to customers on the types of product and services sold, their availability and location, pricing, delivery information and the like. For a long time now, organisations have relied on a variety of paper catalogues, leaflets and brochures that can be sent to prospective customers, handed to them by sales staff, left lying around for interested customers at retail outlets and so on. However, it has always proved extremely difficult to keep these paper-based advertising media up to date, to ensure that they are received by the people who need them, to ensure that the information they contain is accurate for all locations and so on. Brochures, catalogues, CDs and mail-outs, for example, are typically hard to maintain and keep accurate, and can in some circumstances cause more trouble than they are worth if they are inaccurate. However, the **electronic catalogue** (or **e-catalogue**) can provide a solution to some of these problems. The e-catalogue is located on a company's website and allows customers access to accurate product information that is both complete and up to date. From the organisation's perspective, it is relatively easy to keep a website up to date. Customers can simply visit a website and gain information about products and services on offer. It is one of the simplest and least costly ways of making a foray into e-commerce.

Let us consider a simple example. A builder is redeveloping a suburban block, which formerly contained a large single dwelling plus extensive backyard. The block is now zoned as suitable for a triplex development. Timing of the delivery of required building materials is essential to the accurate scheduling of tradespeople. Furthermore, there is comparatively little room on the block for storage of large quantities of materials. Therefore the concrete foundations (the pad) must be *in situ* before the house bricks are delivered. The roofing sections must be delivered especially for the back two units before bricks for a side retaining wall and driveway can be delivered and installed. The roof must be on before the electrical and internal plumbing works can be commenced, and so on. Knowing what materials are available, where they are located and at what price is essential for the builder. Imagine that the roofing sections have already been ordered, their delivery is promised for early tomorrow morning and the roofing contractors are due to start installation tomorrow. The builder decides therefore to place an order for the side retaining wall. A phone call to a local brick manufacturer is made and, following the exchange of information with sales staff, an order is made for twelve palettes of bricks to be delivered before close of business tomorrow. The builder then employs labourers and equipment, such as a bobcat, to start the construction of the retaining wall the following day. It is essential to get the roofing sections delivered before the bricks, as twelve palettes of bricks will fill the driveway and prevent other access.

The following morning there is no sight of the roofing sections. After a phone call to the company involved, the builder is assured that the roofing sections have already left the yard and will be delivered shortly. The roofing contractors meanwhile are hanging around with no work to do. While the builder is out buying lunch, some of the bricks are delivered earlier than expected, and seven palettes are left in the driveway. Then the truck with the roofing sections arrives. But its load is incomplete. The sections for the first and third unit are correct. But the order for the second unit is incomplete.

What should the builder do: scream abuse at the roofing manufacturer for being late and not properly producing his order? Abuse the brick manufacturer for delivering early and for delivering only half his order? Tell the brick manufacturer to come and remove the palettes of bricks? A phone call to the brick manufacturer reveals that they do not have any more stock of the desired brick and that it will be two months before more stock is expected. The roofing manufacturer will not commit to getting the sections for the second unit on site within the next five working days. Whatever course of action is taken, the builder is an unhappy customer, and will incur greater costs in completing this project.

Could an e-catalogue have helped in this situation? A stand-alone e-catalogue might not have helped, but imagine an e-catalogue integrated with the company's back office ERP systems. This would enable a customer online to do a search of the company's inventory to find out what quantities of goods were available, where they were located, delivery costs and schedules, and so on. The e-catalogue, then, serves as the repository of accurate and complete information on company product lines, and so on, and should serve to integrate all product and service information from a variety of sources (paper, CD, etc). Furthermore, customer service staff also have access to this system, so advice they provide to customers who telephone will also be complete and accurate.

Customer self-service systems

The company's website and the e-catalogue are the start of what might collectively be described as **online customer self-service** systems. The aim of such online systems is to enable customers to access all information they need to do business with the company, including information about products and services, inventory levels and locations, price, quality, order forms and the ability to transact online, a help facility and so on. Allowing customers to serve themselves might sound like the opposite of improved customer service. In what ways does self-service help and benefit the customer?

Essentially, these systems allow the customer to take more control of the whole process of selecting goods and services, ordering them, tracking the progress of the order, managing their account details and so on. So, for example, self-service systems enable a customer to access product information and thus make a decision about its suitability, and to check an organisation's inventory levels to see whether there is stock available to fulfil their order at a time convenient to the customer. Customers are also able to place orders online, track the management and fulfilment of their order, and access their account information. In the event that goods need to be returned, this can also be supported as such systems enable tracking of returned goods. These systems do not necessarily replace contact via sales staff, but they do allow a customer to check the veracity of the promises of sales staff via the Internet. The notion of convenience for the customer is central to the concept of online customer self-service. So, although there is a sense in which the customer seeks the service they require from a company, many customers report that the new self-service channel offers greater convenience, flexibility and efficiency. Second, many of these systems allow twenty-four-hour access, to use what for many is a familiar interface (i.e. the web browser) and access via wireless and mobile devices. Thus, decision-making and trading can be conducted at the convenience of the customer.

Amazon.com has made excellent use of these systems. As a potential customer of Amazon, you are able to search for a particular product (let's say a book), to look at its table of contents and sometimes to read a chapter online, to access details of the availability of the book and its price, to order and pay for the book online, and then to track the item as it is being shipped to your required address. Amazon then uses information about your purchases subsequently to make recommendations and suggestions to you for additional purchases, and looks for opportunities for up-selling and cross-selling. Over time, Amazon is also able to build up an accurate picture of every customer's preferences.

Self-service systems are not intended to replace completely the need for call centres (where customers can phone in for service) or face-to-face customer service, but it would be fair to say that a major benefit from the organisation's perspective is shifting some of this activity to the customer and thus decreasing their call centre and customer service costs. There are reports of substantial cost savings to be generated through the effective use of online customer self-service systems (see table 7.1 on p. 194 as an example). The example assumes certain costs associated with providing customer service by phone, via email and via self-service using an online query. It also assumes a level of traffic (monthly contacts) that interacts with the organisation by phone and email. If the implementation of an online customer self-service system facilitates the diversion of, say, 10 per cent of customer service efforts to the online service, then substantial savings can accrue to the organisation.

Some caution needs to be exercised in interpreting these figures, as every organisation will have different levels and volumes of requirement for customer service, and the type of queries dealt with will also vary. But many organisations face repetitive, non-complex queries (e.g. what hours does your store open? Where is the closest store to me? What is the status of my order?), which are easily attended to via the Internet. Furthermore, many organisations find it difficult to ensure that the information and service offered to customers is consistent across all points of contact. Layers of

Table 7.1 ▶ Example of potential monthly savings following customer self-service implementation

	Number	$	Totals
Cost/call		15	
Cost/email		5	
Cost/online query		1	
Current scenario			
Monthly contacts:			
Calls	50 000	15	750 000
Emails	10 000	5	50 000
Monthly contact support costs			**800 000**
Online self-service scenario: 10 per cent call avoidance			
Monthly contacts:			
Calls	45 000	15	675 000
Emails	9 000	5	45 000
Online self-service	6 000	1	6 000
Monthly contact support costs			**726 000**
Monthly savings from self-service			74 000

Source ▶ Tobin 2003, p. 4.

information and access to that information can be made available not only to customers but also to various organisational members or providers of customer service to help ensure that information offered is consistent and accurate (Tobin 2003).

If an organisation also aims to increase revenues through up-selling and cross-selling and through increasing order size, these systems benefit the organisation by making the distribution of marketing materials and other information easier. They can also help an organisation to move into new markets and to attract new customers through the ease of doing business offered to customers.

It would be unwise to assume that all products and services would be equally suited to e-catalogues and customer self-service.

Channel management

A channel in this context is essentially a means of reaching customers. There are multiple channels by which an organisation can reach its customers, and in practice most organisations do not rely on only one channel, using dealers, retailers, paper, fax, phone, personal contact or the company's website (see figure 7.5). The traditional supply chain discussed in the previous chapter is a distribution channel, a means of distributing goods and services to the end consumer. Thus, for example, a typical manufacturer might have its own retail outlets by which it sells direct to end consumers, but it might also (or instead) rely on a network of dealers or retailers to reach its customers. An organisation might also rely on a catalogue that is sent to potential customers by mail and which enables customers to respond by telephone, fax or mail. The organisation might also employ travelling sales staff, who become a conduit of

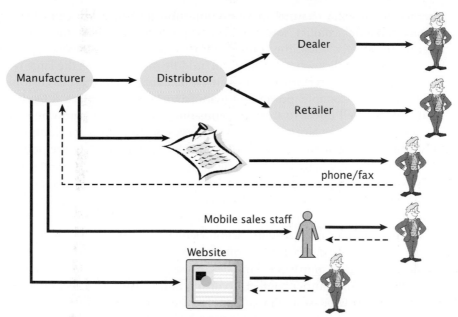

Figure 7.5 ▶ Channels of communication with customers

information between the company and its customers. More recently, organisations have started to adopt electronic means of reaching customers, especially via the Internet and by email.

From one perspective, it seems desirable to have as many ways as possible of reaching one's customers. However, having more channels tends to result in a rapid escalation of complexity and hence increased managerial and administrative overheads. Furthermore the potential for channel conflict to occur increases. Channel conflict is the situation that occurs when an organisation (let's say a manufacturer) adds an additional channel to reach customers that causes upset among existing players in other distribution channels. In the e-commerce world, often this would be selling direct to the customer over the Internet. Various distributors, dealers and retailers currently involved in selling the manufacturer's goods to customers might perceive the extra channel as a threat and a negative development, and express their objections vehemently to the manufacturer. They might also retaliate by refusing to handle the manufacturer's goods any more or by taking other commercially punitive action. Depending on the relative power of the players, this may result in the manufacturer backing down or attempting to find alternatives to the existing network of dealers and retailers. In the early days of e-commerce, reports of channel conflict were quite common.

In the mid 1990s, it was common to hear talk about disintermediation, i.e. the notion that one of the major effects of the Internet in terms of B2C e-commerce would be to cut out the 'middle men' or intermediaries, and allow companies to sell direct to the end consumer. Thus it was widely predicted that businesses like travel agencies, insurance agencies and so on — the classic intermediaries — would disappear as airlines and insurance companies sold direct to their clients. To a large extent this has not happened, as many agencies were in fact adding value for the customer. Indeed, many have in fact reinforced their position by their adoption of the

Internet as an extra channel of communication and possibly extra business transactions. Channel conflict was also widely predicted to affect the adoption of the
Internet negatively. Thus, the countervailing force to disintermediation would result
from channel conflict, whereby powerful 'middle men' (such as the large retail chains,
for example) could exert force on manufacturers not to sell direct to customers via the
Internet. So, for example, power tool manufacturers such as Black & Decker were persuaded not to sell direct to their end consumer by powerful hardware stores such as
Home Depot. Harvey Norman, one of the largest retail outlets for Compaq computers
in Australia, was able to dissuade Compaq from selling direct to the public.

It seems obvious that none of these scenarios is desirable. Channel conflict does
not serve to improve customer service and might result in a negative public image for
some or all of the involved parties. Arguably, information systems that enable appropriate and effective channel management might help to alleviate some of these issues.

Channel management systems acknowledge and support the network of activity
among various players (which is often quite invisible to the end consumer) and
enable all players to 'participate' in sales, irrespective of the channel being employed.
Thus, rather than channel conflict occurring and causing bad feeling among trading
partners, it is now possible that a manufacturer can apparently sell direct to the end
consumer over the Internet, but with the purchased goods actually being supplied by
the closest dealer and delivered to the customer by the distributor usually involved in
the movement of those goods. Therefore IT can enable all players to participate in
activity along the supply chain. Channel management solutions in effect enable companies to sell direct, without disintermediating valued trading partners, as dealers,
retailers and distributors, for example, can still be involved in order management and
fulfilment and can still receive commissions. All channel partners can be offered the
opportunity to track and view the status of orders throughout the order fulfilment
process, and trading partners can also be offered opportunities to sell complementary
goods and services, such as additional warranties and the like. Account details and
inventory information and locations may all be shared among the network of trading
partners. The process of order fulfilment could be designed to maximise the respective
strengths of the trading partners and to bind the trading network even closer together.

Such channel management solutions clearly involve collaborative interorganisational process redesign initiatives of the type described by Hammer (2001). The
negotiation and collaboration involved in such initiatives is in stark contrast to the
adversarial approaches that were being considered in the mid 1990s, and is without
doubt enabled by the deployment of appropriate IT.

Channel management tools can also be used in the execution and management of
marketing and promotional activities, and are useful in tracking the effectiveness of
various activities among multiple trading partners.

Business intelligence, data warehousing and data mining

In the previous chapter, there was a brief discussion of decision support systems and
their role in gathering, storing and manipulating large amounts of data to provide
support for the decision-making activities of managers. These systems probably now

more accurately belong to the area known as **business intelligence**, whereby internal and external data is gathered, stored and analysed to provide accurate information for an organisation. Thus, data from an organisation's internal ERP systems would likely be involved, as would external data, such as information from trading partners, economic trends (macro and micro), seasonality (surges in demand for Christmas or Easter) and so on. Business intelligence tools provide much better forecasts of end consumer demand, which can be fed both upstream and downstream in the supply chain. Such forecasts, together with other statistical decision support analyses, are then used in the design of production, inventory control and distribution systems along the supply chain.

Business intelligence systems rely on the availability of vast amounts of accurate data. Typically an organisation will have a number of separate databases in which pools of relevant data lie, and this data is brought together and combined with external data from trading partners in a data warehouse. The tools and techniques that allow managers to identify trends and patterns and to obtain information on which to base their decision-making are known as data mining tools. Thus, business intelligence, a vital support in corporate strategic analysis and action, is dependent on excellent data warehouses and data mining tools and techniques. The fields of data warehousing and data mining are now important specialist topics in information systems, and a significant body of literature exists for both topics (Kimball et al. 1998; Han & Kamber 2001; Shaw et al. 2001; Thearling 1995; Berson, Smith & Thearling 2000).

Customer relationship management

A chapter discussing the transformation occurring in relationships with customers owing to developments in IT and the Internet could not be complete without mention of **customer relationship management** (CRM). Many of the specific elements previously discussed under the broad heading of IT-enabled demand chains, specifically channel management, customer self-service and business intelligence, all contribute to what is becoming known as CRM (Christopher & Payne 2002). CRM is both a philosophy and an approach to managing the orientation that an organisation adopts to its customers and a suite of software-driven tools and techniques through which an organisation can gather, store, analyse and learn from vast amounts of customer data available to it. Some writers stress the relationship and marketing components of CRM. Payne (2000, p. 2), for example, writes that CRM 'is concerned with the creation, development and enhancement of individualized customer relationships with carefully targeted customers and customer groups resulting in maximising their total customer life-time value'. Those who share Payne's view might also adopt the terms *relationship marketing, customer management* and *one-to-one marketing* as being synonymous with CRM (Peppers, Rogers & Dorf 1999).

A slightly different emphasis is evident when Couldwell (1998, p. 64) writes that CRM is 'a combination of business process and technology that seeks to understand a company's customers from the perspective of who they are, what they do, and what they like'.

Deck (2001, p. 1) offers a more holistic view, which sees CRM as a strategy and a process, comprising many technological components:

> a strategy to learn more about customers' needs and behaviours in order to develop stronger relationships with them...there are many technological components to CRM, but thinking about CRM in primarily technological terms is a mistake...CRM is a process that will help bring together lots of pieces of information about customers, sales, marketing effectiveness, responsiveness and market trends.

Although there is broad agreement on what CRM is, there seems to be a variety of views on what constitutes a CRM initiative in an organisation. In some cases, a CRM initiative seems to involve little more than an organisation paying a little more attention to the needs and preferences of its customers, enabled through the provision of software and databases to customer support staff. However, in other organisations CRM represents a fundamental transformation from being production-oriented to becoming customer-centric, actively aiming to build relationships with its profitable customers and supporting staff with knowledge-enabled CRM tools, including data warehousing, data mining, sales force automation, online customer self-service and call centre technologies (Stone, Woodcock & Wilson 1996; Harvard Business School 2000; Thompson et al. 2000; Ryals & Payne 2001; Ryals & Knox 2001; Ahmed & Buttle 2001; Wilson, Daniel & McDonald 2002; Goodhue, Wixom & Watson 2002; Gray & Byun 2002).

Significance of CRM

CRM now represents very significant expenditure for many organisations. For example, the Gartner Group (2001) estimates that about US$23 billion was spent on CRM projects in 2000. Their estimates suggest that this will rise to US$76 billion by 2005. Large organisations are estimated to be spending between US$15 million and US$30 million per year, with total implementations costing between US$60 and US$130 million. Hence, CRM represents substantial investment, and care needs to be taken that organisations achieve reasonable returns on these investments and feel that adequate business value is being delivered.

However, like so many IT initiatives and large projects, CRM has a questionable track record and is starting to develop a questionable reputation. There have been reports that about 20 per cent of CRM projects are never finished, 55–75 per cent of CRM initiatives fail to deliver the anticipated benefits, and about 60 per cent of managers view their CRM investments as operating failures (Kiely 2001). It is therefore imperative that some of the success factors and issues with CRM implementations are well understood in order to ensure that adequate returns are achieved.

Perspectives and tenets of CRM

CRM seems to represent at least two quite profound shifts in perspective. First, it represents a movement away from a production-centric organisation (i.e. the organisation that is both structured on and based its strategy around the products and services it produces) to a customer-centric organisation (i.e. an organisation that takes as its starting point the needs, wants, values and preferences of its customers and uses them as its focus and orientation). The customer-centric organisation is more concerned with developing individualised and personalised relationships with each customer (hence one-to-one marketing, and the notion of a market of one) and with using the information gained through this relationship over time to learn more about customer preferences and thereby to improve continually on the goods and services offered to customers. Developing individual, learning relationships with customers over time with the aim of increasing customer satisfaction, and building loyalty and retention, lies at the essence of CRM practice (Stone et al. 1996; Moon 2000; Peppers et al. 1999; Harvard Business School 2000; Ryals & Knox 2001; Ahmed & Buttle 2001).

Second, CRM relies on and revolves around the application of sophisticated IT and the Internet to support the marketing and learning activities implied by CRM. Many modern organisations are experiencing the difficulties associated with the commoditisation of mass-produced goods, which almost by definition become difficult to differentiate from those of their competitors. Hence organisations increasingly become very vulnerable to competition based on price. A bundle of goods and services is therefore one of the main ways of differentiating one organisation's offerings from another. However, providing outstanding customer service based on personal contact can prove to be very expensive and is resource intensive, and these expenses are likely to increase substantially over time. Modern IT, and especially the Internet, has provided a key solution to this dilemma. Modern IT enables interactions with customers to be conducted much more cheaply and easily than previously, thus facilitating organisations in their desire to provide excellent service to customers in a cost-effective way. Essentially the costs of collecting, collating, storing, analysing and displaying vast amounts of data have decreased significantly over time, and therefore organisations are in a much better position to use that data, from possibly disparate sources, to learn more about who their customers are, what their customers like and dislike and, most importantly, what each of their customers is actually worth to them. With this knowledge, they are then better placed to target in a cost-effective manner the kinds of service that customers value.

Previously in this chapter it was demonstrated that loyal customers (not just satisfied ones) contribute disproportionately to profitability. IT-enabled tools and techniques are now enabling organisations to learn about their customers, so that not only can an organisation tailor the goods and services it provides to meet the needs of its loyal customers but also the types of services valued by customers that contribute to that loyalty can be delivered via the Internet and other channels in cost-effective ways (Peppard 2000; Ryals & Payne 2001; Gray & Byun 2001; Wilson et al. 2002; Goodhue et al. 2002).

CRM does not imply that an organisation should attempt to meet the needs and demands of all customers, nor that all customers are equally valuable. Rather, CRM is about correctly identifying those loyal customers who contribute disproportionately to profitability and attempting to increase their satisfaction and therefore the retention of such customers. Good CRM initiatives might also recognise that an unprofitable customer might be an extremely profitable customer at a competitor organisation: using business intelligence and CRM systems to detect such instances can also be important.

CRM practice, and consequently the way in which IT should be deployed to support customer centricity, revolves around five major tenets (Thompson et al. 2000; Ryals & Knox 2001; Ryals & Payne 2001; Wilson et al. 2002):

- Customers must be regarded as assets of the organisation.
- Customers will exhibit differences in their needs, preferences, buying behaviour and sensitivity to price and quality variables.
- Not all customers are equally profitable from an organisation's perspective and therefore not all customers are equally desirable.
- By developing an ongoing, learning relationship with customers, organisations can tailor their product and service portfolio to customers not only according to their needs, wants and preferences but also according to their contribution to the organisation's profitability.
- IT and Internet-based technologies are both enablers and facilitators of this process.

So there are a number of key requirements for the successful adoption and implementation of a CRM perspective. Organisations need to reorient themselves from being a product-centric organisation to being more customer-centric. This does not mean that products cease to be of importance, but rather that the starting point of focus is the customer first and then the product offerings. This implies an organisation-wide transformation, which will ultimately involve collecting data about customers at every point of their intersection with the organisation and possibly also its trading partners. The emphasis in marketing activity shifts from the acquisition of new customers towards the retention of customers and building their loyalty over time; hence another focus is on building long-term relationships with customers. All this is made possible through the application of IT and the Internet, both as the means of collecting and analysing data from which to learn about customer preferences and as the means of disseminating information to customer service staff and customers and therefore the provision of the services required and valued by customers.

Role of IT in CRM

CRM software packages share some of the characteristics of ERP systems: they are typically large and comprise a number of integrated modules, from which organisations select those modules suited to their specific customer strategy and requirements. Many of the same debates about customising the software to the organisation or changing the organisation to adapt to the software are also relevant. Essentially IT occupies three major roles in the CRM modules available (see figure 7.6).

At the heart of CRM are database technologies, including the concepts of data warehousing and data mining previously mentioned. It is these technologies that support the collection and collation of large amounts of data about the customer and his/her habits, the bringing together of disparate sources of data about customer activities, and the analysis of that data for trends, buying behaviour and sensitivities, preferences and the like through the use of real-time, user-friendly analytical tools.

Second, IT and the Internet offer opportunities for interaction with the customer and for records to be kept of this interaction. The classic examples of interactivity would include the corporate website and/or portal and the use of call centre technologies. For example, metrics can be obtained about the time spent on each web page, the browsing behaviour, the number of click-throughs from trading partners and associates, what customers are doing and viewing on the website, and so on (Kimball & Merz 2000; Linoff & Berry 2002). Records can be kept of the types of queries associated with customer contact via the call centre, and routine queries can be automated in many cases.

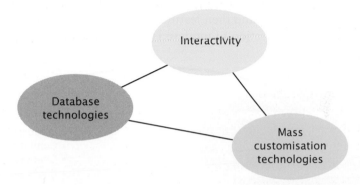

Figure 7.6 ▶ The types of IT facilitating CRM

Third, IT offers the potential for mass customisation, through the use of personal portals for example, where customers can access information pertinent specifically to them (the MyXXX is indicative of the adoption of this type of technology). At MyMonash, for example, students enrolled at Monash University can access their current enrolment status, enrol for a new semester, see personalised examination timetables and their own examination results, pay fines owing, view library catalogues, access a range of student services and so on. Amazon.com provides personalised recommendations of books for readers on the basis of the customer's preferences as indicated by the customer's previous purchases from Amazon and the customer's ratings of books inspected at Amazon's web page. From the customers' perspective, the benefit of mass customisation technologies is that they have access to and only have to deal with information that is relevant to their requirements.

It is fair to say that it is modern IT that makes possible the notion of a market of one, the idea that individualised products and services can be offered to each and every customer. Providing service at this level of personalisation and customisation would be prohibitively expensive without the adoption of appropriate IT. The Internet plays a vital role in this regard. Every new connection to the Internet from an organisation's perspective creates a potential relationship. By understanding the customers and customer segments that an organisation is servicing, much better targeting of products and services can be achieved. It is supporting the organisation both by managing the information about the customer, and in helping to manage the relationship through the provision of cost-effective service.

From figure 7.7 (p. 202), it can be seen that IT is playing two vital roles in the practice of CRM. First, it provides the means by which an organisation can learn about its customers. Through the acquisition and analysis of customer data, the organisation acquires information and knowledge about the preferences and values of its customers and about the value of each customer to the organisation. Thus, over time, it is able to differentiate customers on the basis of their preferences for particular types of goods and services and on the basis of their contribution to the profitability of the organisation. Second, this knowledge allows an organisation to better customise their portfolio of goods and services to the needs of their customers, to establish customer preferences for types of communication (email, phone calls etc.), the channels by which they prefer to interact with the organisation, their sensitivity to price and so on. Thus, an iterative process develops of learning about customers, customising in response to that learning and then learning as a result of the customisation, a process contingent on the application of modern IT and the use of the Internet.

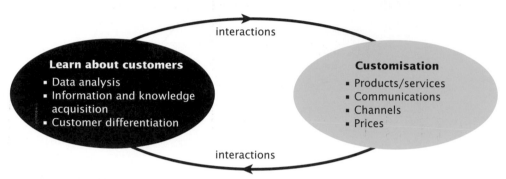

Figure 7.7 ▶ The role of IT in the customer-centric organisation
Source ▶ adapted from Moon 2000, p. 2.

Amazon.com provides an excellent example of an organisation that has used technology for these roles. Amazon has a vast database of stock items and a powerful search engine to help customers search for items of interest or to find a particular item. The level of information can be customised, as customers are prompted as to whether they would like to see more information on a particular product. For customers who are really interested in a particular book, there is often the opportunity to see a table of contents, perhaps to read a chapter and to read reviews and reactions from customers who have already purchased the item. Furthermore, Amazon's software will make suggestions automatically for the customer, based on the current search and for returning customers on the basis of their historical patterns of behaviour. The more the customer accepts these suggestions by clicking on them, the more refined the suggestions will become, and additional suggestions will be made. The Amazon web pages also contain information about availability and price, and there is the opportunity for the customer to customise their choice of delivery mechanisms according to budget and urgency.

Once an order has been made, Amazon uses automated emails to the customer to confirm the order, to confirm the dispatch of the order and to provide information on the tracking of the order (thus eliminating many of the routine enquiries that an organisation's call centre might otherwise have had to deal with). When a problem exists that requires a customer to make contact with Amazon via email, the organisation again uses automated email templates for their responses. Thus, Amazon is able to provide high levels of customer service without the need for employing large numbers of staff to deal with these queries. Behind the scenes, Amazon is able to record a huge amount of data about the behaviour of the customer on the website, the time spent, the number of successful order completions and so on, thus learning how to provide even better service for customers.

It would be wrong to say that CRM is primarily about technology, as developing appropriate strategies, transforming the organisation to a customer-centric orientation and developing excellent processes by which customer service is delivered are all essential ingredients in a CRM initiative. However, it also seems fair to conclude that without the application of modern IT and the advent of the Internet, CRM initiatives would be extremely labour-intensive. It is technology that enables an organisation to get closer to its customers and gain better insights into drivers of customer satisfaction and loyalty and to do so in an economically positive cost/benefit way.

thinking strategically

People or IT: which provides the best service to bank customers?

Lachlan Davenport was in no mood to have the bank he worked for changed by 'newfangled' technologies that added no new business value. He was marketing manager for the Bank of Australia. The bank's profits had plateaued in the last five years, and the CEO, John Dean, had requested that Davenport investigate the possibilities and value of the database marketing approaches of some other rival banks. Dean had suggested that, for a start, Davenport investigate the event-based marketing approach of ValuData, a data warehousing vendor and consulting company that specialised in event-based or event-driven marketing systems.

Roger Kerensky, a partner with ValuData, had explained that good marketing opportunities could be detected in various banking transactions and events if one had the appropriate software to examine transactions and events in a data warehouse of all banking transactions. To accomplish the necessary processing for such an approach the bank should purchase and utilise ValuData's Massively Parallel Processing (MPP) Based Data Warehouse to store and examine every banking transaction every day — indeed every minute or, preferably, every second! — whether this transaction came from the normal banking retail transactions or from transactions in the credit card or wealth businesses of the bank. ValuData's specialised software would allow the bank to detect special events such as the deposit of a large and significant amount of money from a customer, and then include that customer in an appropriate marketing campaign. The software would also coordinate the execution of the campaign.

Lachlan Davenport was not impressed; not immediately anyway. 'All we need,' he said, 'is to know our wealthy customers — those who really contribute to revenue and the bottom line and then focus on them — offering them good, indeed premium service. It's simple! It's based on our values of personal service. Our bank managers have good personal relationships with these people — that's what's key! That's what's fundamental, not information technology. We have basically broken down our customers into gold, silver and bronze, and we have gold, silver and bronze service levels to match. It's simple. You don't need Massively Parallel whatevers to do that!'

The audience of marketing and IT managers seemed impressed by the solid logic of the argument.

Roger Kerensky rose to his feet. 'Yes, you have a good fundamental approach,' he said. 'However, let me show you just one of the ways in which you could improve.

'Let us suppose,' he continued, 'that your customers — and gold, silver and bronze are like this [pointing to figure 7.8] and your rival's customers are like that [again pointing to figure 7.8]. I'm exaggerating the strength of this inverse relationship, of course.

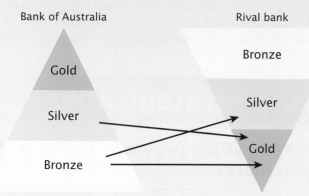

Figure 7.8 ▶ Shared customers

'Clearly,' Kerensky emphasised, 'at least some of your rival's gold and silver customers (very wealthy and quite wealthy) are appearing in your bank as silver or bronze. As we know, many people in Australia have accounts with several banks. But these apparent silver or bronze customers may actually be very wealthy people. How are you going to detect these people and treat them appropriately in terms of the potential opportunity for your bank?'

The group of marketing and IT managers were silent.

'Well,' Kerensky explained, 'our software would be watching transactions from these apparent bronze and silver customers. When, say, a bronze customer deposits a moderately significant dividend cheque, we — or should I say, our software — would notice. The conclusion would be that this deposit possibly indicates a wealthy customer with share portfolio and other investments held at another bank or financial institution. Our software would detect this transaction, pull appropriate data and information from the data warehouse, and determine an appropriate marketing campaign (we have a number of template campaigns) for the customer. The software would email the correct instructions to the right people and coordinate the series of feedbacks and responses with further emails of information and instructions. Your bank could be running 400 or so campaigns a night (with large numbers of individual cases in each) instead of several a week!'

'You mean you would drive our bank managers and call centre personnel's tasks and activities from this data warehouse,' said Davenport with a certain exasperation. 'Our staff respond to people, not computers. We are a very traditional company and proud of it.'

'Another thing,' interrupted Sunil Sharma, the IT director. 'This would be a large IT investment — a very large IT investment! How are we to know whether such an investment in such a radical and dramatic change for our bank will actually pay off for us?'

'Well', responded Davenport, 'if we are to go in the direction that ValuData suggests, we are going to have to think about the implications for the company — in terms of our values, our people and their skills and capabilities and so on. We are also, as Sunil says, going to have to think about how we evaluate such an IT investment.'

The meeting reached a stalemate with some members opposed to the new idea, others in favour of it and a third group still feeling quite uncertain. Lachlan Davenport requested that all managers present at the meeting think carefully and then prepare a brief report on the implications of ValuData's proposal for the bank.

Questions

1. Consider the implications of such an investment in information technology and systems for the bank. Use the framework introduced in figure 5.1 to analyse this proposal.
2. Consider whether such an approach is a CRM approach. Could it be part of a CRM approach?
3. Would you recommend that John Dean should proceed with this investment? Why or why not?

Benefits and challenges in CRM

A well-thought-out, well-designed and well-implemented CRM strategy can cause substantial change to an organisation's operations, but managers who are able to guide their organisations and their people through this transformation successfully can expect substantial returns for the organisation.

From a customer's perspective, CRM programs should result in enhanced service for the customer. This is achieved through improved access to required information and timely updates of that information, including details about products and services, stock availability, price updates, delivery schedules, account information and so on. Access to up-to-date and relevant information enables customers to keep track of their orders and, via online customer self-service systems, to do so at a time and place convenient to them. Customer service staff should also be given access to this information, meaning that if problems or disputes occur, staff are equipped with accurate information that will enable them to resolve these issues rapidly. Information on product and service enhancements and innovations can also be communicated to customers in a timely and cost-effective way. Another benefit of CRM from the customer's perspective is the ability to personalise and customise products and services and for interactions with the organisation to be personalised. Hence a key component of CRM is to use information to provide a better service to customers.

Better service represents added value from the customer's perspective, and therefore CRM aims to increase not just satisfaction but also, through the establishment of a long-term relationship, to increase customer loyalty and thus retention rates. Arguably this will be achieved through the adoption of a proactive rather than a reactive stance to managing customers, and hence one of the benefits of CRM to the organisation is that it should result in existing customer relationships leading to increased revenues for the organisation. With better information about customer behaviour and preferences, organisations can identify opportunities for up-selling and cross-selling and can enhance the customer value proposition through improved customer service, and so profitability can be enhanced if customer retention rates increase over time. A clear aim and benefit of CRM, then, is the identification and retention of profitable customers and establishing a relationship with the organisation that is valued by the customer. If relationships are to be long-lasting, organisations need to recognise and be adaptable to the changing requirements and preferences of their customers over time.

Another major benefit to organisations from CRM is cost reduction. Well-implemented CRM initiatives can reduce the cost of customer service (refer back to table 7.1).

It seems tempting to assume that CRM is right for everyone and that benefits will accrue to all organisations through the adoption of these ideas and techniques. However, although the thinking and practices embodied in CRM might be of benefit to all, wide-scale investment in the expensive technologies that CRM requires might not always be appropriate (see figure 7.9). Organisations can be classified according to the degree of differentiation that exists in terms of their customers' needs. For an organisation to be considered uniform in terms of its customers' needs, all of its customers require the same sorts of products and services, whereas the highly differentiated organisations have customers who are much more idiosyncratic in the precise nature of the goods and services they require. The other dimension used to classify organisations is that of customer valuations, or, in other words, the extent to which the

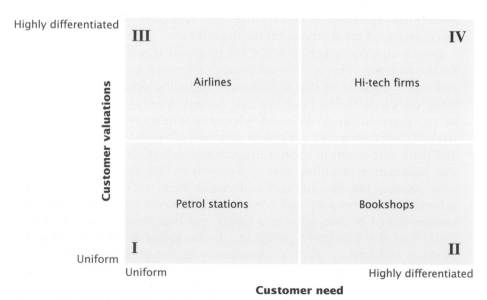

Figure 7.9 ▶ Does CRM apply in all organisations?
Source ▶ adapted from Harvard Management Update 2000, p. 4.

value contributed by customers varies. In organisations where customer valuations are relatively uniform, there is comparatively little difference in value between the most profitable and the least profitable customer groups. By contrast, in organisations with highly differentiated customer valuations, substantial differences exist between the least and most profitable customers.

Are CRM initiatives equally suited to all the quadrants represented in figure 7.9? Research would suggest that they are not (Harvard Management Update 2000). Organisations falling into quadrants II, III and IV are argued to be able to benefit, albeit in somewhat different ways. For a bookshop, for example, CRM applications can help to identify the precise needs of individual customers in terms of the types of books of interest, support excellent search facilities, make relevant suggestions and so on. Although all airline passengers share the same basic need (to be transported somewhere), CRM applications can be used to help airlines identify the profitability of various passenger segments and then to tailor cost-effective levels of service based on the profitability of each customer type. Quadrant IV organisations possibly stand to benefit the most, as CRM applications can help to offer excellent service to customers by identifying different customer interests and providing appropriate service while also enabling the organisation to customise services based on the profitability of a particular client. Figure 7.9 is offered for guidance only. Managers need to be aware that substantial variations among industries and within organisations exist as to the extent to which customers desire and will respond positively to the organisation's attempt to build relationships (Rigby et al. 2002).

Critical success factors in CRM

It was previously mentioned that implementing CRM well is complex and that there are disturbing reports of CRM failures and disappointments. In this regard, CRM shares many characteristics of all IS/IT projects: they promise much; when well-thought out and aligned with appropriate strategies, they can deliver much; but too often aspects of their conception and implementation are inadequate and result in less than satisfactory outcomes for the organisation. In this section, it is proposed to consider some of the critical success factors for CRM. What do organisations and managers need to be aware of if they want to implement CRM successfully?

First of all, successful CRM depends on having an appropriate business and customer strategy in place before deciding on CRM (Accenture 2002; Rigby et al. 2002). Alignment is the key here. Understanding what the organisation wishes to achieve, understanding existing customer segments and understanding how to respond to those customer segments are all essential before any decision about CRM technologies can be made. Throwing technology at a problem does not necessarily solve anything, and a CRM initiative that is clearly aligned with corporate objectives is much more likely to win support from senior executives, which is another critical success factor. For resource-intensive, complex projects that will take years to complete, winning and maintaining executive support is essential. A well-planned, strong business case that demonstrates alignment with business objectives and the benefits for the organisation is a key to obtaining the required support.

It has previously been mentioned that CRM is likely to involve major transformations internally and possibly in trading relationships. Hence, change management is essential. Change that acknowledges that more than changes to the technology is a vital starting point (refer back to figure 5.1). Adopting a customer-centric strategy and orientation will require changes to organisational structure and systems, business processes, skills, training, job descriptions, performance measurement, reward mechanisms and organisational culture as well as the obvious changes to technology (Rigby, Reichheld & Schefter 2002). Part of the cultural change required might be to persuade disparate functions, such as marketing and IT, to work effectively together (Yu 2001).

Before making a decision on software for CRM, it is essential that executives are clear on the aims and objectives of the CRM initiative, on what can be accomplished (given industry and organisational characteristics) and therefore on what capabilities are needed to deliver value to the customer and business value to the organisation. Not all customers have been shown to value relationships, and organisations need to show sensitivity to this. A failure to appreciate the customer's view of the organisation, and the value that that customer places on relationships, can lead to CRM initiatives that only annoy customers and have deleterious consequences for customer loyalty (Rigby, Reichheld & Schefter 2002). A return on investment will be realised only if a proper evaluation is conducted so that it is clearly acknowledged where and how returns will be achieved (Accenture 2002). A realistic time frame for the achievement of adequate return on investment is also implied here.

A good implementation plan for CRM, which includes good project management and prioritised targets for CRM, is another vital component in CRM success.

Concerns with CRM

Although there are many success stories about organisations that have implemented CRM and reports that both they and their customers have benefited, there are some who question CRM. For example, is CRM suited to all organisations? Would our society be comfortable for doctors, dentists, hospitals and lawyers to identify profitable customers and market their services primarily to those groups? Do customers value the relationships built? For example, one study suggests that only 8 per cent of customers feel that they have benefited (as opposed to the organisation) from the implementation of CRM, with about 50 per cent reporting that they did not want a relationship, even one that saved them money (Kiely 2001). So this begs the question of who actually benefits from CRM (and, indeed, who is intended to benefit from CRM)? Consider the following quotations:

> Arrogant marketers think that customers want a relationship with their products and services. But it's a one-sided relationship when a relationship is created fundamentally to cross-sell and up-sell products. (Kiely 2001:4)

> When folks in the industry talk about CRM, they really mean extracting time, information and money from customers. They then call it a 'relationship', but really it's building a system that draws those things out of a customer without giving anything back. (Yu 2001:19)

Clearly, sensitivity must be required if relationships with suppliers are to be re-engineered and win–win outcomes achieved for all concerned.

Summary

Modern organisations are increasingly recognising the importance of customers to the success of their enterprises: surprisingly small shifts in customer loyalty and customer retention rates can have marked impacts on organisational profitability. IT and the Internet have enabled profound changes to the way in which organisations can reach out to their customers via e-catalogues, customer self-service capabilities, channel management and so on. Furthermore, the processing power of IT can help organisations clearly to identify profitable and less profitable customers, better equipping managers to make decisions about the services that should be offered to these respective segments. Combining a business focus on customer retention and profitability with the power of IT and the Internet has resulted in the emergence of customer relationship management (CRM).

Although CRM is essentially a philosophy or perspective on an organisation's orientation to its customers, the collection, analysis and dissemination of the vast amounts of data that drive CRM practice are contingent on the analytical and processing capabilities of modern IT. Adopting an orientation towards customers not only implies technological change but also requires transformation of the business processes by which an organisation reaches out to its customers. Balanced and coordinated change are required if implementation of these CRM systems and practices are to bring the returns that organisations expect. The Internet also provides important ways of delivering service to customers via personalised portals and corporate web pages.

key terms

business intelligence

channel management

customer relationship management

electronic catalogues, e-catalogues

online customer self-service

discussion questions

1. Discuss the relationship between relationship marketing, one-to-one marketing and CRM. How important is each of these in helping an organisation to provide customer satisfaction, to gain customer loyalty and, most importantly, to achieve customer retention?

2. Why is a focus on customers so important for contemporary organisations? How are the Internet and IT contributing to developing closer relationships with customers?

3. Some authors have argued that CRM should not be limited to the sales and marketing function, but should be seen as part of an enterprise-wide customer-centric strategy (Peppard 2000; Ryals & Knox 2001). Discuss the relationship between CRM and business strategy, focusing on the necessity or otherwise of CRM being part of or closely linked to business strategy.

4. Describe data warehousing and data mining and their potential importance in contemporary business. What would you suggest is the role of data warehousing and data mining in establishing an enterprise-wide customer-centric approach to customer management?

5. Discuss the relationship between CRM and organisational structure. In particular, discuss the relationship between CRM and a customer-centric organisational structure. Can CRM be implemented in organisations with product-centric structures?

suggested reading

Payne, A. 2000, 'Customer relationship management. Keynote address to the inaugural meeting of the Customer Management Foundation, London', CRM Forum Resources, http://www.crm-forum.com, pages 1–8, accessed 27 June 2003.

Ryals, L & Knox, S 2001, 'Cross-functional issues in the implementation of relationship marketing through customer relationship management', *European Management Journal*, vol. 19, issue 5, October, pp. 534–42.

Ryals, L & Payne, A 2001, 'Customer relationship management in financial services: towards information-enabled relationship marketing', *Journal of Strategic Marketing*, vol. 9, no. 1, March, pp. 3–47.

Wilson, H, Daniel, E and McDonald, M 2002, 'Factors for success in customer relationship management (CRM) systems', *Journal of Marketing Management*, vol. 18, issue 1–2, pp. 193–219.

references

Accenture 2002, 'The road to CRM riches', http://www.line56.com/research/contributor. asp?ID=18, accessed 29 December 2002.

Ahmed, R & Buttle, F 2001, 'Customer retention: a potentially potent marketing management strategy', *Journal of Strategic Marketing*, vol. 9, no. 1, March, pp. 29–45.

AT Kearney 2001, 'Your customer your boss: a lifecycle perspective on customer relationship management', http://www.atkearney.com, accessed 29 December 2002.

Berson, A, Smith, S & Thearling, K 2000, *Building Data Mining Applications for CRM*, McGraw-Hill, Boston.

Cash, JI 1999, 'Using information technology to improve the lifetime value of customers. Keynote address to the Americas Conference on Information Systems (AMCIS)', 13–15 August, Milwaukee, Wisconsin, Harvard Business School.

Christopher, M & Payne, A 2002, 'Integrating customer relationship management and supply chain management', in M Baker, *The Marketing Book*, Butterworth Heinemann, Oxford.

Couldwell, C 1998, 'A data day battle', *Computing*, 21 May, pp. 64–6.

Deck, S 2001, 'What is CRM? cio.com', Customer Relationship Management Research Center, www.cio.com/Forums/CRM, pp. 1–4, accessed 29 December 2002.

Goodhue, PL, Wixom, BH & Watson, HJ 2002, 'Realising business benefits through CRM: hitting the right target in the right way', *MIS Quarterly Executive*, vol. 1, no. 2, June, pp. 79–96.

Gray, P & Byun, J 2001, 'Customer relationship management', Center for Research on Information Technology and Organisations, University of California, Irvine, CA, www.crito.uci.edu, accessed 27 June 2003.

Hammer, M 2001, 'The superefficient company', *Harvard Business Review*, vol. 79, issue 8, September, pp. 82–91.

Han, J & Kamber, M 2001, 'Data mining: concepts and techniques', Morgan Kaufman Publishers, San Francisco.

Harvard Business School 2000, 'A crash course in CRM', Harvard Management Update, March, Harvard Business School Publishing, Boston.

Kiely, WB 2001, 'CRM: buyer beware', *Marketing and eBusiness*, December.

Kimball, R & Merz, R 2000, *The Data Webhouse Toolkit: Building the Web-enabled Data Warehouse*, John Wiley & Sons, New York.

Kimball, R, Reeves, L, Ross, M & Thornthwaite, W 1998, *The Data Warehouse Lifecycle Toolkit: Expert Methods for Designing, Developing and Deploying Data Warehouses*, John Wiley & Sons, New York.

Kirby, J, Radcliffe, J & Thompson, E 2001, *Management Update: Gartner Introduces the Eight Building Blocks of CRM*, Inside Gartner, August, Document IGG-08222001-03.

Linoff, GS & Berry, MJA 2002, *Mining the Web: Transforming Customer Data*, John Wiley & Sons, New York.

Moon, Y 2000, *Interactive Technologies and Relationship Marketing Strategies*, Harvard Business School Note No. 9-599-101, Harvard Business School Publishing, Boston.

Payne, A 2000, 'Customer relationship management. Keynote address to the inaugural meeting of the Customer Management Foundation, London', CRM Forum Resources, http://www.crm-forum.com, pp. 1–8, accessed 27 June 2003.

Peppard, J 2000, 'Customer relationship management (CRM) in financial services', *European Management Journal*, vol. 18, no. 3, June, pp. 312–27.

Peppers, D, Rogers, M & Dorf, B 1999, 'Is your company ready for one-to-one marketing?', *Harvard Business Review*, vol. 77, issue 1, January–February, pp. 151–60.

Reichheld, FF 1996a, *The Loyalty Effect: The Hidden Force Behind Growth, Profits and Lasting Value*, Harvard Business School Press, Boston.

—1996b, 'Learning from customer defections', *Harvard Business Review*, vol. 74, issue 2, March–April, pp. 56–69.

Reichheld, FF & Kenny, DW 1990, 'The hidden advantages of customer retention', *Journal of Retail Banking*, vol. 12, no. 4, Winter, pp. 19–23.

Rigby, DK, Reichheld, FF & Schefter, P 2002, 'Avoid the four perils of CRM', *Harvard Business Review*, pp. 5–11.

Ryals, L & Knox, S 2001, 'Cross-functional issues in the implementation of relationship marketing through customer relationship management', *European Management Journal*, vol. 19, issue 5, October, pp. 534–42.

Ryals, L & Payne, A 2001, 'Customer relationship management in financial services: towards information-enabled relationship marketing', *Journal of Strategic Marketing*, vol. 9, no. 1, March, pp. 3–47.

Shaw, MJ, Subramaniam, C, Tan, GW & Welge, ME 2001, 'Knowledge management and data mining for marketing', *Decision Support Systems*, vol. 31, pp. 127–37.

Stone, N, Woodcock, N & Wilson, M 1996, 'Managing the change from marketing planning to customer relationship management', *Long Range Planning*, vol. 29, no. 5, pp. 675–83.

Thearling, K 1995, 'From data mining to database marketing', http://www3.shore.net/~kht/text/wp9502/wp9502.htm.

Thompson, K, Ryals, L, Knox, S and Maklan, S 2000, 'Developing relationship marketing through the implementation of customer relationship management technology', in S Leek (ed.), *Proceedings of the IMP 2000 Conference*, Bath.

Tobin, T 2003, 'The value of online self-service. A ServiceWare White Paper', http://www.serviceware.com/whitepapers, accessed 27 June 2003.

Wilson, H, Daniel, E & McDonald, M 2002, 'Factors for success in customer relationship management (CRM) systems', *Journal of Marketing Management*, vol. 18, issues 1–2, pp. 193–219.

Yu, L 2001, 'Successful customer relationship management', *MIT Sloan Management Review*, Summer, pp. 18–19.

case study

The General Insurance Company of Australia: A CRM story

The General Insurance Company of Australia (GICA) is a successful company based in Melbourne, Australia. The company's products cover most aspects of personal insurance, including home, motor and health insurance. The company was founded in 1902. Beginning in 1985, GICA has also begun to provide business and farm insurance, specialising in providing insurance products and services to small businesses and farms.

GICA employs about 500 people, about a hundred of whom are in sales. Unlike some other insurers who use independent agents to sell their products, GICA believed in having full-time salaried employees, who were faithful to the company's vision and values, to sell its products. The sales force is made up of product sales groups, specialising in the various insurance products of home, motor, health, and business and farm. Within each product sales group, there are subgroups specialising in the various sales regions, which included the various cities, regional centres and rural areas of Australia.

GICA has revenues of $120 million per year and profits of $25 million per year. Revenues and profits have been steady for a number of years, but for the last five years they had been declining by about 1 to 2 per cent a year.

Most of the senior management team believe that the increasingly intense competition from the large general insurance companies such as IAG, Allianz Australia and CGU Australia was causing the erosion of revenues and profits. However, some other managers believe that the innovation and change, including the innovative use of IT, that had in recent years been typical of the large insurance companies had been absent from GICA, and this, in part, explained the falling revenues and profits.

The initial CRM initiative

The CEO of GICA, Wayne Bennett, had some sympathy for the idea that it was lack of innovation in customer service, as well as intense competition, that was causing revenue and profits to fall. Having followed the recent interest in the business press concerning customer relationship management (CRM) he believed that CRM had 'something to offer' and was worth investigating. Given that no proposals had come to him from his marketing manager, Josie Chadwick, he had begun an arm's length CRM initiative with Lewis Macmillan and Rob Wong. Lewis Macmillan was a new IT manager, and Rob Wong was the manager in charge of direct marketing. For some time both Lewis and Rob had been keenly interested in CRM. Rob reported to Josie Chadwick, who did not share his enthusiasm for CRM, especially when it involved complex and expensive IT packages.

Lewis and Rob had formed a committee of six middle managers from the sales, marketing and IT departments, and made a case for the purchase of the Sales Force Automation (SFA) module of a midrange CRM package provider called Customer Vision Inc. (CVI). After a very tense meeting with his senior management team, Wayne Bennett secured the approval of his team to let Lewis and Rob go ahead with their suggested CRM applications — a sales information system for the sales department based on mobile computing, and the campaign management system for the direct marketing section of the marketing department.

The CVI 'Customer 1' implementation

Customer Vision's package is called Customer 1. Customer 1 is a suite of systems dedicated to customer relationship management and sales force automation. Customer 1's campaign management system had features that help to guide and manage a sales campaign quite logically. It had such features as automated email reply and some quite useful mathematical and statistical routines that helped one to assess the value of certain direct marketing decisions and activities. Thus, some of Rob Wong's team in direct marketing were enabled to work more efficiently, and some cost savings were made.

Customer 1's Mobile Sales Support System enabled sales reps equipped with small mobile computing devices to upload and download relevant sales and customer information via wireless Internet connections. The system also enabled sales reps to carry out sales transactions remotely. The system implementation required the purchase of some new devices called XDAs from Airwaves Manufacturing Incorporated. The devices are newly released WAP-enabled (wireless application protocol enabled) mobile/PDA devices (mobile personal digital assistants) with 64 MB of memory, a small (13 cm by 7 cm) colour touch-sensitive screen that allows users to input 'writing' via a stylus. Thus sales reps write commands on the screen with the stylus and thus, via the wireless Internet connection, interact with GICA's head office sales and customer information systems to upload and download customer information and sales transaction information.

The initial enthusiasm of Lewis and Rob for the Mobile Sales Support System soon turned to anxiety. The mobile computing system was proving to be very unpopular with the sales force, and sales reps were tending to work around the system when possible and not to work with the system. Hence, despite the considerable cost in terms of hardware devices and software, not to mention training and other costs of introducing the system, it appeared that no business benefits were being realised from the system's introduction. Although Lewis and Rob had argued that there would be a 5 per cent increase in sales revenue due to the system's introduction, after a year of troubled implementation effort there had been no increase in sales. Instead there was a lot of consternation and anger among the sales force regarding

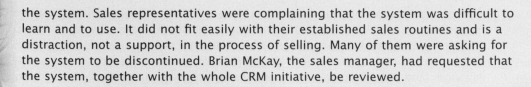

the system. Sales representatives were complaining that the system was difficult to learn and to use. It did not fit easily with their established sales routines and is a distraction, not a support, in the process of selling. Many of them were asking for the system to be discontinued. Brian McKay, the sales manager, had requested that the system, together with the whole CRM initiative, be reviewed.

The review of the CRM initiative

Wayne Bennett felt that it was certainly time to review the CRM initiative, particularly as nothing in the company situation had improved, despite considerable spending on the CRM systems. He gathered his senior management team together for a presentation by Lewis and Rob followed by a presentation by Josie Chadwick. Since she had generally been a negative critic of the CRM initiative, Wayne had asked Josie to try to give some positive suggestions as well as criticisms.

Lewis and Rob detailed the introduction of the campaign management system and the Mobile Sales Support System. They mentioned that although the campaign management system had resulted in some increases in costs, no better revenues from sales campaigns had yet resulted. However, Rob now had an idea for changing the actual process of campaign management in ways such that with a better campaign methodology enabled by the software, he claimed that better targeting of new prospects would be achieved and hence a larger percentage of new customers would result from campaigns. Learning to profit from complex software, he argued, takes time and thoughtful innovation in better business processes.

Lewis reported on the Mobile Sales Support System. Resistance to change brought about by the new system, he said, was to be expected. Perhaps the change management practices of his IT team needed to improve. He was looking into this and had arranged some new training and motivation sessions for sales representatives. He was also talking with the product sales managers about developing a new incentive system together with a new ideal sales process that could be sold to the sales force. The incentives and new sales process would integrate the system's use with sales representatives' routines and pay.

Following the presentation by Rob and Lewis, it was clear that the senior management team was not happy with what had been said. Several senior managers said that Rob and Lewis had been promising 'more of the same' and 'it was not good enough!'

Josie Chadwick then rose to speak. She said that in her view the whole approach to CRM was wrong and that what was needed was to get the basic philosophy of CRM correct. CRM, she said, was about customers, not IT. It involved learning more about what customers valued in the company's products and services and learning how to improve the company's value proposition to both established and new customers. GICA not only made huge assumptions about what was valuable to customers, she argued, but also was very product-centric.

'GICA is not even organised around a customer — GICA needs to be much more customer-centric and to gain one view of each customer,' Josie argued. 'GICA has at least three or four views of each customer,' she said. 'Each John Citizen is a motor insurance customer, a home insurance customer and health insurance customer.' Josie argued that, in this way, the company had three different pictures of each John Citizen and hence had little chance of effective cross-selling. 'Essentially,' she argued, 'we need to be customer-focused and customer-centric.'

'What you are talking about', said Lewis, 'is a data warehouse. Of course we need one.'

'Well, part of it may be a data warehouse of customer data — giving us one view of the customer — but it's much more than that. It is about customer-centric organisational learning, customer-centric business processes, customer-centric organisational structures and, most importantly, customer-centric culture, attitudes and mindsets,' retorted Josie. 'We need to tear down the product silos in this company and organise around the customer, not around products,' she said. 'We need, as I said before, to be customer-centric, not product-centric.'

'Well, I don't know whether we quite need to go that far, Josie,' said Brian McKay, the sales manager. 'I agree we need to be more customer-focused, but tearing down the product sales organisations! Well, that sounds more like revolution and destruction to me than organisational transformation. I think we can profit from some IT in the back office that makes sales processes more efficient and gives us the opportunity to cross-sell. I also think we can profit from some training sessions about customer focus for our back-office people as well as our sales teams, but we have several successfully operating product sales organisations. Why would we want to destroy these proven structures?'

The above conversation continued energetically for some time. Eventually, Wayne Bennett called the meeting to a close, asking all senior managers to reflect on what had been said and then send a short position paper on the CRM initiative to him via email.

After receiving the various position papers from his senior management team, Wayne Bennett felt he was no closer to an effective way to approach the CRM initiative. The suggestions he received ranged all the way from closing down the whole CRM initiative to Josie's view that a total organisational transformation and restructure was necessary in order to profit from CRM. Wayne decided to ask a newly formed consultancy Think! CRM to help him find an effective way forward.

Questions

1. Explain what you believe are the main elements of Josie Chadwick's 'total' approach to CRM. Include in your answer an explanation of the strategy, structure, people, culture, processes and technology aspects of CRM.

2. Brian McKay, the sales manager, has explained to Josie Chadwick that you can have an effective CRM approach without moving away from a product-centric organisational structure. Good sales support from IT systems, together with a data warehousing capability (which includes one view of the customer) and a data mining capability, will deliver good CRM to GICA, according to Brian McKay. Describe your view on Brian McKay's perspective on CRM.

3. What would be your advice to Wayne Bennett regarding the CRM initiative?

4. The GICA Mobile Sales Support System had produced very little business benefits after a year. Explain the role of such mobile computing sales force automation systems in a total CRM initiative. Under what circumstances and in what types of companies would such systems be beneficial?

chapter 8

Strategies for managing information and knowledge in e-business

learning objectives

After reading this chapter, you should be able to:

- understand why managers need to appreciate and manage the information and knowledge resource in an organisation
- define the nature and meaning of the terms *information* and *knowledge*
- describe the role that information and knowledge play in contemporary organisations
- appreciate how information and knowledge can be harnessed to create business value
- appreciate how information and knowledge can be managed as an important corporate resource
- understand the role of IT in knowledge management
- articulate strategies for knowledge management
- understand the importance of becoming a knowledge-based organisation.

chapter overview

This chapter focuses on knowledge management, what it is, why it is important and the role it can play in the development of sustainable competitive advantage in modern organisations. One of the challenges facing managers today is an overabundance of data (and perhaps information) and insufficient time to devote attention to it all. Hence, identifying, filtering, storing and disseminating high-value information and knowledge to those who need it so that they can manage effectively are non-trivial activities in modern organisations. Although IT lies at the heart of many knowledge management initiatives and offers the engine from which intellectual capital can be effectively used in an organisation, it is not itself knowledge management. Good IT will be necessary in implementing knowledge management strategies, but simply installing new technologies does not ensure the development of a knowledge culture in organisations.

Managers need to know and concern themselves with knowledge management as, for most organisations, their knowledge assets and their technical know-how, and their ability to harness them, are the source of their competitive advantage.

If the importance of knowledge is recognised, articulating and implementing sound knowledge management strategies and practices in organisations become an imperative. Knowledge management strategies must be aligned with business strategies, goals and objectives. Therefore the types of knowledge management approaches adopted and resourced in an organisation must be such that the organisation is supported in moving towards desired goals and objectives.

Introduction

In the previous two chapters especially, the focus has been on how organisations can use and share information within the organisation and in both directions along the supply and demand chains to create efficiencies, to increase effectiveness, to compete more effectively in global markets and to create value for customers, all of which imply using information and knowledge to create business value. The focus of this chapter then is not a marked departure from that of the previous two chapters, but rather it represents a reorientation away from suppliers and customers towards the information and knowledge that is gathered, stored, analysed and exchanged both within the organisation and among trading partners to create value for all organisations concerned. The focus switches from the trading partner organisations to the information and knowledge flows.

This topic seems particularly pertinent in this Internet era. In the previous two chapters, the digitisation of the information in the supply chain, the additional channel to reach out to customers, and the application of IT and the Internet to gather, store and manipulate vast amounts of data about transactions and about customers and trading partners were discussed. Increasingly, IT is being applied to that data directly to generate value for an organisation. Hence, IT is not just creating a gigantic database or archive of organisational activity, more and more of which is being conducted electronically, but also modern IT applications enable this data to be 'mined' and used to add value to the organisation. In chapter 7, the role of IT in enabling demand chains to be more rapidly responsive to customer demand and changing consumer trends was emphasised. In addition, IT can take a more proactive role in 'anticipating' customer needs. For example, parents might organise a small savings account for a young child, say aged six. Systems can now predict that when she is 18, parents and/or the child might need a car loan, an education loan or whatever, and proactively suggest this or make offers, either via email or offers on websites, by notifying sales staff, by generating a letter for mail out and so on. In addition, business intelligence systems and data mining can literally 'discover' or reveal patterns, abnormal occurrences and the like from which other information can be deduced and thus activities triggered. For example, systems monitoring all bank transactions will note a sizeable dividend cheque being deposited by a relatively inconsequential customer and conclude that this customer might indeed be wealthy, with considerable assets at another financial institution. The bank is then empowered to plan a targeted and personalised marketing campaign around that knowledge with the aim of encouraging the customer to move their potentially considerable business to the bank. Managing and utilising information and knowledge in this way becomes a direct source of value and possibly also of competitive advantage for an organisation and therefore a business imperative in hypercompetitive markets.

Furthermore, members of an organisation are surrounded by so much data that they would be overwhelmed if they paid attention to it all. The Internet offers limitless opportunities to be exposed to data. Marchand (2000, p. 4) notes that 'the over-abundance of data challenges people in business organisations to manage their time and attention carefully, since both of these resources are in scarce supply'. This comment implies that managers must develop strategies for interpreting data, for screening out data that does not seem relevant, and for utilising data that is relevant to implementing strategies, conducting efficient business operations and the like. The ability to filter data and information thus is an important attribute of managers. Because it is via information technology (IT) and information systems (IS) that managers access a lot of information, then the ways in which IS are designed and implemented and the types of IS/IT investments made are pivotal to shaping the approach to managing and exploiting the information resource in an organisation.

Throughout this book, the importance of information has been implied. Repeatedly, the importance of understanding customers, suppliers, internal operations, an organisation's business environment, its markets, its competitors, its product and service portfolio, and so on has been argued to be at the heart of strategy formulation and exploiting IT to achieve competitive advantage. But where does this understanding come from? It comes from access to timely, relevant and accurate data and information, which when interpreted in the light of personal experience, enables a manager to gain new insights, to confirm previous beliefs, to adopt alternative perspectives, to realise that different ways of acting might be appropriate. Therefore it is through access to accurate, timely and relevant information that managers and organisations create business value, improve their business performance, develop knowledge and skills, and remain competitive and thus viable over time (Marchand 2000).

The point to be emphasised here, however, is that it is information, knowledge and IT that are vital. Investment in IT on its own does not directly contribute to the creation of business value or the derivation of business benefits. The position articulated by Laudon and Laudon (2000) that information and IT have become critical strategic assets of organisations is supported here. But so too is the view of Davenport (1997, p. 3), who writes, 'Information and knowledge are quintessentially human creations, and we will never be good at managing them unless we give people a primary role...The status quo approach to information management, invest in new technologies, period, just doesn't work.'

Why do managers need to worry about information and knowledge?

If it is accepted that information and knowledge are important corporate assets, or at least potentially so, then it seems reasonable to assert that all managers need to understand their responsibilities in terms of the management of this resource. It is not reasonable to expect managers to know and understand all that an IT specialist does, but it is necessary for them to be aware of the importance of information and knowledge in their activities and areas of responsibility and in the implementation of business strategies. Whereas in previous chapters the integrative requirements of organisational transformation were discussed, it is now argued that the integrative use of information (and hence IS/IT) across all facets of business is vital if an organisation is to achieve corporate goals and objectives (Marchand 2000) (see figure 8.1). Therefore managers must appreciate the role and use of information in implementing strategies and in achieving organisational objectives.

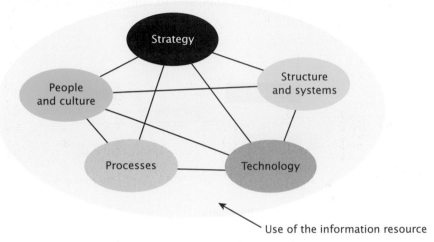

Figure 8.1 ▶ The use of information as an integrative resource

Managers also need to be aware of their own requirements (and those of their subordinates) in terms of information and knowledge. Thus, they should understand their own roles, responsibilities and accountabilities, and the types of decisions they make, the actions they take and the relationships they develop over time, in terms of an informational and knowledge component. Having said this, they also clearly need to appreciate how an organisation currently collects, stores, manages and disseminates information and knowledge, and therefore how effectively organisational members are supported in performing their tasks effectively (Marchand 2000). A mismatch between what they need to know and what information they need to receive and pass on, and the ways in which an organisation handles its information resource, might indicate a need for rigorous IS/IT planning and policy development activities.

If these points are accepted, then it is also important that managers are able to appreciate the capabilities of IS/IT and recognise opportunities to exploit the capabilities of modern technologies to support their business objectives. This does not mean that they should just invest in technology. What it does mean is that they must use their broad knowledge of the business and their need for information to identify areas in which business benefits can accrue from the timely application of IT. Hence opportunities to better manage and use information to enhance the competencies and capabilities of organisational members and thus improve business performance must be balanced against the risks associated with IT investments and opportunity costs (Marchand 2000).

Understanding data, information and knowledge

Arguments have been waged as to the differences between data, information, and knowledge. Without wanting to be pedantic, it is important to be clear about exactly what is being referred to. Generally speaking, data is regarded as being bits of 'stuff', which are meaningless and without significance in their own right until they can be placed in context. Figure 8.2 would be said to contain data, a meaningless collection of points in time and space.

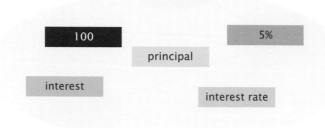

Figure 8.2 ⟩ A collection of data points
Source ⟩ derived from Bellinger 2001, p. 3.

However, points of data can represent information, depending on the context and on the person receiving and interpreting that data. Thus, aided by a process of collection, sorting and summarising data, information emerges in given contexts. The information should literally 'inform' the recipient and/or reduce uncertainty and indecision (Grover & Davenport 2001). So, if, as the recipient of that data, I am aware that the context involves setting up a bank account, and that if my principal is $100, with a 5 per cent interest rate, I will earn $5 interest in one year, then meaningless data becomes meaningful information (see figure 8.3). Or does it? The recipient of the data and the context have much to do with whether information is communicated and becomes useful. But so does the time of communication and whether a decision or action is in some way supported. Thus Galliers (1987, p. 4) defines information in the following way:

> that collection of data which when presented in a meaningful manner and at an appropriate time improves the knowledge of the person receiving it in such a way that he/she is better able to undertake a necessary activity or make a necessary decision.

A key thing to remember here is that one of the main differences between data and information is the necessary involvement of a recipient in the case of information. Information cannot exist independently of the person who receives it, interprets and understands it and is then empowered to act or behave in some way (Liebenau & Backhouse 1990).

Principal	= $100
Interest rate	= 5%
Interest in one year	= $5

Context: opening a bank account

Figure 8.3 ▶ Information in context
Source ▶ derived from Bellinger 2001, p. 3.

What then is knowledge? This is an extremely elusive concept to define adequately in a way that clearly differentiates it from information. Wilson (1996) argues that knowledge is derived by people framing and interpreting information according to some sort of internal processing hierarchy that enables them to take action (Nonaka 1991). Davenport and Prusak (1998, p. 5) develop this notion further in writing that knowledge is

> a fluid mix of framed experience, values, contextual information, and expert insight that provides a framework for evaluating and incorporating new experiences and information. It originates and is applied in the minds of the knowers. In organisations, it often becomes embedded not only in documents and repositories but also in organisational routines, processes, practices and norms.

It might also be argued that knowledge is demonstrated through the recognition and understanding of patterns, similarities and the implications of these. Thus, if we no longer rely on information each year about interest rates and the interest earned in a bank account, but rather can extract and recognise the rules that operate, then this would also be described as knowledge. It is a blend of one's personal experience and expertise, values and the constructs used to interpret the world, information and context used to generate new insights, understandings and/or know-how (see figure 8.4 on page 222). Thus knowledge moves into the realm of strategy, method and practice (Bellinger 2001).

How is this important to the organisation that is effectively exploiting the potential of IT and e-business? Think of the demand chain and the types of forecasting that were involved in efficient and effective demand chains (see chapter 7). Data, information and knowledge are all involved in making those forecasts. The organisation is likely to have historical data on previous sales results and the performance of various goods. When analysed, that data can reveal important information about sales trends, customer preferences and so on. Data and information are also available on industry trends, macro-economic trends, markets, competition, customers (and their satisfaction and loyalty), production capacity and other operational issues, and so on, and an experienced manager would use their frame of reference and know-how to recognise trends, patterns and their implications, such that much better forecasts of demand can be made than would be accomplished by considering just one set of data. In many cases, rules can be written to interpret data, in which case a computer can take over

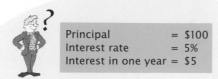

Principal   = \$100
Interest rate   = 5%
Interest in one year = \$5

$$\text{Interest} = \text{Principal} \times \text{Interest rate}$$
$$\text{Principal} + \text{Interest}_1 = \text{Principal}_2$$
$$P_2 + I_2 = P_3$$

Context: a bank account

Figure 8.4 ❯ Creating knowledge
Source ❯ derived from Bellinger 2001, p. 3.

nearly all the information processing involved. In most business contexts, however, a subtle blend of managerial expertise, know-how and interpretive skill needs to be combined with the storage and processing capacity of the computer.

Therefore information and **knowledge management** is all about capturing, storing, manipulating data and information to enhance a manager's ability to gain insights into and understand patterns, trends and relationships and thus to help current decision-making and control activities while helping to envisage and predict the future. It is also concerned with the dissemination of these insights and information to other parties in the organisation who could benefit from them. However, whereas the process of transforming data to information often implies some sort of fairly mechanistic processing (which is well within the realm of a computer) (Grover & Davenport 2001), the process of moving from information to knowledge is totally dependent on the human actors, and it is through these interactions between information and an experienced human actor in a given context that new knowledge is generated.

What is knowledge management?

Having drawn a distinction between data, information and knowledge, it should then be a simple task to define knowledge management clearly. However, one problem is that in common usage, particularly in an IS context, 'knowledge management' is used to cover a range of activities and technologies in an organisation, from efforts to establish a learning culture to database management tools, creating so-called 'knowledge repositories' and so on (Ruggles 1998). At times, this reflects a discipline that has rebadged itself from data-processing systems in the 1960s and 1970s, to information systems in the 1980s and 1990s, and now knowledge management systems. These changes certainly reflect an increase in capability and reach but perhaps do not always indicate a move from data to information to knowledge as differentiated above.

The problem is partly resolved by Grover and Davenport (2001, p. 6), who acknowledge this difficulty but argue that what is emerging is a 'concept of knowledge as a particularly high-value form of information'. Thus, databases, websites and data-processing systems all equip managers with information that supports decision-making and action and help to reduce some of the uncertainly in modern business environments, but rarely in themselves become a complete and stand-alone source of knowledge nor indeed a source of sustainable competitive advantage. In practice they acknowledge that knowledge management has become an inclusive field, which includes data and information, things that are easily stored in repositories (now usually electronic). However, in their view, knowledge management is distinguished by a deliberate attempt to add value to that information, a transformation that might require human judgement, creativity, expertise and experience, and the like; a process differentiated in a sense from information management in the fact that competitiveness might well depend on the effective utilisation of these **knowledge resources** (Grover & Davenport 2001).

For the purposes of this chapter, then, the notion of knowledge as 'high-value information' will be adopted, despite concerns being voiced about this definition. Fahey and Prusak (1998) express concerns that equating knowledge with a type of information can lead to problems, especially when it leads to knowledge management being equated with storage or stocks of knowledge (such as knowledge repositories) rather than being seen as inseparable from human actors who develop, transmit and leverage knowledge. The purpose of studying information and knowledge management stems from its increasing recognition as a key corporate resource and its role in assisting organisations to deliver business value to customers, in seeking efficiencies and in contributing to the organisation's source of competitive advantage, sometimes enabled through deployment of IT, the Internet and associated technologies.

Why focus on knowledge management in e-businesses?

It is interesting to compare the leading industries from a century ago with those of today (see figure 8.5). Whereas the generation of wealth, profitability and sustainability was associated with large-scale heavy industries based on the exploitation of natural resources such as steel, coal, oil and gas, and some manufacturing industries, nowadays these have all largely been replaced as profit leaders in the economy by knowledge-based industries such as the IT industry, media, publishing, film, television, pharmaceuticals, the finance sector and so on, all of which are industries that absolutely depend on their knowledge resources (experience, expertise, innovation and know-how) to remain competitive.

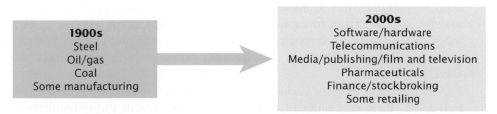

Figure 8.5 ▶ The dominance of knowledge-based industries

Modern success stories then tend to be organisations that excel at utilising their knowledge resources effectively. There are those who argue that in increasingly global economies, knowledge and the ability to learn and innovate are the major sources of competitive advantage and therefore to remain competitive and viable in times of hypercompetition, organisations must learn to manage their intellectual resources effectively (Davenport & Prusak 1998). It is instructive in this context to reflect on the knowledge dimension of the core capabilities and competencies of organisations (Prahalad & Hamel 1990). Also in this context, note Gloor's (2000, p. 9) claim that 'the full benefits of e-business can only be reaped if the knowledge involved in each e-business process is appropriately managed'.

Knowledge management is vital to the extent that it enhances an organisation's ability to accomplish goals and objectives, to become more competitive, to deliver results to important stakeholders and to assist the organisation in becoming better able to cope with change (Bellinger 2001).

Issues and challenges in knowledge management

There are a number of properties and dimensions of knowledge that create challenges when it comes to managing that knowledge as a corporate resource. The first is the tacit–explicit knowledge dichotomy. Essentially **tacit knowledge** resides within individuals with expertise, and it defies most attempts to be fully explicated. Some tacit knowledge can be expressed, but typically we know more than we can express or talk about, evidenced (say) by master craft workers who must demonstrate how something is done as it defies full explication through language (Teece 1998). Tacit knowledge is personal and is inextricably linked to particular contexts. Therefore it is relatively hard to communicate, typically relying on face-to-face contact and correction of errors via feedback. Hence it is very hard to formalise (and therefore to make accessible via computer systems). Tacit knowledge can be classified according to whether it is essentially technical knowledge or 'know-how' or has a cognitive dimension, such as being based on beliefs, values, emotions, perceptions, hunches and mental models (Nonaka 1991). By contrast, **explicit knowledge** lends itself to being codified and documented. Hence it is much easier to communicate and transfer through a wide range of media and can be expressed through formal, shared languages. It does not rely on face-to-face contact for its transfer. This means that it can be stored electronically and transmitted online (Zack 1999b). Clearly both tacit and explicit knowledge are important: the danger, of course, is that it is easier to pay attention to explicit knowledge, perhaps at the expense of tacit knowledge, but it might be through the interactions of tacit and explicit knowledge that the possibility of innovation and learning offers greatest possibilities (Grover & Davenport 2001).

Who possesses or owns knowledge, then? Clearly if it is tacit and resides within the individual, there is a sense in which control resides with the individual. But if the organisation needs to transfer that knowledge and to protect its intellectual asset, how can this be accomplished? Developing communities of practice, in which like-minded individuals willingly exchange knowledge, is one way. But these communities tend to work best if they are self-organising rather than formalised (Walsham 2001; Malholtra 2000), which could be risky in an organisational environment. Other approaches might be embedded in human resource practices in the organisation, whereby recruitment and training procedures and performance measurement and reward systems could all be structured to motivate the exchange and sharing of knowledge (Grover & Davenport 2001).

Understanding the knowledge processes in an organisation could also be helpful in developing organisation-wide knowledge management strategies. Probst, Raub and Romhardt (2000) identify six stages in the knowledge process of an organisation:

- *Identification* (What knowledge do we have? What do we need? Where do our knowledge resources reside?) This stage helps employees to locate sources of knowledge and expertise that they need and to avoid duplication of effort.
- *Acquisition* (What knowledge do we need to acquire or gain access to?) In a competitive business environment, acquiring the right knowledge is critical (for instance, in previous chapters, the knowledge that can be acquired from suppliers, customers and other trading partners was discussed).
- *Development* (How can new knowledge and expertise be developed within the organisation?) This stage has as its focus generating new skills, innovation, developing better processes and so on, or developing the knowledge and expertise required to achieve and surpass business objectives.
- *Sharing and distribution* (Who needs our knowledge about what, where and when? How can distribution of our knowledge resource be facilitated?) Meaningful distribution of knowledge is a key success factor in knowledge management.
- *Utilisation* (How can we ensure that people who need to do so can apply corporate knowledge?) Good distribution mechanisms do not necessarily result in the appropriate utilisation of knowledge in organisations. Other reward and motivational mechanisms might be required to ensure that it is used productively and effectively.
- *Retention* (How can we ensure that required knowledge is not lost to the organisation?) This implies a need for careful documentation and storage of explicit knowledge, but it also implies having human resource policies that encourage human resources to remain loyal to the organisation.

Any strategies developed for knowledge management need to take account of the organisational culture and context, its reliance on high-value information and knowledge, the nature of that knowledge, and the existing and required knowledge processes in an organisation. These ideas will be considered further in the following section.

Strategies for knowledge management

As knowledge is recognised as a key strategic organisational resource, then clearly the need to identify the role that knowledge management plays in an organisation becomes increasingly important. Indeed, in many contexts, developing a knowledge management strategy might well become an integral part of the articulation of the organisation's overall strategy. If organisations recognise that knowledge is essential to their ability to compete, innovate and deliver value to customers, then developing strategies for exploiting **knowledge assets** and resources become essential. This relationship between organisational strategy and the use an organisation makes of its knowledge and intellectual resources is called a **knowledge management strategy** or a knowledge strategy (Zack 1999a). The position adopted here is that the organisation's vision, mission, objectives, goals and strategies should determine and shape the types of strategy (or strategies) for knowledge management that are appropriate to the organisation. Hence there is no 'one size fits all' knowledge management strategy: rather a careful assessment of the idiosyncratic needs and drivers of an organisation must be used as the basis for identifying a knowledge management strategy appropriate to a particular organisation.

> The most important context for guiding knowledge management is the firm's strategy. An organization's strategic context helps to identify knowledge management initiatives that support its purpose or mission, strengthen its competitive position, and create shareholder value. (Zack 1999a, pp. 125–6)

Zack (1999a) goes on to suggest that no matter what the strategic position adopted by the organisation, it must have access to information, skills and expertise, and technical know-how (knowledge assets and resources). The decisions made about the mix of strategy, business processes, products and services, technology and people that it exploits to compete has a profound influence on the types of knowledge resources an organisation requires. But this is limited by those knowledge resources that an organisation currently has. Therefore a gap might arise between what an organisation believes it needs, given its corporate strategy, and those resources it currently has or has access to. Closing that gap is an important element in developing a knowledge management strategy that is aligned with business strategy (refer back to figure 3.16).

Earl (2001) and Hansen, Nohria and Tierney (1999) have identified a number of broad types of approaches to knowledge management that an organisation could adopt, depending on what it is trying to achieve, what this implies about its need to utilise knowledge resources and how it believes that the exploitation of knowledge resources can best be accomplished to meet organisational objectives. These approaches are not to be viewed as mutually exclusive but rather emphasise different beliefs about the way knowledge can be exploited. They are the systems approach, the cartographic approach, the process approach and the organisational approach, all of which are discussed below.

The systems approach

Arguably the systems approach is one of the more common approaches to knowledge management, and it is heavily dependent on IT for its implementation. The systems approach (Earl 2001) or codified approach (Hansen, Nohria & Tierney 1999) is based on the idea that it is possible to capture expert knowledge in a database (or what is often referred to as a knowledge base). Once captured and stored, then essentially this knowledge becomes a resource that can be made available throughout the organisation or to valued trading and business partners, irrespective of geographical location, to whoever needs that type of knowledge. As these systems rely on the ability to articulate knowledge and formalise it, they capture only those aspects of expertise that can be made explicit, or codified. It can therefore be concluded that this approach would be most successful in contexts or domains in which most of the knowledge can be made explicit and stored and presented in a form that is helpful to others without intimate knowledge of a particular context.

Let us consider an example of a systems approach to knowledge management. Donald, Adler & Pratt are a (fictitious) firm of consulting engineers that originated in Australia but which through takeovers now have substantial offices in Singapore, Hong Kong, London, Cologne, Montreal, Los Angeles and Rio de Janeiro. They have a number of divisions, including industrial construction and commercial construction. Their industrial division has repeatedly been awarded prizes for excellence in engineering design and project management. They have developed, and continue to develop, a system that captures high-value information and knowledge about the project tendering process and the project management process in particular. Engineers anywhere in their offices around the world can access these knowledge bases, to look at documents and information pertaining to the tendering process, for example. Thus, the Australian office is known to have developed excellence in preparing documents for tender for projects involving large storage silos for grains, sugar, concrete and so on. Another engineer in Rio de Janeiro is currently preparing a document to tender for a major project involving the construction of wheat storage silos at the port. His starting point can be to use search facilities within the knowledge base, to look at previously successful tenders for similar constructions. Thus, the engineer gains knowledge about the process of costing such major projects, can look for elements of the silo design and construction plans that can be reused, and so on. He can also communicate directly with the engineer at the Australian office if he needs to get a first-hand account of some of the issues, but now it is rarely necessary to have to fly experts around the world for this type of consultation.

What are the advantages for Donald, Adler & Pratt? They believe the productivity of their engineers has increased substantially as they have stopped 'reinventing the wheel' for each new project in a different country. Furthermore, they can now prepare tender documents, for example, in a much shorter time, and are experiencing fewer problems with blow-outs in costing during construction. They have not totally removed the need for specialist engineers to travel to other countries. But rather than using an Australian engineer (say) to direct a project in London, they now use that engineer to develop expertise in London. The knowledge base is the first port of call, and travel is then done only when absolutely necessary. They also believe that there is substantial transfer within the company of intellectual property and know-how. Rather than investing in developing excellence in every office in the world in all dimensions of their work, they can now identify those offices where there is excellence in particular fields and share it worldwide. In the early days of the implementation of this system, there was some resistance from engineers, who felt that they were being devalued. But this issue has largely been overcome through changes made to performance measurement and reward systems, such that engineers now are paid incentives and bonuses when they can demonstrate that their knowledge has been added to the knowledge base and when it is utilised elsewhere in the organisation.

IT plays a critical role in this type of approach. Quite simply, the systems approach to knowledge management cannot function without substantial investment in knowledge base and communications technologies. As this approach is premised on making explicit the knowledge and experience of experts, it relies on good capture, storage, search and display, and communication facilities. Economies then derive from the reuse of this knowledge asset (Hansen, Nohria & Tierney 1999).

The systems approach can work well in fields where expertise and knowledge lend themselves to formalisation and codification. Critical success factors therefore include ensuring that the knowledge captured is accurate, up-to-date and valid, and that knowledge experts participate fully in the development and ongoing maintenance of the knowledge base. In the appropriate domain, and if they are well managed, knowledge bases of this type can make a substantial contribution to building knowledge and intellectual assets and resources in an organisation. However, they would not be as efficacious in contexts involving a high degree of tacit knowledge or in very innovative, unstructured activities.

The cartographic approach

The cartographic approach is offered almost in contradistinction to the systems school. The cartographic approach, or the personalised approach as it is sometimes known (Hansen, Nohria & Tierney 1999), recognises that much intellectual capital is tacit, and hence attempts to codify it and reuse it are often very limited, and indeed limit those who attempt to use it. Therefore the cartographic approach does not attempt to extract the knowledge of experts: rather, it is based on the premise that the best way to share and leverage the knowledge assets of an organisation is to identify who knows what, where they are located and the like, and to list that information in an organisational directory of expertise; hence the notion of 'mapping' an organisation's knowledge resources. A person needing help or advice, or to find out something, can use the directory to locate the source of the knowledge they may be seeking and can then arrange for some sort of personal contact. The 'knower' thus becomes a type of internal consultant, advisor or mentor; the argument being that the organisation's knowledge resource that resides within the head of the expert is most likely to be shared and transferred through person-to-person communication (Earl 2001).

Donald, Adler & Pratt have developed an organisational directory to support their knowledge base. A key support for their knowledge base was the ability to trace the location of the 'knower' and thus to provide opportunities for personal advice and knowledge transfer. Other organisations, however, might adopt this as their major strategy for knowledge management. In engineering contexts, there might be opportunities for reuse of knowledge, but in other contexts, say management, solutions might be highly tailored and personalised. Therefore reuse of knowledge might be less feasible and desirable. Indeed, competitive advantage could come from the ability to tailor solutions and advice specifically for a particular context, in which case experts and their experience and expertise might be better transferred through an apprenticeship type of approach.

IT plays a much more minor role in facilitating the cartographic approach to knowledge management. The role of IT is to help locate people and knowledge via simple databases, directories and/or intranets. In some instances, IT could also play a key role in facilitating communication, via email and the like. This approach to knowledge management could also employ some groupware systems, providing facilities for technology-mediated communication and collaboration. However, as this approach typically recognises the tacit nature of much expertise, it might also be that face-to-face, or at least person-to-person, communication and exchange is preferable.

This cartographic approach works well in contexts in which a high degree of knowledge generated is tacit and therefore does not lend itself readily to being extracted and stored in a database. To be successful, however, it does rely on a culture of sharing and a willingness to engage in meaningful dialogue, and hence reward systems cannot be based on individual knowledge and expertise. Rewards must be developed to act as incentives to be willing to engage with others and share knowledge and experience. A culture that supports communication and the development of communities of practice are essential for the success of this approach to knowledge management (Earl 2001).

The process approach

Another approach articulated by Earl (2001) is the process approach. This approach focuses on core business processes as lying at the heart of long-term business success, and is premised on a view that for world-class performance on various core business processes, people engaged in aspects of those processes must have access to the knowledge they need to be effective in their performance of their related tasks. Through the provision of required knowledge to support the business process, not only does the efficiency and effectiveness of the performance of that process improve but knowledge transfer and learning on the part of the operative can also occur over time. A classic example of this type of approach to knowledge management comes in the area of customer service and the processes an organisation employs to resolve customer complaints, faults and difficulties. In the previous chapter, online customer self-service systems were mentioned. Embedded in these systems is knowledge pertaining to what the organisation knows that a customer will need in order to literally help themselves. Hence FAQs (frequently asked questions) or trouble-shooting diagnostics will be provided to help the customer identify the nature of the issue and possibly to help remedy it. Call centre staff can also be equipped with similar knowledge, and more, so that they can effectively deal with greater complexity and a wider range of issues. They can also be equipped with knowledge of the customer's transaction history with the organisation, as that could also be useful for rapid resolution of concerns.

The process approach is also evidenced in service processes, where field staff move around organisation and homes fixing faults. They might be able to use these knowledge systems to help diagnose problems and problem fixes, to locate the closest spare parts and their costs, delivery schedules and the like, and to access 'stories' from other service staff who have solved particularly challenging or unusual problems. The process approach shares the characteristic of the reuse of explicit knowledge but is much more related to specific business contexts than is implied in the systems approach. Furthermore, the captured explicit knowledge can be supplemented with diagnostics, best practice and contextual information, all of which support the execution of efficient and effective business processes. In a sense, it could be argued that this process approach is a variant of the systems approach.

Again, IT plays an important role, not dissimilar to that of the systems approach. The provision of shared knowledge bases, which are accessible throughout the organisation and at disparate locations, is essential to effectively supporting the knowledge aspects of core business processes.

For this approach to be successful, once again, a culture that values and supports the exchange of information and knowledge is essential. Knowledge must flow from people to the systems and from the system out to people for the process approach to be effective. Systems of this type often require substantial maintenance, and it is through the flows of knowledge among workers that an organisation's intellectual assets and resources are said to increase. However, they do offer the benefit of being able to be implemented on a process-by-process basis, with process-specific knowledge, and hence they could represent manageable projects in an organisation's early foray into knowledge management.

The organisational approach

The organisational approach emphasises the need to create communities of like-minded knowledge workers, and it is therefore reliant on the creation of networks (both technological and human) to create and share knowledge (Earl 2001). This approach has commonalities with the cartographic approach in that it seeks to identify sources of expertise and facilitate the exchange of knowledge between like-minded members of the community. But it also shares characteristics with the systems approach in that there is also reliance on technology to store explicit knowledge and to facilitate communities of practice via groupware, communications and so on. Thus there is a type of 'mix and match' arrangement whereby knowledge management approaches are mixed. There are the codified approaches of explicit, structured knowledge, which is captured and made available through knowledge bases. But the knowledge community also relies on and values the personal exchanges of more tacit knowledge. Members of the community typically share a particular discipline or a reason for coming together to exchange and generate knowledge.

IT therefore plays an important role in the organisational approach. It provides the engine for knowledge bases, communication and collaboration support in the form of groupware technologies to support more personalised interactions, and intranets as repositories of high-value information, and so on. Switching among the various modes is often facilitated by a human facilitator who helps to shape the process of the community of practice.

Like the cartographic approach, this approach works only in cultures that value and encourage the exchange of knowledge. Communities typically work best when they are self-organising rather than formalised (Walsham 2001; Malholtra 2000), so a corporate history of networking, mutual support and the like will be vital to the success of this approach to knowledge management. Creating a community in which all members are comfortable switching between technology-mediated knowledge exchanges and personal knowledge exchanges is also an important factor in the success of this organisational approach.

Selecting an approach to knowledge management

There is no best solution to the challenge of how an organisation best harnesses its knowledge capital, nor how it goes about building and leveraging the knowledge capabilities it requires for future success. The main requirement is that there is a clear understanding of the knowledge requirements implied by a particular business context and strategy and that there is also a clear articulation of the potential contribution that knowledge-based performance and innovation can make (Earl 2001). Then an audit of the organisation's current capability can indicate both strengths to be exploited and weaknesses or gaps, implying a need to acquire or gain access to certain knowledge capital and capabilities. Only when there is a clear picture of how knowledge can contribute to the achievement of organisational goals and objectives is there some certainty that alignment between knowledge management initiatives and business strategy will exist. Hence organisations might also need to go through a careful and deliberate process of figuring out how knowledge capabilities could make a difference to core business processes, to product and service innovation, to the search for efficiencies and effectiveness, and to the delivery of value to customers.

Which specific approach to knowledge management should be adopted should emerge from discussions of which knowledge can support the achievement of business strategy and how knowledge can add value to organisational performance and the audit of current capability. Hansen, Nohria and Tierney (1999) suggest three broad questions to help organisations shape their thinking as to the appropriate knowledge management strategy to adopt. The following three points are the essence of their suggestions:

- Are your products and services standardised or customised? Standardisation lends itself more to codified approaches, such as the systems approach and the process approach. By contrast, customisation is related to the personalisation inherent in the cartographic approach and to some extent in the organisational approach.
- At what stage of maturity are your products and services? Greater maturity is associated with more structured decision-making and greater standardisation and certainty. By contrast, the more innovative a product or service is, the more it is dependent on tacit knowledge and hence relies more on cartographic approaches to knowledge management.
- Is decision-making in your organisation more supported by tacit or explicit knowledge? In organisations in which there is a heavy reliance on tacit knowledge and expertise, low-tech solutions to knowledge management like the cartographic approach might be the most appropriate.

Hansen, Nohria and Tierney (1999) argue that the balance between technologycentred and people-centred approaches must be dependent on an organisation's competitive strategy. Furthermore, successful articulation and implementation of knowledge management strategies is contingent on recognising the role of individuals in knowledge creation and use, to implement reward and career progression structures based on contributions to organisational knowledge, thus creating an information- and knowledge-sharing culture.

thinking strategically

Knowledge management at Building Blocks

Building Blocks is a medium-sized company with offices in Melbourne, Hong Kong and Seoul. It specialises in quantity surveying and project management, and most of its experience comes from large business developments (office blocks, shopping complexes and hotels) and industrial construction (factories, power generation plants and warehouses). Building Blocks has gained a good reputation for the accuracy and timeliness of its estimates and its ability to coordinate the activities of a vast range of professions and trades in developing and executing large projects close to budget and within time limits. Working with engineering consultants and the like, they have on a number of occasions achieved innovative construction or project management approaches that provide substantial cost savings to the investors in these projects. Because of the accuracy of its estimates of quantities of building materials and the scheduling of those requirements, many suppliers of building materials like to work on projects where the project management and quantity surveying is done by Building Blocks, as they can be assured that orders are accurate and required delivery schedules are not constantly being delayed.

Building Blocks has grown very rapidly since its inception in 1994. Its headquarters is still in Melbourne, but it is currently doing most business in Hong Kong, Singapore, Taiwan and Thailand (serviced from the Hong Kong and Seoul offices). In the early days, the partners used to find it easy to chat and exchange gossip and ideas about the current projects they were all working on. Now, however, this is impossible as partners are travelling constantly, many new employees are being taken on in offshore offices and many large building projects are underway in disparate parts of the region. The partners are starting to realise that training of new employees in their procedures and approaches is not as effective as they need it to be. They are also worried that their main source of competitive advantage will be eroded unless they can ensure that new staff are as skilful in their work as the founding partners were.

Questions

1. What sort of knowledge assets and resources exist in Building Blocks? Would you suggest that these resources should now be more formally managed? Why?
2. What knowledge management strategy (systems, cartographic, process or organisational) would you suggest might be the most appropriate for Building Blocks at this stage in their development? Why?
3. What role would IT play in the implementation of this knowledge management approach?
4. What effects might your chosen knowledge management approach have on IS/IT planning?

Becoming a knowledge-based organisation

> Successful companies understand that knowledge management and information technology are not synonymous. (Hauschild, Licht & Stein 2001, p. 81)

Hauschild, Licht and Stein (2001) stress that although IT might play an important part in the knowledge management processes and activities in an organisation, technology on its own will not create an environment in which knowledge is valued, shared and used in supporting organisational activities. Their research suggests that at the core of a successful knowledge management program is a corporate culture that fosters an acknowledgement of the role that knowledge and intellectual property plays in the success of the organisation, and one in which the creation, exchange and utilisation of knowledge are valued and respected. Changing corporate culture is not a simple task, but the creation of financial and other incentives that acknowledge and reward appropriate knowledge behaviour is seen as an essential component of cultural change (Hauschild, Licht & Stein 2001). In addition, attitudes and structures that support the building of knowledge assets and the appropriate allocation of resources might also be important to developing a knowledge-based organisation (Teece 1998). This implies that implementing a knowledge management strategy will require a change management plan, in which job descriptions and tasks, performance measurement and reward systems all change to achieve the knowledge management objectives established for the organisation.

Ensuring that the knowledge management strategy and its implementation are integrated with the organisation's goals and objectives is also essential. Tobin (2001) argues that knowledge management is not a 'project' but rather an ongoing strategic initiative that over time becomes 'invisible' and is absorbed into everyday routines and behaviour at work. Indeed a knowledge management initiative might involve organisational transformation, as was discussed in chapter 5. The framework to support organisational transformation (see figure 8.1) is a useful tool to support thinking about the successful implementation and change management required to embrace a knowledge strategy. For knowledge management initiatives to deliver value and for knowledge management strategies to become highly integrated with e-business strategies, managers need to be aware of the need to balance and blend changes required across strategy structure and systems, technology, processes and, importantly, people and culture.

Benefits of developing a knowledge culture

Organisations rely on the knowledge embedded in activities, processes, systems and routines, indeed in a whole range of behaviour, for their sustainability and success over time. The knowledge an organisation possesses can be embedded in organisational processes (how do we efficiently and innovatively deliver service to customers?), in its technical competencies and know-how (how do we efficiently and effectively design and manufacture quality products?), in its ability to know its customers' needs and preferences and to act efficiently and effectively to meet those needs, and in its ability to understand the capabilities and competencies of its suppliers and trading partners and to harness those through productive relationships (Teece 1998). Not surprisingly, more successful organisations tend to encourage and nurture behaviour in their employees that achieves the creation, use and sharing of knowledge across functional divides (Hauschild, Licht & Stein 2001). Hence the deliberate management and use of knowledge assets is fundamental to innovation, to delivering value to customers and to quality assurance, all of which contribute directly to the organisation's profitability and long-term viability. High-value information, knowledge, know-how and competencies are thus sources of competitive advantage in modern organisations, and, as Teece (1998) points out, it is not just possession of these knowledge assets that underpins competitiveness, it is also an organisation's ability to combine and renew their intellectual and physical assets that drives innovation and creates dynamic capabilities, which are crucial for sustainable competitive advantage.

Summary

This chapter has considered the importance of the effective utilisation of an organisation's information and knowledge. It has argued that in modern business environments, in which an organisation needs to combine product, service, information and relationship in a way that differentiates it from its competitors, knowledge management, the strategies and approaches an organisation adopts to create and build, manage, disseminate and use its knowledge and intellectual resources and technical know-how might be pivotal to its ability to remain competitive. This seems especially apposite as most developed economies move increasingly towards an information-based, service or experience economy.

But given the overabundance of data and information, for this resource to be effectively leveraged to support the achievement of organisational goals and objectives, managing the knowledge resource — making decisions about its capture, storage, manipulation, dissemination and use — is essential. So too are building a culture that values the organisation's knowledge assets and developing human resource policies and procedures, performance measures and reward systems that all develop 'knowledge-friendly' behaviour in employees. Hence the key to knowledge management is to remember a number of things. First, knowledge management is not the same as IT: IT might be important to the effective management of knowledge but in itself cannot deliver knowledge management to an organisation. Second, knowledge is inextricably linked to people, or the knower, and successful knowledge management strategies and approaches must ultimately recognise that it is the interplay between data, information and perhaps explicit knowledge, and the implicit knowledge, experience, intellect and world view of the knower in context, from which benefits can derive for an organisation. Third, it is to recognise that an organisation's knowledge management strategy must be aligned with both its business strategy and its IS/IT strategy. Hence a single approach to knowledge management is not appropriate for all business contexts, but rather any proposed knowledge management initiative in an organisation needs to be able to demonstrate how it can contribute directly to the achievement of corporate goals and objectives.

key terms

explicit knowledge

knowledge asset

knowledge management

knowledge management strategy

knowledge resource

tacit knowledge

discussion questions

1. Distinguish between information management and knowledge management. What is the extent of overlap between these two areas or domains of knowledge?

2. Describe what you believe to be the main components of knowledge management.

3. What are the major success factors of an effective knowledge management initiative in an organisation?

4. What is the role of IS/IT in knowledge management?

5. Describe the main elements of a knowledge strategy. Describe how one might formulate and implement a knowledge strategy. Explain how such a strategy relates to or fits with the business strategy, the information systems strategy and the information technology strategy.

6. Describe how a knowledge management strategy might be viewed as a resource-based strategy. Do you believe this is an appropriate way to view a knowledge management strategy? Why or why not?

7. Suggest how a knowledge culture could be developed in an organisation. Indicate how you would balance the need for cooperation and collaboration against the need for individual creativity, effort and achievement.

suggested reading

Earl, M 2001, 'Knowledge management strategies: toward a taxonomy', *Journal of Management Information Systems*, vol. 18, no. 1, pp. 215–33.

Grover, V & Davenport, T 2001, 'General perspectives on knowledge management: fostering a research agenda', *Journal of Management Information Systems*, vol. 18, no. 1, pp. 5–21.

Hansen, MT, Nohria, N & Tierney, T 1999, 'What's your strategy for managing knowledge?', *Harvard Business Review*, March–April, pp. 106–16.

Ruggles, R 1998, 'The state of the notion: knowledge management in practice', *California Management Review*, vol. 40, no. 3, pp. 80–9.

Zack, MH 1999, 'Developing a knowledge strategy', *California Management Review*, vol. 41, no. 3, pp. 125–45.

references

Bellinger, G 2001, 'Knowledge management — emerging perspectives', http://www.outsights/com/systems/kmgmt/kmgmt.htm, accessed 3 January 2003.

Davenport, TH 1997, *Information Ecology*, Oxford University Press, Oxford.

Davenport, TH & Prusak, L 1998, *Working Knowledge: How Organizations Manage What They Know*, Harvard Business School Press, Boston.

Earl, M 2001, 'Knowledge management strategies: toward a taxonomy', *Journal of Management Information Systems*, vol. 18, no. 1, pp. 215–33.

Fahey, L & Prusak, L 1998, 'The eleven deadly sins of knowledge management', *California Management Review*, vol. 40, no. 3, pp. 265–76.

Galliers, R 1987, *Information Analysis: Selected Readings*, Addison-Wesley, Sydney.

Gloor, P 2000, *Making the e-Business Transformation*, Springer, London.

Grover, V & Davenport, T 2001, 'General perspectives on knowledge management: fostering a research agenda', *Journal of Management Information Systems*, vol. 18, no. 1, pp. 5–21.

Hansen, MT, Nohria, N & Tierney, T 1999, 'What's your strategy for managing knowledge?', *Harvard Business Review*, March–April, pp. 106–16.

Hauschild, S, Licht, T & Stein, W 2001, 'Creating a knowledge culture', *McKinsey Quarterly*, 2001, no. 1, pp. 74–81.

Laudon, KC & Laudon, JP 2000, Management Information Systems: Organisation and Technology in the Networked Enterprise, 6th edn, Prentice Hall, Upper Saddle River, NJ.

Liebenau, J & Backhouse, J 1990, *Understanding Information: An Introduction*, Macmillan, London.

Malholtra, Y 2000, 'Knowledge management for e-business performance: advancing information strategy to "Internet time" ', *Information Strategy: The Executive's Journal*, vol. 16, no. 4, pp. 5–16.

Marchand, D 2000, 'Why information is the responsibility of every manager', in D Marchand (ed.), *Competing with Information*, John Wiley & Sons, Chichester.

Nonaka, I 1991, 'The knowledge-creating company', *Harvard Business Review*, vol. 69, no. 6, November–December, pp. 96–103.

Prahalad, CK & Hamel, G 1990, 'The core competence of the corporation', *Harvard Business Review*, vol. 68, issue 3, May–June, pp. 79–90.

Probst, G, Raub, S & Romhardt, R 2000, *Managing Knowledge: Building Blocks for Success*, John Wiley & Sons, Chichester.

Ruggles, R 1998, 'The state of the notion: knowledge management in practice', *California Management Review*, vol. 40, no. 3, pp. 80–9.

Teece, DJ 1998, 'Capturing value from knowledge assets: the new economy, markets for know-how, and intangible assets', *California Management Review*, vol. 40, no. 3, pp. 55–79.

Tobin, T 2001, 'Eight lessons for knowledge management success. A ServiceWare White Paper', available at http://www.serviceware.com/whitepapers, accessed 6 January 2002.

Walsham, G 2001, 'Knowledge management: the benefits and limitations of computer systems', *European Management Journal*, vol. 19, no. 6, pp. 599–608.

Wilson, DA 1996, *Managing Knowledge*, Butterworth Heinemann, Oxford.

Zack, MH 1999a, 'Developing a knowledge strategy', *California Management Review*, vol. 41, no. 3, pp. 125–45.

—1999b, 'Managing codified knowledge', *Sloan Management Review*, vol. 40, no. 4, pp. 45–58.

case study

Knowledge management at ETM

Rob Lin had completed a Master of Information Management and Systems at Monash University, and Lisa Paterson had completed an MBA at Mt Eliza Business School. Both had completed their courses about ten years ago. After discovering that they shared many professional interests they decided to form a consultancy together. They had both been interested in IT management in their academic courses and furthermore felt that the management of information, information systems and information technology could be improved in industry and government, particularly in the small and medium-sized enterprise (SMEs) sector and in local government throughout Australia. They were particularly interested in establishing IT strategy processes in SMEs. To do this properly, they were aware that, in many cases, to develop a good IT plan with SMEs it would often be necessary to develop an appropriate business strategy process first and then develop the IT strategy processes within, or aligned to, the business strategy processes.

Other IT management processes that Rob and Lisa felt would improve IT management in SMEs were the evaluation and benefits management processes. These processes, they felt, were an essential part of the IT strategy implementation process — essential processes that are often not carried out at all in SMEs, despite the growing amount of quite powerful IT that was appearing in the SME business sector, particularly in the medium-sized firms.

The consultancy had gone particularly well for Rob and Lisa. Their consulting company, now called Essential Technology Management (ETM), was well known throughout Australia, earning revenues of $42 million a year, and employing 120 consultants and thirty support staff. There was a core of experienced consultants, each of whom had been with ETM for seven years or more and had extensive business and IT experience before joining ETM. The rest of the consultants were recent postgraduate students from MBA and Master of Information Management programs. These postgraduates usually had three to five years experience in business, gained through their employment after their undergraduate degrees. Each senior consultant worked with a team of newly graduated consultants.

Four lines of business had evolved within ETM. These lines of business, all specialising in SMEs, were as follows:
- business and IT strategy formulation
- IT evaluation and benefits management
- management of IT-enabled change
- ERP system adoption and implementation.

Then there was a secondary specialisation into industry sector. The industry sectors that ETM specialised in were as follows:
- financial services
- manufacturing
- hospitality and tourism
- local government.

Thus, a particular focus or specialisation for ETM might be IT strategy formulation in SME manufacturing firms.

In the first three lines of business, Rob and Lisa had at first imagined they could set up appropriate processes for IT strategy, evaluation and benefits management for the SME concerned. However, it was found to be easier and more appreciated by client SME firms when Robert and Lisa allocated consultants to help the firms to carry out a particular IT strategic plan, or IS/IT benefits management program, rather than establish an ongoing process. Therefore, although the setting up of good IT management processes remained a goal, ECM received most of its revenues from carrying out consulting projects that had as their outcomes such things as achieving a good IT strategy or benefits management program, rather than in setting up an ongoing process. However, improving the IT management processes, or in other words the IT governance, remained ETM's secondary and longer-term aim for their clients.

Two years ago, hearing about the new interest and focus on knowledge management among academics and other consultants, Rob and Lisa had instituted a knowledge management program in ETM. They had launched ETM's Knowledge Management program during a special weekend retreat at a plush Melbourne hotel. The weekend lectures and workshops reviewed the progress of ETM over the past few years and then looked to knowledge management as the next performance improvement initiative.

Lisa was speaking to the company's consultants. 'Partly ETM consultants are valued because they are ethical, committed to giving value for money and are hard-working. Our consultants are also renowned for being very well educated, articulate and bright. But people also value the knowledge that we have — both from our education and reading, and from our *experience* (emphasised!) on a focused area of business: IT management in SMEs. Who, for example, would know more than our consultants about effectively formulating IT strategy for a medium-sized manufacturing firm in Australia?'

Lisa continued. 'Every one of the consulting projects that we undertake should improve the knowledge base of our company — not only the knowledge of the team on the project but also the knowledge of every consultant in the firm. The more we can increase the efficiency and effectiveness of our learning from our consulting experience, the more knowledgeable our consultants become and hence the more people will value and pay for our services. Knowledge of our four lines of business and our four industry sectors is core to our performance — absolutely critical to our value! Our Knowledge Management initiative will be of value to our senior consultants, but I think it will be hugely valuable to our new consultants just joining us from university.

'We will be establishing a database of the best journal articles and white papers in our areas of interest. These papers will be indexed by line of business and by industry sector, and will be ranked by one of our senior consultant specialists in that line of business and industry sector. The papers will essentially be given a star rating: five stars for a superb, "must-read" paper through to one star for a good but non-essential read.

'We will also establish a methodology for each process: IT strategy formulation, IS/IT evaluation and benefits management, IT-enabled change, and ERP adoption and implementation — our so-called lines of business. These recommended methodological templates will establish a guide to carrying out effective processes. They will also contain guidelines for consultants facilitating these processes. I will let you know who will be in charge of establishing these templates. They will essentially be our best and most experienced practitioners in each area.

'I have also engaged some of the best academics in the country to give us a summary of important issues, challenges and trends in each of our industry sectors. These will be updated for us at regular intervals together with a presentation by the academic concerned each six months.'

Lisa's presentation was enthusiastically received. Many of the younger consultants found that getting knowledge, know-how and expertise from senior consultants was a problem. Part of the problem was the limited time that senior consultants could spend giving coaching, tuition and guidance. Another issue was that the coaching and teaching skills of some of the senior consultants were poor. Hence easily available knowledge directly related to the tasks of the more junior consultants seemed very welcome.

Lisa mentioned that the knowledge databases would be accessible from anywhere over the Internet. This availability was very important, she reasoned, given that the consulting jobs were spread across Australia — particularly some of the local government assignments, which were in quite isolated country towns. Also the culture of the company was to be involved with clients, not with a plush head office. ETM's head office was a very humble and spartan affair based on 'hot-desking'. In each capital city a number of PCs and some desk space were available. Many people worked essentially from home and kept in touch by the Internet and telephone. Head office was in Sydney, but it was no more luxurious than the other capital city addresses. The company got together, however, at least once a year in the annual retreat at a very good hotel — usually in Sydney or Melbourne, but occasionally any other state capitals.

After eighteen months, Rob and Lisa began a systematic review of the knowledge management initiative in ETM. They carried out a set of intensive interviews with a number of their consultants. The general feeling that emerged from those interviews was one of disappointment. Although the knowledge bases were useful, the younger consultants in particular felt that the 'knowledge' in the knowledge bases was bland and superficial. A majority of them felt that many of the senior consultants (and indeed many of the young consultants as well) regarded knowledge about the IT management processes and a special knowledge about how those processes were best customised to the SMEs and particular industry sectors as their personal 'competitive advantage'. The belief that guided their work seemed to be that their knowledge was key to their value and hence to their pay and future promotion. Therefore many of the consultants had a very competitive attitude to other consultants in ETM, and indeed the last thing they were ready to do was share their knowledge and dissipate their 'competitive advantage', either by providing personal tuition to other consultants or by adding genuine knowledge to the knowledge bases.

One of the young consultants whom Rob and Lisa interviewed was Weni Zhao. Weni had been working in ETM for a year in the Evaluation and Benefits Management team specialising in manufacturing SMEs. She had enjoyed her postgraduate studies at Monash University, finding the lectures on IT evaluation and benefits management fascinating and, she thought, relevant to improving what she had seen during her five years employment in manufacturing industry after her undergraduate degree. She had joined ETM with much enthusiasm, looking forward to working in the Evaluation and Benefits Management team — a team with several well-known IT management specialists in benefits realisation. Furthermore the human resources manager for ETM, Ernest Winslow, had told her to be prepared for a steep learning curve. Ernest had told her that ECM was a learning organisation with a collaborative mentoring culture. Weni was to work with several specialists and would soon learn some other ways to implement the best practice in both evaluation of IT projects and benefits realisation.

Weni had found the actual experience of working in ETM quite different from Ernest Winslow's description. She described to Rob and Lisa how much of what Ernest had said was cant and rhetoric. She had spent the year doing rather mundane tasks to help the senior consultants. She was told only what she needed to know to complete the task and no more. Weni thought that this mode of working was followed for more than efficiency reasons. She mentioned that she felt the senior consultants were extremely competitive and very closed with respect to sharing knowledge. Indeed, what was then entered into the knowledge bases of the knowledge initiative in ETM was as little as the consultants felt they could offer without appearing not to support the initiative. Weni was quite bitter about her year at ETM, and felt that the 'failed' (in her opinion) knowledge initiative demonstrated the case.

Rob and Lisa, after finishing the interview with Weni, reflected on her input. They then interviewed Weni's colleagues, who reported that she was very forthright and outspoken. However, they also reported that she was a very bright, articulate and positive person who worked very hard and made a contribution to her team. It seemed that people were very impressed by Weni.

Rob and Lisa thought they might profit from talking further with Weni. They called her back for a further interview and asked her how she thought the situation might be improved. Weni said that she was not sure. She felt that the knowledge management initiative was potentially very helpful but that somehow it wasn't quite working. She remembered that one of her lecturers, Dr June McDonald, had firm and definite views on knowledge management. Indeed Weni had got on very well with Dr McDonald. They were similar characters. Like Weni, Dr McDonald was forthright and outspoken — particularly on knowledge management.

Rob and Lisa contacted Dr June McDonald at Monash University. They asked her to look through their interview data and then to address them and their senior consultants on their knowledge management initiative.

After reviewing the content of the interview data, Dr June McDonald prepared to address the senior consultants. Her opening remarks gave a clear indication of her perspective.

'As a well-known academic paper indicates in its title, IT may inspire knowledge management initiatives, but it cannot deliver knowledge management,' she began. 'There is a very large human resource management component to knowledge management. Indeed the human resource management and organisational culture components of the knowledge management initiative are so important that I wonder how IT has hijacked this new area.

'Tacit knowledge, or knowledge that is difficult to make explicit and record in documents, needs to be transferred by coaching and mentoring — preferably by skilled coaching and mentoring. These human-based activities are a most important component of knowledge management initiatives. And of course good coaching and mentoring will not happen by accident! You need to provide people with the skills (and probably some support) to be able to carry out these activities, and you will need to create an organisational culture in which these activities can thrive.

'Surrounding all knowledge management activities and processes is the social and psychological environment — the organisational culture. You need to develop a culture of learning and knowledge sharing. This is absolutely critical to effective knowledge management.

'One of the steps in creating this culture is to align the payment and reward mechanisms of the company with your expectations of your people in the knowledge management initiative. People need to be rewarded — in tangible ways and in intangible ways — for sharing knowledge. Knowledge sharing and contributing to knowledge bases should be activities that are a natural part of your organisational routines, and these particular activities should be a natural fit with your organisational culture.

'Your policies regarding recruitment and employee retention are also part of knowledge management. You should review your knowledge capability in each area every so often. Is the capability developed enough and mature enough for the particular consulting assignments ahead — and indeed to support our particular business strategy into the future? Are there any gaps in our knowledge needs that we need to address by recruiting a specialist in a particular area? Are we retaining our specialists in each area? Are we vulnerable to "star" specialists in a particular area leaving? And so on. Some of these issues could be addressed via a knowledge strategy.'

As Dr McDonald went on to discuss how to develop a knowledge strategy, it was already clear what her perspective on knowledge management was in the context of ETM. Rob and Lisa were impressed. Both had decided that they would retain Dr McDonald to design some specific additions and changes to ETM's knowledge management initiative so that they could improve their competitive advantage through a superior knowledge capability in the SME's IT management consulting industry.

Questions

1. Critically analyse ETM's knowledge management initiative to date.
2. Critically analyse Dr June McDonald's views on knowledge management.
3. Along the lines of Dr McDonald's criticism, describe the design of a new and more holistic approach to knowledge management in ETM.

chapter 9

Strategic sourcing of resources, capabilities and competencies

learning objectives

After reading this chapter, you should be able to:

- describe the nature and types of capability, resources and competencies that an e-business requires
- understand the essence of core competencies
- appreciate the difference between insourcing, outsourcing and selective sourcing, and the circumstances, situations and strategic contexts in which these would prove to be the preferred option for obtaining required capabilities
- understand the significance of IT outsourcing and its role and contribution to e-businesses
- describe approaches to, reasons for, and benefits and risks of IT outsourcing
- understand the strategic sourcing decision-making process and its evaluation
- identify emerging trends in sourcing arrangements, such as backsourcing, business process outsourcing, e-sourcing and application service providers.

chapter overview

This chapter considers the types of core competencies and capabilities an organisation needs to have to be and remain competitive in an e-business environment characterised by globalisation and rapid change. Faced with such competitive pressures, organisations need to be adaptive to change, to be responsive to changing consumer demands and preferences, and to be able to perform business activities efficiently. Thus, competitiveness is concerned with being able to respond to environmental pressures and trends, but also it relies on an ability to organise and manage required resources and capabilities in an effective and efficient manner. This chapter focuses on the nature of capabilities and competencies, specifically IT capabilities, and how an effective modern organisation needs to acquire these in order to remain competitive and able to deliver value to their customers in e-business environments.

However, the argument developed in this chapter is that an organisation does not necessarily have to develop and manage all required capabilities internally, but rather it can rely on service providers in the business environment. Such arrangements fall within the umbrella term of outsourcing, or relying on the marketplace for provision of required services and capabilities. The motivations, benefits and risks associated with various types of outsourcing arrangements are considered, and guidance is provided on making decisions about effective sourcing arrangements. The chapter concludes by considering future trends in IT sourcing arrangements.

Introduction

The 1990s and beyond have posed a number of challenges for modern organisations. This period has been characterised by rapid technological development and, most notably, by the rapid adoption and diffusion of these developments. Although it could be claimed that the Internet is not exactly a new development, the speed with which substantial proportions of populations have adopted this technology has been unparalleled in history (DeSanctis, Dickson & Price 2001). This in turn has had significant effects on managers in organisations. The pervasiveness of the Internet and the speed of its adoption mean that they ignore it at their peril. However, involvement in e-commerce and e-business is risky and carries no guarantees of business success or paybacks for the investment. In addition, globalisation has increased opportunities and competition, typically resulting in customers who are more demanding in terms of service, quality, price and value offered. One argument is that one of the major challenges for organisations is that they need to be both simultaneously large and small in their thinking, their capabilities and their ability to respond to market changes (Applegate & Collura 2000a). Consider this quote from Jack Welch, former CEO of General Electric, one of the world's largest and most successful enterprises, as he mused on the challenges facing General Electric during the late 1990s and beyond:

> Externally, we faced a world economy that would be characterised by slower growth, with stronger global competitors going after a smaller piece of the pie. Internally, our challenge was even bigger. We had to find a way to combine the power, resources and reach of a large company with the hunger, agility, spirit, and fire of a small one . . . we want to be global and local, big and small, and radically decentralized with centralized reporting and control. If we resolve these contradictions, we create real competitive advantage. (Jack Welch, as reported by Applegate & Collura 2000a, p. 2)

Large, hierarchical organisational designs have typically proved effective in dealing with complexity but cumbersome and bureaucratic when operating in relatively stable, certain business environments. By contrast, small, entrepreneurial-type organisations have often been better equipped to handle dynamic and uncertain business environments but are typically not as well able to deal with complexity (Applegate & Collura 2000a). In global e-businesses, then, the challenge is to combine the efficiency, power, resources and reach of 'big' organisations with the flexibility, speed, agility and responsiveness of 'small' organisations. It can be argued that if all organisations are to attempt to combine simultaneously the benefits of both large and smaller enterprises with few of their drawbacks, they might need to develop or have access to new capabilities, resources and competencies. In addition, it seems vital to consider the role of the Internet and IS/IT in this regard. Networks, telecommunications technologies linking one network to another, ERP systems, flexible integrated databases and the like all contribute to offering organisations new structures, systems and processes by which they can achieve efficiencies (irrespective of size) with speed, flexibility and responsiveness.

There are therefore perhaps three areas in which organisations need to consider and revise their current capabilities in order to remain competitive in the e-business environment. Organisations need capabilities and resources to identify opportunities and to create and communicate visions, goals, objectives and strategies. They then need to allocate the appropriate resources and manage performance so that they achieve the desired goals and objectives. Organisations also need capabilities to innovate and improve, to create excellent core business processes, to establish relationships and systems linking them to key suppliers, trading partners and customers, and to create and manage the information and knowledge resources needed for these purposes. Organisations also need the capabilities to maintain controls without stifling the creativity and innovation, the flexibility, agility and responsiveness, that enable them to remain competitive, to exploit opportunities and to manage uncertainty in the e-business environment (Applegate & Collura 2000b).

This chapter is concerned with the nature and types of information and IS/IT capability, resources and competencies that are required for successful e-businesses and, in particular, to discuss different models and arrangements for sourcing and delivering such capabilities. In particular, it will be argued that the IT capabilities, resources and competencies are essential to e-businesses, and therefore much of the focus of this chapter will be on ways in which organisations can gain access to and develop required IT capabilities to support the achievement of business objectives.

Understanding the notion of core competencies and capabilities

In chapter 3 of this book, the resource-based view or theory of organisations was introduced, in that context in relation to the relevance of resource-based theory to the requirements and process for strategic e-business/IS/IT planning. Essentially chapter 8 on knowledge management was also focused on the notion that effectively harnessing an organisation's intellectual resources allows that organisation to be better able to provide service to customers and to compete in modern business environments. This chapter too is steeped in the theoretical position of the resource-based view, in that it argues that organisations can become more competitive through their ability to access (internally or externally) and exploit required resources, competencies and capabilities. Therefore identifying these required resources, competencies and capabilities and making decisions on which to develop internally and which would be better accessed through external providers is central to delivering business value to customers and achieving organisational objectives. Before proceeding it is important that the key terms **competence** and **capability** are clearly understood.

There are some who see competence and capability as basically synonymous (see Hamel & Prahalad 1994 for example), whereas others like to draw distinctions between the two. For example Peppard, Lambert and Edwards (2000) suggest that capability refers to a strategic level and embraces at a high level the things an organisation must know, have and do in order to achieve its strategic objectives and intent. This is distinguished from competence, a subset of capability, which is directed towards obtaining, managing, effectively utilising and combining the resources required to achieve business objectives. However, for the purposes of this chapter, it is preferred not to make a big distinction. Essentially, the view adopted is that organisational capability is derived from accessing competencies (the ability to do things or 'know-how') and required resources so that business objectives can be achieved.

It is instructive, however, to think about the notion of a core competence, and how competencies are exploited to create business value, as this leads naturally to considerations of where such competencies should be accessed and developed. At the heart of this consideration is to decide which of the organisation's skills, knowledge, processes and activities create unique value for the customer and therefore those that are less pivotal and hence can be accessed through external providers.

Quinn and Hilmer (1994) offer several important insights in this regard. First, they suggest that core competencies should relate not to products or functions but to the cross-functional skills and knowledge embedded in and required for producing excellent products or developing great functions. Thus, core competencies are not the specific products that an organisation produces but are embedded in the knowledge and skills required to produce and deliver those products and in the organisational processes that support their production. In modern organisations, core competencies typically are based on knowledge assets and know-how. Second, core competencies are typically built around sources of added value from the customer's perspective. Identifying what will constitute value from the customer's viewpoint, and building outstanding skills and knowledge in that area, is one way of building core competencies. This implies that building and managing competencies and capabilities is not a static, one-off process but rather is constantly evolving as customer needs, values and preferences evolve over time. Third, as core competence implies excellence, achieving excellence and leadership in all facets of the organisation is impossible. Hence core competencies are typically limited in number and reflect specific activities along the value chain where the organisation can dominate and outperform its competitors and therefore provide unique opportunities for the organisation to leverage its knowledge assets and know-how to offer a unique value proposition for its customers. At the end of the day, core competencies need to be elements that contribute to the value creation process from the customer's perspective (Quinn & Hilmer 1994).

Developing organisational information and IT capabilities

Technical wizardry does not generate sustainable competitive advantage. (Peppard, Lambert & Edwards 2000, p. 295)

It has been recognised for some time that technology on its own is seldom capable of delivering sustainable competitive advantage. Lessons from the 1970s and 1980s suggest that purely IT-delivered strategic advantage is very short lived as rivals are able to copy the functionality of these systems in a relatively short time. Rather, advantage is said to stem from identifying business opportunities and exploiting these with modern IT (Ross, Beath & Goodhue 1996). Deciding whether IT is core to the organisation might then be a matter of deciding whether IT plays a truly strategic role in the exploitation of business opportunities and the delivery of customer value. However, despite the increasing pervasiveness of IT and an organisation's dependency on excellent IT to support and implement business initiatives, arguments can be developed which suggest that it is not IT *per se* that is core or non-core, but rather that some IS capabilities are core to the future exploitation of the IT resource (Feeny & Willcocks 1998).

However, as IT becomes more of a commoditised product that is purchased and then utilised, sources of competitive advantage that derive from IT have less to do with the technical ability to develop particular information systems and technology and more to do with the ability to identify appropriate IT opportunities in an organisation, procure the appropriate information systems software and then implement the system, embedding it efficiently and effectively into the work routines and business processes of the organisation and manage the attendant issues associated with organisational change. The capabilities necessary to carry out effective identification and implementation of information systems are necessary and important capabilities for all managers, not just for information systems and technology managers (Peppard, Lambert & Edwards 2000). Hence having a good IT department within an organisation is not sufficient as these capabilities need to be developed organisation-wide. For example a good marketing information system depends partly on marketing management seeing the information systems opportunity and then assisting the IT department (or perhaps guiding and managing IT) in the effective procurement and implementation of the information system. Marketing management would have a particular role in making sure that the information system contributed to business processes and that it was effectively utilised by marketing personnel. A similar analysis applies with manufacturing, purchasing, quality control and other systems, including enterprise-wide systems that extend across functional specialisations and boundaries. Indeed the contemporary trend is towards enterprise-wide systems that are integrated across the major functional boundaries. Discussions of IT capabilities and competencies have to be undertaken and interpreted organisation-wide, and hence inevitably intersect with other capabilities and competencies.

There have been a number of attempts to consider the types of capabilities required by organisations. Ross, Beath and Goodhue (1996) identify three key IT assets: skilled human resources, a reusable technology base, and a good partnership between IT and the rest of the business. Arguably the quality and balance achieved between these three assets enable and facilitate the required IT processes of planning, delivery of IT services and support infrastructures, and it is the quality of these processes that affects whether IT investments are viewed as delivering business value and the ability of IT to support the achievement of organisational objectives.

Feeny and Willcocks (1998) adopt a similar position in arguing that organisations need to develop and maintain corporate IT capabilities in three areas: articulating and supporting the business and IT visions, making arrangements for the delivery of IT services (via **outsourcing**, **insourcing** or **selective sourcing** strategies), and in building and managing appropriate technology and systems architectures, which is essential if success is to be achieved in the first two. From these three broad areas, they identify nine corporate IT capabilities required for organisations if they are to develop and exploit the I/IS/IT resource as a source of business benefits and competitive advantage (see figure 9.1). An analysis of these capabilities suggests that understanding the role of IT in supporting the business, building relationships between IT staff and the rest of the organisation, and building appropriate infrastructures to support future business development are integral to these capabilities. So too are decisions about who and how IT services will be provided throughout the organisation. This will be elaborated on in subsequent sections of this chapter.

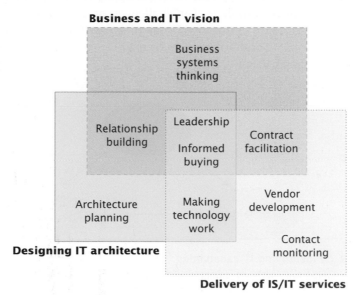

Figure 9.1 ▶ Organisational IS/IT capabilities
Source ▶ Feeny and Willcocks 1998, p. 11.

Peppard, Lambert and Edwards (2000) express reservations about the Feeny and Willcocks framework, arguing that delivering IT services and building architectures are both related to the issue of supplying the desired IT service to an organisation. However, they would essentially support the notions of Ross, Beath and Goodhue (1996) and Feeny and Willcocks (1998) but argue that none of these researchers acknowledge the importance of the use of the information and IS resource. Hence they propose an alternative framework (see figure 9.2 on p. 248), emphasising the importance of business and IT strategising about the information, IS and IT requirements, issues of managing the supply of required IT services, and issues surrounding the use of information, IS and IT.

An interesting dimension to this framework is the emphasis placed on the respective linkages between the three areas. Thus, Peppard, Lambert and Edwards (2000) argue that the linkage between strategy and supply is concerned with developments needed over time in terms of supply required to meet the changing demands and directions of business. Questions about future requirements in terms of systems, infrastructure, information and human resources would be critical here, and, indeed, building infrastructures capable of creating flexibility and adaptability and supporting strategic initiatives can be achieved only through linking infrastructure decisions to business visions and IT strategies (see chapter 3). The linkage between strategy and exploitation implies an emphasis on and concern about the need to translate business goals and objectives into efficient and effective business processes, managerial action-taking and decision-making, which imply effective determination of information requirements and performance measurement and monitoring. It also requires a holistic IT management process for ensuring the realisation of business benefits from IT investments. The linkage between supply and exploitation has often proved to be a contentious area in IS. It covers the need to develop or obtain and implement systems solutions to business problems (or challenges or opportunities) that are used to achieve the organisation's purposes. Developing user-friendly systems that possess the required functionality and access to information is a key concern here, as is training and change management.

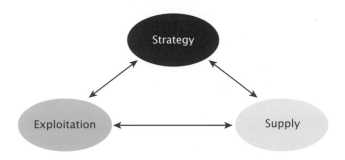

Figure 9.2 ▶ Identifying IT capabilities

Source ▶ adapted from Peppard, Lambert and Edwards 2000, p. 305.

It is also interesting to note that not all these competencies reside in the IT department. Considering what additional skills and resources might be helpful in the IT department might help the organisation to exploit its information and IT resource successfully, but it is not sufficient in itself to deliver competitive advantage and business benefit. Hence thinking about, supplying and using information, IS and IT resources in an organisation need to stretch well beyond the boundaries of the IT department.

The strategy or planning dimension was covered in chapter 3 and will not be revisited here. Subsequent chapters in this book will look further into issues of exploitation. The remainder of this chapter will focus on issues concerning the supply of IT resources in an organisation.

How then should an organisation go about making appropriate arrangements for the supply of IT services and resources? From the previous sections in this chapter, it might be tempting to conclude that if a particular information or IT capability is not regarded as a core competence, it should be obtained from outside the organisation (or outsourced), thus allowing the organisation to focus its efforts on those competencies that are regarded as core. However, decisions with respect to IT sourcing arrangements are not always quite so clear-cut. In the section that follows the issues regarding IT sourcing decisions will be scoped and analysed.

Sourcing required IT capabilities

Historically, IT capabilities have been developed largely in-house, although from time to time organisations would have called on external expertise in the form of consultants, contract programmers and the like. The guiding philosophy generally, however, was to build and/or develop the skill, resource or capability within the organisation. Over the years, few conscious decisions were taken about whether this was an effective strategy. It was simply assumed that an organisation needed an IT department, and it was staffed and resourced accordingly.

As business environments become more competitive and managers pay more attention to the use and allocation of scarce organisational resources, many managers have found themselves viewing modern IT budgets and requests with dismay, alarmed at the size and rate of increase in the IT budget. With time, typically IT requirements in organisations become much more complex, thus increasing the need for IT skills and resources, and therefore budgets escalate. Furthermore, the broader and more complex an organisation's requirements become, the harder it is to equip staff with the range of skills and knowledge they need. At the same time, the business itself has become increasingly dependent on IT, and IT has become increasingly pervasive in the organisation and, in many cases, is driving the core business. It is fair to say that the size of IT departments and the size of IT expenditures during the 1990s could not fail to attract managerial attention, and serious corporate-wide reflection and decision-making were undertaken about whether in-house provision of IT was necessary or was necessarily an efficient use of corporate resources. Consideration was also given to whether IT could be considered a core organisational competency.

In some organisations, decisions were made to access IT skills and capability outside the organisation, through specialised IT businesses and consultancies, who arguably possessed excellent IT skills. This process, of deciding that all or most of an organisation's IT capability is more efficiently purchased in the marketplace, rather than being based, developed and delivered internally, is known as outsourcing. For the purposes of this book, total or full outsourcing will refer to the situation in which about 80 per cent of an organisation's requirements are deliberately obtained externally. Fitzgerald and Willcocks (1994, p. 52) define IS/IT outsourcing as

> commissioning a third party (or a number of third parties) to manage a client organisation's IT assets, people, and/or activities to required results. This can and often does involve a degree of transfer of assets and staff to the third party organisation.

Similarly, Willcocks and Lacity (1998, p. 3) describe information systems and information technology (IS/IT) outsourcing as 'the handing over to third party management of IS/IT assets, resources and/or activity for required results'. Again, similarly, Grover, Teng and Cheon (1998, p. 80) define outsourcing of IS functions as 'the organisational decision to turn over part or all of an organisation's IS functions to external service provider(s) in order for an organisation to achieve its goals'.

For a while there was a trend to total outsourcing arrangements. Over time, however, some concerns were expressed that total outsourcing arrangements were failing to deliver the expected benefits, and this motivated managers to consider other options. Hence the notion of selective sourcing, which means making decisions one at a time about the provision of relatively stand-alone parts of the IT capability, became a favoured approach (Lacity & Hirschheim 1995). Selective sourcing stresses the need to exploit the marketplace when it is capable of delivering required levels of service and functionality more efficiently than is possible through building the capability in-house. However, a selective sourcing strategy will also recognise that some capabilities are much more central to the needs of the organisation and therefore should be kept in-house and carefully developed in keeping with the future business development requirements. A selective sourcing strategy will be said to be in place when decisions are made on a case-by-case basis, and when substantial IT expertise and capability remains in-house.

Lacity and Willcocks (2001) define *selective sourcing* as outsourcing where IT is viewed as a portfolio of activities, some of which are owned and managed internally, some of which are outsourced. Lacity, Willcocks and Feeny (1996) write that the growth of IT outsourcing is increasingly based on selective sourcing, which they say is characterised by short-term contracts of less than five years for specific activities. Selective sourcing locates selected IT services with external providers while still providing between 20 and 80 per cent (the average is closer to 25 per cent) of the IT budget (Lacity, Willcocks & Feeny 1996). The vendor thus becomes responsible for delivering the result of the selectively outsourced IT activities, whereas the consumer remains responsible for delivering the result of the internally managed and provided IT activities. Lacity, Willcocks and Feeny (1996) further contend that selective sourcing meets customers' needs while minimising the risks associated with total outsourcing approaches.

Insourcing, in contrast to outsourcing, means that rather than providing IT service in-house without thinking about whether this represents the best option, an organisation instead has carefully defined its needs, it has tested the performance of its internal IT department against the industry standards and benchmarks, and it has recognised that its IT capability is as good as, if not better than, it can reasonably expect to access in the marketplace. Thus an insourcing decision reflects a conscious testing against accepted performance metrics and consequently deciding to leave the provision of IT services as primarily an in-house capability. Again, a nominal 80 per cent rule would apply here.

Lacity, Willcocks and Feeny (1996) define *total insourcing* as retaining the management and provision of at least 80 per cent of the IT budget internally after evaluating the IT services market. Included in their definition of insourcing is the buying-in of vendor resources to meet a temporary need, such as programmers in the later stages of a new development project or management consultants to facilitate a strategic information systems planning process.

In some circumstances, outsourcing fails to deliver the required level of service, or business strategies change, for example, suggesting that existing outsourcing arrangements are no longer satisfactory for the organisation. This leaves the organisation with a number of choices. They can do nothing and hope the problems might resolve themselves, they can renegotiate the contract to deliver new desired levels of service, or they can start to repopulate an internal IT department and move towards internally providing the outsourced services and functionality. When organisations decide to bring back in-house capabilities that had been once outsourced, this process is known as **backsourcing** (Lacity & Willcocks 2001).

None of these approaches to the provision of IT services is inherently good or bad. They simply represent different approaches to obtaining organisational services and capabilities in IT and different perspectives on how that can best be achieved. Generally in organisations, all functions including IT are under pressure to become leaner and more efficient while delivering the same or increased levels of service. At the same time, the IT function is buffeted by technological innovation and change, requiring constantly broadening and shifting skill sets and demand for IT capabilities. Organisations move more towards adoption of virtual organising principles or strategic business networks where increasingly the delivery of the customer value proposition is a responsibility shared among a number of cooperating organisations (see chapter 10 of this book). All these forces require the planning and building of flexible IT infrastructures and architectures that not only meet the demands of business today but will also accommodate business growth and development in future. Thus, as IT becomes more pervasive and diffused in organisations, the IT environment becomes more complex yet also more essential to the development and implementation of business strategy and more tightly interconnected with core business processes and operations. Different perspectives therefore emerge as to how best deal with increasing demands for service, technological change and technologically driven innovation and change. It might be extremely difficult to offer the best of services and skills in all areas. Decisions about outsourcing, insourcing and/or selective sourcing are very much about how to achieve the desired levels of competence, expertise and capability in IT and how to manage the increasing complexity of IT in modern organisations.

Approaches to sourcing IT capabilities in e-business

Table 9.1 (p. 252) neatly encapsulates some of the broad approaches that organisations are adopting to sourcing their IT requirements (Lacity & Willcocks 2001).

Organisations adopting an 'in-house commitment' approach whereby the majority or all of their IT requirements are sourced internally typically do so because they believe that IT is at the core of their business and is a valued strategic asset. IT would generally be viewed as providing a source of competitive advantage. Furthermore, this approach suggests that if IT people are employees of the firm, they are more likely to share the organisation's vision, to be loyal and to be committed to playing their part in the achievement of organisational goals and objectives. However, there is always the risk that the IT function might become too insular, inwardly focused and unresponsive and might fail to keep up-to-date if they become totally secure in the organisation.

When adopting a 'selective sourcing' approach, an organisation is typically seeking good returns for its investment, or value for money. The organisation using this mode of outsourcing is seeking the best provider of a particular IT service on a case-by-case basis and is committed to that primarily, rather than feeling any particular loyalty to in-house IT staff and capability or to existing outsourcing partners or vendors. These organisations simply seek the best option to suit a particular business need or circumstance. This can result in a substantial part of the required IT services being provided internally, with the remainder being farmed out to multiple IT **outsourcing vendors**. Although this approach might optimise local IT service provision, it could result in integration issues as multiple vendors and system solutions are involved. In addition, it could give rise to a substantial management overhead, and the organisation needs to manage multiple, often very complex outsourcing contracts and arrangements. Care needs to be taken to balance increasing complexity against always seeking best of breed solutions (the best possible solution).

Table 9.1 ▶ Approaches to sourcing of IT capabilities

	In-house commitment	Selective sourcing	Total outsourcing (i)	Total outsourcing (ii)
ATTITUDE	Core strategic asset	Mixed portfolio	Non-core, necessary cost	World-class provision
PROVIDERS	IT employees loyal to the business	'Horses for courses'	Vendor	'Strategic partner'
EMPHASIS	'Value focus'	'Value for money'	'Money'	'Added value'
RISKS	High cost, insular, unresponsive	Management overhead	Exploitation by suppliers	Unbalanced risk/ reward/ innovation

Source ▶ Lacity and Willcocks 2001, p. 312.

Organisations can adopt a 'total outsourcing' approach for two quite different reasons, which result in quite different behaviour, attitudes and outcomes. In the first scenario, a total outsourcing approach can be adopted because IT is regarded as a non-core part of the business and is seen as a necessary cost; a necessary evil, so to speak. IT is not seen as making a strategic contribution, nor is it seen as contributing to future business growth, development and innovation, and hence building IT capability internally is not a priority. In such cases, organisations do not see the benefits and value of building expensive capabilities internally and so seek efficient providers in the marketplace for those IT services that they feel obliged to have. Low-cost solutions are the order of the day. The risk in these cases is that the opportunities for starting to see IT in any other light are limited, and an organisation might fail to respond to changing business pressures. Furthermore, placing themselves in the hands of outsourcing vendors for the total supply of required IT services increases the risk of exploitation and manipulation.

By contrast, organisations can also adopt a total outsourcing policy but have a completely different view of IT. Some organisations view IT as absolutely central to their current competitiveness and to their future business growth and development. IT innovation is therefore viewed as being inextricably linked to innovation and business performance. However, executives might also feel that, given the pivotal role of IT in their organisation, they need access to the very best the world has to offer in terms of IT services. Hence they seek a world-class IT outsourcing vendor, who becomes a strategic partner of the organisation. The emphasis in such cases is not so much on cost reduction and efficiency but rather on adding business value and effectiveness through seeking the best partner the market can offer. Although this sounds quite reasonable, the problem here is that an organisation becomes dependent on external parties for the provision of mission-critical services, profit motives are not necessarily shared, and hence a contract becomes the only recourse when services disappoint or business requirements change. This could be a source of considerable risk for the organisation. Another issue is that the organisation fails to build any of the requisite IT capability in-house over time, thus reducing their opportunity to learn about this strategic resource. Furthermore, establishing an appropriate environment that encourages and reaps the benefits from innovation in IT and IT-enabled business processes can become problematic.

The intention here is not to argue that one position is better than another, although this latter position is regarded as having a high risk associated with it and perhaps not looking at the optimal long-term solution for the organisation. Rather, the intention in presenting these different approaches is to suggest that organisations should be aware and clear that different options exist and consider what they are trying to achieve with respect to IT in their organisation over time, and thus which of these options provides a sensible arrangement for the provision of IT services and the building of required IT capabilities.

What can be outsourced?

The approach adopted to IT sourcing arrangements does not limit what can be outsourced. In full outsourcing arrangements, all, or nearly all, IT and e-commerce operations and capabilities are outsourced. In other arrangements, organisations might choose to outsource applications development or implementation or systems maintenance and support activities. In other situations, networks and telecommunications requirements might be outsourced. Other organisations feel that their training and staff development needs can easily be outsourced to specialists in those areas. Process re-engineering and the accompanying IT support could be outsourced. So too could strategy formulation. There are no rules governing what can or should be outsourced. The objective is to find the optimal mix of arrangements that facilitate the efficient and effective delivery of required levels of IT service, so that the organisation builds and develops the IT capabilities it needs to be competitive.

In general terms, however, it can be observed that the heuristic that guided early outsourcing decisions was that activities and services regarded as non-core and which clearly provide support to the organisation should be outsourced. Hence cleaning services and canteen facilities were often early candidates for outsourcing arrangements, whereas critical customer-facing business processes, strategy formulation activities and the like tended to be kept in-house. This trend embraced the idea that non-core but strategic assets and services, such as IT in many organisations, should or could be outsourced. In some organisations now, consideration is being given to outsourcing core and strategic assets and services, such as production operations, logistics, marketing and sales, and the like.

What motivates outsourcing or selective sourcing arrangements?

It is fair to say that many possible motives can drive outsourcing decisions. In this section some of the more common ones will be discussed.

▶ Cost

Repeated research tends to indicate that the main reason for outsourcing was associated with costs: either the outsourcing decision was seen to help reduce the cost of delivering the required level of IT service to the organisation, or the decision was motivated by a desire to achieve better control of the costs of the function. The IT function is notoriously expensive in organisations, and these costs are often viewed as difficult to predict and control. Outsourcing is often viewed as a way of benefiting from greater efficiencies perceived to operate through a competitive marketplace, and the outsourcing contract was viewed as a device for better monitoring, control and indeed understanding of the costs involved in providing IT services. It was also seen as adding predictability to the cost of this important function. Hence, in many outsourcing decisions, there is an element of gaining control over a difficult to manage function while trying to maximise flexibility.

Allied to the issue of IT costs is the perception of many managers that IT does not deliver business benefits proportional to the amount spent on it. It is sometimes difficult to measure the returns on investments in IT, but irrespective of whether or not IT is delivering business benefits, uncertainty in the minds of decision-makers as to whether it is or is not can lead to outsourcing being viewed as a good option. Hence entering an outsourcing arrangement can be seen as a way of improving levels of service (and therefore better demonstrating the contribution IT makes to the business) while establishing a fixed cost for the provision of that service. In organisations where a fractious relationship exists between IT and the rest of the business and a lack of trust prevails in dealings between IT and the rest of the business, external experts might be more persuasive about the business case they can articulate in terms of the contribution IT makes to business performance.

▶ Refocusing staff

The other dimension of this issue of delivering business value is that by outsourcing most of an IT department's typical service, an organisation is able to maintain a smaller core of staff who can concentrate solely on high value-adding activities for IT, rather than focusing only on day-by-day maintenance and operational-level issues. BP offers an interesting example of this type of approach (see figure 9.3). Before outsourcing, their IT staff comprised 1600 people. The main focus was on building and supporting infrastructure, applications development, implementation, maintenance and support, with comparatively little attention or emphasis being placed on strategic thinking and planning the IT assets. After much of the more day-to-day operations were outsourced, BP retained a core IT staff of 150, whose main priority was to act as consultants to the rest of the organisation, suggesting and planning strategic applications of IT in the respective business units. This was argued to have offered much improved outcomes and a better investment for BP, as remaining IT staff concentrated on IT activities that add high value for the company (Lacity & Willcocks 2001).

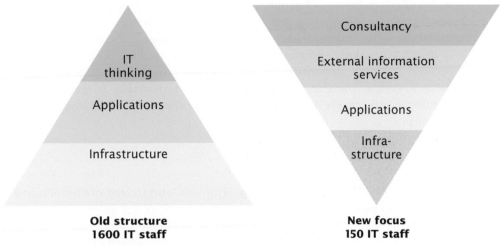

Old structure
1600 IT staff

New focus
150 IT staff

Figure 9.3 ▶ Reorienting the focus of IT services in BP
Source ▶ Lacity and Willcocks 2001, p. 223.

▶ Changing business strategy

Another driver of the outsourcing decision is a changing business strategy. This driver is usually associated with rapid change in the business or technological environment. In considering the use and deployment of organisational resources, it was previously mentioned that organisations need to identify and nurture their core competencies, and that business strategy must be cognizant of those competencies so that they are exploited in such a way as to deliver value to the business. A philosophy of this type might suggest therefore that all non-core activities should be outsourced, allowing an organisation to reduce its complexity and avoid increased diffusion of its activities, and to exploit its capabilities in a few core areas. This reason for outsourcing emphasises the need to improve business performance by outsourcing all non-core activities. In organisations in which IT is not regarded as a core competency, outsourcing IT can be seen as an attractive option as it allows greater focus on those dimensions that are regarded as core, thus leading to improved business focus.

Pilkington Glass decided to outsource much of its IT function while it implemented a large-scale change in IT platform. Its logic was quite simple: it would be almost impossible to conduct normal business (requiring substantial IT support) while implementing and undergoing widespread IT-induced change. Outsourcing was seen as a way of continuing normal business operations using the resources of an external provider, while internally key IT staff were organising and implementing major IT change (Turban, McLean & Wetherbe 1999).

Outsourcing of IT can also be driven by a change in business direction and internal restructuring. Some organisations view outsourcing as a way of more rapidly introducing the re-engineering of core business processes supported and enabled by the latest IT.

▶ Access to state-of-the-art technology

The Pilkington Glass example is a case of the 'old' being outsourced while the 'new' was handled in-house. Outsourcing can be undertaken for almost the reverse reason: external outsourcing vendors are seen as having access to state-of-the-art technology, skills and expertise. A decision to outsource therefore can be seen as a way of accessing skills and resources not currently available in-house. This might be especially the case in smaller IT departments where it is almost impossible to achieve a critical mass in all required areas. Outsourcing to gain access to new technologies and skills helps also to reduce the risks of technologically driven innovation.

▶ Cash flow

It was previously mentioned that outsourcing can, and indeed often does, involve the transfer to the outsourcing vendor of many organisational assets, such as hardware, software, licenses and skilled IT staff. Thus outsourcing often does represent a cash infusion into the organisation, which can in some circumstances, especially in companies experiencing short-term cash flow problems, help the cash flow situation without losing access to IT capability. Furthermore, such a transfer of assets might release capital resources for other purposes in the organisation.

▶ Popular trend

Needless to say, there is an element of fashion in outsourcing decisions in some circumstances. In other words, because there are so many reports of outsourcing deals representing substantial cost savings for organisations, many managers feel that they too must pursue such benefits. Lacity and Hirschheim (1993) refer to the 'bandwagon effect': outsourcing to jump on the bandwagon, rather than establishing a persuasive business case or proposition. Some managers also feel that the IT function is difficult to control. Not only are the costs seen as escalating, without associated escalation of business benefits in some cases, but also widespread user complaints and the like might lead to a perception that the IT department is not service-oriented and is difficult to control and manage. Outsourcing is seen therefore as a simple and attractive way of getting rid of a troublesome function (Lacity & Hirschheim 1993; Willcocks & Lacity 1998).

Risks and failures in outsourcing arrangements

It might be tempting to conclude from the previous discussion that once the IT function has been outsourced, benefits start to flow back to the organisation. This sadly is not always the case, as there are many attendant risks associated with outsourcing, and reports of failure or disappointment with the performance of the outsourcing vendor are not uncommon. For example, statistics cited by Lacity and Willcocks (1998) suggest that two out of every three contracts will be regarded a failure, and nearly 25 per cent of all contracts will be terminated.

Contractual issues

Problematic contracts are a major factor contributing to the risk associated with outsourcing. It is difficult to lay down in a contract all aspects of the day-to-day behaviour involved in an effective outsourcing relationship that satisfies all parties. Issues that need specification in the contract are as follows:

- the IT services to be outsourced
- the required service levels for particular services
- the IT personnel and other corporate technology assets involved in transfer to the vendor
- the fees payable for services, including variations applying to contracted service levels
- the skills and experience of the personnel provided by the vendor to look after the various aspects of service provision
- expected levels of IT and business process innovation
- dispute resolution and 'divorce' issues and procedures.

The legal definition of particular service levels and the monitoring and evaluation provisions associated with them can sometimes be problematic. This becomes even more difficult when, as is often the case, these issues change subtly or even significantly given changing business conditions and thus changing information and information systems needs.

Major issues surrounding outsourcing arrangements are often associated with contractual incompleteness (not all eventualities have been recognised and allowed for within the contract) and contract complexity (recognising the first problem, contracts are written to cover any imaginable possibility and hence become overly complex, bureaucratic and totally inflexible). A lack of attention to detail can be just as damaging as excessive zeal in terms of detail, and care must be taken to achieve the required level of flexibility in the contract while ensuring reasonableness from both parties when it comes to the delivery of services and fees charged.

Increased dependency on external skills

Another risk is associated with increased dependency on people outside the organisation for service. While the relationship is working well, this seems unproblematic, but given the problems alluded to above, it can easily become an issue for the organisation. Concerns of this type can result from a poor contract or inadequate planning of requirements before entering into the contract. Some organisations find that goals and objectives established for the outsourcing initiatives are immeasurable, and this becomes very problematic when issues of contract performance are assessed. Often issues to do with contracts stem from poor contract management skills (are the remaining IT staff equipped with the necessary skills to manage complex contracts?), a lack of relationship building (the contract becomes the only vehicle for resolving disagreements) and poor communication, both between the organisation and its outsourcing vendor and between affected parties in the organisation itself. Problems of this type can stem from personnel changes: in the early stages of the relationship, efforts to communicate are made, but with staff turnover and the like, these channels of communication might be lost.

Loss of skills and knowledge

Another risk with outsourcing, particularly when the arrangement involves the transfer of staff to the outsourcing vendor, can be a loss of skills and knowledge from the organisation, which in modern environments can become a real issue. Sometimes organisations outsource IT, believing that IT is not core to their business, and at first the implications of a loss of skills, expertise and knowledge is not regarded as problematic. But as more and more organisations seek to exploit the potentialities of the Internet in seeking efficiencies and effectiveness gains, or business strategy changes, and so on, then the result might be the realisation that IT did play or needs to play a strategic role, and the organisation finds itself locked into a contract that might no longer suit its requirements.

Unrealistic contract negotiations

Recall that the single most common factor for outsourcing was to reduce or at least control costs. Organisations approaching outsourcing with this mindset typically do not set about the negotiation process looking for ways to help the vendor to make a profit. Rather they typically try to achieve a very good price for themselves and seem to resent any attempt by the vendor to make a profit at their expense. Vendors in this situation might then, once the contract has been signed, look for ways of achieving a reasonable profit from the deal, looking for creative ways to interpret aspects of the contract, allowing service to degrade slightly and so on. This type of situation has been referred to as 'the Winner's Curse' (Kern, Willcocks & van Heck 2002). Hence, if an organisation is intent on 'winning' from the outsourcing deal, it might pay insufficient attention to the need of the vendor to 'win' also, recognising that the vendor must be allowed to be profitable is essential if outsourcing initiatives are to be successful over time.

Hidden costs

Many organisations learn that outsourcing arrangements do not deliver the cost saving expected or forecast, particularly in the long term. This often occurs because of a number of hidden costs that plague this sort of arrangement. First, many organisations fail to factor in the costs of locating a suitable vendor and negotiating and entering into a contract with that vendor. This can be a very costly process, particularly when it might also involve establishing sound performance metrics for the IT department before starting the negotiations. Second, the costs associated with transitioning to the vendor are often not factored into the equation. Initially, many organisations experience disruption and a degradation of IT service levels as the vendor is getting to know the organisation and its requirements. Help must be given to the vendor in order to familiarise them with required service levels and support, key business processes, technology issues and so on as soon as possible. If the vendor then has a change in staff, the organisation might go through the same process many times, essentially providing training to staff of the outsourcing vendor. This could be repeated many times in some circumstances and can represent a substantial hidden cost to the organisation.

There are also so-called hidden costs associated with the contract management process. Fulfilling all contractual obligations, building relationships, bargaining with vendors and negotiating contract changes and variations can, and often is, a resource-intensive business and is often more difficult than people anticipated. Turban, McLean and Wetherbe (1999) cite a number of instances where contract management proved much more costly and difficult for the organisation than they had imagined. If higher costs and greater effort are involved in contract management than were anticipated, then clearly cost saving will be eroded. Finally, in those cases where the organisation ultimately decides to bring the IT function back in-house (backsourcing) for a variety of reasons, there is an enormous cost associated with transitioning back in-house.

Decision-making about strategic sourcing

There is clearly a lot at stake when organisations make decisions about **strategic sourcing** of IT services. It is important therefore that executives charged with making decisions about IT are informed about the implications and consequences of particular sourcing decisions and strategies recommended for their organisations. Some frameworks have been derived to assist decision-makers to take carefully thought through decisions about outsourcing.

Lacity, Willcocks and Feeny (1996) offer the decision-maker three separate matrices, which emphasise the need to consider the outsourcing decision from a number of different perspectives, namely, from a business perspective, from an economic perspective and from a technology perspective. These three matrices are reproduced in figure 9.4 (p. 260). Thus, for example, the business factors matrix suggests that if a particular IT project under consideration is absolutely critical to business operations, and if it is expected to provide a source of competitive advantage, then the best strategy would be to develop it in-house. The other matrices can be interpreted in a similar way.

These matrices have been used to encourage thinking creatively about the issue at hand and to consider an option from a number of different perspectives. The problem for decision-makers, however, is that by considering a particular project from the perspective in each of the matrices, it is entirely possible that conflicting recommendations might be made. For example, if the previous example is extended (the critical differentiator should be insourced), it could emerge that our IT management practices are lagging and that we have a small-ish IT department (i.e. of subcritical mass), and therefore the economic perspective suggests that an outsource decision might be appropriate. On the one hand, this is a strength as it could help decision-makers to recognise that outsourcing decisions are full of tensions, multiple and conflicting objectives and possible contradictions, and hence are very difficult to make. But on the other hand, little advice or help is offered to the decision-maker in terms of resolving these contradictions.

An alternative approach is offered by Insinga and Werle (2000), who put forward a single matrix to support the outsourcing decision, essentially based on the value to the business or potential to achieve a competitive advantage from a particular IT activity and the extent to which the organisation already has the capability internally to perform that activity (see figure 9.5).

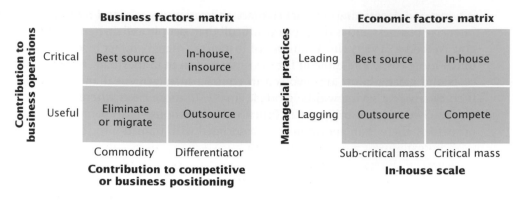

Figure 9.4 ▶ Three different perspectives from which to analyse outsourcing decisions
Source ▶ Lacity, Willcocks and Feeny 1996, pp. 19, 21 and 24.

	Internal capability of enterprise to perform in comparison with competitors			
Absolutely	1 Get capability	2 Build strength	3 Do in-house	*Key activities*
Probably	4a Partner	5a Partner	6a Do in-house	*Emerging activities*
		5b Collaborate		
	4b Collaborate	5c Share risk	6b Share risk	
Possibly	7 Buy	8a Develop second source (external)	9a Make it a profit centre	*Basic activities*
			9b Consider selling/buying	
		8b Buy		
Not likely	10 Buy	11 Exit/buy (sell, abandon or allow to weaken)	12 Consider selling/buying	*Commodity activities*
None				

Potential for activity to yield competitive advantage (vertical axis)

Internal capability of enterprise to perform in comparison with competitors

Figure 9.5 ▶ Outsourcing decisions linked to value and capabilities
Source ▶ Insinga and Werle 2000, p. 61.

Insinga and Werle (2000) argue that in broad terms, four types of activities, each contributing differently to the organisation's potential to achieve competitive advantage, can be identified. Thus, key activities are those that provide a competitive advantage, emerging activities are those thought to have the potential to provide competitive advantage, basic activities are essential for staying in business but are not generally regarded as a source of competitive advantage, and commodity activities are commonly available in the marketplace and cannot provide a source of competitive advantage to anyone.

The organisation's ability to perform a particular activity can be assessed as weak, moderate or strong. The resultant matrix (see figure 9.5) provides guidance in planning IT activities. In cell 1, therefore, an organisation is deemed to have little capability to perform an activity judged to be certain to deliver competitive advantage, and hence the recommendation is that the capability should be obtained and developed within the organisation. For emerging activities (cells 4–6), some uncertainty is acknowledged as to the likelihood that a particular activity will become a source of competitive advantage. For highly probable activities (i.e. those moving upwards towards key activities), there are different recommendations from those that seem to be moving down towards basic activities. Thus, for an activity that is probably going to deliver advantage but for which the organisation has little capability, the recommendation is to form a partnership that will allow for later acquisition of the capability in order not to be placed at a disadvantage. By contrast, when there is more likelihood that the activity will become basic, the recommendation is to collaborate with a capable enterprise to limit the risks and strengthen the organisation's position without a full-scale commitment to developing the capability.

It is not proposed to describe in detail each of the cells in the matrix (refer to the original paper by Insinga and Werle (2000)). The point to be made here is that this matrix offers a connection between IT outsourcing decisions, current internal capabilities, the potential for an activity to deliver a source of competitive advantage, and business strategy. It also helps to highlight an organisation's current levels and area of capabilities and competencies with respect to IT and therefore could help management to realise areas that need development in the organisation and others where cost saving and asset shedding could be achieved without compromising the performance of the organisation.

thinking strategically

Precision Instruments to outsource its ERP implementation?

Precision Instruments is a medium-sized business specialising in the installation and maintenance of high-tech precision measurement equipment. They have been very successful of late and have grown rapidly. However, rapid growth has caused problems for them, too: most of their existing information systems are unable to cope with the increased processing demands, and they are completely unable to automate information exchanges between different systems. Precision Instruments has just appointed an IT manager, who oversees the performance of the company's small IT team of twelve. In his previous role, the IT manager had worked as a consultant for an ERP vendor.

The IT manager presented a business case to the general manager outlining his recommendation to implement an ERP system. He recommended InteGrate, an ERP package designed specifically for medium-sized enterprises. One of the very attractive features of InteGrate, argued the IT manager, is its ability to link directly to web-based front office systems. This feature was very attractive to the staff at Precision Instruments as they believed a source of competitive advantage to them was the new web-based system by which they provide service and information via a secure website to their valued customers.

InteGrate offered the possibility of automating flows of information to this website and, in so doing, smoothing out internal operations, particularly in improving the maintenance scheduling for the many clients. It would thus become the engine room of the company and be inextricably linked to corporate success. The general manager, however, had heard of ERP failures and was concerned that this system acquisition and implementation should avoid that fate.

Questions

1. Should Precision Instruments outsource the acquisition, development and implementation of their proposed ERP system? Why? Justify your rationale using Insinga and Werle's outsourcing framework.
2. What about maintenance and operations of this system? Justify your answer.
3. Is Precision Instruments well advised to build an IT department internally, or should they adopt a total outsourcing strategy to access the required IT capabilities? Be prepared to justify your answer.
4. Discuss the broad categories of IT capabilities that Precision Instruments will need to maintain and extend its successful position in the marketplace.

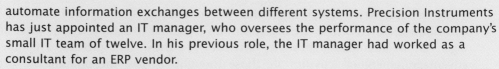

Towards best practice in outsourcing

Evidence suggests that more recently signed outsourcing contracts typically achieve better returns and cost savings for organisations than did contracts signed some years ago (Lacity & Willcocks 1998). This suggests that organisations are learning more about the foundations of successful outsourcing decisions and how better to manage contracts if outsourcing seems to be the desirable option. In this section, it is proposed to consider some of these lessons and some of the factors that seem to be associated with reaching successful and appropriate outsourcing decisions.

Contracts are essential

Essentially three types of sourcing contracts have been identified: fee-for-service, strategic alliances or partnerships, and buy-in contracts. Fee-for-service contracts are just that: fully defined requirements, levels of service, agreed performance measurements, penalties for non-performance and price for service, specified over specific periods. Fee-for-service contracts seem to be most appropriate for stable and mature technologies, in situations in which organisations can be reasonably sure of stable requirements over the period of the contract. However, in situations in which organisations struggle to define requirements, or where IT activities are associated with immature or unstable technologies, adequately defining the services required and therefore the fees to be charged can prove problematic (Lacity & Willcocks 1998). Opportunistic vendors could use contract variations to charge excess fees, but by contrast, client organisations could be unrealistic in expecting contract variations at no fee because activities had been 'forgotten'.

Strategic alliances or partnerships exist when there is interdependence and a long-term relationship is planned, when all parties have attributes and resources of value to contribute, when there might be cross-organisational investment, and where there is strategic significance associated with the relationship by both parties (Lacity & Willcocks 1998). The issue of strategic alliances and partnerships will be dealt with more fully in the following chapter. Summing up overall, however, we can say that many outsourcing arrangements of this type have suffered from problems and difficulties, or at least have not lived up to expectations (Lacity & Willcocks 1998).

Buy-in contracts are effectively an insourcing arrangement, as buying in involves obtaining extra capabilities from a vendor(s) to supplement existing internal capabilities. Arrangements of this type work well when organisations need access to the expertise of the vendor and to foster learning in the organisation but they could not draw up a fee-for-service contract as requirements could not be fully specified. Technology transfer is an important aspect of buy-in arrangements (Lacity, Willcocks & Feeny 1996).

Whatever the exact arrangements, a sound contract, one that is understandable, reasonable, well thought-out and measurable, and one that aims for flexibility where possible, is essential to successful ongoing operations. Experts, such as lawyers, consultants and outsourcing process managers, could be important in the process of leading to and writing an outsourcing contract. Creating a sound process whereby alternative bids are evaluated (including a bid from the internal IT department) is essential. So too are establishing clear performance measures and then ensuring that data is collected to allow categorical establishment of whether performance has been adequate.

Allow the vendor to be profitable

Outsourcing arrangements based on adversarial win–lose philosophy are rarely successful. Organisations need to appreciate that while they might wish to access the best possible service for the lowest fee they can negotiate, at the end of the day a successful relationship relies on the vendor being able to make a reasonable profit while delivering required levels of service (Kern, Willcocks & van Heck 2002). Win–win scenarios are thus associated with more successful contractual relationships. Successful relationships are often based on a notion of 'sharing the pain and the gain' or building in incentives for excellent performance and penalties for below-standard performance.

Contract management

Another essential ingredient in successful outsourcing initiatives is for the organisation outsourcing to ensure it has adequate contract management skills in-house. Keeping track of vendor performance, managing contract variations, resolving disputes and carefully auditing contract performance are all associated with successful contracts (Hirschheim 2003).

Change management

Moving to a partial or substantial outsourcing arrangement involves significant change in an organisation. Managing the transition to the vendor is essential. So too is caring for staff who might be moving to the employment of the vendor. Ensuring that expectations are reasonable, throughout all business units, among IT staff and on the part of the vendor, is essential if the change is to be successfully negotiated.

Retain IT management skills

Even when outsourcing involves a substantial proportion of the IT services required by an organisation, it is essential to retain a small team of specialist IT planners and managers. Understanding the role of IT in an industry and the contribution it could make to future business growth and development, ensuring that IT is appropriately used throughout the organisation and ensuring that IT is used to support the achievement of business goals and objectives are all essential activities that should never be outsourced.

Trends in outsourcing

After more than a decade of substantial IT outsourcing arrangements, what trends are emerging? It seems fair to say that many of the large-scale, total outsourcing initiatives that were characteristic of the early to mid 1990s are now up for renewal, and some executives are questioning whether arrangements of this type continue to meet the needs and objectives of their organisations.

Research seems to indicate that outsourcing will continue, but expectations are that prices will come down in response to increased competition among outsourcing vendors and the growing attraction of offshore outsourcing. Competition among outsourcing vendors is also likely to drive service levels up. Given these trends, we are also likely to see outsourcing evaluations involve more careful thought and analysis before deciding what to outsource and what capabilities and services to retain in-house. It is also predicted that outsourcing decisions will be recognised as having a strategic dimension, and outsourcing adoption will be driven more by the need to access particular expertise and competencies rather than being driven primarily by cost savings (O'Neill 2001).

Contract renegotiation

Many contracts are being renegotiated. The sort of changes typically being demanded revolve around more flexibility, better measurement of performance and better monitoring of contract performance. Some very large, complex contracts are still being signed, but there is less naivety about the terms of the contract. Complexity often forces vendors into partnering arrangements with other vendors to obtain the requisite skills and expertise required to maintain required service levels for the client.

Backsourcing

Some organisations are deciding not to continue with large-scale outsourcing but to rebuild some IT capability internally and hence set about recruiting and rebuilding the IT department, a process known as backsourcing or reinsourcing. This might be the result of disillusionment with outsourcing as contracts at times fail to deliver expected cost savings and required service levels or a fundamental change in the role and nature of the contribution IT can make to the business (cio.com 2003).

Netsourcing

Netsourcing (sometimes referred to as e-sourcing) refers to obtaining the entire e-business infrastructure requirements from a single vendor, who delivers all required services via the Internet. One of the challenges facing businesses offering round-the-clock fully transactional e-commerce is the need for $24 \times 7 \times 52$ availability as many organisations experience surges or unpredictability in demand. Therefore establishing required levels of infrastructure (including networks and telecommunications), skills, service and support can be difficult, and doing so appropriately might be beyond the existing internal capabilities of the IT department. Netsourcing offers a complete infrastructure and provides a flexible model for businesses with full capability e-commerce websites without multiple contracts and accountabilities and without difficulties in contract management. Netsourcing vendors typically bundle network services, hosting of mission-critical systems, hardware and systems software, infrastructure integration, technical support and business continuity planning and services, all within a single contract from a single provider with clear accountabilities and performance measures. Clients can adopt a 'pay as you use' model (i.e. businesses pay only for the traffic and usage of the services provided on a monthly basis, for example) or they can enter into standard contracting or rental arrangements. The choice might depend on the netsourcing vendor and on predictability of the need for services on the part of the client business (cio.com 2000).

Application service providers

Application service providers (ASPs) are in many regards similar to the netsourcing model described above and could probably be included in that section. Typically, with an ASP, applications software is provided to a client by an ASP for a regular rental or on a user-pays basis. Users of that software can access the application from their workplace or remotely via the Internet, and access for business partners, valued trading partners and the like can also be accommodated. Some ASPs provide their own applications, whereas others host applications from other software companies, such as SAP, Oracle and e-Piphany. Whereas netsourcers stress a single provider for the entire IT/e-business infrastructure, ASPs might provide parts of services and are not confined only to the infrastructure required for Internet-based trading or service delivery. So an ASP might provide ERP functionality or CRM functionality and so on. Although the ASPs usually rely on the Internet for the delivery of service to their clients, the services offered do not relate only to Internet commerce. Furthermore, whereas the netsourcing approach stresses a total service, ASPs offer more flexibility in that the ownership of hardware, networks and databases might rest with the client company and might not even be offered as part of the service of the ASP. ASPs are especially attractive to medium-sized and larger small enterprises that need more than a few networked PCs but struggle to find the money to pay for full ERP or CRM systems and functionality (Dzubeck 1999) and who lack the internal IT resources to support such applications fully (Morency 1999).

Four major types of ASP are identified: full services ASPs (very similar to the netsourcing model above), whereby the client has only to manage the relationship with the ASP; managed service providers, who provide the technology infrastructure and basic software maintenance while the client owns and manages the software; infrastructure providers, who own and manage the technology infrastructure only; and software providers, who own and manage everything to do with the applications while control of and responsibility for the technology infrastructure remains with the client (cio.com 2002).

The major advantages of the ASP are a lower cost of entry and a shorter set-up time for businesses needing IT functionality. The rental or pay-for-use costing model also often proves to be less expensive than acquisition. It also removes the need for as many IT staff as might otherwise be needed (Marshall 2003). However, problems can occur with ASPs. Rarely will ASPs provide anything other than the standard software functionality, which might not suit specific business needs. There might also be problems related to security, data integrity and confidentiality, and business continuity planning and management. Organisations that rely on the full ASP model are often also left without internal IT capability to provide support. Hence strong service-level agreements are required, and might be necessary to ensure the delivery of appropriate levels of service and support (cio.com 2002).

Business process outsourcing

Another growing trend is that of business process outsourcing (BPO). BPO can be defined as 'contracting with an external organization for providing a business process or function' (Linder, Cantrell & Crist 2002). Processes suitable for outsourcing to a BPO vendor include human resources, finance and accounting, training and customer relationship management. Despite the name, it can be noted from these activities that BPO more often refers to outsourcing a function rather than a specific process. However, Keen (2002) emphasises that BPO should emphasise the process aspects, and argues that BPO involves a selective or best sourcing approach (i.e. find the best source for a range of capabilities and activities) for key processes in the business value chain. In this, Keen (2002) includes supply chain, customer demand chain and relationship management, product and service innovation, and so on.

Keen also argues that BPO has a slightly different emphasis from outsourcing. Whereas outsourcing might literally stress the 'out', or getting someone outside the organisation to do something or take control of something, BPO stresses relationships or alliances, with the notion that client and vendor should collaborate and contribute distinctive offerings and mutually supportive and necessary capabilities for a successful and distinctively BPO arrangement. Hence benefits of BPO include operational excellence (i.e. gaining access to better capabilities than the organisation possesses internally while still leveraging internal sources of excellence), financial efficiency through reducing capital tied up in inefficient activities and process elements, building capabilities in a cost-effective manner, gaining responsiveness to change and supporting innovation (Keen 2002).

Summary

Some capabilities are central or core to an organisation's purposes. These capabilities are usually developed within organisational boundaries and, together with assets or resources such as IT, money and physical assets, core capabilities underpin the business processes or activities that essentially earn revenues for the organisation. Other capabilities, together with their associated business processes, are regarded as non-core and are often thought of as better carried out by some other organisation. Information systems, human resource management functions (including management of employee benefits), canteen and cleaning functions, and so on are typically viewed as potentially non-core. These may often be turned over to another organisation to perform, a process known as outsourcing.

In some organisations, information systems and information technology are often regarded as non-core capabilities and activities and therefore are viewed as candidates for outsourcing. In recent times, however, there has been a trend to outsourcing some core activities in the expectation that competition among service deliverers will lower costs and improve service. Outsourcing of core activities is therefore motivated by looking for best-of-breed solutions at competitive prices.

However, simplistic total outsourcing of IS/IT has proved to be problematic. Many early mega-deals involving the total outsourcing of IS/IT got into substantial difficulties and failed to live up to expectations and did not deliver the expected results and service. As research began to indicate that a more carefully considered approach to outsourcing was justified and could lead to better outcomes, outsourcing practice began to change. Outsourcing IS/IT began to be viewed as a decision that had some strategic elements, which needed careful consideration. Total outsourcing practice gave way to a more considered selective sourcing strategy, whereby typically IS/IT that was considered more strategic or critical to business operations or a source of competitive advantage was insourced whereas the more commodity-like applications and services less likely to contribute directly to business competitiveness were outsourced. A key principle was that IS/IT was a portfolio of capabilities and activities that should be sourced competitively from the marketplace. That marketplace was seen as being made up of both the internal IS/IT function and external outsourcing vendors.

New trends are emerging in the practice of outsourcing. One important trend among these is business process outsourcing whereby an organisation, instead of outsourcing the IS/IT component of a business process, outsources all elements required to make up that business process. This allows the outsourcing vendor to optimise the business process by focusing its capabilities, resources and knowledge on the whole process, including the linkages between the information systems and the human activities involved in the process.

key terms

application service provider
backsourcing
capability
competence (core competence)
insourcing
netsourcing

outsourcing
outsourcing vendor
selective sourcing
strategic alliance
strategic sourcing

discussion questions

1. Discuss the notion that non-core processes and activities should be outsourced whereas core processes and activities should be provided in-house. In particular mention some problems and limitations with this notion.

2. Describe the risks and potential problems involved in IS/IT outsourcing. Are these risks and problems ameliorated or exaggerated in the cases of netsourcing and the use of applications service providers (ASPs)?

3. Describe selective sourcing. What are the advantages of selective sourcing over total outsourcing? Describe the frameworks (business, economic and technical) of Lacity, Willcocks and Feeny (1996) regarding decision-making with respect to selective sourcing. (See Lacity, Willcocks & Feeny 1996.)

4. What are the major IS/IT capabilities? (See Feeny & Willcocks 1998.) Peppard, Lambert and Edwards (2000) argue that the necessary information and IS/IT capabilities for an organisation are actually organisational capabilities, not merely capabilities of the IS/IT department. Explain and critique Peppard's view on this matter. What implications does Peppard's view have for IS/IT outsourcing behaviour in organisations?

5. Describe business process outsourcing (BPO). Describe the possible advantages of BPO over conventional IS/IT outsourcing. What are the problems and limitations of BPO?

suggested reading

Insinga, RC & Werle, MJ 2000, 'Linking outsourcing to business strategy', *Academy of Management Executive*, vol. 14, no. 4, pp. 58–70.

Kern, T, Willcocks, LP & van Heck, E 2002, 'The winner's curse: strategies for avoiding relational trauma', *California Management Review*, vol. 44, no. 2, Winter, pp. 47–69.

Lacity, MC & Willcocks, LP 1998, 'An empirical investigation of information technology sourcing practices: lessons from experience', *MIS Quarterly*, September, pp. 363–408.

Lacity, MC, Willcocks, LP & Feeny, DF 1996, 'The value of selective IT sourcing', *Sloan Management Review*, vol. 37, issue 3, Spring, pp. 13–25.

Peppard, J, Lambert, R & Edwards, C 2000, 'Whose job is it anyway? Organizational information competencies for value creation', *Information Systems Journal*, vol. 10, no. 4, pp. 291–322.

Willcocks, LP & Lacity, MC 1998, 'The sourcing and outsourcing of IS: shock of the new?', in LP Willcocks & MC Lacity (eds) 1998, *Strategic Sourcing of Information Systems: Perspectives and Practices*, John Wiley & Sons, Chichester.

references

Applegate, LM & Collura, M 2000a, *Developing E-business Capabilities: Building E-businesses*, Harvard Business School Publishing, Boston.

—2000b, *E-business Value Framework and Tables*, Harvard Business School Publishing, Boston.

cio.com 2000, 'Netsourcing, the new look of outsourcing', available at http://www.cio.com/sponsors/080100_intira.html, accessed 10 March 2003.

—2002, 'Application service provider', http://www.cio.com/summaries/outsourcing/asp/inex.html?action=print, accessed 19 March 2003.

—2003, 'Bringing IT back home', CIO magazine, 1 March, available at http://www.cio.com/archive/030103/home_content.html?printversion=yes, accessed 20 March 2003.

DeSanctis, G, Dickson, G & Price, R 2001, 'Information technology management: perspective, focus, and change in the twenty-first century', in G Dickson & G DeSanctis (eds), *Information Technology and the Future Enterprise: New Models for Managers*, Prentice Hall, Upper Saddle River, NJ.

Dzubeck, F 1999, 'Application service providers: an old idea made new', http://www.nwfusion.com/cgi-bin/mailto/x/cgi, accessed 19 March 2003.

Feeny, DF & Willcocks, LP 1998, 'Core IS capabilities for exploiting information technology', *Sloan Management Review*, vol. 39, issue 3, Spring, pp. 9–21.

Fitzgerald, G & Willcocks, L 1994, 'Relationships in outsourcing: contracts and partnerships', in WRJ Baets (ed.) 1994, Proceedings of the Second European Conference on Information Systems, Nijenrode University, The Netherlands, Nijenrode University Press, Breukelen, pp. 51–63.

Grover, V, Teng, JTC & Cheon, MJ 1998, 'Towards a theoretically based contingency model of information systems outsourcing', in LP Willcocks & MC Lacity (eds) 1998, *Strategic Sourcing of Information Systems: Perspectives and Practices*, John Wiley & Sons, Chichester, pp. 79–101.

Hamel, G & Prahalad, CK 1994, *Competing for the Future*, Harvard Business School Press, Boston.

Hirschheim, R 2003, 'Strategies for the effective sourcing of IT', SIMS Seminar Series, Monash University, 21 February 2003, available at www.sims.monash.edu.au/research/seminar/index.html.

Insinga, RC & Werle, MJ 2000, 'Linking outsourcing to business strategy', *Academy of Management Executive*, vol. 14, no. 4, pp. 58–70.

Keen, PGW 2002, 'Business process outsourcing. Computer Sciences Corporation, Virginia', available at http://www.csc.com/solutions/businessprocessoutsourcing/knowledgelibrary/uploads/915_1.pdf, accessed 10 March 2003.

Kern, T, Willcocks, LP & van Heck, E 2002, 'The winner's curse: strategies for avoiding relational trauma', *California Management Review*, vol. 44, no. 2, Winter, pp. 47–69.

Lacity, MC & Hirschheim, R 1993, *Information Systems Outsourcing: Myths, Metaphors and Realities*, John Wiley & Sons, Chichester.

—1995, *Beyond the Information Systems Outsourcing Bandwagon: The Insourcing Response*, John Wiley & Sons, Chichester.

Lacity, MC & Willcocks, LP 1998, 'An empirical investigation of information technology sourcing practices: lessons from experience', *MIS Quarterly*, September, pp. 363–408.

—2001, *Global Information Technology Outsourcing*, John Wiley & Sons, Chichester.

Lacity, MC, Willcocks, LP & Feeny, DF 1996, 'The value of selective IT sourcing', *Sloan Management Review*, vol. 37, issue 3, Spring, pp. 13–25.

Linder, J, Cantrell, S & Crist, S 2002, 'Business process outsourcing big bang: creating value in an expanding universe. Accenture', http://managementconsult.profpages.nl/man_bib/rap/accenture09.html, accessed 10 March 2003.

Marshall, B 2003, 'How ASPs work', http://www.howstuffworks.com/asp.htm/printable, accessed 19 March 2003.

Morency, J 1999, 'Application service providers and e-business', http:www.nwfusion.com/cgi-bin/mailto/x.cgi, accessed 10 March 2003.

O'Neill, R 2001, 'Strategic view — outsourcing backlash?', http://www.misweb.com/magarticle.asp?doc_id=19403&rgid=7&listed_months=0, accessed 19 March 2003.

Peppard, J, Lambert, R & Edwards, C 2000, 'Whose job is it anyway? Organizational information competencies for value creation', *Information Systems Journal*, vol. 10, no. 4, pp. 291–322.

Quinn, JB & Hilmer, FG 1994, 'Strategic outsourcing', *Sloan Management Review*, vol. 36, no. 4, pp. 43–55.

Ross, JW, Beath, CM & Goodhue, DL 1996, Develop long-term competitiveness through IT assets', *Sloan Management Review*, vol. 38, no. 1, pp. 31–42.

Turban, E, McLean, E & Wetherbe, J 1999, *Information Technology for Management: Making Connections for Strategic Advantage*, 2nd edn, John Wiley & Sons, New York.

Willcocks, LP & Lacity, MC 1998, 'The sourcing and outsourcing of IS: shock of the new?', in LP Willcocks & MC Lacity (eds) 1998, *Strategic Sourcing of Information Systems: Perspectives and Practices*, John Wiley & Sons, Chichester, pp. 1–41.

case study

Security Printing Australia: an outsourcing story

Security Printing Australia (SPA) had been founded in 1892 in Melbourne. By the beginning of the twenty-first century the company produced a range of security products from financial documents to plastic cards with sophisticated security features. The workforce had grown from approximately twenty employees at the beginning of the twentieth century to about 950 employees by the beginning of the twenty-first century. Sales revenues were currently running at about $120 million per year.

SPA had been established to produce personalised cheques for the early Australian banking system. It soon had become profitable and had added the capability of producing postage stamps for the postal system in the first years of the twentieth century. Personalised cheques were still a major product line, and postage stamp printing had expanded to include postage stamp production for a number of countries in Africa and Asia.

New lines of financial document printing included the printing of bonds, promissory notes, gift vouchers and travellers cheques. Security features built into these products included watermarks, foil images and holograms.

In the 1980s SPA began to produce plastic cards with inbuilt security features. These cards ranged from bank-related transaction and credit cards to ID cards to smart cards for mobile telephony and pay phone use. These cards featured a range of sophisticated security characteristics such as holograms, magnetic strips, security patterns, signature panels and photographic data. To gain full advantage from the advanced technology-based security features it built into its cards, SPA advertised regularly and frequently to the business world that they keep abreast of the latest technology in cards. The security card business is the fastest-growing part of SPA's business.

The SPA manufacturing establishment or factory worked around the clock, twenty-four hours a day, seven days a week. There were three eight-hour shifts per day. The front office employees and a sales force, however, worked standard office hours.

The 'e-business/e-commerce revolution' of the late 1990s had provided SPA with a new business opportunity. Bringing together its formidable graphic design skills and its information technology capabilities, SPA had launched a web page design and web page implementation business. In its advertisements for this business, SPA promised to design and create an attractive, fast-loading website using the latest Internet technologies, including 128-bit encrypted e-commerce facilities, such as product catalogues, 'virtual shopping cart' technology and full purchase and payment transactional capabilities. Also provided was a password-protected hits counter that provided a full set of online statistics.

The web page design initiative was second only to the plastic security card business in terms of the company's growth rate. To ensure that this successful initiative provided a full e-business/e-commerce service to business, SPA had partnered with E-Business Outsourcing Ltd (EOL), a successful new business in Melbourne that had commenced business in 1996. EOL offered to implement, run, maintain and enhance a company's website for them. They also offered to develop, maintain and run a basic 'back office' set of systems for an organisation.

The information technology department of SPA had been established in the late 1960s, when computers began to be used in the cheque personalisation business. Through the years some members of the IT department had developed a very good knowledge of how to use IT to build security into printed products and cards. Two members of the IT department, Jane Weld and William Thorpe, were recognised specialists at utilising IT in this way. Jane and William had built the Direct Security Encrypting and Embedding Applications Suite, a set of specialised computer routines or applications for use in developing digital security applications for embedding IT-based security features into printed products and plastic cards. They also had developed a set of computer applications that they had called the Smart Card Encoding Applications Suite of computer routines or applications for developing IT applications for embedding security and other functionality into smart cards.

Apart from those people with a specialised knowledge of security applications, the rest of the IT department had developed and implemented a number of business-based information systems through the years. All of the systems had been developed in-house. Some of the systems were quite standard, such as the financial accounting system and the manufacturing cost accounting system. However, some of the systems were focused on SPA's printing production processes and were regarded by most of the senior management as a key part of SPA's business competitiveness and its commitment to the highest quality security products at a reasonable price.

The information systems thought to be particularly significant to SPA's production processes attaining high quality and a reasonable price were the quality control system, the production scheduling and finite capacity planning system, and the computer-driven direct-encode cheque personalisation system. Some of the senior managers also included the purchasing system, the job estimation system and the sales forecasting system as having special features that contributed to SPA's business competitiveness. However, there was by no means unanimity on this issue.

There was quite general agreement that the order entry system, the sales statistics system, the inventory management system, the fixed assets system, the HR management support system, the capital investment appraisal decision support system and the payroll system were all fairly standard systems — or at least it was believed that they could be replaced by standard systems. It was believed that the special routines and features embedded in some of the systems were not essential to the conduct of business and delivered few business benefits to SPA.

Although the service provided by the IT department to the rest of SPA was generally regarded as of a high standard, the costs of IT had been rising quite rapidly over the last few years. Depending on what was taken into account in the costing, the total cost of IT services seemed to be rising at between 5 and 10 per cent a year. The CIO, Rens Peetoom, had, however, assured the CEO, Martin Christopher, that SPA was getting value for money from the IT department.

A solution to the problem of rising IT costs had been suggested to Martin Christopher by Vijay Sharma, the CEO of EOL. It was that EOL look after the 'standard' systems (finance, accounting and so on) for a fixed price. Help desk services would be provided along with application system maintenance and enhancements.

Rens Peetoom was meeting with Martin Christopher regarding the EOL outsourcing proposal. Rens was feeling somewhat defensive. He began the conversation. 'The IT department not only provides an excellent and dedicated service regarding routine IT applications, but we also provide creative solutions to production scheduling and capacity planning problems, to quality control problems and many other problem situations. We also contribute to the smooth running of this business in many tangible and intangible ways.'

'I hear you, Rens,' said Martin, 'but EOL is only going to look after "standard" IT systems — of course we will have to define what EOL and us mean by "standard"...'

Rens interrupted rather agitatedly. 'Yes, Martin, but my department is quite efficient...No! Efficient and effective at looking after "standard" systems — not only during the day shift either...'

'Well, look,' said Martin, 'I want to open the whole IT outsourcing question a little more! I have been speaking with IT Global, a world-class outsourcing company...'

Rens interrupted again. 'Yes, Martin, world class at driving one-sided outsourcing agreements!'

Martin was now becoming annoyed. 'Hang on, Rens,' he said. 'We have to make a rational analysis of this. IT Global is offering us a total solution, and I wanted to look at that in an objective way from the perspective of our whole business — not just the perspective of the IT department. IT Global is one of the world dominant IT outsourcing companies. They have world-class people and capabilities in IT — that is their business, that is their core competence.

'I have had some initial conversations with Chuck Siboni, their Australian representative. Chuck maintains they can not only look after our "standard" applications but can also deal with our manufacturing applications and our specialist security applications. They have a large number of specialists in these areas in the US headquarters in New York, and in some of their branch offices in the European capitals like London and Rome. They are reputed to be first rate — we can tap into their world-class IT knowledge and into their knowledge of best practice in IT! I also hope that they will help us to innovate better — how could we hope to innovate better by ourselves? You know, we need to keep innovating in this business. I am impressed by them, Rens — I have read some excellent reviews of their work. Chuck also impresses me.'

Rens was surprised and somewhat shocked at this new development. 'Well', he said, 'I'll need time to respond to this. My first thoughts are that my people are not only experts in manufacturing and security applications but also they really know not only our industry but also our company in some detail.'

Martin began speaking in a more conciliatory manner. 'Look, I know there are many things to think over here. I would like you to prepare a paper for me on the options open to us. I want us to try to consider all viable options objectively and to determine an IT outsourcing — no, better — an IT sourcing strategy. We will consider the future for our people in this — Chuck has told me that in many of the outsourcing deals he has worked on, he has found ways to permit surplus staff to move to IT Global. Chuck feels that some such arrangement could operate here if we go for his total outsourcing strategy.

'I know this is a complex and — in many ways — difficult issue for you. However, I have contacted Dr James Munkres from Monash University and he will help you prepare your paper. I must tell you that I have also asked William Massey, our CFO, also to prepare a paper on our options. As you know, William is very positive about outsourcing, particularly outsourcing IT.'

Rens left the CEO's office feeling rather gloomy. However, his spirits picked up after he had a conversation with Dr Munkres. Dr Munkres has suggested that his initial feelings in looking at the situation at SPA were that a number of positive options are available that involve substantial future involvement of the IT department. Feeling more positive himself, Rens scheduled several more meetings with Dr Munkres.

Questions

1. What are the major issues to be taken into account when approaching outsourcing of IT at SPA?

2. Discuss the option of outsourcing 'standard' systems to EOL and keeping the rest of the IT applications and services in-house. If this is the option taken by SPA, can you guard against the IT department becoming complacent and bureaucratic?

3. Discuss the option of outsourcing all of IT services, IT management, IT development and enhancement and IT operations to IT Global. Can you avoid becoming too dependent on IT Global? Is this a worry? What about the problems of new product development or product improvement, where part of the product development or improvement is dependent on IT?

4. Discuss the issue of including innovation in IT and in business processes in the outsourcing deal with IT Global. What are the potential problems, risks and benefits of this aspect of the outsourcing deal?

chapter 10

E-business and strategic business networks

learning objectives

After reading this chapter, you should be able to:

- appreciate the global business and technology trends that are driving the formation of strategic business alliances and changing assumptions about contemporary business environments
- define the fundamental characteristics of strategic business networks, or virtual organisations, and understand their role and importance in contemporary businesses
- understand the role that strategic business networks play in delivering customer value
- articulate some of the critical success factors for managing strategic business networks
- appreciate the nature of planning in strategic business networks
- articulate the requirements of building alliance and strategic business network competencies.

chapter overview

This chapter[1] is concerned with discussing the key features of the current hypercompetitive business environment and the resultant impetus for organisations to enter into a variety of collaborative trading arrangements, generically referred to as strategic business networks. These are collaborating groups of organisations that come together to exploit short-term — or possibly long-term — business opportunities: such collaborating groups of organisations are often also called virtual organisations, since although they show what is apparently one face to the customer, they are in reality groups of organisations. Such forms of organisations are argued to be useful in business environments where globalisation, increasingly affluent, knowledgeable and demanding consumers, and the effects of the Internet and other communications technologies are driving organisations to consider the benefits of focusing on core competencies and on relying on a range of partnerships and alliances for the provision of other key goods and services required for the delivery of the customer value proposition. Strategic business networks or virtual organisations are seen as a way of managing complexity and uncertainty and of improving competitive positioning in the contemporary business world. The formation of such alliances has important implications for creating customer value, and it forces organisations to rethink basic strategies about seeking efficiencies and effectiveness gains along their supply chains.

Adopting a strategy of forming strategic business networks requires changes to management strategies. Critical success factors for these arrangements involve the ability to develop a shared purpose and vision, the development of extraordinary levels of trust between trading partners and the willingness to share risk for the venture among all participants. Care needs also to be taken to ensure that the very strengths of the strategic business network do not become its weaknesses. Planning in such environments needs to be rethought, and organisations must take care to develop the competencies and capabilities required (both managerial and technical) if the organisation is to negotiate a strategic business network successfully and then to use that network as a major business initiative. A number of different types of strategic business network can be identified, although some contain weaknesses in their fundamental logic, which is depressing their rate of adoption in the broader business community.

Introduction

At the outset of this chapter, it is important to consider the nature of the business environment in which most organisations now operate and to consider whether technology, specifically the Internet and associated technologies, is playing a role in fundamentally changing the realities of the business environments in which organisations now operate.

The trend to globalisation provides organisations with a larger marketplace and the opportunity to specialise by developing core competencies (Hamel & Prahalad 1994; Masifern & Vila 1998; Strassmann 1997). Globalisation breaks down barriers between countries, organisations and individuals. It is driven by political, economic and technological factors, such as the demise of communism, the removal of trade tariffs and free trade agreements, and the rapid advance in telecommunications technologies and the Internet (Kotter 1996). However, globalisation also creates more competition because global operators can enter local markets because there are fewer barriers (Kotter 1996). These advantages and disadvantages, as well as an increasing rate of change and sudden, unpredictable change, present most organisations with a confusing mix of increasing opportunities, challenges (Sambamurthy 2002), complexity and uncertainty.

Along with the trends that accompany globalisation, in many developed countries people are becoming increasingly affluent, and this brings with it changes to the traditional business environment. Not only does it imply that there are new and larger markets developing and becoming accessible to organisations, but it might also imply that customer needs, preferences and expectations change, again forcing an increase in the responsiveness and flexibility of modern organisations. Hence many businesses are under pressure to adapt quickly, to innovate and to change in response to changing consumer demands and needs. In addition, it means that for many organisations there are increased pressures to communicate and work effectively and cooperatively with suppliers and business partners, often at geographically remote locations. Not only are customers becoming more demanding but they are also often in possession of more information, making them much more knowledgeable and discerning in their decisions.

In part at least, this has been enabled and driven through improvements to computer technologies and telecommunications, along with the growth and diffusion of the Internet and associated technologies. Hence businesses can reasonably easily develop much greater connectivity both internally and externally, among suppliers, business customers, partners and so on. In the previous chapter, the idea that the Internet can now help manage netsourcing and outsourcing arrangements in which increasingly non-core activities are provided to the organisation by best of breed providers was discussed, and it provides a good example of this phenomenon. Both the diffusion and infusion of new technologies have resulted in a shrinking of our expectations in terms of time, as most individuals and organisations are increasingly feeling under pressure to react and respond quickly to changes and trends.

In dealing with such complexity and change, typically the need for information and knowledge increases, while at the same time the likelihood of finding all requisite knowledge and skills within one person decreases. Therefore contemporary organisations are much more likely to be reliant on teams of skilled individuals, each possessing different but complementary skills and knowledge. These individuals might be drawn from within an organisation, but many organisations are now witnessing and experiencing the increasing likelihood that some team members come from outside the organisation and belong to quite separate organisations or entities. In other words, the requirement for organisations and individuals within them to become more cooperative and collaborative increases. The ability of these teams to share knowledge and information via knowledge bases was discussed in chapter 8. In chapter 9, types of outsourcing arrangements whereby such skills and attributes are accessed via the external marketplace were discussed. However, the key issue to be addressed in this chapter is the implication that increasingly, organisations must enter into a variety of contracts, arrangements and relationships with external service and goods providers in order to remain innovative and competitive in the challenging business environment that confronts them today. Business success (profitably delivering value to customers) could be contingent on identifying, developing and managing relationships with other organisations to contribute in various ways to the process of creating value. So, in modern business environments, the trend has been for organisations to move away from the traditional vertically integrated model to the **virtual organisation** (VO) or the **strategic business network** (SBN) (Pearlson 2001).

Formation of strategic business networks or virtual organisations

One response to the challenges of modern business environments is to form virtual organisations or strategic business networks as a way to manage environmental uncertainty, improve competitive positioning and to be better placed jointly to withstand environmental pressures (Finnegan, Galliers & Powell 1998). For example, Prahalad (1995, p. v) argues that 'firms are competing, not as stand-alone entities, but as a "family of firms"', acknowledging the vital role of supplier relationships in maintaining organisational competitiveness. In addition, Li and Williams (1999) argue that, in order to survive and prosper, organisations will have to focus on core competencies and to share expertise and risks with business partners. These points are confirmed by Kanter (1994, p. 96), who writes:

> Alliances between companies, whether they are from different parts of the world or different ends of the supply chain, are a fact of life in business today ... In the global economy, a well-developed ability to create and sustain fruitful collaborations gives companies a significant competitive leg up.

Forming a variety of **business alliances** is both an important and increasing trend for many organisations (Volkoff, Chan & Newson 1999) and a strategic device for dealing with the challenge of modern business environments while also retaining flexibility and adaptability (Kelly 1998). Another reason to enter into such collaborative relationships might be to create added value for customers (Brandenburger & Nalebuff 1996). This can happen because each partner brings its own set of skills, resources and competencies, which are jointly valued by the customer (Marshall et al. 1999b). Although improved customer satisfaction might be an important reason to form the collaboration, there is also the potential for a stream of opportunities to be realised together over a period of time (Kanter 1994). **Interorganisational collaboration** can therefore provide greater stability in business relationships and switching costs for all parties concerned, perhaps an attractive proposition in challenging times. However, it should be noted that increased stability might hamper the need and desire for flexibility and adaptability (Li & Williams 1999).

Most researchers would argue that IT plays an important role in enabling these strategic alliances (Nixon, Hitt & Ricart i Costa 1998; Kraut et al. 1998). Telecommunications technologies and interorganisational systems (IOS) are an important component of the strategic business network and can:

- reduce costs and improve the efficiency of transactions (Swatman & Swatman 1992)
- facilitate communication, information quality and information provision (Scala & McGrath 1993; Li & Williams 1999)
- improve the competitive positioning of the collaborating partners (Marshall et al. 1999b).

Therefore skill, foresight and excellence in exploiting IT is necessary to be able to build strategic business networks successfully.

The business environment that is rapidly developing (if it is not already a reality) is one in which the respective fates of collaborating enterprises become increasingly intermingled and interdependent (Marshall et al. 1999b) as organisations build relationships of varying degrees of strength and commitment with suppliers, business customers, business partners, end consumers and even competitors (Wigand, Picot & Reichwald 1997). This development has caused business environments to be described as an 'interconnected ecology of firms' (Moore 1996) or 'symbiotic networks' (Volkoff, Chan & Newson 1999) (see figure 10.1).

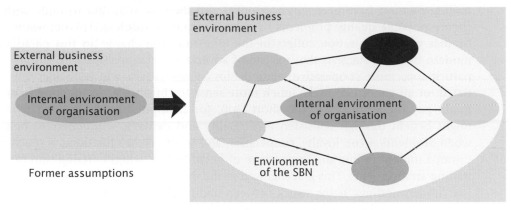

External business environment

External business environment

Internal environment of organisation

Former assumptions

Internal environment of organisation

Environment of the SBN

Current and future assumptions

Figure 10.1 ▶ Changing assumptions about business environments
Source ▶ McKay and Marshall 2001, p. 28.

Implications of the adoption of strategic business networks or virtual organisations

This trend of increased reliance on strategic business networks, alliances and contractual arrangements has important implications. First, analysing and understanding the business and its environment shifts from a focus on the organisation itself (that which is contained within traditional notions of the organisational boundary) to recognising that the focus of analysis needs not only to incorporate the organisation but should also encompass surrounding business partners, collaborators, outsourcing vendors, valued members of relationships and cooperatives, and so on (see figure 10.2, p. 280). Understanding competitive and environmental trends likewise means broadening horizons to include all those external organisations and entities that contribute to the ultimate delivery of value to customers.

Thinking about building relationships with trading partners is also undergoing something of a paradigm shift. Take, for example, transacting with major suppliers. Traditional business thinking advised that a manager should seek the lowest possible price for the best (or most suitable) quality, wait as long as possible before paying accounts to the suppliers, and complain vociferously if ever there were defective items, discrepancies in ordered and delivered quantities of goods, or late delivery and so on. Procurement managers could sometimes feel absolutely triumphant at obtaining really good deals (usually meaning low cost) for their organisation. Indeed, it is tempting to conclude that negotiations like this result in desirable outcomes for the organisation. But look at this from the suppliers' perspective. They might feel resentful that pressure has been exerted to get prices lower than they can sensibly offer and remain viable businesses, and are therefore likely to look for other customers. Your business might then become a lower priority (hence late delivery of goods as other trading partners have been given priority) and they are reluctant to trade with you (hence possible quality problems or erratic delivery schedules). The net result could be that your organisation suffers in the long run. The change in this paradigm in modern business suggests that instead of adversarial relationships with supply chain participants, more cooperative relationships in which win–win outcomes are negotiated for all concerned make much more sense for businesses in the long term. You might pay higher prices in the short term, for example, but in the long term you might benefit through consistency of quality and delivery, willingness to help out when problems occur, loyalty, cooperation and so on. Hence the trend is much more towards understanding the importance of 'relationship' when entering into business trading arrangements. This is recognised in the increasing use of alliances and formalised 'understandings' being struck between trading partners along a supply chain. The ultimate aim and recognition of such deals is that ultimately the end consumer and customers of the organisation can be better served (and hence contribute more value to the organisation) through relationships of this type.

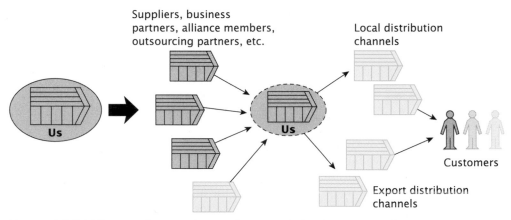

Figure 10.2 ▶ The growing trend towards strategic business networks

Trading relationships and customer value

How can entering into relationships or forming networks of organisations support the delivery of value to the customer and thus help to ensure long-term viability for the organisation? In previous chapters, implicit in many of our discussions was the argument captured in figure 10.3. If an organisation is going to achieve its objectives in the long term, it must deliver value to customers: the customer needs to derive satisfaction (on which they in effect place an economic value). In order to achieve this, an organisation must have a thorough understanding of the needs and wants of their customers, the nature and capabilities of their competitors and so on. In other words, to be successful in the long term, an organisation must meet the needs and wants of its customers more effectively and efficiently than do its competitors.

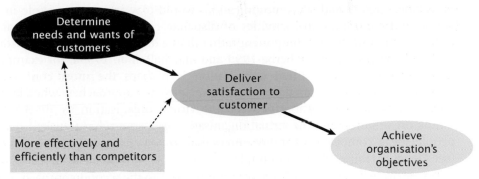

Figure 10.3 ▶ Achieving organisational objectives through delivery of customer value

Another perspective suggests that customer satisfaction and loyalty depend on the delivery of a 'bundle' of goods and services, at an appropriate price and quality level. The challenge for the organisation is obtaining or accessing and then using the requisite capabilities, knowledge and skills in order to deliver that bundle of goods and services. In many organisations, there is a recognition that perhaps greater efficiencies and effectiveness gains can be achieved through accessing some of those capabilities, skills and knowledge through external organisations who become close, cooperative trading partners who contribute quite directly to the delivery of customer value. The resultant webs of cooperating and trading organisations have been called strategic business networks (McKay & Marshall 2001), business webs or b-webs (Tapscott 2001), value networks or strategic networks (Gulati, Nohria & Zaheer 2000) or virtual organisations (Chesborough & Teece 1996). Creating and maintaining these strategic business networks (SBNs) or virtual organisations (VOs) has therefore become a major strategic thrust of many organisations.

The essence of strategic business networks or virtual organisations

If one carefully examines the literature on strategic business networks and the virtual organisation, it appears that three types of approach are taken to this particular concept. For some, a virtual organisation is essentially an electronic one, an online organisation. Proponents of this position offer Amazon.com and eBay.com as examples of organisations that have been created primarily to exist in and exploit the opportunities offered by the World Wide Web and cyberspace. This so-called virtual, or electronic, organisation is discussed in contradistinction to the traditional 'bricks and mortar' retail outlet (Czerniawska & Potter 1998). An alternative to this first definition is to present the virtual organisation as an organisational structure based primarily on the notion of collaborating entities that come together to share competencies, skills, knowledge and other resources for the purpose of producing a particular service or good, or of taking advantage of a particular opportunity. Although there is the clear expectation that IT and telecommunications would play an important role in coordinating and controlling the activities of disparate components of the virtual organisation, IT becomes a key component rather than a distinguishing characteristic per se (see Turban, McLean & Wetherbe 1999 and Marshall et al. 1999a, for example). The third approach to the virtual organisation is perhaps the most confusing. This approach represents an amalgam of the previous two approaches, whereby authors move almost interchangeably between the virtual organisation as an electronic or online organisation and the virtual organisation as a somewhat transient network of people, ideas, competencies and resources that come together for a particular purpose (see Siebel & House 1999 for example).

The position adopted in this chapter corresponds to the second approach discussed. As a precursor to more detailed discussion, a virtual organisation can be defined as being

> composed of several business partners sharing costs and resources for the purpose of producing a product or service...can be temporary...or it can be permanent. Each partner contributes complementary resources that reflect its strengths, and determines its role in the virtual corporation. (Turban, McLean & Wetherbe 1999, p. 142)

This stance suggests a need to discuss the essential and fundamental attributes of the virtual organisation more fully.

Agility

A key characteristic of the virtual organisation is its adaptability and flexibility in the face of turbulent business environments, a condition sometimes described as **agility** (Metes, Gundry & Bradish 1998). Virtual organisations are capable of rapid and adaptable response to changing markets whether these arise as a result of globalisation, changing cost structures, changing customer needs and wants, or other similar reasons (Goldman, Nagel & Preiss 1995). Virtual organisations use existing organisational structures from one or more existing organisations, combining these in creative ways to forge new organisational capabilities and competencies, thus averting the need to recruit, train and forge new work teams, buy new equipment and buildings, and work through a period of organisational learning (Magretta 1998). Thus, allied with its agility, an important attribute of the virtual organisation is argued to be its more effective utilisation of existing resources, thus creating an important source of competitive advantage (Turban, McLean & Wetherbe 1999).

The formation of business partnerships and alliances is therefore pivotal to the concept of the virtual organisation (Grenier & Metes 1995; Henning 1998). Acquiring and/or developing all the required resources and competencies in order to avail itself of windows of opportunity can be both too time-consuming and too costly to be an appropriate response for organisations acting on their own. In other words, in the brief period of time available to exploit business opportunities, a single organisation might not have the time or the financial resources available to obtain and/or develop the needed skills, infrastructure and resources, nor to develop efficient business processes. However, access to the required knowledge, skills, resources and infrastructure might be available through entering into alliances or partnerships with all, or only a part, of other organisations. This notion is captured pictorially in figure 10.4.

Virtual organisation

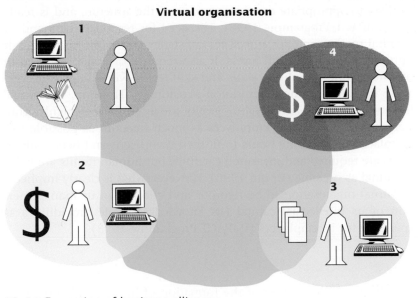

Figure 10.4 ▶ Formation of business alliances
Source ▶ adapted from Marshall, McKay and Burn 2001, p. 173.

Thus organisation 1 on its own might not have the capability to take advantage of a particular perceived business opportunity. But by working cooperatively and synergistically with others, a virtual organisation (depicted by the shaded area) could be formed to exploit that opportunity. By each contributing different knowledge, skills and resources, the virtual organisation formed by the cooperative leveraging of assets and resources in organisations 1, 2, 3 and 4 might be highly successful in availing itself for a time of the original business opportunity.

Human resources

Key components of the agility ascribed to and required of virtual organisations are its human resources and the management practices associated with those human resources (Pfeffer 1998). The needs and requirements of virtual organisations demand that each employee has the skills to contribute directly to the value chain of product and service design, production, marketing and distribution, thus contributing directly to the bottom line. As each member of the virtual organisation contributes to its core competencies, the resultant team of human resources would be anticipated to be excellent, geared appropriately and directly towards exploiting a particular opportunity, and therefore better collectively than any of the contributing organisations could be expected to be on their own (Turban, McLean & Wetherbe 1999). Employees must also be capable of learning new skills, be positive to the need for constant change and tolerant of ambiguity and uncertainty in their working lives as well as sensitive to the possibly changing needs and wants of the organisation's customers.

For this to be achieved, virtual organisations are characterised by the empowerment of their employees, whereby decision-making, responsibility and accountability is devolved to appropriate component parts of the structure and is readily accepted as such (IMPACT Programme 1998). The need for responsiveness and competitiveness in global markets implies a need for constancy and excellence in the development of appropriate skills and skill levels. It also requires of employees that they accommodate their work procedures, skills and skill levels, work times and even working lives to the demands of the organisation's customers. However, the virtual organisation also rewards skilled and psychologically tough employees highly. This is done both financially and by giving employees as much freedom as possible to structure their workplaces and working hours to fit their own needs and personalities. Outputs and results are required and measured carefully, but human inputs are left as much to the individual as possible (Coutu 1998). However, what is clearly implied is the need for the virtual organisation to be rigorous and effective in its management and exploitation of its intellectual capital (its knowledge) while providing a satisfying work experience for its employees (IMPACT Programme 1998).

Geographical dispersion

Implicit in this description of the formation of business alliances is the notion that various components of the virtual organisation might well be geographically dispersed, giving rise to the challenge of communication and coordination among different time zones, different locations, different cultures and different languages (IMPACT Programme 1998). This is illustrated in figure 10.5 and typically implies a need for excellent IT to support communication and coordination throughout the virtual organisation.

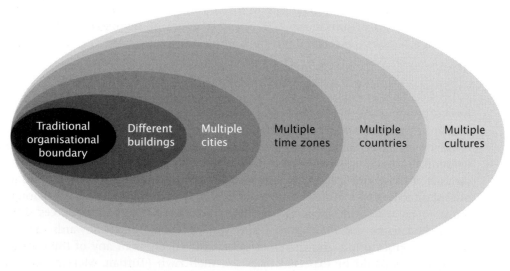

Figure 10.5 ▶ Characteristic dispersion of the virtual organisation
Source ▶ Marshall, McKay and Burn 2001, p. 174.

Cost-effective administration

Agility and responsiveness also imply a need for cost-effective administration and an absence of heavy, clumsy bureaucratic practices that would appear to be the very antithesis of the agile virtual organisation. The needs of a centralised administration should impede the work of those involved in creating value for the organisation as little as possible, and the inertia, heaviness and clumsiness associated with the bureaucratic hierarchical organisation of the late twentieth century should be avoided at all costs. Any unnecessary administrative activities should be minimised or abolished altogether. Administrative work is done as efficiently as possible by as few staff as possible. Where administrative overheads can be carried by those staff directly involved in the value-creating activities of the virtual organisation, this might be preferable since they will do only what administration is directly useful and needed by them and their team, and when it is necessary for them to cease a certain activity because it is no longer viable, the administrative activity winds down naturally and without the difficulties of reducing or reassigning central administrative staffs (Goldman, Nagel & Preiss 1995; Benjamin & Wigand 1995). It is essential that the organisation retain its ability to respond and adapt to changing conditions, and high administrative overheads and/or slow and bureaucratic procedures can always threaten this essential characteristic.

Accepting change

Acknowledging the transient nature of business opportunities in contemporary business environments, virtual organisations are opportunistic and avail themselves of profitable business circumstances even if they are apparently temporary. There is an acceptance of, even an enthusiasm for, change and uncertainty with respect to its products and services, its customer base, its structure and scope, and in its very approach to doing business (IMPACT Programme 1998). This characteristic means that virtual organisations are at ease with the idea of porous and changing organisational boundaries, changing their skills and skill levels through outsourcing and alliances. In these ways virtual organisations incorporate the competencies of other organisations' employees so as to adapt and change their skills base quickly and thus take advantage of emerging business opportunities.

Reliance on IT

Underpinning and enabling the opportunistic behaviour of virtual organisations, and coordinating and managing disparate resources and activities in the virtual organisation's supply chain going right through to the customer, is a heavy reliance on IT and communications technologies. IT supports some of the new organisational alliances and forms necessary to design and produce new goods and services quickly and provides a fast and convenient channel through which to promote and inform potential customers of developments in the organisation's products and services and to accept and process sales to customers (Metes, Gundry & Bradish 1998; Benjamin & Wigand 1995). These new technologies provide the information and communication framework necessary for the anywhere anytime work that takes place in virtual organisations (Upton & McAfee 1996).

In addition, it must be noted that virtual organisations are information intensive (Grenier & Metes 1995) and hence might well be expected to be heavily reliant on information technology. However, it must be acknowledged that the virtual organisation can exist without heavy reliance on IT (Sor 1999), although it is generally acknowledged that in most cases, IT will occupy an important position.

Essential characteristics of a virtual organisation

The virtual organisation is put forward as a low-cost, highly responsive and adaptable way to organise and compete in the face of extreme turbulence and uncertainty in the business environment. The essential characteristics of the virtual organisation have been argued to be:
- agility, adaptability, flexibility and responsiveness to changing requirements and conditions and therefore the formation of business alliances of varying degrees of permanence
- dispersion of component parts
- empowerment of staff, stewardship of expertise, know-how and knowledge (intellectual capital)
- cost-effective administration, low levels of bureaucracy, and effectiveness in utilisation of resources
- opportunistic behaviour, embracing change and uncertainty
- high infusion of IT to support business processes and knowledge workers.

The practical implications for managers of adopting the virtual organisation structure and the strategy of virtual organising in their organisations need to be considered further. It is important to note in passing that as soon as one mentions managing in a virtual organisation, or of adopting virtual organising as a deliberate strategy, there is a sense in which one is almost inevitably talking about interorganisational management and therefore about the coordinated and cooperative behaviour and endeavours of actors/managers who originate in different organisations and who, after a period of time, might again actually be in different organisations.

Critical success factors in managing strategic business networks

Many of the defining characteristics of the virtual organisation sound delightfully and seductively simple, indeed obvious, on paper. Yet it would seem that a number of important managerial tasks must be accomplished if the virtual organisation is to function effectively. People in the virtual organisation are drawn from different sources but are likely to be working in teams and therefore need to find a shared purpose or vision in order to arrive at successful outcomes and results. The shared purpose or vision serves as a 'glue' for the virtual organisation (Hedberg et al. 1994; Wiesenfeld, Raghuram & Garud 1998), and it also serves as the life blood of the virtual organisation as the existence of the virtual organisation depends on the existence of a raison d'être: when the desired results have been achieved and the purpose accomplished, then the virtual organisation dissolves as there is no longer glue to hold the structure together. A key function for management and organisational members therefore would seem to be quickly to identify and seize ownership of this **shared purpose and vision**.

However, in order that the purpose may be genuinely shared and for linkages to operate unimpeded, extraordinary levels of **trust** must exist. Indeed, Lipnack and Stamps (1998) suggest that in the virtual organisation, trust must function to replace the usual rules, procedures and policies that dictate the behaviour of the more traditional hierarchical and bureaucratic organisations. With a trusting relationship in place among virtual organisation members, there is also a requirement for the risk(s) associated with the joint initiative (i.e. inherent in the purpose of the virtual organisation) to be shared. In traditional organisational structures, risk is typically totally the preserve of a single organisation, which alone tends to implement measures to manage its exposure to risk. The more interdependent the nature of the virtual organisation's activities, the more risk must be seen to be and accepted as shared. If risk is to be shared, and high levels of trust maintained, then clearly the purpose of the virtual organisation must be such that all members benefit in more ways than they would from remaining outside the virtual organisation relationship. Hence the successful virtual organisation relies on the ability of the alliance to offer benefits to individual members in terms of increased productivity, increased revenues, increased profitability, increased market share and the like (Friedman 1998).

Fundamental critical success factors for the virtual organisation can therefore be posited as being a shared purpose, a trusting relationship, a willingness to share risk and a mutual benefit being derived from the virtual organisation's existence. This is illustrated in figure 10.6.

Hence it is argued that a successful virtual organisation is very much based on the notion that mutual benefit for the parties involved is derived through the timely and appropriate initiation and formation of alliances to take advantage of possibly short-lived business opportunities. But for the alliances to operate in an efficacious manner providing benefits to all concerned, the very important assumption is made that management activity has achieved the requisite level of shared vision and purpose, a high degree of trust among virtual organisation members and an acceptance and understanding that risk is to be shared among those standing to benefit.

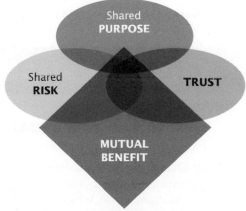

Figure 10.6 ▶ Critical success factors for the virtual organisation

Source ▶ Marshall, McKay and Burn 2001, p. 178.

Some caution needs to be exercised at this point, for the virtual organisation and virtual organising should not be presented as the way of the future, almost akin to a business imperative for the successful enterprise in this internetworked era. Many of the characteristics, strategies and claims for the virtual organisation are conceptually appealing. Yet there seems to be a range of challenges for managers to nurture a successful business within the conceptual framework of a virtual organisation, and some would argue that many of the strengths and powerful characteristics of the virtual organisation also tend to render it vulnerable and therefore can be a source of weakness (Chesborough & Teece 1996). Chesborough and Teece (1996) identify a number of such potential tensions in the virtual organisation concept. Table 10.1 summarises some of these tensions.

Table 10.1 ▶ Inherent tensions in the behaviour of the virtual organisation

Strengths	How strengths become weaknesses
Opportunistic, entrepreneurial, risk-taking	Personal incentives and rewards for risk-taking increase, leading to self-interest in behaviour, etc., making coordination and cooperation among parties more difficult.
Mutual trust, shared risk, opportunistic	When conflicts or misunderstandings do arise, or unforeseen opportunities work to favour some of the parties more than others, few established procedures for negotiation and conflict resolution exist.
Opportunistic	The spirit that drives parties to collaborate might also cause virtual organisations to fragment if one or more of the parties deliberately act to exploit more benefits for themselves than for the other parties.

Source ▶ Marshall, McKay and Burn 2001, p. 178.

thinking strategically

Should Liz go virtual?

Liz Gisborne graduated from university with a masters degree in information systems about eight years ago, and spent the first year working for a relatively small IS consultancy firm, which contained about ten partners. She loved the work, formed many good contacts and established a close working relationship with a number of the client organisations she had consulted for. However, she disliked not being able to control the quality of all the work done by staff in that consultancy, and so, with the encouragement of her friends and family, she decided to form her own small business. So Liz Gisborne Consulting was born. She was the sole consultant, and received help with accounts and some of the administrative aspects of the business from her husband, part time. She loved the work, she loved knowing exactly what was being done, and she soon developed a loyal clientele, all of whom thought her work and advice in the area of strategic IS planning and IS management was first rate. Her reputation grew, and she had more and more offers of consultancy work, mostly from medium-sized organisations. Over time, she found it necessary to start blending business strategic planning with her existing strengths in IS planning, as she often found that organisations in need of an IS plan also needed some fundamental business thinking and strategising. As her reputation and success grew, the clamour for her to take on staff, train them in her approaches and expand the business also grew.

Liz often discussed this problem with her husband, and on each occasion she resolved to remain as a sole operator, valuing the independence and sense of control that it brought to her. However, there were disadvantages associated with her stance. Increasingly, she was being asked to tender for large projects, such as doing a strategic IS plan for an entire government department like the Ministry for Justice or Ministry for Education, which were large complex organisations requiring intensive large-scale planning. Time and effort (both of which were precious to Liz) were spent preparing responses to tender documents and preparing proposals, only to find that either large consultancies such as Price Waterhouse Coopers or Ernst & Young were being offered the job or that the organisation was looking for a wall-to-wall service (i.e. one consultancy that could not only do an IS plan but could also draw up an enterprise architecture, do a technology plan, and manage and oversee the procurement, development and implementation of required systems). Liz simply did not have the requisite knowledge and skills or the resources to offer such a breadth of skills.

However, she had some very close friends from her days at university who did possess such skills. For example one friend, Tony, was acknowledged as a technical wizard and was very insightful in developing sound technology strategies for organisations, and another friend, Hermione, was an astute project manager. It occurred to Liz one day that perhaps she, Tony and Hermione could form a strategic business network, or virtual organisation, to enable each of them to work cooperatively together to better compete against the larger, established consultancies. Liz felt that with her excellent contacts, reputation and skills in business and IS strategy, Tony's vision and skills with IT, and Hermione's strengths in IS/IT procurement and project management, together they could form a formidable team. However, she knew from chats with each of them that they did not want bureaucratic arrangements governing a formalised partnership. Liz also recognised that these large opportunities would only come along every so often and that sustaining their usual sources of income was probably vital. Liz has arranged to meet Tony and Hermione in a few days to canvass their thoughts about creating a virtual organisation.

Questions

1. Advise Liz. Do you think she should enter into a virtual organisation with Tony and Hermione? How would they each benefit? Would there be any drawbacks or disadvantages for them in such an arrangement?

2. What factors might be important if this venture were to be successful? How would you suggest this arrangement is managed?

3. What infrastructure and other costs might a virtual organisation of Liz, Tony and Hermione incur?

4. How attractive would it be to a prospective customer for work to be performed by a virtual organisation such as the one proposed between Liz, Tony and Hermione? Would the customer need to know? What might the customers' concerns be, and how would you suggest that Liz should allay their concerns?

5. Analyse and describe how the SBN or virtual organisation of Liz, Tony and Hermione could compete with a large and possibly bureaucratic consultancy. What would be possible sources of competitive advantage for Liz, Tony and Hermione?

Planning in strategic business networks or virtual organisations

McKay and Marshall (2001) give the example of three enterprises (A, B and C) that have recognised the mutual benefits of collaborating in some way and acknowledged the contribution that each can make. These three enterprises have formally entered into some sort of deal or contractual arrangement and are now trying to make the collaboration work. This process must involve discovering differences, negotiating and creating mechanisms to resolve differences, which would require internal changes to be made to the three collaborators.

A, B and C also bring three discrete internal business environments to the relationship. As A, B and C work together to reconcile different goals and approaches, a network business environment in which A, B and C collaborate is created.

Becoming part of an emergent network business environment is likely to cause changes to the individual internal business environments because A, B and C's interaction with the external business environment is (as far as the extent of their collaboration is concerned) conducted via the network business environment. Figure 10.7 illustrates this point.

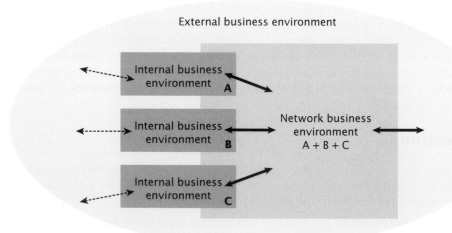

Figure 10.7 ▶ Emergent network business environment
Source ▶ McKay and Marshall 2001, p. 30.

Collaboration will develop on at least three levels as the strategic business network matures (McKay & Marshall 2001). At a strategic level, a shared vision, purpose, goals and objectives for the collaboration should be developed. This will be an ongoing activity throughout the life of the strategic business network. At a tactical level, collaboration and planning for specific projects should occur, and strategies for knowledge management and knowledge transfer should be put in place. At an operational level, mechanisms need to be in place to ensure that staff have information resources and support required to accomplish these tasks (Kanter 1994).

If these developments were occurring within a single organisation, or business unit, they would be considered during a strategic information systems planning (SISP) exercise. In a SISP exercise the organisation's existing IS/IT assets are noted and evaluated and a statement of future information, IS and IT needs is written. Likewise, if the strategic business network is to be anything more than transient, an SISP exercise should be undertaken. Furthermore, IS/IT might itself be the enabling mechanism by which such collaboration in a strategic business network is made possible (McKay & Marshall 2001).

When planning an SISP required for a strategic business network, internal and external IT environments must also be considered. Figure 10.7 could therefore be adapted, simply replacing 'business' with 'IT' (McKay & Marshall 2001). Out of A, B and C's individual IT environments emerges a network IT environment, which in turn will have implications for the internal IT environments of A, B and C. These implications include compatibility of the respective IT environments, compatibility of management attitudes to IS/IT, and the use of and reliance on consultants.

A revised framework for SISPs in strategic business networks is shown in figure 10.8.

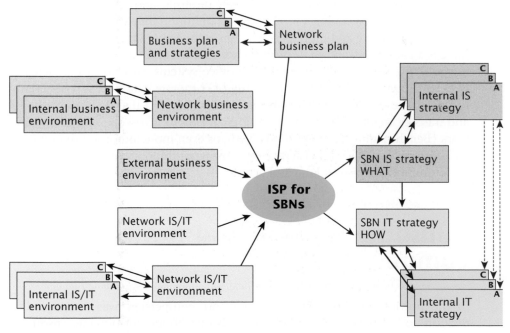

Figure 10.8 ▶ Revised framework to support SISP in SBNs
Source ▶ McKay and Marshall 2001, p. 31.

There are parallel changes to the results of the SISP. Once completed, a strategy for the strategic business network will be written that describes future information and IS requirements for the strategic business network. This strategy will be limited and shaped by the respective internal IS strategies of A, B and C, which in turn will be affected by the SBN's strategy.

Issues in strategic business networks

Typically the decision to seek out alliance opportunities stems from a recognition that the customer value proposition could be delivered more effectively and efficiently by interconnected networks of organisations cooperating and collaborating in a seamless fashion. Multiple organisations in a sense need to start to think and behave as though they were one. This means that organisations need to appreciate that in the strategic business network, business processes are no longer defined internally by an organisation but must be conceptualised and managed as though the one process flowed through multiple organisations (Hammer 2001).

An appropriate technical infrastructure, usually based around Internet technologies, is obviously an essential ingredient in achieving this. There must be no technical impediment to $24 \times 7 \times 365$ trading, no technical impediment to the rapid and seamless interchange of data, expertise and so on. Hence decisions need to be made about the adoption of the technical architecture that is essential to the successful operation of the strategic business network. Typically, scalability is one element in the choice of infrastructure. The infrastructure needs to be sufficiently flexible to allow for rapid growth and changes in demand and processing requirements. An open systems platform that supports collaboration between multiple trading partners and eases the introduction of new trading partners is also an important element. As mobile technologies become more and more pervasive, an architecture that supports a mobile workforce is an added advantage. Technical choices must also take into account the need to integrate the system with internal back office systems, such as ERP systems and the like. Furthermore, the concept of security of corporate data needs to be rethought, as security issues must now also take into account the fact that data-processing, storage and transfer might be occurring at multiple locations across the strategic business network (Benchmarking Partners 2000). Perhaps even more important than the technical architecture, however, is the change in managerial mindset and competencies needed to accommodate this thinking and acting.

Building alliance and network competencies

In the previous chapter, the notion of core competency was introduced, and in relation to e-business competencies, decisions about outsourcing, insourcing and selective sourcing were discussed. Arguably, specific competencies exist for the initiation, formation and ongoing management of alliances and strategic business networks, which we have already argued to be key management strategies and practices for the e-business environment. Spekman, Isabella and MacAvoy (2000) define a number of categories of alliance competencies, and these will be used as the basis for the discussion in this section.

Alliance or SBN know-how

Clearly, know-how refers to specific industry- or production-related skills and knowledge. But Spekman, Isabella and MacAvoy (2000) also use 'know-how' in the sense of knowledge about and skills in the management of all aspects of SBNs or alliances. Included in alliance know-how are such competencies as understanding the implications of alliances for the strategic direction of the organisation, cross-alliance visioning, engaging in interorganisational strategic dialogue, partner selection, ability to assess degrees of complementarity in partners, negotiation skills (looking for win–win outcomes), building consensus around the goals of the alliances, and so on. Competence at handling the dissolution of the SBN might also be important.

Alliance-friendly structures and processes

In many of the chapters in this book, the notion of seamlessly delivering goods and services across the entire value chain to customers in response to customer demand, needs and preferences has been emphasised. These sorts of activities are vital for successful e-businesses, and implicit in the success of such arrangements are systems, processes and structures that enable this to occur. Hence another alliance area of competence is the willingness and infrastructure to support sharing of information and knowledge and therefore to encourage learning, both within an organisation and including critical constituencies such as suppliers, business partners, customers and the like. Supportive processes and structures are essential if the entire supply chain is to become truly integrated and therefore to rely on collaborative activity to deliver on the value proposition for customers.

Mindset

Spekman, Isabella and MacAvoy (2000) and Benchmarking Partners (2000) both emphasise that a change in mindset to one that embraces partnerships and SBNs and is therefore able to benefit effectively from the ability to leverage the skills, capabilities and resources of others is another essential area of competence in the formation and management of alliances. Included in this change of mindset is the ability to build commitment and trust, to foster and nurture relationships, to encourage teamwork and the like.

Adequate depth in management

A challenge for SBNs is that often decisions about the formation of the alliance were made by senior executives, who understand the rationale behind the decision and enthusiastically embrace the changes implied in operating. However, people throughout the organisation, and particularly those who interact with alliance partners, also need to appreciate the importance of the alliance to all players, to have the skills to work cooperatively across traditional organisational boundaries, and to have the alliance mindset previously referred to inculcated into day-to-day practices and behaviour.

Learning

Part of the learning area of competence requires an organisation to institutionalise the mechanisms and values of an alliance-friendly mindset and behaviour. These need to be spread across the organisation to ensure that the entire organisation works cooperatively with all members of the SBN in order to achieve the alliance's goals and objectives.

Types of strategic business network

So far in this chapter the discussion has proceeded almost as if strategic business networks were a unitary concept. This is far from being the truth as strategic business networks can adopt a variety of forms for a variety of purposes. For example the network created by eBay brings together a variety of players to create a marketplace for the exchange of goods and services at desirable prices. By contrast, Amazon.com serves as a coordinator and aggregator of a variety of services, many of which are delivered by separate organisations, to effect excellent matching of customer needs, effective and efficient transactions, and excellence in order fulfilment. Fedex relies on network capabilities to deliver excellence in distribution and logistics (Tapscott, Ticoll & Lowy 1999).

Perhaps a more generic and common term for one type of strategic business network is the B2B e-marketplace or e-hub (Kaplan & Sawhney 2000). Essentially, the **B2B marketplace** is an electronic forum in which multiple buyers and sellers can come together electronically to trade and exchange goods and services. The business model of the B2B marketplace is essentially that of an intermediary (see chapter 2), serving to create value for their members by aggregating buyers and sellers, thus creating marketplace liquidity and lowering transaction costs (Wise & Morrison 2000). These e-marketplaces might offer a combination of services, including some of the following: information exchange, digital catalogues, online auctions, logistics planning and distribution, supply chain planning, product design and collaboration (Laseter, Long & Capers 2001). There are a variety of ownership models from independent marketplaces (although these are generally not proving to be successful), consortia or industry-sponsored marketplaces (in which groups of industry players come together to create a forum for the exchange of goods and services), and private networks, which serve to facilitate electronic transactions, typically along the supply chain for members of this private network.

It is fair to say that such B2B marketplaces have not generally proved as popular as was once predicted (Copacino & Dik 2001). The thinking behind these B2B exchanges was sometimes flawed. For instance, buyers might have been happy to find many suppliers bidding against one another to offer the cheapest price in these B2B markets, but this runs counter to much of the current thinking on buyer–supplier relations (negotiate a win–win scenario) and does not make participation for the supplier a particularly attractive proposition. Furthermore, as previously discussed in this chapter, getting the lowest price might not serve an organisation's best interests in the long run. Generally speaking, the costs of participation (transaction fees for buyers, content management fees for suppliers, and integration costs shared across the network) proved much higher than anticipated, and networks of this type generally failed to attract the volume of participants required to make them viable in the long term (Copacino & Dik 2001).

The message therefore is very clear. There are no guarantees of success in B2B marketplaces. Organisations recognising a need to enter into collaborative trading relationships must be very clear on what they wish to achieve through entering into strategic business network arrangements and must be also sure that the delivery of the customer value proposition is enhanced through such a relationship. Adaptability and flexibility are keys to success in this regard. Copacino and Dik (2001) argue that organisations need to create a portfolio of dynamically managed strategic business networks through which they align their needs for enhanced capability with their business needs and drivers. However, with strategic business networks, it might not be the case that if some are good, then more are better. For example, effectively managing and maintaining strategic business networks comes with a management overhead. Managerial resources must be allocated to take responsibility for the alliance, and every new alliance entered into makes it increasingly difficult to rationalise business processes and activities across multiple organisations and multiple alliances. Furthermore, as more and more organisations enter into alliances to help them manage effectively in **hypercompetitive business environments**, then a shortage of good, unaligned partners might actually develop, resulting in either entering into an alliance with a partner of doubtful quality (which cancels out the whole purpose of the alliance) or starting to compete to attract organisations into the alliance, resulting in a competitive atmosphere rather than a cooperative one. The final problem has to do with loss of control and autonomy. With every strategic business network, the destiny of the firm is intertwined with the destiny of the strategic business network. Over time, too many such arrangements might result in the needs of the organisation always being subordinated to the needs of the strategic business network (Gomes-Casseres 1993).

Summary

With the increasing globalisation of business and the increasing use of information and communication technologies, we are seeing the emergence of an increasingly interconnected and interdependent world of business. This, together with an increasing use of outsourcing to source capabilities beyond the boundaries of the organisation is leading to the development of new forms of organisation and some new principles of organisational design, called virtual organising and the virtual organisation or strategic business network.

SBNs or VOs share a number of characteristics including agility, adaptability and flexibility, geographical dispersion, empowerment of staff and stewardship of expertise and intellectual capital, cost-effective administration and ability to embrace change and uncertainty. Many SBNs rely heavily on IT and the Internet for the coordination and support of knowledge and work activities.

Planning in such environments is important, yet challenging, as it must span and take into account multiple internal IT and business environments and histories, but it may be vital if the SBN is central to the delivery of value to the customer. Allied with the issue of planning is that of developing SBN and alliance competencies and capabilities, such as understanding the vision, purpose, and objectives of the SBN, making appropriate cultural changes, valuing organisation learning, appropriate management of relationships, and so on.

key terms

agility	interorganisational collaboration
B2B marketplace	shared purpose and vision
business alliance	strategic business network
hypercompetitive business environments	trust
	virtual organisation

discussion questions

1. Discuss the business trends that have led to the growth of virtual organising and to the emergence of the virtual organisation or the strategic business network as an effective organisational form.

2. What are the essential characteristics of virtual organisations or strategic business networks? Discuss the advantages and disadvantages, issues and challenges of this form of organising business.

3. What are the critical success factors for an effective virtual organisation? In what way do each of these success factors affect the operation of the virtual organisation or strategic business network?

4. Explain how strategic planning and strategic information systems planning might take place in a virtual organisation or strategic business network. How could you ensure that these visioning and planning activities were effectively carried out? Are there any particular difficulties in implementing strategic plans in virtual organisations or strategic business networks?

5. Describe the factors that led to the emergence of B2B marketplaces. What are the strengths and weaknesses of this form of organisation? Why did many of the B2B marketplaces fail?

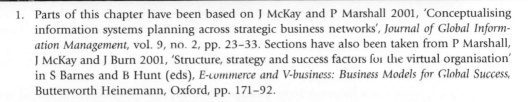

note

1. Parts of this chapter have been based on J McKay and P Marshall 2001, 'Conceptualising information systems planning across strategic business networks', *Journal of Global Information Management*, vol. 9, no. 2, pp. 23–33. Sections have also been taken from P Marshall, J McKay and J Burn 2001, 'Structure, strategy and success factors for the virtual organisation' in S Barnes and B Hunt (eds), *E-commerce and V-business: Business Models for Global Success*, Butterworth Heinemann, Oxford, pp. 171–92.

suggested reading

Chesborough, HW & Teece, DJ 1996, 'When is virtual virtuous?', *Harvard Business Review*, vol. 74, no. 1, pp. 65–73.

Gulati, R, Nohria, N & Zaheer, A 2000, 'Strategic networks', *Strategic Management Journal*, vol. 21 (2000), pp. 203–15.

Marshall, P, McKay, J, Burn, J & Wild, M 1999, 'The essence and logic of the virtual organisation', in D Haseman & DL Nazareth (eds), *Proceedings of the Fifth Americas Conference on Information Systems*, Milwaukee, Wisconsin, 13–15 August 2001, pp. 594–6.

McKay, J & Marshall, P 2001, 'Conceptualising information systems planning across strategic business networks', *Journal of Global Information Management*, vol. 9, no. 2, pp. 23–33.

Upton, DM & McAfee, A 1996, 'The real virtual factory', *Harvard Business Review*, July/August, pp. 123–33.

Wise, R & Morrison, D 2000, 'Beyond the exchange: the future of B2B', *Harvard Business Review*, vol. 78, issue 6, November–December, pp. 86–96.

references

Benchmarking Partners 2000, 'Driving business value through e-collaboration', available at www.benchmarking.com, accessed 14 April 2003.

Benjamin, R & Wigand, R 1995, 'Electronic markets and virtual value chains on the information superhighway', *Sloan Management Review*, Winter, pp. 62–72.

Brandenburger, AM & Nalebuff, BJ 1996, *Co-opetition*, Doubleday, New York.

Chesborough, HW & Teece, DJ 1996, 'When is virtual virtuous?', *Harvard Business Review*, vol. 74, no. 1, pp. 65–73.

Copacino, WC & Dik, RW 2001, 'Why B2B e-markets are here to stay', *Outlook 2001*, no. 2, accessed at www.accenture.com on 12 April 2003.

Coutu, DL 1998, 'Organization: trust in virtual teams', *Harvard Business Review*, vol. 76, no. 3, pp. 20–1.

Czerniawska, F & Potter, G 1998, *Business in a Virtual World*, Macmillan, London.

Finnegan, P, Galliers, RD & Powell, P 1998, 'Systems planning in an electronic commerce environment in Europe: rethinking current approaches', *Electronic Markets*, vol. 8, no. 2, pp. 35–8.

Friedman, LG 1998, 'The elusive strategic alliance', in P Lloyd & P Boyle (eds), *Web-Weaving: Intranets, Extranets and Strategic Alliances*, Butterworth Heinemann, Oxford, pp. 109–16.

Goldman, SL, Nagel, RN & Preiss, K 1995, *Agile Competitors and Virtual Organizations: Strategies for Enriching the Customer*, Van Nostrand Reinhold, New York.

Gomes-Casseres, B 1993, *Managing International Alliances: Conceptual Framework*, Harvard Business School (9-793-133), Harvard Business School Press, Boston.

Grenier, R & Metes, G 1995, *Going Virtual: Moving Your Organization into the 21st Century*, Prentice Hall, Upper Saddle River, NJ.

Gulati, R, Nohria, N & Zaheer, A 2000, 'Strategic networks', *Strategic Management Journal*, vol. 21 (2000), pp. 203–15.

Hamel, G & Prahalad, CK 1994, *Competing for the Future*, Harvard Business School Press, Boston.

Hammer, M 2001, 'The superefficient company', *Harvard Business Review*, September, pp. 82–91.

Hedberg, B, Dahlgren, G, Hansson, J & Olve, N 1994, *Virtual Organizations and Beyond: Discover Imaginary Systems*, John Wiley & Sons, Chichester.

Henning, K 1998, *The Digital Enterprise: How Digitisation is Redefining Business*, Random House, London.

IMPACT Programme (1998), 'Exploiting the wired-up world: best practice in managing virtual organisations', available at www.achieve.ch, accessed 17 July 1999.

Kanter, RM 1994, 'Collaborative advantage', *Harvard Business Review*, July–August, pp. 96–108.

Kaplan, S & Sawhney, M 2000, 'E-hubs: the new B2B marketplaces', *Harvard Business Review*, vol. 78, issue 3, May–June, pp. 97–103.

Kelly, K 1998, *New Rules for the New Economy*, Viking, London.

Kotter, JP 1996, *Leading Change*, Harvard Business School Press, Boston.

Kraut, R, Steinfield, C, Chan, A, Butler, B & Hoag, A 1998, 'Coordination and virtualization: the role of electronic networks and personal relationships', *Journal of Computer Mediated Communication*, vol. 3, no. 4, pp. 1–35.

Laseter, T, Long, B & Capers, C 2001, 'B2B benchmark: the state of electronic exchanges', *Strategy + Business*, issue 25, Fourth Quarter, available at http://www.strategy-business.com, accessed 26 March 2003.

Li, F & Williams, H 1999, 'Interfirm collaboration through interfirm networks', *Information Systems Journal*, vol. 9, no. 2, pp. 103–15.

Lipnack, J & Stamps, J 1998, 'Why virtual teams?', in P Lloyd & P Boyle (eds), *Web-Weaving: Intranets, Extranets and Strategic Alliances*, Butterworth-Heinemann, Oxford.

Magretta, J 1998, 'The power of virtual integration: an interview with Dell Computer's Michael Dell', *Harvard Business Review*, March/April, pp. 73–84.

Marshall, P, Burn, J, Wild, M & McKay, J 1999a, 'Virtual organisations: structure and strategic positioning', *Proceedings of the 7th European Conference on Information Systems*, Copenhagen Business School, Copenhagen, 23–25 June 1999, pp. 482–95.

—1999b, 'The essence and logic of the virtual organisation', in D Haseman & DL Nazareth (eds), *Proceedings of the Fifth Americas Conference on Information Systems*, Milwaukee, Wisconsin, 13–15 August 2001, pp. 594–6.

Marshall, P, McKay, J & Burn, J 2001, 'Structure, strategy and success factors for the virtual organization', in S Barnes & B Hunt (eds), *E-commerce and V-business: Business Models for Global Success*, Butterworth Heinemann, London, pp. 171–92.

Masifern, E & Vila, J 1998, 'Interconnected mindsets: Strategic thinking and the strategy concept', in MA Hitt et al. (eds), *New Managerial Mindsets: Organizational Transformation and Strategy Implementation*, John Wiley & Sons, Chichester, pp. 15–34.

McKay, J & Marshall, P 2001, 'Conceptualising information systems planning across strategic business networks', *Journal of Global Information Management*, vol. 9, no. 2, pp. 23–33.

Metes, G, Gundry, J & Bradish, P 1998, *Agile Networking: Competing through the Internet and Intranets*, Prentice Hall, Upper Saddle River, NJ.

Moore, JF 1996, *The Death of Competition: Leadership and Strategy in the Age of Business Ecosystems*, Harper Business, New York.

Nixon, RD, Hitt, MA & Ricart i Costa, JE 1998, 'New managerial mindsets and strategic change in the new frontier', in MA Hitt et al. (eds), *New Managerial Mindsets: Organizational Transformation and Strategy Implementation*, John Wiley & Sons, Chichester, pp. 1–12.

Pearlson, KE 2001, *Managing and Using Information Systems: A Strategic Approach*, John Wiley & Sons, New York.

Pfeffer, J 1998, *The Human Equation*, Harvard Business School Press, Boston.

Prahalad, CK 1995, 'Weak signals versus strong paradigms', *Journal of Marketing Research*, vol. 32, pp. iii–viii.

Sambamurthy, V 2002, 'Business strategy in hypercompetitive environments: rethinking the logic of IT differentiation', in RW Zmud (ed.), *Framing the Domains of IT Management*, Pinnaflex Educational Resources, Cincinnati, OH., pp. 245–61.

Scala, S & McGrath, R 1993, 'Advantages and disadvantages of electronic data interchange: an industry perspective', *Information & Management*, vol. 25, pp. 85–91.

Siebel, TM & House, P 1999, *Cyber Rules: Strategies for Excelling at E-business*, Currency/Doubleday, New York.

Sor, R 1999, 'Virtual organizations: a case study of the housing construction industry in Western Australia', B Hope & P Yoong (eds), *Proceedings of the 10th Australasian Conference on Information Systems*, 1–3 December 1999, Victoria University of Wellington, vol. 2, pp. 825–36.

Spekman, RE, Isabella, LA with MacAvoy, TC 2000, *Alliance Competence: Maximising the Value of Your Partnerships*, John Wiley & Sons, New York.

Strassmann, PA 1997, *The Squandered Computer*, Information Economics Press, New Canaan, CT.

Swatman, PMC & Swatman, PA 1992, 'EDI system integration: a definition and literature survey', *The Information Society*, vol. 8, pp. 169–205.

Tapscott, D 2001, 'Strategy in a networked world', *Strategy + Business*, vol. 24, pp. 1–8.

Tapscott, D, Ticoll, D & Lowy, A 1999, 'The rise of the business web', *Business 2.0*, November, pp. 1–7.

Turban, E, McLean, E & Wetherbe, J 1999, *Information Technology for Management*, 2nd edn, John Wiley & Sons, New York.

Upton, DM & McAfee, A 1996, 'The real virtual factory', *Harvard Business Review*, July/August, pp. 123–33.

Volkoff, O, Chan, YE & Newson, EFP 1999, 'Leading the development and implementation of collaborative interorganizational systems', *Information & Management*, vol. 35, no. 2, pp. 63–75.

Wiesenfeld, BM, Raghuram, S & Garud, R 1998, 'Communication patterns as determinants of organizational identification in a virtual organization', *Journal of Computer Mediated Communication*, vol. 3, no. 4, pp. 1–21.

Wigand, R, Picot, A & Reichwald, R 1997, *Information, Organization and Management: Expanding Markets and Corporate Markets*, John Wiley & Sons, Chichester.

Wise, R & Morrison, D 2000, 'Beyond the exchange: the future of B2B', *Harvard Business Review*, vol. 78, issue 6, November–December, pp. 86–96.

case study

The Manufacturing Ideas Company — an exercise in SBNs

David Dummit and Richard Foote were IT consultants who were interested in providing value-added IT support to manufacturing companies. Their consultancy, called Advanced Approaches to Manufacturing Excellence (AAME), was headquartered in Melbourne, but they also had a Sydney office. Twelve IT specialists, ranging from technical specialists in computer-aided manufacturing (CAM) through to manufacturing management specialists, worked for David and Richard's consultancy.

David and Richard had helped a number of manufacturing companies to implement materials requirements planning (MRP) software packages. In doing so they had noted some shortcomings in the support for capacity-constrained production scheduling. Over time they had developed a method for capacity-constrained scheduling. They had explained the method to Walter Rudin, the ex-CEO of Melbourne Metal Manufacturers, a large job shop manufacturing enterprise in Melbourne. Walter was not only an astute businessman but also an extremely wealthy one. He was very impressed by David and Richard's idea and was prepared to create and fund a software business that would develop and market the software.

David, Richard and Walter had prepared a business plan, and Walter, together with some other wealthy investors, had provided the funds for the business, which they had called the Manufacturing Ideas Company (MIC). MIC had begun its existence in a small office adjacent to AAME.

MIC had begun with the recruitment of three computer programmers, all highly capable in writing both C++ and Java code. Progress was slow, but quality computer routines were beginning to take shape. After eighteen months, however, only 30 per cent of the production scheduling software had been completed. Impatient with this progress, Walter had called a meeting with David and Richard.

The three greeted each other at the restaurant where they had decided to meet at the end of what had been a long working day for David and Richard. Walter, still fresh from a day walking in a local park and reflecting on the new business venture, began to speak.

'We must move fast. Faster than we are. My contacts have told me that Monash University has established a research centre of manufacturing excellence. They have hired a German professor by the name of Karl Weierstrass, who has an excellent reputation in computer applications for manufacturing management. Indeed he is reputed to have very similar ideas to you guys regarding computer-based production scheduling. We believe that they are going to embark on a similar software product to the one we have planned. We need to do two things: speed up the computer coding of your production scheduling method and, secondly, recruit a really good marketing and sales team. We need to get the new team on board soon so that they can come up to speed with our ideas, understand the capabilities inherent in the software application and plan the marketing and sales of our product. After that they will be well prepared to hit the ground running when it comes to marketing and selling the product.

'Yes — as with all innovations and innovative products, we have to be first to market. Yes indeed, we have to move fast!'

The three business partners discussed Walter's ideas. Although they felt Walter was exaggerating the threat from the Monash University research centre, David and Richard agreed to recruit three to five new programmers (depending on the availability of quality capable people) together with a project manager. They also agreed to recruit a good marketing manager and begin to look for a sales team.

Three months passed. David and Richard were becoming quite anxious about being able to obtain quality people. They had used Professional People, a specialist Australian recruitment firm. However, after three months, because of their commitment to quality, they had only managed to recruit one more programmer. Walter, however, was becoming increasingly impatient and annoyed at what he perceived to be a lack of action. He called another meeting.

Walter had brought a French consultant, Henri Lebesgue, with him to the meeting. Henri was a founding member of Virtual Organising Incorporated (VOI), a Sydney consultancy. David and Richard had heard of Henri. However, they regarded virtual organising as a somewhat impractical management fad.

After being formally introduced by Walter, Henri began to speak. 'Virtual organising is an approach to business that creates business capability quickly. It creates lean and effective business units without the usual growth in bureaucracy that occurs as businesses grow larger.

'Walter has explained your problem to me. You essentially need to grow several capabilities very quickly. VOI has extensive contacts with firms in the software industry, and indeed in many other industries. Many of these are very positive about virtual organising. Our contacts are very responsive to business opportunities that involve innovation, innovative ideas and innovative products.

'I have a very simple solution for you! This is hardly rocket science so let me explain very simply and directly. Walter has confided the nature of your product to me — broadly anyway. I have sounded out some companies with the capabilities you need. Note — existing capabilities! You do not need to recruit people, induct them, train them and then house them in expensive city office space. These capabilities already exist in mature teams of people who work well together. All you need to do is tap into them. Of course they are not all in Melbourne — well, in fact none of them are in Melbourne. But with today's communication possibilities — e-mail and the Internet, fax, telephone, videoconferencing and so on — you can coordinate these co-workers or colleagues.'

'Yes', said David, suspicious of having to create and sustain relationships to a number of companies scattered across the globe, 'but at a real management overhead cost. There is possibly a real relationship management problem here.'

'Well, yes, perhaps,' said Henri, 'but I think I have a solution to that issue as well.'

'I hope so,' said David.

'Well, let Henri outline his specific solution. Let us hear his specific ideas and then examine them — before rushing to judgement,' said Walter, very aware that David and Richard were conservative in their business perspective and outlook.

'Yes indeed,' said Henri. 'Let me be specific. You obviously need some more programming expertise. There is an Indian software company headquartered in

Bangalore, called IT solutions, that has a large number of well-educated and capable Java and C++ programmers. They speak English fluently and have worked with IT teams in Europe, the USA and Australia. They have videoconferencing facilities for meetings and are quite experienced in the use of such facilities. I suggest this is where you source your IT capabilities. They will assign the number of programmers that you need for this task. They have more than enough skilled programmers — they just await your specifications! Of course you will have to negotiate a deal with them — but you'll find their rates and charges very competitive with Australian rates and charges — very competitive indeed! — for the skills you need.

'Now let us turn to your need for project and program management skills. There is a firm in Perth, Western Australia, that has an excellent record in providing project management capabilities for software projects. The firm is called The Project Management Office (TPMO). TPMO will negotiate to have a project manager relocate to Melbourne for you if you wish, or (and I think this is the preferable option for you) they will project-manage at a distance, using e-mail, the Internet, fax and the occasional audio conference or videoconference for communication. I think this distance option will work well for you, and it is very much less expensive than having someone on site. Now, these guys are really up with the world's best practice in project management. You can't do better than TPMO — they really focus on project management, they are up with the latest ideas, they are always learning and training in better skills and the latest techniques. I can really recommend them for this particular capability. There is no way you could do better via recruitment. These guys are real specialists.

'Now, you need to market the software product. You need to advertise in the right places and in the right way, and you need to plan your promotions and sales campaigns very effectively, I believe — this is a very important part of the success of your product. I think you need — separate from a sales capability — a real marketing professional. Indeed, there is a Sydney firm called the Marketing Professionals that can contract with you to give you this capability. Since you possibly could not utilise a really professional marketing manager full time (for very long, anyway) I think this is a way to obtain a professional marketing capability.

'However, you also need a sales capability. Software Australia Limited (SAL) is a Brisbane firm that sells a number of software products. They have a professional sales team in each of the capital cities and major regional centres in Australia. Indeed they cover Brisbane, Sydney, Newcastle, Wollongong and Melbourne very well — and that coverage reaches most of the manufacturing companies in Australia.

'That, however, is not the end of the sales issue. From conversations I have had with Walter, it is clear that your product is world-class — an advance in ideas and concepts that is quite new and revolutionary worldwide, not just in Australia. Walter and I believe you should tap into a global sales capability covering Europe and the USA at least. So I have contacted Software Associates (SA) of Boston, USA. Subject to a positive outcome from a more detailed evaluation of your product, SA are willing to enter into a contract with you, such that they will sell the product and you obtain a royalty or a commission. I think I can help structure quite a good deal for you that really covers the major European markets and the US market.

'We thus have this picture of relationships,' said Henri, pointing to a diagram he had brought with him [see figure 10.9]. 'These relationships, taken together, give you the capabilities you need to go forward.'

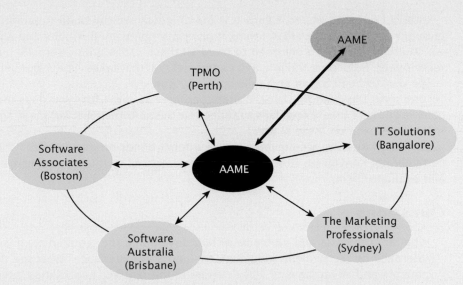

Figure 10.9 ▶ A proposal for a virtual organisation

Richard was amazed at the solution Henri had put forward. He was also a little exasperated. He began speaking rather loudly and critically. 'Look, I haven't quite taken all this in yet, but I can see what David meant about a relationship management issue or problem. It is one thing to manage all these skills and capabilities where everyone works for the same company and everyone is largely housed in the same building. But, given Henri's solution, how on earth do you manage all these relationships and still get an effective business going forward in a coherent and coordinated manner?'

'Coordination! A motivated group of people moving a business forward! Why, of course! That's why you have managers!' retorted Henri. 'What else is management for?'

Richard countered. 'Well, yes, but there are so many arm's-length relationships here. You are really making management difficult.'

'Look,' said Henri, trying to build some consensus, 'I think I have the person who can really bring this together. Helena Riemann is an experienced "relationship manager". She is currently working for New Holland Lager, a company that manufactures and distributes beer and wine across Australia. New Holland Lager owns a large chain of hotels. It leases the hotels to franchisees who have a lot of independence but who are essentially operating under a management framework provided by New Holland Lager. New Holland Lager also provides all the hotels' IT capability to them, including the websites. This is done via an outsourcing relationship to Global Information Management, the US-based IT outsourcing vendor. Managing these relationships is quite a skill, and Helena does it very well. However, she has been in this job for more than ten years and wishes to move on. I've already sounded her out for the job of "relationship manager" at MIC. With Helena managing these arm's-length relationships (as you call them) under your guidance I believe you guys will succeed with your business — and succeed quickly. I know that Walter has confidence in this solution.'

'Indeed I do,' said Walter. 'I think it is the only way we can build capability quickly enough — but more than that, I think it gives our company flexibility and agility that we could not achieve if one tried to build all these capabilities internally by recruitment, induction, training and experience. All that takes time. No, I believe this is the way to build a lean and agile company quickly.'

Turning to David and Richard, Walter continued, 'Look, I fear you guys are not convinced. Let's take a few days to reflect on this and then we will meet again to make a decision on these matters.'

David and Richard, who favoured a very direct hands-on management style, were certainly not convinced. However, they were prepared to think through these ideas and evaluate them.

Questions

1. What are the costs and problems of MIC developing the required capabilities internally by recruitment, induction, training and experience? What are the benefits and advantages of MIC developing the required capabilities internally?

2. What are the costs and problems of MIC developing the required capabilities via the virtual organising solution as proposed by Henri Lebesgue? What are the benefits and advantages of Henri Lebesgue's solution?

3. David and Richard come to the second meeting with Henri Lebesgue with a modified solution. They reject the idea of a project manager and a marketing manager being obtained via virtual organising. These tasks, they feel, are part of the 'hands-on management' of the business and require an in-house professional recruited for and paid by MIC and therefore dedicated to their company for these roles. However, they are quite amenable to getting some programming expertise via a contractual relationship, as long as the programmers work in MIC's office along with MIC's programming team. They feel that the sales team for Australia could be hired and paid largely by commission — again being employees under MIC's managerial direction. David and Richard, however, are willing to enter into a royalty and commission agreement with Software Associates of Boston to cover sales in Europe and the USA.

   Evaluate David and Richard's proposal. How do you feel it compares to Henri Lebesgue's original proposal?

chapter 11

Mobile computing

learning objectives

After reading this chapter, you should be able to:

- demonstrate an understanding of mobile computing and its potential contribution to e-businesses
- understand the main features and characteristics of mobile computing devices
- appreciate the forces in business and society that are driving the adoption of mobile computing and m-commerce
- understand many of the issues, challenges and difficulties associated with mobility
- appreciate the major types of application that are delivering business benefits through mobile computing
- recognise the need to develop strategies for mobile computing and m-commerce that are in alignment with organisational goals, objectives and strategies
- understand some of the major trends with mobile, pervasive and ubiquitous computing.

chapter overview

There is increasing interest in the possibilities of m-commerce and mobile computing, and a real risk that the hype that fuelled e-commerce and ultimately resulted in the dotcom crash could be repeated in m-commerce and mobile computing. This chapter aims to take a reality check on m-commerce and mobile computing and to assess the major issues and potential that mobility has to offer organisations and individuals. The factors driving the trend towards mobile technologies are considered, along with the potential benefits for organisations from the adoption and integration of appropriate m-commerce and mobile computing applications, infrastructure and technologies. However, it is argued that an applications focus or a technology focus is inappropriate for organisations adopting mobile technologies. Rather, a carefully thought-through strategy that has been developed after an analysis of business needs and with the knowledge of a full appraisal of the strengths and limitations of m-commerce and mobile computing is required, one that is deliberately aligned with corporate goals, objectives and strategies. The chapter discusses the major issues that managers need to understand before moving to adopt mobile technologies.

Introduction

Information technology (IT) is often seen as a key enabler of contemporary business and is frequently argued to be a source of competitive advantage. With successive innovations and development, IT has become more and more pervasive within the business domain. Some argue that the move towards increased mobility in computing technology is a fundamentally new development in IT and therefore represents the latest era or wave of computing (Weiser 1998; Barbero 2001; Lyytinen & Yoo 2002a). As Lyytinen and Yoo (2002a) note, in little more than the forty years that has seen the adoption of computer technology in organisations, there has been a move from mainframe computers that occupy a room to desktop personal computers, portable personal computers and, in recent years, the emergence of truly mobile, compact devices that help to organise and support key business processes and personal activities on a daily basis. Arguably, the trend towards mobile technologies offers organisations and individuals the opportunity to access and exchange information and to engage in commercial activities free from the usual constraints of time and location (Lyytinen & Yoo 2002a; Scheepers & McKay 2003). Davis (2002) describes this phenomenon as 'anytime/anyplace computing'.

This trend might also have been fuelled by the explosion of e-commerce in the mid 1990s, with the ubiquitous nature of the Internet driving a demand for access that is not to be tied to desktops but is available literally at the convenience of the user, whenever or wherever the user desires. The question to consider, then, is whether m-commerce and mobile computing will have similar effects on organisations as e-commerce and e-business have done in the last decade. Although there is little doubt that there was an enormous amount of hype surrounding e-commerce and the Internet, there is no doubt that, among other things, the Internet and e-commerce applications enabled many organisations fundamentally to change the way they could interact and transact with customers (both end consumers and business customers) and the way in which supply chains could be organised and managed. Internal arrangements for the dissemination and storage of critical corporate data and knowledge also changed fundamentally. E-commerce and e-business, therefore, as we have discussed throughout this book, had quite profound effects on business strategy, on IS/IT strategy and on our conceptualisation of what was possible with IT within organisational contexts.

Of interest in this chapter, then, is to consider the characteristics and possibilities presented by the emergence of mobile technologies and to contemplate whether they too will have similar substantial effects on the ways in which organisations think about service delivery, operational efficiency and the organisation of corporate resources to achieve business goals. Those who view mobile computing as the next era of computing undoubtedly would argue that m-commerce and mobile computing are likely to change the ways organisations and individuals access and provide information and services, and therefore major effects on business strategy can be expected (Fano & Gershman 2002). However, a careful analysis of the issues and potential are essential if organisations are to integrate mobile technologies successfully into their competitive and operational armoury.

Definition of terms

As was discovered and discussed in the early chapters of this book with regard to e-commerce and e-business, there is no widespread agreement when it comes to the use and meaning of terminology relating to mobile computing. Hence a proliferation of terms, including *m-commerce, mobile computing, mobile electronic commerce, m-business* and *mobile technology,* has accompanied the technological advances that enable mobile computing. Sometimes these terms are used almost interchangeably, yet other writers draw fine distinctions between them.

Perhaps the two most common terms are *mobile computing* and *m-commerce.* **Mobile computing** literally refers to the ability to move computer services around with individuals as they themselves move around their world (Lyytinen & Yoo 2002a). This can be accomplished through the use of mobile technologies, including such items as mobile phones, personal digital assistants (PDAs), handheld computers and other handheld devices, such as scanning devices, and so on. Similarly, **m-commerce** is commonly defined as 'the buying and selling of goods and services using wireless handheld devices such as mobile telephones or personal data assistants (PDAs)' (UNCTAD 2002, p. 89), thus emphasising the commercial, transaction-based nature of m-commerce. Sadeh (2002) is less focused on the transaction side, arguing that *m-commerce* refers to an emerging set of applications and services that are accessible from Internet-enabled mobile devices. In contrast, Tsalgatidou and Pitoura (2001) use *mobile e-commerce* to include any type of Internet-enabled transaction of economic value that uses a mobile device and wireless telecommunications networks. Gilbert and Kendall (2003) prefer to use the term *mobile data services* in a similar way, stressing the need to deliver and access content and conduct transactions via mobile devices.

Paavilainen (2002) adds complexity by differentiating between three different terms. He uses *mobile business* as the broadest term, referring simply to the exchange of goods, services and information via mobile technologies. Used in this way, mobile business (or m-business) includes transactions, communication and exchanges that could not be described as commercial in nature. However, Paavilainen (2002, p. 1) discusses what he calls the 'mobile Internet', which refers to any mobile device that can access the Internet, irrespective of time and location. He argues that this serves to emphasise the potential synergies that could exist between mobile technologies and the ubiquity of the Internet, suggesting that the three main elements of the **mobile Internet** are communication facilities, commerce and value-added services. *M-commerce* is reserved only for commercially based transactions conducted via the mobile Internet.

Others offer a more technical definition of mobile computing and m-commerce, using underlying technology platforms as the basis for defining mobile computing. For example, Xu, Teo and Wang (2003) argue that a combination of wireless web-based technologies, such as wireless application protocol (WAP), I-mode, or general packet radio service (GPRS), and text-based technologies, such as short message service (SMS), form the basis of defining mobile computing and m-commerce.

For the purposes of this chapter, m-commerce will be used for transactions with a monetary value or, quite literally, commercial transactions conducted via mobile devices, and mobile computing will be used to include the range of other possibilities for interaction and communication and accessing services via mobile devices.

Drivers of mobile computing

Mobile computing and m-commerce have seen very rapid growth world-wide in the last few years. Estimates suggest that there are now more than a billion mobile phone users, and it is expected that they sent about 100 billion SMS (short message service) messages annually by the end of 2002 (UNCTAD 2002; Xu, Teo & Wang 2003). Barbero (2001) reports that the sales from m-commerce in the USA are likely to total about $21 billion over the four years from 1998. However, despite the impressive growth figures, it emerges that B2E (business to employee) uses of mobile technologies are outstripping growth in m-commerce. The Industry Standard (cited in synchrologic.com) reports that there has been a decline of about 33 per cent in consumer interest in m-commerce, as issues associated with the small screen size in mobile phones and relatively slow transmission speeds have limited consumer interest. (Limitations in m-commerce and mobile devices are discussed later in this chapter.) However, increasingly organisations are realising that B2E applications could potentially deliver greater benefits and that by providing staff with any of a range of mobile devices, they can improve their access to required corporate information. Organisations have also realised that they can experience high levels of productivity increases and improvements in customer service levels and, at times, achieve extraordinary returns from these investments (synchrologic.com 2001).

A number of forces appear to be driving the adoption of mobile computing. First of all, there has been the emergence of a service economy and customer service as a differentiator in highly competitive industries and marketplaces, whereby demand for service anytime anywhere is helping to increase demands for m-commerce and the mobile Internet. Time-starved but resource-rich individuals are increasingly expecting mobile technologies to support the performance of a range of tasks at their convenience.

Another substantial factor has been both the rapid adoption of mobile phone technology and a proliferation of mobile devices available, combined with an improvement in the power, capabilities and functionality of those devices (UNCTAD 2002). Over time, there has been an increase in the number of companies launching mobile devices, which, despite rapid growth in this market, results in price pressures, increased competition and the provision of more choice for consumers at affordable prices. At the same time, the processing power of these devices has typically increased, supporting a broader array of applications, while they have tended to become lighter and smaller and are able to offer colour as a result of improved battery technology (UNCTAD 2002). The Gartner Group (2001) estimates, for example, that by 2004 the average office worker will carry and/or own at least three mobile devices.

Hence there is an imperative for organisations to consider the potential productivity increases and service benefits that can be derived through the adoption and exploitation of mobile computing. Organisations with a substantial mobile workforce (e.g. sales and field service staff, transportation workers, managers in charge of large geographical areas and the like) or whose business relies on the movement and tracking of large numbers of goods and services (transportation services, distributors, home health care and so on) can use such devices to access and retrieve accurate and timely corporate information, to receive schedules and instructions from head office without having to lose time travelling to and from corporate headquarters, and so on (Barbero 2001). As the power of these mobile devices increases, their ability to handle a broader range of 'serious' business applications will increase, thus encouraging businesses to think strategically about the possibilities of cost reductions on core business processes and productivity gains among field workers.

Increases in telecommuting and decentralised workforces, which are growing trends in themselves, are also fuelling interest in m-commerce and mobile computing. Concerns about security and the possibilities of pandemics are causing organisations to reassess their areas of vulnerability and their risk management strategies, and these, coupled with the increasing availability and power of mobile devices, are helping to increase telecommuting and challenge popular notions of where knowledge workers need to be located (Lyytinen & Yoo 2002b; synchrologic.com 2001; Barbero 2001).

Lyytinen and Yoo (2002b) argue that the increasing emphasis on information and knowledge as a source of competitive advantage is also helping to increase the adoption of mobile computing, as knowledge workers involved in global value chains need to access, create and assimilate information and knowledge from a range of Internet sources and virtual communities freed from constraints of desktop computing. Hence the trend towards knowledge as a factor of production and organisational learning as a core competence, globalisation, and the increased experimentation with and use of virtual teams and virtual communities of practice will all serve to drive the adoption of mobile computing.

May (2001) argues that pressured lifestyles might be also driving the move to m-commerce and the adoption of mobile computing. Hence making productive use of 'dead' time (time spent in airport lounges, travelling by public transport to and from work, and so on) is attractive to busy managers (Perry et al. 2001). So too is the ability to mix work and social demands and requirements. Hence the busy executive can pay personal bills, access emails, upload the latest sales data and check on the welfare of children all while waiting in an airport lounge.

Another driver of m-commerce has been favourable changes in the cost of ownership associated with mobile computing. Over time, the price:performance ratio of mobile devices has been dropping, but organisations are still concerned about achieving an ROI and the total costs incurred through moving towards supporting a mobile workforce with mobile devices (synchrologic.com 2001). Gartner (2001) suggests that about 40 per cent of the costs to organisations are associated with end-user activities in synchronising mobile devices with the organisation's desktops or servers and that organisations must factor in the costs of providing support, networks, replacement units, training, software costs, building a mobile infrastructure and managerial overheads when calculating their expected returns from such a move to mobile computing. Nonetheless, as costs decrease, and mobile infrastructures become established and can be written off against a number of mobile applications, the total cost of ownership is expected to fall, thus making the move to mobility more affordable and more attractive to many organisations (synchrologic.com 2001).

Main features and characteristics of mobile computing

Mobile devices share a number of characteristics that influence the way they are used and what they are used for. For example Gilbert and Kendall (2003) note that such devices are truly and readily portable (and hence a debate could be held as to whether laptops are accurately described as mobile devices), are intensely personal in the sense that they are seldom used by others, and are often characterised by using networks that are always on (Gilbert & Kendal 2003).

Technological advance in the field of mobile computing has been rapid so that it is now quite feasible for organisations to adopt mobile devices to run serious and strategic business applications. Declining equipment and connection costs, technical improvements in quality, reliability and efficiency, and the convenience offered owing to the mobility factor have all been cited as drivers of adoption in organisational contexts (Francis 1997, as cited by Scheepers & McKay 2003). Although it could be argued that the need for travel has been minimised through the improved telecommunication and the Internet, the need to travel to a range of locations for work purposes where services need to be delivered remains for many organisations. Hence, for mobile workers (especially mobile sales staff and field service staff), the ability to remain connected to head office and receive the information they need to do their jobs effectively without regularly having to return physically for updates is one particular benefit of mobile computing (Barbero 2001). Mobile technologies can dramatically increase access in real time to data, information and computer-processing power for knowledge workers (Davis 2002). This means that mobile workers can rely on more accurate information (exact stock levels, pricing, status of orders, delivery schedules and production schedules for example) and can remotely record details of transactions and services performed and/or required, thus removing the need for duplicate or subsequent recording of such activity. This can have many positive effects, among which would be improved customer service, improved relationships with customers and suppliers, streamlined and more efficient operations, and the like (Leung & Antypas 2001).

Mobile devices share a number of characteristics that must be understood and appreciated if they are to be successfully implemented in organisational contexts for the conduct of key business activities. First, they are small in size, compact and relatively lightweight and therefore are readily portable. Second, some argue that mobile devices are characterised by being easy to switch on and almost instantaneously ready for use (referred to as 'zero boot time' (Paavilainen 2002)). For example PDAs and mobile phones require a single button to be pushed to be ready to work, in stark contrast to laptops, which still need to go through relatively lengthy boot procedures before they are ready for use. Increasingly also mobile technologies represent a convergence of mobile telephone technology and Internet technologies, thus removing the need for wired networks for the exchange of information and to gain access to other value-added services (UNCTAD 2002; Pearson & Nelson 2003).

Their size, instant connectivity and portability result in mobile devices being characterised above all else by convenience (Paavilainen 2002) and, within the constraints of network coverage, such devices should be available for use independent of location and time.

Reasons for adoption of mobile computing

A number of reasons for the adoption of m-commerce and mobile computing can be suggested. Provided that applications take note of the characteristics of mobile devices mentioned in the previous section and are designed accordingly, then there are important business imperatives that should drive the uptake of mobile computing. There are widely acknowledged to be three broad benefits and advantages that can be achieved for organisations adopting m-commerce and mobile technologies. These include, first, increasing the productivity of workers, especially mobile and/or knowledge workers, second, cutting costs associated with key business processes through automating part of that process, and third, achieving a competitive advantage through improved service provision, faster response times, differentiation and so on (Leung & Antypas 2001; synchrologic.com 2001).

Increasing the productivity of mobile workers

Sales force automation (SFA) technologies, one example of the use of mobile computing to support the activity of mobile sales staff, provide many examples of how the productivity of mobile staff can be boosted through the appropriate deployment of mobile devices. SFA tools can decrease the time spent in administrative tasks and increase the currency and accuracy of the information that sales staff take into meetings with clients, meaning that the sales staff have more time for potentially revenue-producing meetings with clients (AvantGo 2003) and are therefore better equipped to provide value-adding service to their clients (being better informed about the status of orders, inventory levels, delivery schedules, pricing, new product launches, product information and so on). This is potentially a source of differentiation in competitive marketplaces (synchrologic.com 2001).

Similar benefits can be reported through regularly obtaining updates on daily work schedules without the need for the field officer to return to base, being able to download and upload up-to-date reports of customer services (both performed and required), resulting in better utilisation of field staff time, more timely and accurate billing for service, more complete records being kept and so on, and an automation of data entry requirements, thus saving clerical staff time (Leung & Antypas 2001; Scheepers & McKay 2003).

Cost-cutting achieved through automation of business processes

Providing access to corporate systems, reports and required corporate data electronically can remove the need to post such information to field staff. By equipping staff with relatively simple mobile devices, and providing synchronisation facilities to allow such reports to be downloaded, companies can achieve substantial cost savings without compromising on the information provided to support their field staff. One large US manufacturer saved US$3000 per year per sales representative through providing detailed sales analyses in this way, adding millions of dollars annually to the corporate balance sheet (synchrologic.com 2001). Used appropriately, it is not uncommon for applications of this type to achieve a return on investment within comparatively short periods of time.

Achieving competitive advantage

Mobile devices can also be used to increase the speed by which a key service can be performed, to improve responsiveness and to provide value-added services for customers, among other things; all of which are examples of how mobile computing can provide an opportunity for one organisation to outperform its rivals in speed, cost structures, service quality, flexibility and so on. An example is provided by a national fast food restaurant chain. By using mobile devices to support daily uploads of sales performance at regional branches, administrative staff at corporate headquarters can, on a daily basis, analyse the effectiveness of marketing campaigns and thus make adjustments and so on, on the basis of analyses performed (synchrologic.com 2001).

Value propositions and mobile computing

Davis (2002) argues that potential business benefits are associated with the access to information provided to knowledge workers, and this should be significant as more and more businesses find themselves operating in the information-intensive, knowledge-based service sector. The types of benefits that exist include a removal of time and place constraints and hence the notion of anytime, anywhere computing (Davis 2002), improved access to decision-makers and much improved access to information needed to complete work and provide excellent customer service.

It does seem reasonable to assert that the notion of critical mass is significant in the arena of mobile computing, much as it was reported to be with e-commerce and the adoption of the Internet, and hence a potential conundrum exists. As Gilbert and Kendall (2003) note, success with these mobile innovations, and therefore their capability to deliver on promises of the delivery of business value, is contingent on the adoption of the technology by a critical mass. But enticing a critical mass to adopt implies the need to deliver value and services that are desired and welcomed by users, such that behavioural changes are effected, including the willingness to adopt the new technology, use it as intended, and apply it to support and enable routine business activities.

Value propositions are derived from the relationships between the bundle of product, service and information that an organisation offers, and consumer purchases, and the extent to which this bundle satisfies consumer needs (Clarke 2001). In comparing the particular value associated with mobile technologies with other information technologies such as e-commerce, Clarke (2001) identifies four unique value propositions that could be derived from the use of mobile technologies. These include exploiting the concepts of ubiquity (the exchange of information and performance of transactions from any location in real time), convenience (activities can be performed at the user's convenience), localisation (contacts and exchanges can be based around knowing the location of a particular mobile device) and personalisation (the ability to receive and access personalised information and services). These four value propositions are seen to derive from an exchange between an organisation and a consumer, with the conceptualisation resting upon the use of mobile technologies on the part of the consumer. Hence, they are all examples of a B2C transaction, with value needing to be derived by the customer in order for the type of transaction to be sustained. However, as previously discussed, B2E applications are argued to offer greater promise for the delivery of organisational value than B2C exchanges, and hence the concept of a value proposition needs to be reconceptualised from an internal organisational perspective.

In the context of many organisations, internal members of staff are using mobile technologies in B2E-type exchanges and transactions to accomplish work tasks, which might or might not involve direct interaction with the customer. For example, warehouse staff might use mobile devices to monitor and control inventory levels and movements. In the situation illustrated in figure 11.1, mobile field staff use mobile technologies to gain access to information needed to support their interactions with customers, with the mobile device serving almost as a conduit between the mobile staff member and head office, in order to support the service delivery to the customer. Thus, the mobile device might not be adopted to create value directly from the customer's perspective but rather to create value from a purely internal perspective (between mobile staff and head office), as a result of which value is added for the customer.

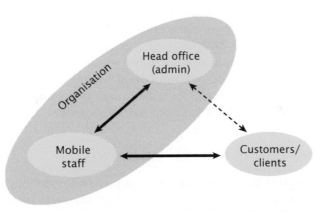

Figure 11.1 ▶ The internal value proposition arising from B2E exchanges

Success with m-commerce applications is not guaranteed. First, organisations need to plan carefully and to consider whether an m-business strategy is well suited to supporting the achievement of their organisational goals and objectives. Once there is certainty that such an initiative is appropriate, then the organisation needs to consider technical issues and potential limitations. Failure to take into account the range of relevant business, sociocultural and technical issues and limitations could result in the delivery of fewer business benefits to the organisation. However, viewing a move to mobile technologies as offering too limited a range of benefits to the organisation can inevitably limit the benefits derived after implementation and understate the potential benefits that could be achieved.

Mobile computing applications and trends

UNCTAD (2001) identify a number of characteristics and advantages of m-commerce and mobile computing applications that are argued to underpin successful business applications and implementations. Mobile computing applications must support immediacy, or the ability to access information and services as and when desired. Thus, successful applications will be cognisant of the need to be available twenty-four hours a day, seven days a week (24/7) from any location, or, as Davis (2002) described it, 'anytime/anyplace'. M-commerce and mobile computing applications are therefore characterised by simplicity and speed in terms of completing a transaction. Typically they are not designed for lengthy periods of 'surfing' but rather for short, sharp exchanges (Paavilainen 2002). Second, they are characterised by connectivity, or the notion of the 'always on' networks. Third, such applications often rely on the deployment of positioning technologies, and therefore the location of users or items of interest (whether they are staff, customers or goods) can be readily established and location-specific services can be made available. Fourth is the characteristic of data portability, or the ability to download information to mobile devices. Such data can then be carried around and accessed when needed, such as during meetings.

Such m-commerce applications can be broadly divided into two types: applications designed to support commercial transactions between businesses and individual consumers (the extension of e-commerce to mobile devices), and B2E applications, or those applications that link an organisation with its employees wherever they need to work and perform critical business activities. In discussing specific types of applications, it should be remembered that many of those applications can be used successfully for both B2C and B2E applications.

SMS and communication services

One of the most common and successful applications developed for mobile phones is SMS (short message service), which allows short messages of up to 160 alphanumeric characters to be sent. SMS is undergoing exponential growth rates. The 30 billion messages sent in 2001 grew to about 100 billion in 2002 (Xu, Teo & Wang 2003), and about 50 per cent of mobile phone users send SMS messages daily in most regions of the world (UNCTAD 2002). SMS messaging applications actually underpin many of the applications discussed subsequently.

Micro payments

A growing trend is for the use of mobile devices to make what are called micro payments, examples of which would include parking meters, vending machines, subscriptions and memberships (new and renewals), purchasing petrol and so on. With mobile phones, the charges can simply be added to mobile phone accounts. UNCTAD

(2002) has forecast that such micro payments will reach US$200 billion worldwide by 2005. There are developments in linking such payments with existing debit and credit cards, and this would imply that, in time, other mobile devices could be used to make such micro payments.

Financial services

Another growing area is accessing a range of financial services via mobile devices. Currently, it is possible to buy and sell shares and securities via mobile phones, and in some cases it is possible to receive quotations for insurance, submit personal details and pay for insurance via mobile phones. This is viewed as a growing trend. It is argued that m-commerce will provide a low-cost but very widespread market of potential customers for such services, potentially allowing insurance companies to focus on lower-end, cheaper products and services and customer service via the delivery of information and accessing of personal details via mobile networks (UNCTAD 2002). Many banks are currently considering the business case for developing a range of mobile banking services.

Information services

For a small charge (usually to mobile phone accounts), users can gain access to a range of information services including weather reports, news headlines, localised, real-time traffic reports, bus and train timetables, stock market information and so on. Increasingly, too, there is the ability to personalise such news and information services, so that fans of Arsenal, for example, are alerted to their team's news and match results, travel industry representatives are sent regular reports on the progress of alarming epidemics, personal investors are informed of the performance of their portfolio of investments, people looking for flats and houses are notified when suitable properties become available, and so on. Hence it is predicted that more personalised and event-driven content will be available via mobile devices. For example, a particular event, such as a stock market fall of more than 1 per cent, will trigger messages to be sent to select mobile phone users.

Logistics

One area with a potential for huge growth in applications is that of logistics, which is broadly defined here to include all aspects of warehousing, transportation, movement of physical goods, importing and exporting, and associated services. There are estimates that logistics adds between 12 and 20 per cent to the final cost of an item, and therefore any potential savings in this area are of great interest and importance in competitive marketplaces.

Efficiencies can be accrued through the use of handheld and mobile devices to track goods, check inventory levels, expedite customs clearance, manage the movement of goods and identify locations of orders, both by timely access to information and through a reduction in administrative and data entry activities. Furthermore, as in Australia and most other countries, transport is often multimodal in that it can involve ship, road and air, smoothing the interfaces between modes, reducing data entry requirements, and facilitating greater efficiencies and improved service levels, which can offer substantial benefits to trading partners (UNCTAD 2002).

Sales force automation and wireless customer relationship management

Customer relationship management (CRM) was earlier identified as an important area of growth in enterprise systems that enables organisations to gain better insights into the preferences and needs of their customers and thus to establish longer-lasting and better relationships with their customers. CRM initiatives and systems often help organisations to take a customer-centric view and are often premised upon an ability to draw together a vast amount of data related to customers from disparate sources within and outside the organisation in order to tailor goods and services appropriately. Company sales staff are often very reliant on the outputs from CRM systems and, increasingly, with sales forces moving about in the field, a range of mobile devices will be adopted to support their activities. Sales force automation (SFA) tools have been delivered via hand-held devices, laptops, modems and the Internet for some time now, but increasingly, mobile devices will enable real-time access to corporate data, and this will be achieved via wireless networks and a range of smaller, genuinely mobile devices (Speier & Venkatesh 2003; Morgan & Inks 2001; Erffmeyer & Johnson 2001).

Mobile CRM tools and technologies allow for real-time data synchronisation (rather than periodic, say daily) and therefore will also allow access to customer information, purchase history, product information, technical documentation, order status reports and the like. Equipping mobile sales and service staff with such information is argued to enable them to provide a better, more informed service direct to customers in a timely fashion. The other dimension of wireless CRM, however, is the ability to locate customers via their own mobile devices and to market services to them according to their location. This is considered to be a huge growth area, and will thus be discussed in the next section.

Location-based marketing and services

Some people describe location-based services as the 'killer app' of m-commerce (Paavilainen 2002). In essence, GPS technology will be employed so that the location of mobile devices can be ascertained at any point of time, triggering both the sending and receiving of messages dependent on location. This can be used for marketing purposes, so that consumers could be notified of 'specials' as they walk around shopping malls and so on (Xu, Teo & Wang 2003). However, arguably this has the potential to annoy customers just as much as to attract them.

Possibly more serious applications of location-sensitive technologies are for such things as roadside services, emergency services in case of accidents, remote diagnosis of vehicle troubles, location-sensitive maps, traffic reports and alternative route information, tracing of stolen cars and so on (Paavilainen 2002).

thinking strategically

Delivering value with m-commerce

Read the following mini-cases, and then decide whether the proposed m-commerce investment sounds as if it will deliver value to customers and value to the business.

Beer Co.

A large, established brewery (Beer Co.) is considering the purchase of mobile technologies for their sales staff. The proposed m-commerce application would involve handheld devices that would enable sales staff to look into stock levels, customer purchasing history, customer credit rating, order status and so on. The beer market is mature and experiences growth rates associated with population increases only, rather than due to an increasing market. There are three established players, all of which share roughly equal shares of the market. Beer Co. has very good forecasting systems, which show seasonal trends in beer consumption following well-known and established patterns, and production is closely linked to that trend data. Production is stable throughout the year, so product stock-outs do not occur unless there is a major breakdown in the production line. The only perturbations to the system occur with the opening of new hotels or restaurants, but a stable, predictable pattern of ordering is usually quickly established even at these new premises.

Repair Co.

Repair Co. is also thinking about investing in an m-commerce application for their service staff. The proposed system would allow remote workers maintaining or repairing equipment at a customer's premises to do the following:

- access diagnostic information about the likely source of the error from the equipment manufacturer's database
- find the location and establish the availability of spare parts, once the problem has been diagnosed
- place an order for the spare part
- receive information about the expected delivery date of the spare part to the customer's site
- schedule a repair technician to revisit the customer's premises when the spare part is available
- organise billing of the customer, based on the service performed, parts required and hours spent on the job by field service staff.

There is no similar system in place. Currently the repair technicians have mobile phones, with which they can phone administrative staff and ask them to find out where a spare part might be located. Details about hours on the job, services performed and parts required are manually written in a book and a copy is given to administrative staff when the field staff next return to head office.

Sometimes equipment can be out of action for several days, and no one can inform the customer when it might be repaired.

Questions

1. Would you recommend Beer Co. invest in this new mobile computing application? What would be the benefit to Beer Co.?
2. Would you recommend Repair Co. proceed with the proposed investment? What would the benefits of this new m-commerce application be?

Other personal services

Mobile technologies will be able to support the achievement of a range of other personal needs, such as being used to activate or deactivate alarm systems remotely (say, to allow a child to enter the home after school without the parent being physically present to unlock the door), for making a host of appointments and possibly in the future as part of the democratic process of voting. In addition, mobile devices will support purchasing of goods and services, ticketing and reservations for a range of services, games, music, betting and other entertainment activities.

Issues in mobile computing

Organisations need to take note of a number of potential issues and challenges if they are to benefit from mobile computing and take advantage of the opportunities it offers while being careful to manage some unintended or potentially negative consequences. These can be divided into technical issues, socio-professional issues and a range of regulatory and legal issues, mainly privacy and security.

Technical issues

Among the technical concerns are such issues as security of corporate data on mobile devices (Tsalgatigou & Pitoura 2001), a lack of standards, as the market is considered too immature for one dominant standard to have emerged (Barbero 2001; Pearson & Nelson 2003), bandwidth and interoperability concerns (Leung & Antypas 2001), and limitations of existing handheld mobile devices (small displays, length of time required and difficulty in completing lengthy tasks, and so on) (Leung & Antypas 2001; Tsalgatigou & Pitoura 2001). These limitations sometimes relate to physical restrictions associated with mobile devices, such as the small screen size, rather tedious and clumsy data entry (via styluses or keyboards), and a fairly slow transmission speed. In addition, these devices, especially those with Internet enablement, are reasonably expensive and are moderately complex to use, and currently there are still rather restricted services and content available for consumers to access (Pearson & Nelson 2003).

In addition, there have been interconnection issues between fixed-line phone companies (often long-established wealthy companies) and newer competitive mobile operators competing for market share in a burgeoning marketplace. Regulation by governments has sometimes been necessary to manage these issues and charges. Arguably for organisations to implement these mobile technologies successfully, care must be taken to manage and minimise the potential technical limitations through careful planning and design, and attention must be given to business change issues if they wish to exploit the potential offered by mobility and derive business value from their investments.

Socio-professional issues

Socio-professional issues arise from changes that mobility potentially bring to the way in which people do their jobs and to the potential for problems to occur at the boundary between professional and personal life. For example, while enabling the conduct of business and performance of work tasks free from constraints of office hours, the potential arises for individuals to blur the boundaries between work and home, for computing and work tasks to intrude into personal space and time, which needs careful management to ensure that workers take the breaks they need and so on (Davis 2002). Second, knowledge workers might suffer from information overload or something akin to a paralysis because they have access to just far too much information. Third, with the increased ease of communications, decisions might be escalated to more senior managers simply because it is easy to do so (Davis 2002).

Privacy issues

In developed countries, governments have long been concerned with balancing the rights of the individual to privacy of personal information against the needs of others to store and access that data. There was an upsurge of concern in this respect with the advent of the Internet, with many rightly expressing concerns about personal details being stored and potentially used without the owner of that information necessarily being aware of or consenting to such use. With the advent of a range of mobile devices and applications that use, store and exchange information, the potential for personal information and other privacy concerns to be violated is clear and must be a growing concern. Location-based devices that can in effect track movements of individuals are one major concern in this respect, and there seems to be a fine line between monitoring for safety and welfare purposes and surveillance.

Security concerns

Associated with privacy concerns are those of security. Security has often been cited as a major inhibitor of the adoption of e-commerce (Poon & Swatman 1999), with concerns being expressed over the security of networks for sensitive personal and financial information. If anything, security concerns about mobile devices and networks are likely to be increased in a mobile environment (Pearson & Nelson 2003). Any breaches of security can cause a corruption of corporate data and loss of consumer confidence and the misuse of personal data. In addition, mobile devices are easy to lose and are easily stolen and misused, particularly if they contain sensitive personal information, passwords and the like. Mobile devices are also prone to attack from viruses similar to those that plague computer networks from time to time.

Developing a mobile strategy

To achieve the business benefits previously identified for mobile computing, careful planning and strategising is necessary if organisations are to capitalise on these new technologies and gain an advantage in competitive marketplaces. It is stressed that the best outcomes are only seldom achieved through a focus first and foremost on the mobile devices available. Hence a sound starting point is not to try to think about available mobile technologies and to try to find a use for them in an organisation. Rather, developing a successful **mobile strategy** involves, first of all, identifying a business problem that could be solved or ameliorated through the application of mobile technologies or to articulate a clear need based on a sound, sustainable business case where added value for the organisation can be demonstrated in some way (Paavilainen 2002). Creative thinking is important here. But obvious target problems that might be improved through the appropriate use of mobile computing would include problems associated with core business processes (are bottlenecks or high costs associated with portions of core business processes, which imply that greater efficiencies could be achieved?), with the management and productivity of mobile staff (can the productivity or service provided by mobile staff improve through greater and more timely access to corporate information?), and where the storage, movement and management of goods is critical to the success of the enterprise (can efficiencies be achieved or service levels improved through timely access to information about the location and inventory levels of particular items?). Achieving alignment between mobile strategies and initiatives is just as important as the need for alignment between IS/e-commerce strategies discussed in chapter 3 of this book.

Understanding the value drivers of an organisation, and therefore recognising those opportunities for m-commerce and mobile computing that will have the most impact on the organisation, is vital. Hence organisations need to understand whether greatest value can be achieved through cost savings, decreased inventory, increased inventory turnover, improved quality, improved productivity of human resources or improved relationships with mobile staff, subcontractors and business partners, and so on (Paavilainen 2002). Understanding value drivers can help to identify crucial mobile applications, as opposed to fashion-driven investments. In as much as e-commerce enabled fundamental changes in the way organisations could interact with customers, achieve efficiencies in the supply chain and improve internal operations, mobile computing offers similar abilities to leverage existing infrastructure for greater business benefit. With mobility, it might be possible to achieve greater efficiencies along supply chains, greater intimacy with customers and so on. The skill of the corporate strategist in identifying high value-added applications is critical.

It is also appropriate to attempt to take a high-level corporate view of mobile computing and to avoid looking at specific applications as stand-alone, single uses of **mobile technology**. Hence it might be more appropriate for an organisation to recognise the need to develop a standard mobile infrastructure that supports all their current and future mobile computing initiatives, rather than adopt a piecemeal approach to the adoption of mobile technologies. This is important and has been associated with reducing the total cost of ownership (TCO) of mobile computing and might therefore be associated with the delivery of much more attractive business benefits than adopting a case-by-case approach (synchrologic.com 2002; Gartner Group 2001).

As previously discussed, substantial business benefits are more likely, at least in the short term, to occur from B2E applications rather than from m-commerce applications. Hence in articulating a mobile strategy, it might be important to bear in mind the likely sources of business value from the application of mobile computing: mobile devices might boost mobile staff productivity, they might result in cost reductions through re-engineering and automating existing business processes, they might result in the delivery of improved and more valued services to customers, and they might offer a source of competitive advantage to an organisation.

As is the case with most IT initiatives, it is wise to start relatively small and simple, to avoid creeping requirements and blow-out of costs and scope of the initiative, to focus on areas of high and more certain added value and to prototype or pilot these initiatives in targeted areas of the organisation before rolling them out organisation-wide. The characteristics of mobile devices need to be clearly understood in articulating a mobile business strategy. Clarke (2001) argues that success for organisations with a substantial e-commerce component in their business portfolio might require the articulation of an effective consumer-oriented mobile strategy.

Future trends

As mentioned earlier, many argue that mobile computing and the adoption in business of m-commerce represent the next wave of computing. Many pundits, however, look beyond current mobile technologies and see further progress in coming years in the areas of **pervasive computing** and **ubiquitous computing**. The relationships between mobile, pervasive and ubiquitous computing are illustrated in figure 11.2. Lyytinen and Yoo (2002a) have classified various fields of computing to illustrate some of the trends that have been, and are, occurring with respect to the use of technology for business and social activities. Their classification involves consideration of two dimensions: first, the degree to which computing is mobile, and second, the extent to which it is embedded in the environment (the computer chips in washing machines, diagnostic chips in photocopiers and the like, for example, are much more embedded than a desktop personal computer). Traditional business computing is argued to be relatively immobile and is not embedded in the environment to any great extent. Mobile technologies, by contrast, support the concept of anytime, anywhere computing but are still not embedded in our environment. Pervasive computing has a high degree of embeddedness but at this stage is not mobile (it does not move around with the user). Pervasive computing implies that the computer can obtain information from its environment and act on it. Examples of pervasive computing would be various sensing devices, heating controls that can sense the room temperature and the rate of change in order to adjust the degree of heating or cooling required, and so on.

Ubiquitous computing shares the embeddedness and functionality of pervasive computing with mobility. This would mean that pervasive computing functionality would be built into items we wear or carry round with us, learning and remembering from past experiences and services used (see figure 11.2) (Lyytinen & Yoo 2002a). Ubiquitous computing applications offer some real challenges to systems analysts and designers. For example, they must be able to adapt dynamically as the requirements of the user's task change, meaning that they must be able to respond and adapt to changing technological capabilities in their environment. As the ubiquitous computing application will inevitably impact on social interactions, a host of issues regarding privacy and security, the ownership of data and the uses to which data can be put need to be resolved (Banavar & Bernstein 2002).

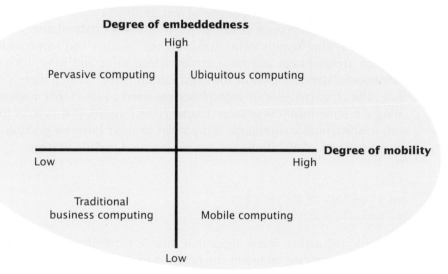

Figure 11.2 ▶ The relationships between mobile computing, pervasive computing and ubiquitous computing

Source ▶ Lyytinen and Yoo 2002a.

Clearly, technical, social and organisational changes and challenges will be associated with trends of this sort as they emerge. Issues like how such applications and service are designed and implemented must be addressed, and the underlying computer architecture required to support such devices (Banavar & Bernstein 2002). Potential changes to social structures and interactions will need to be carefully considered, as will the organisational change issues associated with the adoption of these new forms of computing (Grudin 2002; Lyytinen & Yoo 2002a). Fano and Gershman (2002) argue that ubiquitous computing has the potential to change the nature of interactions between business and their customers (and business partners and the like) in much the same way that e-commerce enabled organisations to form and manage relationships with customers in different ways. For example, a challenge for business has always been accessing their customers at an appropriate time and in an appropriate manner. Ubiquitous computing has the potential to remove the problem of gaining access, but perhaps increases the challenges of establishing the right time and right manner.

If such devices and concepts are to gain widespread acceptance in our communities and offer positive experiences to individuals and organisations, then the utility of such environments must be thoroughly tested and validated from a variety of perspectives (Banavar & Bernstein 2002). We are a long way yet from being able to accomplish this, and advances are most likely to come from identifying social and business needs rather than from creating technological visions and solutions.

Summary

This chapter considers a range of issues associated with mobile computing, and presents the view that m-commerce and mobile computing offer an advance on e-commerce by extending the ubiquity of the Internet to wireless networks and mobile people, making computing power, corporate information and a range of services accessible anytime anywhere via a host of mobile devices. Mobile computing has the potential to offer substantial benefits to individuals and organisations and, like e-commerce, when appropriately applied it has the potential to improve flows along the supply chain, offer staff better access to corporate data irrespective of their location, reduce travel time for employees and hence increase their productivity, and positively influence the delivery of services to customers. However, there are a number of important limitations with mobile devices, such as small screen size, relatively slow transmission speeds and the like, and these need to be taken into account in designing applications suited to existing mobile technologies.

For real business value to be delivered, however, it is argued that a coherent mobile strategy needs to be developed, one that clearly stems from a perceived business need or opportunity and therefore can be shown to be aligned with business goals, objectives and strategies. Although mobile computing will in the future be augmented by pervasive and ubiquitous concepts, careful thought and development needs to be given to these concepts so that they enhance the human condition rather than impoverish it.

key terms

m-commerce

mobile computing

mobile internet

mobile strategy

mobile technology

pervasive computing

ubiquitous computing

discussion questions

1. What is m-commerce? What is mobile computing? How does m-commerce differ from mobile computing? What are the drivers and motivators of m-commerce? How do these differ from the drivers and motivators of e-commerce? What are the drivers and motivators of mobile computing?

2. What is pervasive computing? What is ubiquitous computing? How do these differ from m-commerce and mobile computing? What are the drivers and motivators of pervasive and ubiquitous computing? What are the likely benefits to be derived from each?

3. What benefits are corporations likely to derive from mobile computing? What are the characteristics of those enterprises that will gain most from adopting mobile computing?

4. Describe how you would make sure that mobile, pervasive and ubiquitous computing applications were appropriately considered in your organisation's strategic IS planning exercise. Would you adapt any of the frameworks, models and techniques of strategic IS planning to encourage thinking about mobile, pervasive and ubiquitous technology applications?

5. Give examples of some possible mobile computing applications to the following areas:
   (i) logistics
   (ii) sales force automation
   (iii) location-based marketing and services.

suggested reading

Clarke, I 2001, 'Emerging value propositions for m-commerce', *Journal of Business Strategies*, vol. 18, no. 2, pp. 133–48.

Lyytinen, K & Yoo, Y 2002a, 'Issues and challenges in ubiquitous computing', *Communications of the ACM*, vol. 45, no. 12, pp. 63–5.

—2002b, 'Research commentary: the next wave of nomadic computing', *Information Systems Research*, vol. 13, no. 4, pp. 377–89.

Paavilainen, J 2002, *Mobile Business Strategies: Understanding the Technologies and Opportunities*, IT Press (Pearson Education), London.

Perry, M, O'Hara, K, Sellen, A, Brown, B & Harper, R 2001, 'Dealing with mobility: understanding access anytime, anywhere', *ACM Transactions on Computer–Human Interaction*, vol. 8, no. 4, pp. 323–47.

Sadeh, N 2002, *M-commerce: Technologies, Services, and Business Models*, John Wiley & Sons, New York.

synchrologic.com 2001, 'The future of enterprise mobile computing. Synchrologic Executive White Paper', available online at www.synchrologic.com, accessed 4 June 2003.

references

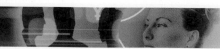

AvantGo 2003, 'Know your ROI . . . Building the business case for mobile SFA. AvantGo White Paper', available from www.avantgo.com, accessed 3 June 2003.

Banavar, G & Bernstein, A 2002, 'Software infrastructure and design challenges for ubiquitous computing applications', *Communications of the ACM*, vol. 45, no. 12, pp. 92–6.

Barbero, M 2001, 'Preparing to ride the wireless wave', *Journal of Business Strategy*, September–October, pp. 10–12.

Clarke, I 2001, 'Emerging value propositions for m-commerce', *Journal of Business Strategies*, vol. 18, no. 2, pp. 133–48.

Davis, GB 2002, 'Anytime/anyplace computing and the future of knowledge work', *Communications of the ACM*, vol. 45, no. 12, pp. 67–73.

Erffmeyer, RC & Johnson, DA 2001, 'An exploratory study of sales force automation practices: expectations and realities', *Journal of Personal Selling and Sales Management*, vol. 21, no. 2, pp. 167–75.

Fano, A & Gershman, A 2002, 'The future of business services', *Communications of the ACM*, vol. 45, no. 12, pp. 83–7.

Gartner Group 2001, 'Mobile device management and synchronization: take control or lose control', *Gartner Symposium ITxpo*, October 2001.

Gilbert, AL & Kendall, JD 2003, 'A marketing model for mobile wireless services', *Proceedings of the 36th Hawaii International Conference on Systems Sciences*, IEEE Computer Society, pp. 1–9.

Grudin, J 2002, 'Group dynamics and ubiquitous computing', *Communications of the ACM*, vol. 45, no. 12, pp. 74–8.

Leung, K & Antypas, J 2001, 'Improving returns on m-commerce investments', *Journal of Business Strategy*, September–October, pp. 12–13.

Lyytinen, K & Yoo, Y 2002a, 'Issues and challenges in ubiquitous computing', *Communications of the ACM*, vol. 45, no. 12, pp. 63–5.

—2002b, 'Research commentary: the next wave of nomadic computing', *Information Systems Research*, vol. 13, no. 4, pp. 377–89.

May, P 2001, *Mobile Commerce: Opportunities, Applications and Technologies of Wireless Business*, Cambridge University Press, New York.

Morgan, AJ & Inks, SA 2001, 'Technology and the sales force: increasing acceptance of sales force automation', *Industrial Marketing Management* vol. 30, no. 5, pp. 463–72.

Paavilainen, J 2002, *Mobile Business Strategies: Understanding the Technologies and Opportunities*, IT Press (Pearson Education), London.

Pearson, C & Nelson, E 2003, 'mBusiness: the world within your grasp', *PriceWaterhouseCoopers*, available online www.pwc.com, accessed 4 June 2003.

Perry, M, O'Hara, K, Sellen, A, Brown, B & Harper, R 2001, 'Dealing with mobility: understanding access anytime, anywhere', *ACM Transactions on Computer–Human Interaction*, vol. 8, no. 4, pp. 323–47.

Poon, S & Swatman, PMC 1999, 'An exploratory study of small business Internet commerce issues', *Information & Management*, vol. 35, no. 1, pp. 9–18.

Sadeh, N 2002, *M-commerce: Technologies, Services, and Business Models*, John Wiley & Sons, New York.

Scheepers, H & McKay, J 2003, 'Improving the delivery of business value from mobile technologies: an empirical assessment of implementation outcomes'. Paper accepted for presentation at Workshop on eBusiness (WeB2003), Seattle, Washington, December 2003.

Speier, C & Venkatesh, V 2002, 'The hidden minefields in the adoption of sales force automation technologies', *Journal of Marketing*, vol. 66, no. 3, pp. 98–111.

synchrologic.com 2001, 'The future of enterprise mobile computing. Synchrologic Executive White Paper', available online at www.synchrologic.com, accessed 4 June 2003.

Tsalgatidou, A & Pitoura, E 2001, 'Business models and transactions in mobile electronic commerce: requirements and properties', *Computer Networks*, vol. 37, 2001, pp. 221–36.

United Nations Conference on Trade and Development (UNCTAD) 2002, *E-commerce and Development Report*, UNCTAD Secretariat, United Nations, New York and Geneva.

Weiser, M 1998, 'The future of ubiquitous computing in campus', *Communications of the ACM*, vol. 41, no. 1, pp. 41–2.

Xu, H, Teo, HH and Wang, H 2003, 'Foundations of SMS success: lessons from SMS messaging and co-opetition', *Proceedings of the 36th Hawaii International Conference on Systems Sciences*, IEEE Computer Society, pp. 1–10.

case study

Mobile computing in the Farm Machinery Mechanical Company

The Farm Machinery Mechanical Company (FMM) had been founded in 1920. The company provided expert and quality repairs to all forms of farm machinery from tractors to combine harvesters, wherever such repairs were needed in Australia. It promised a quick resolution to breakdowns on location and performed regular maintenance checkups on farm machinery on location.

FMM was based in Sydney but had offices in all state capital cities in Australia. It also had small offices in many regional centres and large country towns across the continent. It held a small inventory of important farm machinery parts in most of these offices.

FMM had two major competitors. One was the Ag Repair Company (AR) of Perth. AR had offices in Perth and Adelaide and in a number of large country towns in Western Australia and South Australia. It provided a reasonable service at a very low cost. The management and workforce of FMM felt that the service was too 'low-cost' and that the quality of work done by AR mechanics was very poor. However, the low cost of the AR repairs was attracting business away from FMM.

Croptech was a Brisbane-based farm machinery repair company that served farmers in the eastern states of Australia. It had a reputation for speed and efficiency and for quality work. Its prices were about on a par with those of FMM.

Revenues for FMM in 2003 had been $360 million, down 10 per cent on 2002 and down 12 per cent on 2001. The management of FMM blamed, in part at least, the drought conditions of the past few years. However, they noted that in the same period Croptech's revenues had remained constant and AR's had increased substantially. Thus FMM's management was keen to look for ways of cutting costs in order to be able to reduce prices while keeping profits reasonable.

FMM was in the process of working through its strategic information systems plan. There had been general acceptance that two new projects were needed. One was to upgrade the accounting and financial systems, and the other was to improve and enhance the inventory control system that monitored, controlled and advised on replenishments for FMM's distributed inventories of machinery parts. Both systems enhancements were accepted as necessary improvements to FMM's portfolio of information systems.

André Tychonoff, FMM's CIO, was trying to help the senior management systems planning group to uncover possible new IT investment opportunities. 'In thinking about new IT investment opportunities we need a vision and a motivating idea. I think such an idea is the Gartner Group's idea of the "real-time organisation". This is an organisation that has all of its information online and integrated, so that when an event occurs, say a person buys a product and pays for it, for example, then the information from that transaction is entered into the integrated corporate information system and all the necessary processing is done immediately. All the necessary fields of information are also updated, thus updating all reports. So for the product that was bought, the corresponding inventory field is decremented by one, the report on sales for that product is increased by one, and the various accounting information is updated according to the dollars involved in the sale. So all the information in online reports is actual and up-to-the-minute. All "information slack" is removed. We then have the best decision-making information possible, and our financial transactions are being carried out as soon as possible.

'We could slowly move towards the "real-time organisation" as we upgrade our systems and invest in new systems. It will not happen immediately, but as we move towards it we move closer and closer to "friction-free" business — business is never delayed or compromised by not having the latest information to hand!

'If we think this through for FMM, one system I can think of as fitting a move towards the ideal of the "real-time organisation" is a system that gives our mechanics, our front-line people, a mobile office in their vehicles. The system would be based on a laptop computer plus printer in their vehicles, with the system having a wireless connection to the Internet. If we need to monitor their location for any reason we could have a GPS location-based system. Our mechanics could then access all the information they needed — technical or commercial — from the very field, shed or paddock in which they were repairing the farm machinery.'

'Well, now I've heard everything!' said Ernst Zermelo, FMM's chief operations officer. 'Here we are struggling to make reasonable profits, trying to cut costs and you suggest...well...look, it's good to have your visionary ideas, André, but we also need some reality.'

'Hang on, Ernst!' said George Stokes, FMM's CFO. 'I know CFOs are the last people credited with appreciating "visions" — but there may be something to André's idea.'

'I imagine', continued George, 'the mechanics with their mobile computer — with a wireless connection to the Internet — and their printer in their vehicles, and perhaps each having a PDA, or similar device that is connected wirelessly to the laptop, so that they can take the PDA right up to the worksite. Indeed, even with this pretty lavish amount of technology, the system might well be able to pay for itself.

'First, it will be easier to get scheduling and rescheduling information out to everyone. We have 400 or so mechanics, and scheduling them requires a considerable administrative effort. With a group email address, this could be much easier. Thus, our schedule of jobs to be done could be easily updated. The same applies to availability of parts from inventory and so on.

'Second, our expert system on farm machinery repair could be accessed anywhere. We have stopped publishing and updating paper versions of this owing to the cost, but our mechanics, at present, can access the Internet only from regional and country town offices — and, in a few cases, from their homes. Feedback from our mechanics regarding the system — replete as it is with easy-to-follow diagrams, graphics and photos, with audio output and step-by-step guidance — is that they

prefer the system to manuals. They rate the system as really contributing to their capability to repair farm machinery. That system would be present to all mechanics right at the place of need.

'Administrative details on each job could be input via the mobile devices to our work record system and to our billing, invoicing and accounting systems. So, instead of the mechanics writing down details for later entry, it would be done immediately, at the place of work. If we could also encourage customers to utilise the Internet to settle their accounts with us — either directly or through their bank's website, then all administrative and financial processing could be done very efficiently and very soon after the job was finished.

'Further to efficient administrative processes, we could capture, via the mobile systems, the mechanics' usage and needs regarding machinery parts. At present, we are slow to respond to the mechanics' inventory needs, and when we do the inventory, usage and status falls through the cracks somewhere between a central inventory location and the farm where the repairs are happening. With the mobile computing system, we could better track inventory through the system, thus having fewer inconvenient stock-outs and providing better service.

'Then, I think when we examine closely all the functions that the system could carry out in support of our mechanics and on behalf of our customers, the next question we ask is — well, given each mechanic with the mobile office — do we really need so many local offices in country towns? There are several hundred of these offices across Australia. It would really be worth examining whether we still need these offices if each mechanic had a mobile office.'

James Sylvester, FMM's CEO, then entered the discussion. 'This is very interesting,' he reflected. 'At present our country offices are centres for customer inquiries and for customer requests for assistance. The offices also serve as stockholding points and as communication centres, including Internet access for local mechanics. If the mechanics are to take over all these functions, then we will have to assume some extra responsibilities and duties. The problem is that they are already feeling stretched. Also, they are quite strongly unionised. However, this system is well worth pursuing further.'

The strategic information systems planning session then continued looking for other systems opportunities.

Questions

1. What you think of André Tychonoff's thorough portrayal of the 'real-time organisation' as a future ideal for FMM? Evaluate this ideal.

2. Evaluate, in principle, the proposal for 'mobile offices' for FMM consisting of laptop computer, printer and PDA, together with wireless Internet connection. What are the costs and benefits (in principle) of such a system? List what detailed costs and benefits you would seek to calculate in evaluating this system.

3. Would you, in principle, support such a system being investigated further? Why? Do you feel such a system is unlikely to be suitable for this company when it is seeking to reduce costs? Why?

4. Describe the major challenges that you feel FMM faces in introducing this system in such a way that the benefits outweigh the costs. Be sure to take account of intangible benefits.

chapter 12

IT governance: delivering value from e-business

learning objectives

After reading this chapter, you should be able to:

- understand and appreciate the ways in which IT and e-business investments can deliver value to organisations
- define the notion of IT governance and appreciate the importance of governance in the delivery of value from organisational IT investment
- understand both the objectives and characteristics of IT governance and appreciate effective IT governance mechanisms
- appreciate the difficulties in evaluating IT investments
- understand some of the major methodologies for IT/e-business evaluation and proactive benefits management.

   Note that in this chapter we will be using 'IT' in the general sense of referring to information, information systems and information technology. This follows the general usage of the term *IT governance* as referring to the governance of matters pertaining to information, information systems and information technology.

chapter overview

Implicit throughout this book has been the issue of how to ensure that IT and the Internet are deployed in organisations in a manner that ensures optimum business benefits are derived. This chapter explicitly turns its attention to this issue: how can organisations implement and manage IT to ensure that expected benefits are derived from IT investments and that value accrues to the organisation? The argument developed throughout this chapter suggests that there are a number of key practices and processes that organisations should put in place. First, sound and effective IT governance (consisting of principles, structures, processes and procedures) need to be put in place. IT governance helps to ensure alignment of business and IS/IT strategies and investments, that IT opportunities (such as that presented by the advent of the Internet) are recognised and exploited in a timely manner, that IT-related risks are recognised and managed effectively, all contributing ultimately to ensuring the delivery of business value from IT.

   Second, effective IT governance requires effective evaluation of IT investments and resources and proactive management of the anticipated benefits from IT, thus ensuring, as far as is possible, the realisation of actual benefits from IT investments. This chapter briefly identifies some key approaches to IT evaluation and discusses their strengths and weaknesses in the light of a number of issues surrounding the evaluation of IT in general.

Third, the chapter discusses the notion of IT benefits management and argues that benefits management and IT evaluation need to be closely linked and integrated with IT strategy if business value is to be derived from IT investments over time. A framework to support the integration of IT strategy formulation, evaluation and benefits management, the IT Evaluation and Benefits Management Lifecycle, is presented and analysed.

Introduction

In many of the chapters in this book thus far, the message has been clear: in many cases, the success of an enterprise is now dependent on IT. Facing global competition and more informed consumers successfully will often depend, at least in part, on how well an organisation is able to harness the potentiality of IT, the Internet and associated technologies in creating products and services in an effective and efficient way, in developing streamlined business processes and activities by which those products and services are produced and delivered, by creating effective relationships with business partners, suppliers and customers throughout strategic business networks, by delivering excellent value-adding services to end consumers, and so on. Hence IT now needs to be woven through the very fabric of the organisation. How well this is done and the positive outcomes that ensue for the organisation are often referred to as the **business value** of IT. Business value from IT has to do with efficiency gains (for example increased throughputs and/or decreased costs), effectiveness gains (for example improved customer service) and/or the improvements brought about through the timely and appropriate application and exploitation of information and IT.

The role of IT has changed substantially over the decades, and whereas most IT investments in the 1960s and 1970s were geared towards cost efficiencies, it seems reasonable to assert that investments are now often geared towards revenue generation or effectiveness gains, such as can be derived through IT investments that contribute to improved quality and quality controls, the ability to customise product and services, increasing speed and responsiveness to customer needs and wants, and gaining access to new markets via the Internet, for example. Think about many of the types of IT investments that have emerged since the advent of e-business and the Internet that have been discussed throughout this book. Many of the IT applications considered have to do with the formation of strategic business networks, which change industry and organisational structures (see chapter 10); many had to do with building IT applications to reach directly into supplier organisations and to change interfaces with customers and end consumers (chapters 6 and 7), thus fundamentally altering core business processes, supply chains and distribution channels, and notions of customer service. When IT investments are primarily geared towards automation, then often business benefits are clear in terms of reduced head counts, increased throughputs and so on. However, the notion of benefit or business value is much less obvious when we talk about IT investments to improve service or relationships, and hence value becomes more intangible, less direct, and more interwoven and diffused across a range of organisational activities.

Building required **IT capabilities** in organisations today is a complex task. Organisations require IT that will deliver fast, accurate, secure, reliable and quality information and information processing where needed throughout an enterprise. Investments are also needed to help knowledge workers share valuable knowledge and expertise throughout the organisation in a timely manner. Capabilities are also required to ensure that core business processes and activities are implemented in a cost-effective and efficient manner, delivering cost savings, increased throughputs and increased productivity to the enterprise. So too are IT capabilities that will enhance the effectiveness of the organisation, through systems that serve to create closer ties with suppliers, customers, business and alliance partners, and the like. Opportunities for IT innovation and exploitation must also be seized by means of timely and appropriate IT investments. The returns for organisations that accomplish this successfully are obvious, as are the penalties for organisations that fail to derive reasonable business value from their IT investments.

However, concerns have been voiced about the value derived from IT expenditures and whether organisations are achieving an acceptable payoff for their considerable investments (Willcocks 1996). For example, the literature reports repeated findings of the failure of IT to deliver the anticipated business benefits (Thorp 1998; Ward, Taylor & Bond 1996). There are quite frequent reports of systems failure and disappointments, which result in business losses to the organisation, a damaged external reputation if reported in the media, and a damaged reputation of the IT department internally, as senior executives lose their faith in the **IT function**'s ability to deliver business value from IT investments. Furthermore, senior executives are often puzzled and concerned by reports that their IT infrastructure is unable to accommodate business change and future development, that reasonably new investments are already considered to be obsolete and that integration issues (i.e. linking one system to another one so that data can be seamlessly exchanged and stored between the two systems) plague new initiatives, requiring costly fixes and causing delays to implementation. This situation must be of great concern given the potential value that can be derived from well-planned and executed IT initiatives.

Why does this occur? In some instances, the problem is created because senior business executives leave IT decisions to their CIO or senior IT managers. Perhaps this is because managers feel that they lack the necessary expertise and knowledge to be able to make good decisions regarding IT (they cannot decipher 'technobabble' and believe they need to know programming languages and network protocols in order to make good decisions), and they often feel inadequate when confronted with very technical proposals. Perhaps too there are historical factors, as the IT function was often created as a separate entity in organisations, and functional barriers serve to mean that IT activities get less scrutiny than other activities in the business, such as finance.

Developing the organisation-wide capabilities necessary to exploit the IT resource effectively must become a priority for organisations, as must putting in place the requisite governance mechanisms (principles, structures, processes and procedures) to ensure that IT investments deliver the anticipated benefits and value to the organisation while IT-related risks are managed appropriately. It is too important a risk for it to remain the preserve of technicians, and business managers must involve themselves in developing sound business cases for all IT investments. Understanding what constitutes good governance of IT and e-business-related investments is vital to business success in contemporary business environments.

Understanding IT governance

Closely allied to the concerns mentioned in the previous section about the ability of IT to deliver value to the business is the question of how best an organisation should organise and manage its IT function and the provision of IT services in order to enhance rather than hinder the achievement of business goals and objectives. **IT governance** is concerned with just this: it refers to the mechanisms (principles, processes, structures and procedures) that an organisation implements, institutionalises, monitors and controls in order to ensure that business value is derived from IT investments and that IT-related risks are appropriately managed (Korac-Kakabadse & Kakabadse 2001; IT Governance Institute 2001).

Shane, Lafferty & Beasley (1999) argue that the aim of effective IT governance is to ensure that IT is managed from an organisation-wide perspective so that it contributes to the achievement of enterprise goals and objectives. Taking this a little further, Korac-Kakabadse and Kakabadse (2001) suggest that IT governance concentrates on the 'relationships and processes to develop, direct and control IT resources in order to achieve the enterprise's goals through value adding contributions, which account for balancing risk versus return', The aims of IT governance thus become to direct all IT endeavours in the organisation and to develop a vision and strategic direction for IT, which ensures that IT objectives are achieved, that IT-related risks are identified and managed appropriately, and that an organisation's IT resources and capabilities are being exploited effectively and responsibly in order to deliver value to stakeholders in the organisation (IT Governance Institute 2001). Indeed, the IT Governance Institute (2001, p. 6) defines IT governance as 'the leadership, organisational structures and processes that ensure that the organisation's IT sustains and extends the organisation's strategies and objectives'. Implicit in these definitions and aims are the need for effective relationships to be built between IT and the rest of the business (Ward & Peppard 1996; Peppard & Ward 1999; Peppard 2001), the need for effective IT management processes to be established, and the need for IT structures and decision-making authorities to facilitate the effective exploitation of the IT resource in an organisation. Pivotal to effective IT governance is to ensure that IT's performance meets certain objectives, as follows:

- to enable and enhance the organisation by exploiting opportunities
- to be in alignment with enterprise objectives and to deliver anticipated benefits from IT investments
- to utilise IT resources and capabilities efficiently and effectively such that business value is delivered to the organisation

- to identify and manage IT-related risk effectively (IT Governance Institute 2001, p. 10).

Therefore it is our contention that good IT governance processes accomplish at least three broad objectives: they support an environment for the exercise and exploitation of IT resources and capabilities; they provide a framework for the fruitful exploration and explication of relationships between the IT function and the rest of the organisation; and they underpin a series of organisational routines and procedures through which the business value of IT is realised and IT risk contained.

Decision making about IT and e-business investments

A key part of IT governance revolves around ensuring that good decisions are made about the use of organisational resources on IT projects and initiatives. Decisions have to be made about a number of issues, including:

- high-level principles that will dictate and guide the use of IT throughout an organisation (referred to in chapter 3 as IT maxims)
- IT strategy and how it can be ensured that IT initiatives are well aligned and integrated with business imperatives and directions
- building a flexible and robust IT infrastructure to facilitate e-business initiatives, and to enable shared services throughout the enterprise to be delivered in a cost-effective manner
- required business applications, what is required and how it should be sourced and implemented
- how limited financial resources will be allocated to various competing IT initiatives to derive the best outcomes and value for the organisation (Weill & Woodham 2002, Broadbent 2002).

Good governance implies that structures are in place to ensure that these decisions are made by the people best qualified to make those assessments, and research suggests that not all IT decisions should be made at the same organisational level by the same people. Generally speaking, the more technical decisions relating to choice of IT infrastructure and architecture should be made by the **chief information officer** (CIO), supported by IT specialists, who are fully cognisant of the technical and business ramifications of decisions made. All other decisions, whenever there is an intersection between IT and the rest of the business, should be made through a coalition of the CIO and other **C-level managers** (chief executive officer (CEO), chief operations officer (COO), chief financial officer (CFO), etc), after contributions to the decisions have been sought by business unit managers, or process owners and the like (Weill & Woodham 2002).

Effective IT governance mechanisms

A number of structures, processes and relationships need to be built in order to ensure that IT and e-business initiatives ultimately deliver value to the organisation's stakeholders, including customers, suppliers, business network partners and so on. Some of these arrangements (Broadbent 2002) are discussed on the following page.

IT executive committees

'IT executive committees' are so named as they are generally made up of only the most senior managers in an organisation. These committees would therefore be composed of the CIO, CEO, COO, CFO and so on, and would report directly to the board of directors on significant IT matters. The executive committee would also take responsibility for developing sound governance processes for effective planning, monitoring and controlling of IT initiatives to ensure the delivery of benefits to the organisation.

Project management

Many organisations would also have a structure in place to ensure excellence in the management of IT projects. This might be initiated by a business projects office (a centralised mechanism for dealing with all business projects) or through sound procedures and mechanisms for ensuring good management and governance of all IT projects.

Capital approval committees

Capital approval committees might operate at the level of the business unit in an organisation, and would be charged with responsibility for making the initial approval for IT and e-business proposals. Before being checked by the executive committee, for example, any proposal would first have been approved by the capital approval committee. The approval process would involve checking that the proposal was directly relevant to the achievement of business goals and objectives and therefore directly related, aligned and integrated with business directions.

Relationship builders

Governance can also be affected through the building of deliberate and effective relationships between IT and the rest of the business. This can be left to happen informally, but many organisations are now preferring to appoint relationships managers who act as boundary riders between IT and business units.

Characteristics of good IT governance

Organisations that practise good governance of their IT and e-business initiatives tend to exhibit a number of important characteristics. Their IT strategies tend to be more focused and more overtly supportive of key business initiatives and drivers. These organisations have much clearer business objectives for their IT investments and, through sound structural and processual devices, ensure that relevant stakeholders are aware of those desired business objectives. It is the norm in these organisations for non-IT senior executives to be aware of the potential of IT and to be actively involved in its governance. Effective IT processes in terms of IT strategy formulation, **IT evaluation** and IT **benefits realisation** are formally established and well understood, and help to ensure that positive outcomes result from IT investments. In addition, this means there are fewer occurrences of 'cowboy' behaviour with respect to IT, meaning that IT projects are thoughtfully constructed and in alignment with business thrusts (Broadbent 2002).

IT governance processes

The IT Governance Institute (2001) provides a high-level view of some of the processes involved in good governance (see figure 12.1). Effective governance has as its starting point establishing objectives for the use of technology and for the IT function in an organisation. Included among these objectives would be statements and goals for the alignment of IT investments and activities with business directions and strategic objectives, namely:

- proactively seeking opportunities to exploit IT
- implementing processes to ensure that IT investments are adequately evaluated both pre- and post-investment, that anticipated benefits realised and that **IT risks** are identified and effectively managed
- ensuring that IT resources are responsibly used throughout the enterprise.

Resultant IT activities and investments would be geared towards seeking efficiencies for the organisation, increasing the effectiveness of the organisation through increased automation and building an infrastructure that supports not only current needs for IT services but also future growth and flexibility. IT activities need to be subject to scrutiny, and hence performance measures must be set and assessed against the objectives established for IT. This might necessitate some fine-tuning of the direction IT has been taking, which will be reflected in resultant IT activities. Thus, a loop of setting objectives, comparing performance against those objectives, and redirecting efforts and activities when necessary lies at the heart of an effective IT governance process.

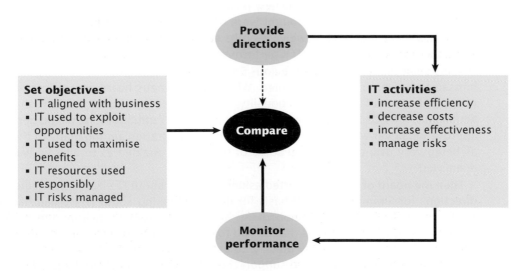

Figure 12.1 ▶ High-level view of effective governance processes

Source ▶ adapted from IT Governance Institute 2001.

In order to implement this high-level view of governance, organisations require a combination of principles that determine the way in which IT will be used in an organisation (IT Maxims — see Broadbent & Weill 1997), an integrated set of mechanisms or structures by which the locus of decision-making authority and responsibility is allocated in an organisation (see discussion on IT governance mechanisms previously in this chapter) (Weill & Woodham 2002), and a set of deliberate processes by which IT activity can be monitored and controlled, IT risks managed and the benefits from IT investments realised for the organisation (see figure 12.2).

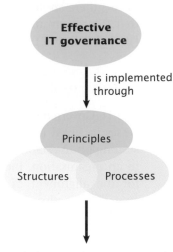

is implemented through

with the aim of monitoring and controlling IT investments and associated activities to ensure the delivery of business value from IT

Figure 12.2 ▶ Implementing IT governance in organisations

thinking strategically

Louis Pudelin set to sort out IT at Simmons

Simmons is a stockbroking firm, and it has just been through the process of replacing its CIO for perceived non-performance. Louis Pudelin has just been appointed as the new CIO. Before being offered the new position he was acquainted with the problems that Simmons' management thought were occurring with the previous CIO. It was made very clear that within twelve months senior executives and the board would expect a dramatic reversal of IT's performance and service provision.

Louis soon realised that the previous CIO, Mattheus Bernard, had actually believed himself to be very customer-oriented. Whenever Mattheus heard complaints or requests from staff for new functionality, IT and new systems, he would rush into action and, provided there were no requests for huge IT initiatives, he would generally approve whatever was requested. Mattheus had a reputation among many of the staff as being very user-oriented, and some of them were puzzled as to why he was dismissed.

Then the board of directors started asking Mattheus about IT visions, strategies and directions for Simmons and the basis for decision-making about IT. He had had to admit that he hadn't really developed any, he was just intent on meeting the requests of users. Louis Pudelin figured that he had to come up with some documentation and plans for the board reasonably quickly, to assure them that IT expenditure would be devoted to initiatives that would support the achievement of business objectives and to ensure that IT-related risk was managed appropriately. However, it seemed that he would need to put a lot into place to satisfy senior executives and board members.

Questions

1. What would you suggest that Louis attempt to do to improve the use and management of IT at Simmons?
2. What types of decision-making structures, mechanisms and processes should Louis recommend to the board? How would those structures help manage IT-related risk?
3. How would the articulation of business and IT maxims help to improve IT governance at Simmons?

The authors have undertaken research in large organisations to determine the relevant processes that organisations need to formally define, establish and implement in order to achieve good IT governance. It is not our view that these can be considered in compete isolation from the other aspects of governance (setting principles, establishing structures and mechanisms), so although our interest was on understanding the processes of governance, inevitably our discussions with managers took a more holistic perspective. Four important managerial actions were identified, which seemed pivotal to the successful exploitation of IT in an organisation, and from these, the associated IT governance processes that arguably would be necessary to monitor and ensure that IT management activities produced the desired and expected outcomes for the organisation were derived (see table 12.1).

Table 12.1 ▶ Key IT governance processes

IT managerial action	IT governance process
• Seek IT opportunities and align and embed IT with business strategy	**ALIGN** • Create and implement mechanisms that enable the planning of an optimal IS portfolio to ensure that strong alignment exists between business imperatives and IT investments
• Source and implement the portfolio of information system solutions necessary to optimally support the achievement of strategic business goals	**ACQUIRE** • Optimally source and procure business solutions and systems to enable the realisation of the IS portfolio
• Evaluate the performance of IT, particularly in terms of the delivery of business value, and manage IT-related risks	**EVALUATE** • Create and implement mechanisms to ensure that rigorous evaluation of IT is conducted to ensure that a compelling business case exists and that business benefits will be derived • Create and implement mechanisms to ensure that IT-related risks are correctly identified and appropriately managed and controlled
• Realise the benefits from IT investments	**BENEFIT** • Create and implement mechanisms that support the proactive realisation and ongoing management of benefits derived from IT investments

Ribbers, Peterson and Parker (2002) and Sambamurthy (2002) argue that in current competitive environments, IT governance needs to be based on lateral decision-making processes throughout the enterprise that, among other things, serve to integrate decision-making about IT into the day-to-day decision-making and action-taking behaviour of business. Ribbers, Peterson and Parker (2002, p. 1) note that 'organizations use a number of structural alternatives for IT governance...the question remains, however, what process mechanisms are required for IT governance in contemporary business environments.' If it is accepted that business success is inextricably linked to the ability to innovate using IT and to harness requisite IT capabilities on an organisation-wide basis, excellence in IT management and excellence in IT governance seem to be vital ingredients in the exploitation of IT for enhanced business performance.

Although the specific activities, processes and structures for overseeing and managing the acquisition of IT varied from organisation to organisation, in all organisations included in our research there emerged an interlinked pattern of IT governance processes of planning and alignment, acquisition (or procurement), evaluation and **benefits management**, which broadly can be associated with five main integrated phases of management activity in acquiring IT business solutions (see figure 12.3). These processes are the central or key IT governance processes that organisations need to establish in order to achieve an effective processual architecture for IT governance. Each of these key IT governance processes is briefly discussed below.

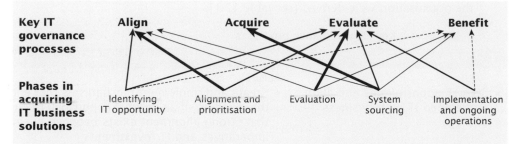

Figure 12.3 ▶ IT governance processes in action. Increased strength of relationships is indicated by darker and thicker lines.

▶ Phase 1: identifying IT opportunities

In all the organisations included in our research, CIOs were very clear on the need for any proposed IT investment to be demonstrably supportive of business goals and objectives and on the need for a compelling **business case** to be articulated before any IT investment would even be contemplated.

In all organisations, the ideas for IT investments in most circumstances originated either from the strategic business units (SBUs) or from joint interaction between IT and the SBUs, but did not arise from the IT department on its own. The only exception to this was in the case of IT infrastructure investment proposals, which were more likely to have originated within the IT department (Weill & Woodham 2002). However, the IT department was involved in the very early stages in the development of initial ideas. Thus, the initiation of IT investments is now regarded as a business responsibility, and the development of the early business case is seen also as a responsibility of the SBU, although the IT department does provide support and assistance in this process, particularly in terms of what is feasible, practicable and 'doable' in terms of the organisation's current IT infrastructure, IT skill set and existing IT capabilities. The output of this first phase is an initial business case for a specific IT investment proposal, which has been through some preliminary identification of anticipated costs and business benefits. Sponsorship for the proposal from within the business unit must have been identified.

Phase 2: alignment and prioritisation

Once an SBU believes it has built a compelling business case and a sponsor for the project has been identified, typically organisations then require the proposal to be scrutinised by a higher-level entity or committee, usually associated with strategic planning. This might be some sort of steering committee, it might be conducted within the corporate strategy department, or it might be an independent business project office, but all reported some higher-level scrutiny of the SBU proposals. Very large proposals could go to the board for scrutiny. All the CIOs interviewed reported formal IT planning processes and mechanisms in their organisations, with the typical planning cycle being one year (with a three- to five-year time frame). However, these plans and strategies were subject to more frequent reviews, often three- or six-monthly, whereby business goals, objectives and priorities were re-evaluated and then IT initiatives re-evaluated in the light of possibly changing business initiatives. It was during this process of strategic planning and review that new proposals for IT investments were considered. Very careful scrutiny of each proposal is conducted to ensure that any resultant IT investment would be aligned and consistent with strategic business imperatives and that responsibilities for costs and the delivery of business benefits was clearly identified. Sensitivity to IT projects failing to deliver on business benefits and exceeding budgets was evident, and attempts had been made in all organisations in our sample to effect governance mechanisms to try to prevent costly (and damaging public) failures with IT projects.

Projects that survived this process were those that could clearly be shown to be aligned with business goals and objectives. Successful initiatives were then prioritised on the basis of the extent to which they were seen to be directly related to key business initiatives and according to their perceived ability to deliver value to the business. For large initiatives (say, those project proposals in excess of $500 000), the organisations in our sample were on average willing to spend between $20 000 and $30 000 to get to the point of proceeding with or killing off the initiative.

Phase 3: evaluation

At this stage, successful projects were typically exposed to more rigorous cost–benefit analysis and the like. Thus, although the projects surviving to phase 3 were seen as aligned with business strategy, yet more rigorous assessment of the costs and the likely benefits was considered necessary. One CIO interviewed described this scrutiny as 'applying a blowtorch to investment proposals'. Typical of the sentiments expressed are the words of one manager who said, 'We don't like surprises.' The CIOs were very aware of the apparent ease with which IT projects could get out of control and hence were careful in conducting rigorous investigation and analysis to prevent this wherever possible. Again, it was not uncommon with very large projects (say, more than $1 000 000) for perhaps $200 000–$300 000 to be spent in refining and confirming the project's scope, its costs and its likely benefits.

At this phase, risk profiles were developed for all projects, as risk management was seen as one key aspect of successful project implementations. It was not generally the case that high-risk projects were given lower priorities or abandoned, but rather that higher risk projects needed to deliver greater benefits to the business and hence additional efforts to ensure the realisation of those benefits was essential.

All the CIOs interviewed expressed concerns with their ability to deal effectively with intangible business benefits during these detailed attempts to evaluate proposals. Generally speaking, they did not try to allocate dollar values to intangibles, but this did mean that there was still considerable uncertainty as to the benefit or value associated with particular initiatives. Concerns were also expressed about the time required to realise benefits: costs were generally easier to identify and were largely experienced early in the life of the system, whereas benefits often took some time to be realised. Another factor in the delivery of benefits had to do with business change: some CIOs felt that during the six to twelve months typically required to deliver a project, business change was likely to have occurred, which reduced the possibility of benefits being realised as business assumptions and requirements had changed. The CIOs also commented that it was often difficult to attribute benefits solely to IT: hence benefits were often derived from business change initiatives, of which IT was just one component, and therefore being specific about the benefits realised from just the IT component of that change was extremely difficult to articulate with any precision. The usual problems of enthusiastic project sponsors overstating benefits and understating costs were evident in most of the organisations interviewed.

Projects at this stage were still subject to being terminated. Many of the CIOs stated that if considerable doubts still existed about the ability of the organisation to implement a viable system, then they would have no hesitation in cancelling the project at this stage.

Phase 4: system sourcing

Phase 4 saw the acquisition of the system, with CIOs facing the dilemmas of the build versus buy dichotomy. Thus systems could be sourced through an in-house development project, but more often it involved procuring packages and customising them to suit in-house business processes, possibly from a number of different vendors. Customisation was sometimes done in-house, but at other times it was left to the software vendor or a recognised consultant to do.

In five of the six organisations interviewed for this research, the 'buy' model was the preferred, but not the sole, approach. The reason stated for this was that generally packaged software was seen as a cheaper option, it was seen as more predictable, and it generally took less time to implement a working system. In the sixth organisation where the norm was to develop systems in-house, and in the other five organisations in those cases where they decided to build in-house rather than buy software, there were a number of compelling reasons why this was done. First, CIOs reported that peculiarities of their business sometimes meant that purchasing systems were not appropriate. Many could identify business circumstances and processes that meant that available software packages were a very poor fit. For example, one CIO had implemented an ERP package, but found that the production and manufacturing module simply did not suit their industry-specific production processes. Consequently their production control system and the like were developed in-house, or alternative modules were sourced from another software company, and interfaces and integration issues were dealt with in-house. Others, particularly those associated with the finance and insurance sectors, argued that packages sourced from vendors based in the USA, for example, did not fit adequately with the Australian business environment, specifically Australian tax laws and regulatory requirements. The third reason stated for preferring in-house development occurred when there was heavy IT involvement in the product/service mix of the company. For example, in the insurance and financial sectors, CIOs reported that IT support and enablement could no longer be separated from the company's products and services. In such cases, in-house development was often the preferred approach.

Irrespective of the build or procure decision, ongoing evaluation and scrutiny of the acquisition process was the norm during phase 4. All organisations reported rigorous governance structural mechanisms for their major IT projects. The specifics varied but essentially involved either regular reviews by a steering committee or the involvement of a business project office that oversaw the progress of each IT project. Although the evaluation conducted in phase 3 had typically sorted out suspect projects, it was not impossible for a project to be terminated at phase 4 if the entities charged with overseeing the projects felt that costs were escalating, business benefits were less likely to be realised or the business need was changing and so on.

Many of the CIOs attributed these structural and processual aspects of governance to reducing the number of runaway projects. The CIOs acknowledged that not all projects were implemented on time and within budget, but did feel that careful management of the project from a business perspective has delivered much better results for their organisations. Most stated that now between 60 and 80 per cent of projects were on time and between about 70 and 80 per cent were within budget, both figures having shown substantial improvements in recent years.

Phase 5: implementation and ongoing operations

Some CIOs described a rigorous process of post-implementation reviews, driven by the business sponsors of the project, with some inputs from IT. Part of this was a review of typical measures of project management success (on time, within budget, to specification and quality requirements). By contrast, some managers felt that extensive post-implementation reviews consumed resources that were needed elsewhere, and another admitted that although they were important, post-implementation reviews were not routinely done. However, many of the CIOs interviewed typically recognised the perhaps more important requirement to assess the delivery of business benefits (i.e. were the systems, once implemented, actually realising the benefits identified pre-investment for the business?). A few in our sample organisations had pro-active benefits management processes in place, but most conceded that this was an important area in which they needed to improve, and some were concerned about the resources required to undertake such a benefits realisation process. The issue being grappled with here is that, as CIOs, they felt torn between the potential to derive greater benefits from the existing investments and diverting resources to exploiting other IT opportunities. Interestingly, our CIOs tended to adopt the satisficing position (i.e. that delivering, say, 80 per cent of expected benefits was probably good enough and that the resources consumed in trying to achieve 100 per cent or more would be better diverted elsewhere).

The CIOs in this study were aware of proactive benefits realisation. They were aware that looking to enabling business changes and activities such as motivating users to use the system involved by appropriate recognition and reward mechanisms, changing organisational roles and responsibilities, awareness raising regarding the organisational logic and rationale of the systems and so on, could help to achieve business benefits, particularly if these activities were carried out according to some more effective and logical plan of attack. However, the interviewees admitted that this aspect of governance was not well established, and that they had not established an effective process of benefits realisation as part of the accepted routines of the organisation. Such benefits realisation activities as did occur were owing to the initiative and thoughtfulness of the particular project manager and not to a formal established process being accepted as part of the organisational environment.

Importance of relationships in effective IT governance

Despite the importance of IT and e-business to most contemporary organisations, often IT is not well regarded by senior executives, and at times a fractious relationship can exist between IT and the rest of the business. However, from the previous discussion, it seems apparent that the CIO is a key determinant in the effective exploitation of the IT resource, and hence it seems reasonable to argue that a sound relationship needs to exist between the CIO, as representative of IT in the organisation, and senior executives and SBU managers, as key consumers of IT services and arbiters of IT performance.

Despite the advances of IT and e-business, concerns are being voiced about the value derived from IT expenditures and whether organisations are achieving an acceptable payoff from their considerable investments (Willcocks 1996). For example, the literature reports repeated findings of the failure of IT to deliver the anticipated business benefits (Thorp 1998; Ward, Taylor & Bond 1996). However, there are conflicting findings in the research (Willcocks 1996; Willcocks & Lester 1999), and considerable doubts have been expressed about the efficacy of existing, explicit measures and measurement frameworks of the value of IT (van der Zee 2002). The problem compounds as the types of value associated with IT investment become associated more with revenue increase and other more esoteric benefits rather than cost displacement (Keen 1991), and hence business benefits tend to be more intangible, less direct and more interwoven and diffused among a range of organisational activities. Indeed, as the pervasiveness and mobility of IT investments increase, this problem is likely to increase rather than diminish.

Peppard, Lambert and Edwards (2000) note that when IT 'disappoints' and there is uncertainty among management as to its benefits and value to the organisation, the dominant perspective in the literature attributes these shortcomings to the IT function. Remedies therefore are also sought in the IT function, and the notion of value creation from IT investments is thus also attached to the IT function. When this is coupled with a techno-centric view of IT (i.e. the view that technology itself can deliver business value), then the 'remedies' are, in all likelihood, going to further disappoint with few desired organisational impacts and business benefits. There is a view, however, that internal organisational processes and activities are key determinants of the delivery of value from IT investments, rather than the technology itself (Tallon, Kraemer & Gurbaxani 2000) and that the access to information and knowledge that is facilitated via IT and the ways information and IT are used to accomplish tasks, goals and objectives are essential ingredients in the overall value creation process. Thinking from an organisational perspective (i.e. that information and IT are corporate resources and therefore need to be managed along with other valuable corporate resources, rather than being seen as falling exclusively within the preserve of the IT function) therefore seems vital if IT is to be effectively utilised to support the achievement of organisational goals and deliver value to the organisation. Developing the organisation-wide capabilities necessary to exploit the IT resource effectively must then become a priority for organisations, as must putting in place the requisite governance mechanisms (principles, structures, processes and procedures) to ensure that IT investments deliver the anticipated benefits and value to the organisation while IT-related risks are managed appropriately.

A number of reasons can be posited as to why there are concerns and perceptions of an inadequate rate of return on investment in IT. First, it could be that there has been an inappropriate investment in and use of information, IS and IT in organisations and hence concerns about the value of such investments. One often-cited example of this stems from a failure to link IT investments with business objectives and strategy initiatives (Edwards, Ward & Bytheway 1995; Hochstrasser & Griffiths 1991). Alternatively, it could be symptomatic of a lack of business and/or IT planning or ineffective planning. Over time, a failure to achieve alignment of IT strategies and business strategies could be argued to contribute to disappointing perceptions of IT's contribution to business performance. Second, it could be that current evaluation processes are either inadequate (or non-existent in some organisations) or that inappropriate evaluation techniques are being used (Willcocks & Lester 1997). Perhaps a lack of confidence in the tools available leads to less than satisfactory practices. Third, it could also be that an inadequate rate of return on IT investments arises because managerial procedures put in place to ensure the realisation of benefits from IT are not adequate (Ward, Taylor & Bond 1996; Remenyi, Money & Twite 1993). Expected benefits are nearly always identified pre-investment for new systems and technology, but rarely is proactive behaviour adopted and changes made to support the post-implementation realisation and evaluation of these anticipated benefits (Thorp 1998). Fourth, inadequate IT governance structures and processes could lead to disappointing outcomes and perceptions of a gap between IT and the rest of the organisation (Ward & Peppard 1996; Peppard & Ward 1999). Hence building sound relationships between IT and the rest of the business is at the heart of fully utilising the IT resource for strategic benefits.

Research suggests that the CIO plays a vital role in determining the perceptions of non-IT managers about IT in an organisation, and therefore the CIO is essential to ensuring that senior executives appreciate the contribution of IT and e-business to their organisation and are supportive of major IT initiatives (Earl & Feeny 1994; Feeny, Edwards & Simpson 1992). CIOs need to focus on developing dialogues with senior managers in order to better understand the business, its strategic drivers, likely future scenarios and so on. Understanding this means that the CIO and the IT department can ensure the relevance of IT initiatives and activities to the achievement of key business goals. Getting the dialogue started depends somewhat on the position of the CIO in the organisational hierarchy, and therefore the CEO is well advised to put the CIO on the senior executive committee, thus demonstrating to all the importance of IT and the regard with which the CIO is held in the organisation. This also aids in the formation of informal alliances, relationships and networks between the CIO and key business executives.

CIOs are thus better positioned to talk informally to executives about the role and success of IT in other situations: for example, the CIO might describe a highly successful e-business initiative, which could be emulated in his/her organisation to achieve similar successes. CIOs must be sure that other senior executives know about and understand the performance of IT and its role in and contribution to business success, as this helps to build a shared vision for IT among organisational units. Thus, the CEO behaving as though IT were central to the enterprise, not an adjunct, and the CIO behaving as though business imperatives and needs are central to and the most important focus of IT operations and investments, will more likely lead to the existence of a strong relationship and the achievement of better outcomes for the organisation from its IT investments.

The importance of evaluation of IT investments

Evaluating IT investments is concerned with attempting to figure out how well a particular investment is meeting expectations, objectives and needs (Farbey, Land & Targett 1999; Hirschheim & Smithson 1987). It involves using quantitative and qualitative means to establish whether IT is delivering value to an organisation (Willcocks 1992). IT evaluation is important for a number of reasons, not the least of which is the concern frequently voiced by senior executives that they are unsure whether their IT expenditure is benefiting the business and are uncertain whether the organisation is achieving a reasonable return on investment (ROI) from IT. When one considers that IT accounts for about 45 per cent of all investments by large organisations (Devaraj & Kohli 2002) (in certain industries this figure is closer to 50 per cent); (van der Zee 2002), then it seems reasonable to assert that evaluating that investment for the purposes of ensuring that value is being created for stakeholders is important. Evaluation is therefore necessary pre-investment in order to justify large-scale expenditure on IT initiatives, including essential IT projects, IT infrastructures needed to create the building blocks for the rest of the organisation, and for strategic IT initiatives that might affect the competitive position of the organisation or the way it interacts with its customers, for example. Post-implementation, evaluation should play a key role in establishing whether the system is contributing adequately to business performance and that it is meeting the objectives established for the investment and delivering benefits to the business. In addition, increasingly IT is not a stand-alone venture but should be regarded as a part of large business change initiatives, and hence evaluation becomes an important tool in justifying and assessing the contribution of IT to those broader business initiatives.

However, it is far from clear that traditional accounting measures such as cost–benefit analysis and return on investment are adequate to provide an accurate assessment of the contribution of IT to the business. Difficulties in establishing the value of IT have given rise to one of the great conundrums of modern business, known as the productivity paradox (Willcocks & Lester 1999). Intuitively, most people feel that IT makes us more productive, enables us to be more efficient at work, and so on. On a case-by-case basis, there have been spectacular successes from using IT to increase throughputs, for example, which might lead to productivity increases. However, when one considers overall economic performance, IT does not consistently seem to result in productivity increases. For example, figures cited by *The Economist* (1999) suggest that from 1960 to 1973, at a time when there was comparatively less investment in IT than currently, productivity increased by an average of 4.5 per cent per annum. Productivity increased by only 1.5 per cent per annum between 1973 and 1995 in spite of greatly increased investment in IT during that period. For many of us, this is counterintuitive. Part of the dilemma can be explained by considering the move from an industrially based economy to a service-based economy. If an organisation is manufacturing cars, for example, measuring inputs against outputs is relatively easy to do. However, consider healthcare services. Defining the services offered, identifying all the inputs and outputs, specifying required levels of service quality and so on becomes very complex and intricate. It is also much harder to identify a direct link between inputs, outputs and outcomes. IT generally falls into the service category when it comes to evaluation.

Besides the challenges previously identified, there are a number of other possible explanations for the productivity paradox. Some argue that long learning curves accompany the introduction of any new technology, citing the changes that came with the Industrial Revolution and the introduction of electricity into factories as examples where forty to fifty years of learning was required before organisations effectively utilised these changes and derived substantial benefits from them (*The Economist* 1999; David 1990). This might suggest that we have still much to learn about how to utilise IT efficiently and effectively in organisations. There has been a tendency to computerise existing processes and practices without fundamentally altering ways of working and utilising information. E-commerce might indeed be a driving force in recognising new possibilities in this regard as a result of technological innovation.

Second, the productivity paradox might be explained by rather uneven results with respect to IT, whereby gains achieved from IT in one system are offset by losses occurred by poor practices elsewhere. For example, very few organisations can claim that they have never lost money or had a 'disaster' with respect to IT. Thus gains achieved from, say, computerising their supply chain might be offset by losses incurred through an unsuccessful CRM implementation, for example. Allied to this might be questionable management practices and employee behaviour with respect to IT. For example, the ease of word-processing and printing could encourage the production of multiple, almost identical versions of documents and spending excessive time on formatting and refinements that do not add to quality and certainly do not contribute to increased productivity, and so on. It can be concluded that, given the apparent difficulty of establishing the value of IT and the unevenness of research findings in this area, the value that IT contributes varies enormously from organisation to organisation. Thus an organisation's managerial practices with respect to IT seem to have a substantial influence on the overall effectiveness of IT and its contribution to that organisation and therefore its value (Tallon, Kraemer & Gurbaxani 2000).

It appears that achieving alignment between IT and business initiatives is imperative if IT is to deliver value to the organisation. Hence, in achieving value, it is imperative that clear objectives for IT — derived overtly and directly from business objectives — exist and are implemented via effective management practice and effective IT governance. Establishing a good working relationship between the CIO and other senior executives is vital if a clear understanding of business imperatives is to be achieved and translated into IT initiatives. Some studies suggest that a federal approach to IT structures and decision-making (with some centralised controls but localised flexibility) is also important to achieving better ROI for IT (Broadbent 2002; Earl et al. 1996). Attention to matters of quality is vital, as is the re-engineering of processes so that IT can be fully exploited to achieve greater efficiencies and effectiveness gains for the organisation. Benchmarking is another way of ensuring good management practices with respect to IT. For example considerations of IT expenditure levels against other similar organisations provides one indication of organisational performance, but a more detailed analysis of the structure of IT costs (the proportions spent on hardware, software, consultancies and so on) could also indicate where and how improvements could be made. The perceptions of end-users and managers as to the effectiveness of IT might also give insights into IT's performance. Hence attending to issues of IT management practice (including the evaluation of IT and the realisation of anticipated IT benefits) and IT governance are pivotal to the derivation of IT value in an organisation.

Issues and difficulties in IT evaluation

In the 1960s and early 1970s, the prime role of IT was to automate routine information processing and, in so doing, often head count reductions were achieved in basic clerical jobs. Thus, in some early IT systems, it was evident that the implementation of the system had resulted in obvious and measurable head count reductions, and hence calculating ROI or cost–benefit analyses was relatively easy. However, with rapid advances in IT capabilities, and changes in the role of IT in organisations, accurate evaluation has become much more problematic. It is more difficult to assess the effects of systems designed to improve customer service or influence marketplaces, as there are so many more intervening variables that might have affected the influence of the IT investment. This problem becomes even more evident as IT is used to link the supply chain or to change the structure of industries, as the driver of organisational innovation and as an integrator across trading networks. Hence costs and benefits have to be tracked across functional and organisational boundaries. Furthermore, the nature of benefits derived from IT investments (and hence also organisational expectations of IT) are changing, from efficiency and effectiveness gains within functional areas to embrace the benefits of competitive advantage achieved through changing the relative powers of players within an industry, cooperative advantage achieved through the successful formation of strategic business alliances and trading networks, through to providing better support for decision-making through the timely delivery of sophisticated analyses of vast amounts of corporate data, knowledge management and the like.

Evaluation and management practice must now consider the costs and benefits that are derived from organisational transformation initiatives in which IT plays a key role. This IT evaluation becomes more important (as expenditure on IT increases rapidly) but simultaneously also more difficult, as the effects of IT become increasingly intangible and interwoven with a host of organisational change initiatives into the fabric of the organisation. ROI techniques and cost–benefit analyses are reasonably effective evaluation tools when the prime purpose of IT investments is to reduce costs or increase throughputs, but finding tools and techniques that are adequate for organisation-wide, often intangible benefits, such as competitive or cooperative advantage, diversification and innovation, and the like, has proved extremely problematic.

Approaches to IT evaluation

Despite the importance of evaluation to the recognition of IT's contribution to the business, research suggests that, all too often, evaluation is not given sufficient attention. For example Ward and Peppard (2002) cite studies that found that only about 50 per cent of IT projects were subjected to any rigorous pre-investment evaluation, and of these only about 50 per cent used a recognised financial appraisal technique. Often evaluation proved to be inadequate, and businesses were frequently unaware of whether they were deriving benefits from their IT investments. Of the financial appraisal techniques in use, techniques based on return on investment and cost–benefit analysis are the most common. There are too many approaches for them all to receive adequate coverage in this chapter. Rather, a few select ones will be briefly considered, and interested readers can follow up by referring to specified readings at the end of the chapter.

Return on investment

All return on investment (ROI) techniques are premised on the idea that over time all investments should yield a positive return (in other words, the utility or benefits they provide should outweigh their costs). ROI approaches work reasonably well when evaluating IT investments that are expected either to generate direct savings or to generate direct benefits. Direct is an important word here, and it means that literally: the effect of the system must be a reduction in head count following the automation of routine work, for example, or enabling a task to be performed much more quickly, such as point-of-sale scanning devices in supermarkets, where there is a direct increase in speed over the traditional machines, which required the cost of an item to be entered manually. In cases where there is a direct saving or direct benefit, then estimates of savings and/or benefits can be either demonstrated (and hence measured reasonably accurately) or accurately calculated, and there is relatively low uncertainty regarding the outcomes.

However, ROI does not work as well when it is difficult to express benefits and savings in cash flow terms, or when there is considerable uncertainty about estimates and calculations, which is often the case when intangible benefits are involved (Farbey, Land & Targett 1999).

Cost–benefit analysis

Cost–benefit analysis (C/B) analysis is an attempt to overcome some of the limitations of ROI, in that it does attempt to overcome the problem of valuing intangibles by providing the ability to identify surrogate measures for intangible benefits. So, for example, if a proposed investment is argued to increase job satisfaction through improved easy access to data, then surrogate measures for increased satisfaction might be a reduced turnover in staff, a reduction in recruitment and training costs, and the like. Cost–benefit analysis is an improvement in situations where many of the benefits from IT are intangible, and it is particularly useful where there is agreement among the management team on the surrogate measures used. When there is uncertainty about the surrogate measures, or on the intrinsic value of intangible benefits, this approach proves to be much more problematic. It is also of concern when there is uncertainty surrounding the realisation of these intangible benefits (Farbey, Land & Targett 1999).

Investment mapping

Other approaches are geared more towards building shared understanding of the value of IT or in generating a dialogue about the direction of IT initiatives. 'Investment mapping' (Peters 1994) might be classified as one such approach (see figure 12.4). Investment mapping broadly looks at the purpose or orientation of investments (to build infrastructure, to improve business processes or to influence the market in some way) against the types of benefits expected from the investment (enhanced productivity, risk reduction or business expansion). Proposed IT investments can then be mapped against proposed initiatives based on business strategy. If alignment has been achieved between IT and business initiatives, the considerable overlap of the mapping would be expected. Thus figure 12.4 would suggest a situation in which poor alignment had been achieved.

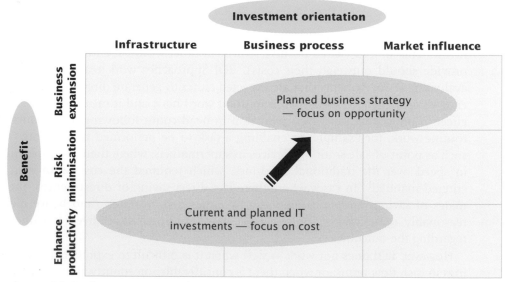

Figure 12.4 ▶ Investment mapping
Source ▶ Willcocks 1994, p. 369.

Information economics

Developed by Parker, Benson and Trainor (1988), information economics (IE) is an attempt to cover a much broader range of issues than can be accommodated by purely financial metrics like ROI and C/B. Proponents of information economics argue that the value derived from IT is made up of a composite of benefits from financial measures, the benefits associated with the impact of the IT on the business domain, and improvements made within the technology domain itself (see figure 12.5). A weighted factors analysis approach is used to put ratings and weightings on the relative contribution and importance of various items within each of those three domains. Factors and objectives considered important by managers can be built into the IE model, and the ratings and weightings used reflect managerial concerns and beliefs about the importance of particular elements. The weighted factors analysis incorporated into IE allows for sensitivity analysis to be conducted, and it can allow for the influence of different ratings and weightings to be computed and noted. Specifically for e-commerce, Avram (2001) suggested that another dimension needed to be built into IE, that of customer value. Research in this area is continuing.

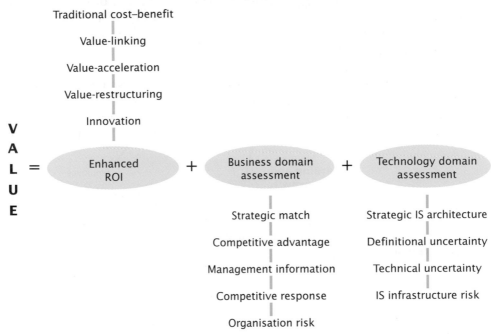

Figure 12.5 ▶ Information economics
Source ▶ Willcocks 1994, p. 376.

Balanced scorecard

The balanced scorecard (BSC) (Kaplan & Norton 2001) rejects the idea that ROI and financial metrics are the only ones important in organisations, arguing instead that investing in people, skills and capabilities, creating databases and so on are all absolutely essential for the future success of the organisation. Thus the BSC offers a series

of interlinked measures that are derived from both short-term operational requirements and long-term vision and strategy (see figure 12.6). Furthermore, the BSC in
fact recognises that financial measures are lagging indicators, meaning that problems
have already occurred when they are reflected in financial figures. Therefore a combination of lagging and leading indicators provides management with a better sense of
how an organisation is really performing (Dutta & Manzoni 1999). More recently, van
Grembergen (2003) has attempted to use the BSC to show the multifarious effects
and benefits of IT investments, and this provides a promising new approach to the
effective evaluation of IT investments.

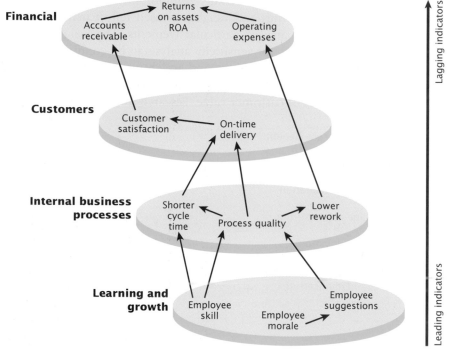

Figure 12.6 ▶ The logic of the balanced scorecard
Source ▶ Dutta and Manzoni 1999, p. 215.

Managing the realisation of e-business benefits

It might be that an inadequate rate of return on IT investments arises because
adequate managerial procedures to ensure the realisation of benefits from IT are not
put in place (Ward & Peppard 2002; Remenyi, Money & Twite 1993). Expected
benefits are nearly always identified pre-investment for new systems and technology,
but rarely is proactive behaviour adopted and changes made to support the post-
implementation realisation and evaluation of these anticipated benefits (Thorp 1998).
So a formal benefits management process, one that ensures that anticipated benefits

identified pre-investment are actually realised post-implementation, might be necessary (Ward, Taylor & Bond 1996). The challenge for managers, then, is to identify upfront the costs and benefits of an IT project and to attempt to quantify these benefits so that the feasibility of the project can be assessed. But post-implementation, it is essential that the effect of changes brought about by the introduction of IT are evaluated so that it can be determined whether benefits are being realised and then managerial actions planned to ensure that they are. Thus, evaluation is required throughout the life of any particular system or technology, but the nature of the evaluation is likely to change at various stages as the focus changes from anticipating benefits to realising benefits (see figure 12.7).

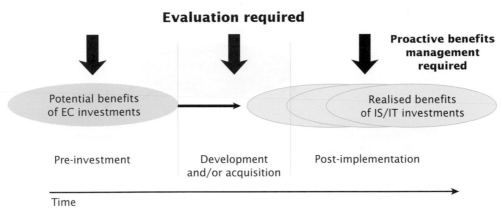

Evaluation required

Figure 12.7 ▶ Ongoing evaluation of IT investments

Comparatively few formal approaches are available for the proactive management of benefits (Thorp 1998 and Remenyi, Money & Twite 1993 are exceptions). One of the more generic approaches is offered by Ward, Taylor and Bond (1996), who proposed a process model for benefits realisation (see figure 12.8, p. 352). We argue that benefits realisation should not be left to chance but rather should be managed more carefully via a structured approach running in parallel with the acquisition of IT investments. The approach recognises five stages with possible iterations.

During the first stage, the potential benefits from an IT investment are identified and attempts made to identify suitable business measures (both financial and non-financial) by which these can be quantified. At this stage it is also vital to understand the interconnections between the technology and the effects it will have, the changes to the business and the business objectives for the particular investment proposed. During stage 2, specific responsibilities for realising the benefits are allocated, and required business changes necessary for benefits to be realised are identified and planned for. In addition, the time scale in which the benefits will accrue is identified. Stage 2 also considers costs, as the total cost of an IT project involves not only the IT development/acquisition and ongoing operations costs but also costs of business change, training and so on. In stage 3, the plan is executed along with the implementation of the new IS/IT. The measures identified in stage 1 are now used to review the effects of the implementation, with emphasis being placed on the benefits associated with business-technology change, not on traditional measures of project management success. The results of the implemented benefits plan are reviewed in stage 4, and opportunities for realising additional benefits are noted. Benefits not achieved are reviewed, and recommendations are made to improve the situation. Negative effects of the new implementation, or disbenefits, are also identified, and actions are taken to remedy the problems caused. Learning from successes and failures at this stage is also valued, and in stage 5, the potential for further benefits to be achieved is considered, possibly resulting in changes to measures and so on (Ward, Taylor & Bond 1996).

The emphasis of this approach is not on project management success nor on technological accomplishment, but is solely focused on the proactive identification and management of business benefits from IT investments, arguing that this is more likely to be achieved if systematically planned for rather than being left somewhat to chance.

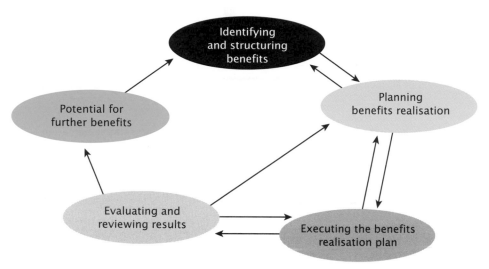

Figure 12.8 ▶ The benefits management process model
Source ▶ Ward and Peppard 2002, p. 442.

Benefits management is practised by some large successful organisations, but it is the contention of the authors that too often the realisation of benefits is not adequately performed in many organisations. This might contribute to executive perceptions that IT is not delivering on the value it promises in many instances.

The IT evaluation and benefits management lifecycle

There are at least three key issues that will impact on perceptions of the value of IT investments:

- that appropriate levels of business and IT planning are undertaken, with the express aim of ensuring that proposals and priorities for IT investment are aligned with corporate visions, strategies and objectives (see chapter 3)

- that wide-ranging, qualitative and quantitative evaluation procedures and techniques to assess performance on a range of measures are adopted throughout the lifecycle of IT, and that the outcomes of this evaluation are actively fed into managerial decision-making and action about ongoing investment in that IT
- that organisations implement explicit procedures to ensure that adequate pre-investment consideration of benefits anticipated from IT is undertaken and, more importantly, that after implementation of that IT, procedures are put in place deliberately to ensure that anticipated benefits are actively realised and managed over time (see figure 12.9).

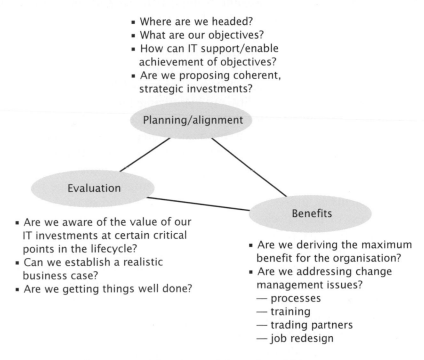

- Where are we headed?
- What are our objectives?
- How can IT support/enable achievement of objectives?
- Are we proposing coherent, strategic investments?

Planning/alignment

Evaluation

Benefits

- Are we aware of the value of our IT investments at certain critical points in the lifecycle?
- Can we establish a realistic business case?
- Are we getting things well done?

- Are we deriving the maximum benefit for the organisation?
- Are we addressing change management issues?
  — processes
  — training
  — trading partners
  — job redesign

Figure 12.9 ▶ Broadening considerations of the value of IT

This section will briefly describe and analyse a framework to achieve adequate linkage between IT planning, evaluation of investments on an ongoing basis, and the active realisation of benefits to the organisation over time. This framework is called the IT Evaluation and Benefits Management Lifecycle (McKay & Marshall 2001), and it shows how to integrate planning, evaluation and benefits management activities. It is argued that this mix of planning, evaluation and benefits management is vital, as each of these components adopts a somewhat different (albeit important) focus, and the position adopted in this chapter reflects our belief in a need to meld or simultaneously juggle these three perspectives if the IT resource is to be more effectively utilised. Procedures for the active realisation of the benefits from IT investments should, together with procedures for the evaluation of such investments, be built into the routines and rituals of organisations, thus enabling an informed adaptive response to the problems of achieving ongoing value from IT investments.

Strategic planning and thinking about IT therefore support finding answers for — or at least contemplating — key questions about business directions, objectives and considerations of how IT can either support or enable the achievement of objectives and of whether a suite of coherent, strategic investments in IT is being proposed. Evaluation of IT enables greater certainty as to the 'value' of IT investments, and by extending the evaluation process throughout the system's lifecycle, the dynamic nature of the worth of IT can be established and therefore managed. Establishing a sound business case for new and continuing investments is an important concern of evaluation. In managing benefits, our concern focuses more on harnessing potential benefits, ensuring that they become realised benefits and, in so doing, recognising that the realisation of benefits needs to be considered in the context of a raft of organisational change initiatives. Our conviction is that management thinking and routine practice needs to link these sometimes disparate activities.

How does this work in practice? The first step in our integrated approach involves establishing strategic alignment between proposed IT investments and business strategy, assessing initial feasibility, and identifying and structuring benefits. Arguably, bi-directional flows and relationships exist here (see figure 12.10 (a)). Thus, demonstrably close alignment between business strategy and IT initiatives is likely to enhance perceptions of potential benefits from IT investments and therefore improve the likelihood that the project feasibility can be securely grounded in a strong business case. By contrast, doubts about feasibility might encourage reconsideration of potential benefits or, indeed, the extent of alignment and so on.

This process of proactively 'flickering' between notions of achievement of objectives, possible benefits, possible costs and risk arguably supports the prioritisation of a suite of potential investments, which must, in turn, be subjected to a more comprehensive feasibility study. Feasibility will be impacted one way or the other as understandings of potential benefits are enhanced, with the potential existing that heightened sensitivity with respect to benefits could affect priorities for investments. Fluidity in investigating, considering and reviewing information regarding priorities, feasibility and expected benefits is expected (see figure 12.10 (a) and (b)).

Assuming that a 'go' decision is reached, the process of systems analysis (including the establishment of requirements) and design must proceed (arguably irrespective of whether a 'develop' or 'buy and tailor' decision is reached). Systems development (used here to include a 'buy' option) is itself a fluid process, and therefore design decisions and changes need to be reviewed against whether alignment with business objectives has been undesirably affected (the problem of scope creep), whether decisions and changes affect expected benefits positively or negatively and therefore whether feasibility is in any sense compromised (see figure 12.10 (c)).

The IT investment must go through a process of implementation and testing, ultimately with the aim of becoming a fully operational system. A variety of perspectives or measures need to be adopted to enhance management of the realisation and delivery of business benefits, to answer questions of the business impact and technical quality of an investment, ultimately leading to making decisions about the future of the investment (e.g. should we continue to maintain the system? Does it need to be enhanced in order to continue to support the achievement of business objectives? Should it be replaced? Would it be beneficial to outsource its operations?). Any concerns about the impact on business, technical quality and/or a failure to deliver continuous benefits might well result in 'outsourcing' or 'replace' decisions. This in turn implies a need for renewed planning and assessment of the business requirements and drivers to take place (see figure 12.10 (d)).

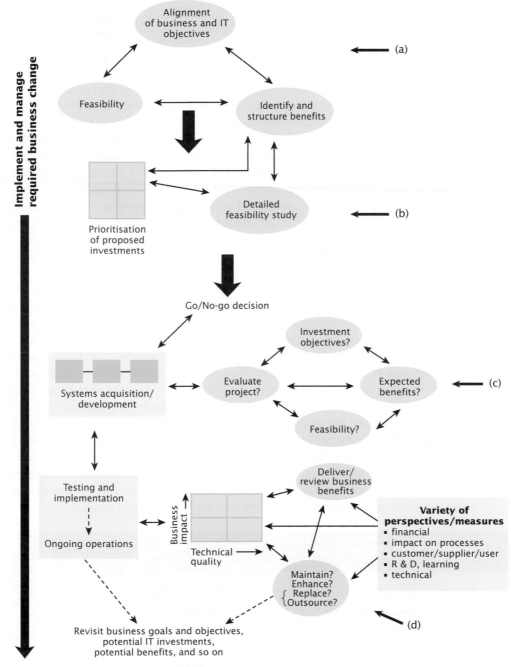

Figure 12.10 ▶ The IT Evaluation and Benefits Management Lifecycle

Source ▶ McKay and Marshall 2001, p. 52.

The IT Evaluation and Benefits Management Lifecycle is thus complete, with one important omission. Earlier it was argued that benefits from IT would be realised only if appropriate organisational changes to support the technological change were planned, implemented and managed. To complete our cycle, therefore, this vital dimension of change management is added to the diagram.

Summary

This chapter has concentrated on consideration of whether IT and e-commerce investment delivers value to a business and, more specifically, on the practices and structures in organisations that can help to ensure that IT investments do in fact realise value for the organisation. Value could take the form of increased efficiencies, improved effectiveness, improved customer relationships and the like. At the heart of the issue of delivering value from IT and e-commerce investments is the notion of IT governance. IT governance refers to the principles, structures and processes put in place to ensure that IT strategy and therefore IT investments are aligned with business goals and objectives, that the risks associated with IT initiatives are identified and managed appropriately, and that appropriate controls on the actions of the CIO and the IT department are in place. This chapter develops a definition of effective IT governance, and considers effective governance mechanisms in organisations, including how decisions are made about IT investments, and discusses effective governance processes that all organisations should look to implement. Effective relationships between IT (CIO) and the rest of the business (CEO) are a key element in establishing effective governance routines in organisations.

Also associated with good governance, and with having insights into whether or not IT investments are delivering value to the organisation are the contentious issues of IT evaluation and benefits management. The chapter argues that sound evaluation of IT and e-commerce investments is essential to ensure the delivery of business value, but acknowledges that there are many difficulties in evaluating IT, especially as it moves more and more into the strategic arena, where many of the benefits are considered intangible. An assessment is made of a number of the more common approaches to IT evaluation and benefits management. An argument is then developed for an IT Evaluation and Benefits Management Lifecycle, which proposes an ongoing cycle of strategic thinking, prioritising systems, evaluating the investments throughout their lifecycle while proactively managing the process of benefits realisation.

key terms

benefits management

benefits realisation

business case

business value

chief information officer (CIO)

C-level managers

IT capabilities

IT evaluation

IT function

IT governance

IT risks

1. What is IT governance? How does it differ from IT management?

2. Describe some possible structures for IT governance. Detail the decision-making processes and relationships in each case.

3. Outline the major processes that you feel an organisation should have formally defined as part of effective framework for IT governance. Why is a formal definition of the key management processes an important part of IT governance?

4. What are the major capabilities an organisation needs in order to effectively exploit IT? Why is it important that these capabilities or competencies exist throughout the organisation rather than just being located in the IT department? Why is developing organisation-wide capabilities to exploit the IT resource an important aspect of IT governance?

5. Explain why developing a good relationship between IT and the rest of the business is important to IT governance. Does the benefit of this relationship work both ways? That is, does a good relationship between IT and the rest of the business contribute good IT governance and good IT governance contribute to a good relationship? Explain the nature and importance of this relationship between IT governance and a good IT–'rest of the business' relationship.

suggested reading

Broadbent, M & Weill, P 1997, 'Management by maxim: how business and IT managers can create IT infrastructures', *Sloan Management Review*, vol. 38, no. 3, pp. 77–92.

Earl, MJ & Feeny, DF 1994, 'Is your CIO adding value?', *Sloan Management Review*, vol. 35, issue 3, Spring, pp. 11–20.

Farbey, B, Land, F & Targett, D 1999, 'IS evaluation: a process for bringing together benefits, costs, and risks', in WL Currie & R Galliers (eds), *Rethinking Management Information Systems: An Interdisciplinary Perspective*, Oxford University Press, Oxford, pp. 204–28.

IT Governance Institute 2001, 'Broad briefing on IT governance', available online at www.itgovernance.org, accessed 5 June 2003.

Weill, P & Woodham, R 2002, *Don't Just Lead, Govern: Implementing Effective IT Governance*, Center for Information Systems Research Working Paper No. 326, Sloan School of Management, Cambridge, MA.

references

Avram, G 2001, 'Evaluation of investments in e-commerce in the Romanian business environment', avalaible online at http://www.iteva.rug.nl/ejise/vol4/papers/Gabriela%20Avram. htm, accessed 26 May 2003.

Broadbent, M 2002, 'Creating effective IT governance', Gartner Symposium ITXpo 2002, 6–11 October, Walt Disney World, Orlando, FL, pp. 1–20.

Broadbent, M & Weill, P 1997, 'Management by maxim: how business and IT managers can create IT infrastructures', *Sloan Management Review*, vol. 38, no. 3, pp. 77–92.

David, P 1990, 'The dynamo and the computer: a historical perspective on the modern productivity paradox', *American Economic Review*, May, pp. 335–61.

Devaraj, S & Kohli, R 2002, *The IT Payoff: Measuring the Business Value of Information Technology Investments*, Financial Times Prentice Hall, New York.

Dutta, S & Manzoni, JF 1999, *Process Re-engineering, Organizational Change and Performance Improvement* (Insead Global Management Series), McGraw-Hill/Irwin, Boston.

Earl, MJ, Edwards, B & Feeny, DF 1996, 'Configuring the IS function in complex organizations', in MJ Earl (ed.) *Information Management: The Organizational Dimension*, Oxford University Press, Oxford.

Earl, MJ & Feeny, DF 1994, 'Is your CIO adding value?', *Sloan Management Review*, vol. 35, issue 3, Spring, pp. 11–20.

Economist, The 1999, *Economics: Making Sense of the Modern Economy*, Profile Books, London.

Edwards, C, Ward, J & Bytheway, A 1995, *The Essence of Information Systems*, 2nd edn, Prentice Hall, London.

Farbey, B, Land, F & Targett, D 1999, 'IS evaluation: a process for bringing together benefits, costs, and risks', in WL Currie & R Galliers (eds) 1999, *Rethinking Management Information Systems: An Interdisciplinary Perspective*, Oxford University Press, Oxford, pp. 204–28.

Feeny, D, Edwards, B & Simpson, K 1992, 'Understanding the CEO/CIO relationship', *MIS Quarterly*, vol. 16, issue 4, pp. 435–48.

Hirschheim, R & Smithson, S 1987, 'Information systems evaluation: myth and reality' in R Galliers (ed.) 1987, *Information Analysis: Selected Readings*, Addison-Wesley, Sydney, pp. 367–80.

Hochstrasser, B & Griffiths, C 1991, *Controlling IT Investment: Strategy and Management*, Chapman & Hall, London.

IT Governance Institute 2001, 'Broad briefing on IT governance', available online at www. itgovernance.org, accessed 5 June 2003.

Kaplan, RS & Norton, DP 2001, *The Strategy-focused Organization: How Balanced Scorecard Companies Thrive in the New Business Environment*, Harvard Business School Press, Boston.

Keen, PGW 1991, *Shaping the Future: Business Design Through Information Technology*, Harvard Business School Press, Boston.

Korac-Kakabadse, N & Kakabadse, A 2001, 'IS/IT governance: need for an integrated model', *Corporate Governance*, vol. 1, no. 4, pp. 9–11.

McKay, J & Marshall, P 2001, 'The IT evaluation and benefits management life cycle', in W Van Grembergen (ed.), *IT Evaluation Methods and Management*, Idea Publishing Group, Hershey, PA, pp. 44–56.

Parker, MM, Benson, RJ & Trainor, HE 1988, *Information Economics: Linking Business Performance and Information Technology*, Pearson Higher Education, London.

Peppard, J 2001, 'Bridging the gap between the IS organisation and the rest of the business: plotting a route', *Information Systems Journal*, vol. 11, no. 3, pp. 249–70.

Peppard, J, Lambert, R & Edwards, C 2000, 'Whose job is it anyway? Organizational information competencies for value creation', *Information Systems Journal*, vol. 10, no. 4, pp. 291–322.

Peppard, J & Ward, J 1999, 'Mind the gap: diagnosing the relationship between the IT organization and the rest of the business', *Journal of Strategic Information Systems*, vol. 8, no. 1, pp. 29–60.

Peters, G 1994, 'Evaluating your computer investment strategy', in L Willcocks (ed.), *Information Management: Evaluation of Information Systems Investments*, Chapman & Hall, London, pp. 99–112.

Remenyi, DSJ, Money, A & Twite, A 1993, *A Guide to Measuring and Managing IT Benefits*, 2nd edn, NCC Blackwell, Oxford.

Ribbers, PMA, Peterson, RR & Parker, MM 2002, 'Designing information technology governance processes: diagnosing contemporary practices and competing theories', *Proceedings of the 35th Annual Hawaii International Conference on Systems Sciences*, IEEE Computer Society, pp. 1–12.

Sambamurthy, V 2002, 'Business strategy in hypercompetitive environments: rethinking the logic of IT differentiation', in RW Zmud (ed.), *Framing the Domains of IT Management*, Pinnaflex Educational Resources, Cincinnati, OH, pp. 245–61.

Shane, B, Lafferty, P & Beasley, T 1999, 'IM/IT governance framework', *Optimum: The Journal of Public Sector Management*, vol. 29, no. 2/3, pp. 30–5.

Tallon, PP, Kraemer, KL & Gurbaxani, V 2000, 'Executives' perceptions of the business value of information technology: a process-oriented approach', *Journal of Management Information Systems*, vol. 16, no. 4, pp. 145–73.

Thorp, J 1998, *The Information Paradox: Realizing the Business Benefits of Information Technology*, McGraw-Hill, Toronto.

Van der Zee, H 2002, *Measuring the Value of Information Technology*, Idea Publishing Group, Hershey, PA.

Van Grembergen, W 2003, 'The balanced scorecard and IT governance', available online at www.itgovernance.org/balscorecard.pdf, accessed 15 June 2003.

Ward, J & Griffiths, P 1996, *Strategic Planning for Information Systems*, 2nd edn, John Wiley & Sons, Chichester.

Ward, J & Peppard, J 1996, 'Reconciling the IT/business relationship: a troubled marriage in need of guidance', *Journal of Strategic Information Systems*, vol. 5, issue 1, pp. 37–65.

—2002, *Strategic Planning for Information Systems*, 3rd edn, John Wiley & Sons, Chichester.

Ward, J, Taylor, P & Bond, P 1996, 'Evaluation and realisation of IS/IT benefits: an empirical study of current practice', *European Journal of Information Systems*, vol. 4, 1996, pp. 214–25.

Weill, P & Woodham, R 2002, *Don't Just Lead, Govern: Implementing Effective IT Governance*, Center for Information Systems Research Working Paper No. 326, Sloan School of Management, Cambridge, MA.

Willcocks, L 1992, 'Evaluating information technology investments: research findings and reappraisal', *Journal of Information Systems*, vol. 2, pp. 243–68.

—1994, 'Managing information technology evaluation — techniques and processes', in RG Galliers & BSH Baker (eds), *Strategic Information Management: Challenges and Strategies in Managing Information Systems*, Butterworth Heinemann, Oxford, pp. 362–81.

—1996, 'Introduction: beyond the IT productivity paradox', in L Willcocks (ed.), *Investing in Information Systems: Evaluation and Management*, Chapman & Hall, London, pp. 1–12.

Willcocks, L & Lester, S 1997, 'Assessing IT productivity: any way out of the labyrinth?', in L Willcocks, DF Feeny & G Islei (eds), *Managing IT as a Strategic Resource*, McGraw-Hill, London, pp. 64–93.

—1999, 'Information technology: transformer or sink hole?', in LP Willcocks and S Lester (eds), *Beyond the IT Productivity Paradox*, John Wiley & Sons, Chichester, pp. 1–36.

case study

Pantonic: the need for IT governance

Pantonic is a Melbourne-based manufacturer of patent medicines and vitamins. It was established in 1920 by the Heine-Borel family of Melbourne, and had a reputation for quality manufacturing. The manufacture of some of the simple health products was outsourced to Vital Products Limited (VPL), which focused on low-cost manufacture of health products.

Pantonic was a medium-sized to large firm by Australian standards. Revenues had grown to $220 million in 2003. Employee numbers had grown from twenty to thirty people in the 1920s to about 550 employees in 2003. However, after rapid growth of 14–18 per cent between the 1920s and the 1980s, growth in the 1990s had slowed to 2–3 per cent. The situation had become even worse with the turn of the century, and the early 2000s had shown 0 to –2 per cent growth. Furthermore, the cost of manufacture had been rising, as had IS/IT costs. At the same time, profit margins on Pantonic products were being squeezed by several international competitors who, as part of their globalisation drives, had targeted Australia as a developed economy where margins for health products are relatively high.

Pantonic's IT department had grown significantly during the 1990s. It now comprised twenty-six people, almost all of whom were skilled programmers. Two members of the IT department were skilled systems analysts and project managers, who were more comfortable than most of their colleagues with interacting with the business on such matters as requirements definition and systems analysis and design.

The CEO, Peter Heine-Borel, had been dissatisfied with the IT department for some time. However, the company's recent poor growth and profit performance, together with the increasing cost of manufacture, had caused him to focus on several areas that he saw as problematic. Among these was IS/IT. Peter had called his senior managers together, including the CIO, Adi Fubini, to begin an evaluation of the IT function.

After formalities, Peter began talking to his senior management team. 'As you know, I think we seem to be spending a lot on IT. We spend an amount that is about 12 per cent of our sales revenue on IT. It seems, from some investigations that I have carried out, that our competitors are only spending between 2 per cent to 5 per cent on IT. This seems to indicate that we might be spending too much. But how do we tell? How do we know how much is enough or appropriate?'

'Yes, but we are getting good value from our systems!' interjected Adi. 'Look at the support our specially built production scheduling and capacity planning systems give to manufacturing, for example.'

'Yes, Adi and his team work endlessly and tirelessly to help us plan and monitor our manufacturing processes. The system we have is expertly and carefully tailored and customised to our production methods and processes. I don't know what we would do without the support of his IT team,' added Helena Dedekind, the manufacturing manager.

'Well, yes, but look,' responded Peter, 'I am not so sure we're getting added business value from IT. We have had our share of cost and time overruns. We currently have trouble with some of the systems designed to assist our customers. So there are current problems with our IT. But beyond that, how do we know that we are investing our time, money and effort in the right set of systems? How do we know our information systems investments are well targeted? We ought to review our IT activities and practices.'

The meeting then discussed the recent history of IT practices in the company. It soon became clear that although Helena Dedekind supported Adi Fubini's IT department, the rest of the senior management team had significant concerns about the IT practices.

The meeting ranged over general concerns with the IT department. Discussion was dominated by Felix Klein, the marketing manager, Arthur Cayley, the sales manager, and, to a lesser extent, George Cantor, the finance manager. They pointed out that, from the viewpoints of their respective departments, the IT department looked very technical and insulated from real business pressures. The company's IT professionals, they felt, were interested in the technical aspects of IT and, indeed, were quite highly technically skilled, by all reports. However, the IT department's professionals did not respond well to the real pressures of the business. They seemed content to believe that these issues were the concern of marketing, sales, finance and other departments, but not them. Indeed, Felix and Arthur felt that the IT department had a certain 'regal complacency' about it.

Felix and Arthur continued their criticism for some time, after which George mentioned that he supported them both. 'Furthermore,' said George grimly, 'they don't even speak our language!'

From the perspective of Felix and Arthur, although there were some technically very clever manufacturing and manufacturing control systems, the marketing and sales systems, which were becoming critical in their industry, were not getting their rightful share of attention. Despite protests from Adi Fubini, Felix and Arthur held their ground as they felt very strongly about the issue of complacency and lack of commercial awareness in the IT department. When he entered the conversation, George Cantor firmly supported Felix and Arthur.

Peter Heine-Borel then asked his senior managers to be more specific in their criticisms. Indeed, to improve the tone of the meeting, which had turned decidedly negative, he asked for both praise and criticism.

Helena Dedekind mentioned that the production scheduling system, which had been written by the IT department and implemented as a joint project between IT and manufacturing, was turning out to be a great success. The system featured finite capacity constrained production scheduling, a feature that, on examination, SAP had lacked. The system gave very detailed work centre loading reports. In some cases, the system was interfaced to production machinery and had some very effective controls on manufacturing quality and output. Yes, the system had taken between ten and twelve months longer than had initially been planned. But many of the complexities of the manufacturing control environment, particularly some scheduling subtleties, had not been anticipated.

'You could never have planned such a complex undertaking as a complete manufacturing control system for our production,' said Helena, 'especially with all our technical and legal quality checks and constraints!'

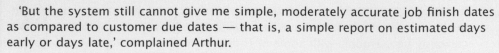

'But the system still cannot give me simple, moderately accurate job finish dates as compared to customer due dates — that is, a simple report on estimated days early or days late,' complained Arthur.

'That is coming,' said Adi. 'The complexities of the production scheduling and production quality control have kept us involved in the manufacturing aspects of the system. We just haven't had the resources to devote to your sales report.'

'Well, I suppose the same applies to my manufacturing cost reports', said George, rather bitterly. 'You gather all the actual production times in your schedule report, and yet you cannot produce our manufacturing costing reports. In finance and accounting there is considerable resentment that you are not helping in this direction. We just do not know why you are not working with us on this.'

'Well, if you had any idea of our commitments...' began Adi.

'Well, look, let's steady things a bit,' interjected Peter. 'I think it is clear from this meeting that Adi needs to attend our weekly executive meetings. I know we have always had the view that senior management need not be concerned with the details of technology, but maybe that was a naive and limited view. There appear to be aspects of the planning and management of technology that are essential to the effective general management of this firm. We need to get an overview of where IT fits into our activities.

'So where are we? Well, let us accept that the manufacturing control system is looking like it will be a success. What about Pantonic's customer systems initiative?'

The customer systems initiative (CSI) had been proposed by Felix Klein as a way of increasing customer loyalty and 'buy-in' to Pantonic. Under the CSI, Pantonic offered free systems to its customers, many of whom were small pharmacies or small pharmacy chains that did not have internal IT professionals. The systems offered included a store layout and stock control system that gave guidance and advice on shelf space to be devoted to particular items as well as guidance on stock levels based on cost and sales data (including trend analysis of costs and sales). Also included was an online ordering system linked to Pantonic's online catalogue and e-commerce sales system.

Pantonic's IT department had worked on the CSI for about a year. The marketing department had held great hopes for the system. Expectation had also been high among Pantonic's customers after the company had run a publicity campaign advertising the CSI and detailing its functionality to major customers. However, trials of the system with several customers had revealed some problems.

Several of the customers reported that the requirements for the store layout and stock control system were not well met. They did not have easy access to the data in the form required by the system, and the reports were not helpful or easy to interpret. Indeed the language used in the system was not typical of the business language of the industry. Several reports, which customers said would have been very helpful for store layout and stock control, were not provided at all. Similar complaints were made with respect to online ordering. It also appeared that the system was not user-friendly and indeed was quite difficult to use.

Adi Fubini thought that the only real issue underlying these problems was that some of the sales people who had been trained in the system by the IT department needed to spend more time training staff at the pharmacies. However, Felix Klein thought that the situation was much more serious. He felt that the requirements specification for the system had been badly done by Adi's staff, and it needed to be reworked after the systems analysts had acquired a better grasp of the business requirements of the pharmacies. Felix claimed that Adi's systems analysts lacked a real understanding of — and indeed patience with and interest in — business issues generally, preferring instead to focus on the (to them) more interesting technical issues.

'We have wireless mobile data capture and other mobile computing bells and whistles in the systems for the pharmacies, together with some serious misunderstandings of the most basic business issues,' said Felix, summing up, obviously exasperated.

Adi was quick to respond. 'Look, Felix! We would be able to do a better job of requirements determination if some of your sales people would put in some serious time and effort with my analysts,' he said sharply. 'The path to a good CSI is a two-way street. This effort should be a partnership. My analysts have been slaving alone on this one, and they need some business input from your people.'

Felix snapped back. 'My people do not understand this technology — indeed they're not paid to understand this technology! They have told you what they can. They now have to get on with their work — and your guys have to do theirs!'

The meeting then moved on to discuss several other systems. Finance and purchasing thought that the systems they felt were important had been given less focus, less attention and less investment of resources than they thought the systems merited. They also felt that the requirements determination or business specification of the systems had been poorly done. Furthermore, necessary evaluations of system development progress and system implementation progress either had not taken place or had been done very peremptorily. Also, finance and purchasing argued that during the implementation of the systems Adi Fubini's systems analysts and project managers had focused solely on implementing the systems on time, on budget and according to technical specifications. They had neglected the all-important raison d'être for the systems: the business benefits. In defence of his systems analysts and project managers, Adi cited the fact that his analysts were overworked and that they were not given help they needed from managers in finance and purchasing in understanding the business requirements.

The meeting by this time had been going on for the best part of three hours. Peter Heine-Borel called the meeting to order, saying that he wished to summarise the issues and point the way to an improvement in the current situation. 'Well, we have certainly raised, and indeed begun to analyse and elucidate, a number of important issues surrounding some of the IT investments or projects,' began Peter.

'And, indeed, we have to deal with all these issues — some of them quite promptly. However, since I do not want us to have a meeting like this every few months, I think we need to deal with some broader issues — we need to take an overall perspective on what is happening here. Information technology has become too important, too complex and too expensive for us to deal with it on a project-by-project basis. We need some overall framework that defines how we should deal with IT. Indeed, we need a governance framework for IT.

'We first need some fundamental principles that define our overall approach to IT and what we expect from it. Then we need some structures and processes that define our approach and procedures for IT. Then we could use it to define a working approach — a governance framework — for IT in this company.'

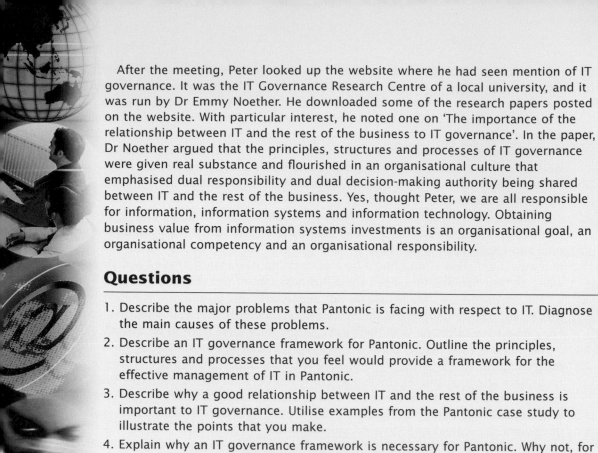

After the meeting, Peter looked up the website where he had seen mention of IT governance. It was the IT Governance Research Centre of a local university, and it was run by Dr Emmy Noether. He downloaded some of the research papers posted on the website. With particular interest, he noted one on 'The importance of the relationship between IT and the rest of the business to IT governance'. In the paper, Dr Noether argued that the principles, structures and processes of IT governance were given real substance and flourished in an organisational culture that emphasised dual responsibility and dual decision-making authority being shared between IT and the rest of the business. Yes, thought Peter, we are all responsible for information, information systems and information technology. Obtaining business value from information systems investments is an organisational goal, an organisational competency and an organisational responsibility.

Questions

1. Describe the major problems that Pantonic is facing with respect to IT. Diagnose the main causes of these problems.

2. Describe an IT governance framework for Pantonic. Outline the principles, structures and processes that you feel would provide a framework for the effective management of IT in Pantonic.

3. Describe why a good relationship between IT and the rest of the business is important to IT governance. Utilise examples from the Pantonic case study to illustrate the points that you make.

4. Explain why an IT governance framework is necessary for Pantonic. Why not, for example, simply attend to the immediate problems in each IT project, thus solving the problems very directly?

index